A

NEW TRANSLATION

OF

JOB, ECCLESIASTES,

AND

THE CANTICLES,

WITH

INTRODUCTIONS, AND NOTES, CHIEFLY EXPLANATORY.

By GEORGE R. NOYES, D.D.,

HANCOCK PROFESSOR OF HEBREW, ETC., AND DEXTER LECTURER IN HARVARD UNIVERSITY.

FIFTH EDITION,

Carefully Revised, with Additional Notes.

BOSTON:

AMERICAN UNITARIAN ASSOCIATION.

1874.

CONTENTS.

THE BOOK OF JOB.

INTRODUCTION TO JOB.

THE work, which it is the design of the present volume to illustrate, is in many respects one of the most remarkable productions of any age or country. It is, without doubt, in its general plan, as well as in the rhythmical construction and high poetic character of its language, the elaborate work of a skilful artist. Deep thought and long-continued study must have been united with genius in its production. Yet has it, in a much higher degree than most compositions, the freshness of an unstudied effusion of the soul of the author; a soul full of the sublimest conceptions of the Parent of nature and his glorious works, and of true and deep sympathy with all that is great and amiable in the character, and affecting in the condition, of man. The imagination of the author seems to have ranged freely through every part of the universe, and to have enriched itself from almost every department of nature and of art. Whether he attempt to describe the residence of Him "who maintaineth peace in his high places," or "the land of darkness and the shadow of death;" the passions and pursuits of man, or the nature and features of the animal creation; the phenomena of the air and the heavens, or the dark operations of the miner, — he is ever familiar with his subject, and seems to tell us what his eyes have seen and his ears have heard. And not more remarkable are the richness and vigor of his imagination than his power in representing the deep emotions and the tender affections of the soul. Admirable, too, in a poem of so high antiquity, is the skill with which he makes all the delineations of the human heart, and all the descriptions of external nature, subservient to the illustration of one important moral subject; thus uniting the attributes of the poet and philosopher. It is true that we miss the perfection of Grecian art in the structure of the work of a Hebrew poet who wrote more than a century before Æschylus; and his plan required him to set forth the general workings of the human heart, rather than to delineate the nicer shades of human character. It was in harmony with the ethical nature of the composition, that his characters should make speeches, rather than converse. Yet no one can fail to perceive the unity of design which pervades the work, and the adaptation of the various parts of it to its completion.

The first place among the Hebrew poets has usually been assigned to Isaiah. But in what respect the Great Unknown, the author of the Book of Job, can be regarded as inferior to any Hebrew poet, or any other poet, unless perhaps we except Shakspeare, I am at a loss to conceive. In comprehensiveness of thought, and in richness and strength of imagination, he seems to me to be unsurpassed; and in depth and tenderness of feeling to be incomparable, when we consider that female loveliness constitutes no part of the interest of the work. Almost every Christian poet has felt his influence in respect both to thought and expression. But to delineate the excellences and beauties of the Book of Job is a task far beyond my capacity. They must be understood and felt, rather than described.

There has been much discussion in former times, in regard to the particular department of poetry and literature under which the Book of Job should be classed. Undue importance has without doubt been attached to this question; and the scope and spirit of the work have in a degree been lost sight of, in the eagerness with which different writers have sought to establish its claim to the appellation of epic or dramatic, or its place in a particular department of poetical composition. The truth is, that there is nothing which bears an exact resemblance to it in Grecian, Roman, or modern literature. It has something in common, not only with different forms of composition, but with different departments of literature. Those who have given it the appellation of an epic poem have applied to it a term the least suited to its character, and the most unjust to its claims as a work of art. They have made unimportant circumstances, in regard to its form, of more consequence than its substantial character, spirit, and design. Nothing can be more evident than the fact, that to excite interest in the personal fortunes of Job, as the hero of a poem, was not the principal design of the writer. Still less was it his design to unfold characteristic traits in the other personages introduced into the work. Some, indeed, have discovered, as they supposed, striking characteristic traits in Eliphaz the Temanite, Bildad the Shuhite, and Zophar the Naamathite; and have pointed out the different degrees of severity which they exhibited towards their friend in his distress. It appears to me that these writers have drawn largely on their own imaginations to make their opinions probable. There is, no doubt, some diversity in the manner and substance of the discourses of the friends of Job. The author may have put the longest and best speeches into the mouth of an inhabitant of a city so famous for its wisdom as Teman; * and to Elihu, whom some regard as thrust into the place he occupies by a later writer than the author, he certainly assigns, at least in the beginning of Elihu's speech, and in the preambles in chap. xxxiii. 1–9, 31–33, xxxiv. 2–4, xxxv. 2–4, the language of a young man who has made rather an extravagant estimate of his abilities and his consequence. But I seek in vain for evidence that the author made it a principal object to excite an interest in the actions or characters of the personages whom he introduces. He had little dramatic power.

There is more plausibility in the views of those who have regarded and named the Book of Job a dramatic poem. For, undoubtedly, the character of Job has a tragic interest, and reminds one of the most interesting characters of Grecian tragedy, suffering by the will of the gods or the necessities of fate, especially the Prometheus Vinctus of Æschylus. In regard to its form, there is something that resembles dialogue, — though the persons taking part in it make speeches rather than converse, — and something that bears a distant resemblance to a prologue and an epilogue. The author has also skilfully introduced into various parts of the work hints having reference to the final issue of

* Jer. xlix. 7.

the fortunes of Job, similar to those which occur in the best of the Greek tragedies, such as the Œdipus Tyrannus. (See chap. viii. 6, 7; xvi. 19; xix. 25, &c., compared with chap. xlii.) Still, to give the name of a drama or a tragedy to this production is to give it a name from what is incidental to it, rather than from its pervading spirit and prominent design. To call it a poem of any kind fails to suggest the characteristic feature of the work, though it contains poetry, which perhaps has never been surpassed.

If we have regard to the main design, the substance and spirit of the work, we shall refer it to the department of moral or religious philosophy. It contains the moral or religious philosophy of the time when it was produced. It is rather a philosophical religious discussion in a poetical form than an epic or dramatic poem. It is more nearly allied to the Essay on Man than to Paradise Lost, or Prometheus Vinctus. It is the effusion of the mind and heart of the author upon a moral subject which has agitated the human bosom in every age. Still, the author was a poet as well as a religious philosopher. In the mode of presenting the subject to his readers, he aimed, like other poets, to move the human feelings by exhibitions of passion and scenes of distress, and to please the taste by the sublime flights of his imagination. He aimed to give the highest interest to his subject by clothing his thoughts in the loftiest language of poetry, and arranging them in the measured rhythm which is one of the characteristics of Hebrew poetry.

It might be interesting to analyze the pure religious doctrines which the author held, and, with wonderful liberality for one of the Jewish nation, ascribed to Arabians; but such an analysis is hardly necessary in an introduction to the book. It seems particularly remarkable that he should ascribe Divine inspiration to Eliphaz the Temanite. (See chap. iv. 12–21.)

The special subject of this unique production is the ways of Providence in regard to the distribution of good and evil in the world, in connection with the doctrine of a righteous retribution in the present life, such as seemed to be contained in the Jewish religion. It sets forth the struggle between faith in the perfect government of God, or in a righteous retribution in the present life, and the various doubts excited in the soul of man by what it feels or sees of human misery, and by what it knows of the prosperity of the contemners of God. These doubts the author expresses in strong and irreverent language from the lips of Job; while the received doctrine of an exact earthly retribution, which pervades the Jewish religion, is maintained and reiterated by the personages introduced as the friends of Job.

The subject is one which comes home to men's business and bosoms. Even under the light of Christianity, perhaps there are few who have not in peculiar seasons felt a conflict between faith in the perfect government of God, and various feelings excited in their minds by what they have experienced or witnessed of human suffering. The pains of the innocent, — of those who cannot discern their right hand from their left hand, — the protracted calamities which are often the lot of the righteous, and the prosperity which often crowns the designs of the wicked, have at times excited wonder, perplexity, and doubt in almost every thoughtful mind. We, as Christians, silence our doubts, and confirm our faith, by what experience teaches us of the general wisdom and benevolence of the Creator, by the consideration that affliction comes from the same merciful hand which is the source of all the good that we have ever enjoyed, by the perception of the moral and religious influences of adversity, and especially by the hope of the joy to be realized in a better world, which is set before those who endure to the end. The apostle could say for the consolation of himself and his fellow-sufferers, "For I reckon that the sufferings of this present time are not worthy to be compared with the glory which shall be revealed in us." And every Christian knows that the Captain of his salvation ascended to his throne of glory from the ignominious cross. The cross is the great source of the Christian's consolation. But let us suppose ourselves to be deprived of those sources of consolation which are peculiar to a disciple of Christ, and we may conceive of the state of mind of the author of the Book of Job, upon whom the Sun of righteousness had never dawned. Is it strange that the soul of a pious Jew, who lived before "life and immortality were brought to light through the gospel," should have been agitated by the conflict between such a faith in temporal retribution as his religion seemed to require, and the doubts and murmurings excited by what he felt and saw of the calamities of the righteous, and witnessed of the prosperity of the wicked? One of the most enlightened of the Romans, when called to mourn the early loss of the children of his hopes, was led, as he says, almost "to accuse the gods, and to exclaim, that no Providence governed the world." An Arabic poet, quoted by Dr. Pococke,* writes: —

Quot intellectu præstantes in angustias rediguntur,
Et summè stolidos invenies prospere agentes!
Hoc est quod animos perplexos relinquit,
Et egregiè doctos Sadducæos reddit.

"How many wise men are reduced to distress,
And how many fools will you find in prosperity!
It is this that leaves the mind in perplexity,
And makes Sadducees of very learned men."

We think that many have stated too strongly the argument for the immortality of the soul, drawn from the apparent inequalities of the present state. To maintain that there is little or no retribution in this part of the Creator's dominions appears to me not the best way of proving that there will be a perfect one in another part of them. Nor is such a representation true. To a very important extent, "we still have justice here." But the sentiments referred to above, respecting the limited retributions of the present life, may serve to illustrate the mental condition of a pious man of exalted genius, who appears to have had no conception, or at least no belief, of a state after death that was desirable in comparison with the present life.

In Ps. lxxiii. we have the thoughts which passed through the mind of another upon the same subject: —

"Yet my feet almost gave way;
My steps had well nigh slipped:
For I was envious of the profane,
When I saw the prosperity of the wicked," &c.

Ps. xxxvii. may also be considered as being upon the same subject, and so likewise the Book of Ecclesiastes; though a more sceptical spirit seems to pervade the latter than either of the psalms above mentioned, or the Book of Job.

* Not. in Port. Mos. c. vii. Opp. p. 214.

Such being the subject which filled the mind of the author of this book, the question arises, how he has treated it, or what he aimed to accomplish in regard to it. That in his own view he had solved all the difficulties which embarrass the human understanding in regard to the subject is not very probable. But that he proposed to establish some definite truths in relation to it, as well as to inculcate the duty of entire submission to God, and unreserved faith in him, is, I think, clear. I do not believe, with De Wette, that he meant to leave the subject an utter mystery, and merely to bring man to a helpless consciousness of his ignorance. The prologue and epilogue, which this writer admits to be genuine, to say nothing of the speech of Elihu, refute such an opinion. The most prominent part of the author's design is, indeed, to enforce the duty of unqualified submission to the will of God, and of reverential faith amid all the difficulties which perplex the understanding in relation to the government of God. But a part of it is also to illustrate the truth, that moral character is not to be inferred from outward condition (see chap. xxxiii. 19–28); that afflictions are designed as the trial of piety, and as means for its advancement; and that they lead in the end to higher good than would otherwise be obtained; and thus to assert eternal providence, and justify the ways of God to man. And, while he enforces the duty of entire submission to God, he incidentally intimates that unfounded censures and unkind treatment of a friend in distress are more offensive to the Deity than those expressions of impatience which affliction may wring from the lips of the pious.*

The author aims to show, that, in the distribution of good and evil in the world, God is sometimes influenced by reasons which man can neither discover nor comprehend, and not solely by the merit or demerit of his creatures; that the righteous are often afflicted, and the wicked prospered: but that this course of providence is perfectly consistent with wisdom, justice, and goodness in the Deity, though man is unable to discern the reasons of it; that afflictions are often intended as the trials of piety and the means of moral improvement; that man is an incompetent judge of the Divine dispensations; that, instead of rashly daring to pene-

* Chap. xlii. 7.

trate or to censure the counsels of his Creator, it is his duty to submit to his will, to reverence his character, and to obey his laws; and that the end will prove the wisdom as well as the obligation and the happy consequences of such submission, reverence, and obedience.

In this view, I have taken the whole book, as we now have it, to be genuine. I think this supposition is attended with the fewest difficulties. Those who discard the speech of Elihu, the twenty-eighth chapter and part of the twenty-seventh, and the prose introduction and conclusion, must give, of course, an account of it somewhat different. They imagine that by the exclusion of these portions they give greater unity to the composition. But where did they learn that every poem must have perfect unity, or even perfect consistency?

In order to accomplish the design, or express the views, which I have exhibited, in such a manner that his work should possess the highest interest for his readers, the author employs a form of composition resembling that of the drama. He brings forward a personage, celebrated probably in the traditions of his country on account of the distinguished excellence of his character, and the marvellous vicissitudes through which he had passed. In the delineation of the character and fortunes of this personage, he uses the liberty of a poet in stating every thing in extremes, or in painting every thing in the broadest colors, that he might thus the better illustrate the moral truth, and accomplish the moral purpose, which he had in view.

He introduces to the reader an inhabitant of the land of Uz, in the northern part of Arabia, equally distinguished by his piety and his prosperity. He was pronounced by the Searcher of hearts an upright and good man; and he was surrounded by a happy family, and was the most wealthy of all the inhabitants of the East.

If virtue and piety could in any case be a security against calamity, then must Job's prosperity have been lasting. Who ever had more reason for expecting continued prosperity, the favor of men, and the smiles of Providence? "But, when he looked for good, evil came." A single day produces a complete reverse in his condition, and reduces him from the height of prosperity to the lowest depths of misery. He is stripped of his possessions. His children, a numerous family, for whom he had never forgotten to offer to God a morning sacrifice, are buried under the ruins of their houses, which a hurricane levels with the ground; and, finally, he is afflicted, in his own person, with a most loathsome and dangerous disease. Thus the best man in the world has become the most miserable man in the world.

The reader is made acquainted in the outset with the cause of the afflictions of Job. At an assembly of the sons of God, — that is, the inhabitants of heaven, — in the presence of the Governor of the world, an evil spirit, Satan, the adversary or accuser in the court of heaven, had come, on his return from an excursion over the earth, to present himself before God, or to stand in readiness to receive his commands. Jehovah puts the question to Satan, whether he had taken notice of the model of human excellence exhibited in the character of his servant Job, and sets forth the praise of this good man in terms so emphatic as to excite the envy and ill-will of that suspicious accuser of his brethren. Satan intimates that selfishness is the sole motive of Job's obedience; that it was with views of profit, and not from sentiments of reverence toward God, that he paid him an outward service; that, if Jehovah should take away the possessions of him whom he believed so faithful, he would at once renounce his service. "Doth Job fear God for nought?" To establish the truth of what he had said in commendation of his servant, Jehovah is represented as giving permission to Satan to put the piety of Job to the test, by taking away at once all his possessions and all his children. But the evil spirit gains no triumph. Job remains true to his allegiance. He sins not even with his lips. There is yet another assembly of the heavenly spirits; and here the hateful spirit, the disbeliever in human virtue, persists in maintaining that it is the love of life, the dearest of all possessions to man, which retains Job in his allegiance. Satan therefore is represented as having permission to take from Job all that can be called life, except the mere consciousness of existence and the ability to express his sentiments in the condition to which he is reduced, by the infliction of a most loathsome disease. And yet the good man, in this lowest point of depression, is represented as remaining patient so long, that when his wife, whom Satan appears to have spared to him for no good purpose, tempts him to renounce his allegiance to God, he calmly answers, "Shall we receive good at the hand of God, and shall we not receive evil?" Thus far he did not sin with his lips.

But when the fame of Job's sufferings had spread abroad, and had drawn around him a company of his friends, who had left their distant homes to sympathize with him in his calamities, he is represented as giving vehement utterance to his long-repressed impatience, and pouring out his complaints and doubts in rash language, with which the reader would hardly be able to sympathize, were it not for the account which has been given of the cause of his afflictions in the introductory chapters.

But the friends of Job, who of course are not acquainted with the cause of his sufferings in the occurrences of the heavenly assembly, are thrown into amazement at the condition in which they find their friend, and the expressions uttered by him whom they had heretofore looked upon as a wise and good man. They are silent while they witness only his dreadful sufferings; but, when they hear the vehement and rash complaints which are extorted from him by the severity of his distress, they refrain no longer from expressing their sentiments respecting the cause of his calamities. They ascribe them to his sins. Thus commences a discussion respecting the causes of human sufferings between Job and his friends. They are represented as holding the doctrine of a strict and perfect retribution in the present life; as maintaining that misery always implies guilt; and hence, instead of bringing him comfort and consolation, they accuse him of having merited his misfortunes by secret wickedness. They exhort him to repentance, as if he were a great sinner suffering the just punishment of his crimes.

Job repels their insinuations with indignation, and firmly maintains his innocence. He knows not why he suffers. He complains of severe treatment, and asserts that God afflicts equally the righteous and the wicked. His friends are offended with the sentiments to which he gives utterance, and undertake to vindicate the conduct of the Deity towards him. They repeat with greater asperity their charges of wickedness and impiety, and even go so far as to accuse him of particular crimes. But the more they press their accusations, the more confident is he in his assertions of his innocence, or of the justice of his cause. He avows his conviction that God will one day manifest himself as the vindicator of his character. He appeals to him as the witness of his sincerity; denies the constancy, and even the frequency, of his judgments upon wicked men; and boldly asks for an opportunity of pleading his cause with his Creator, confident that he should be acquitted before any righteous tribunal. His friends are reduced to silence; Bildad closing their remarks by a few general maxims respecting the greatness of God and the frailty of man, and Zophar not undertaking to say any thing.

The spirit of Job is somewhat softened by their silence; and he retracts some of the sentiments, which, in the anguish of his spirit, and the heat of controversy, he had inconsiderately uttered. "He proceeds with calm confidence like a lion among his defeated enemies." He shows that he was able to speak of the perfections of God, and to express all that was true in the positions of his opponents, in a better style than any of them. He now admits, what before he seemed to deny, that wicked men are often visited by severe punishment. But from his main position he does not retreat, that misery is not always the consequence of wickedness, and that God has a hidden wisdom in regard to the distribution of happiness and misery, which it is impossible for man to fathom. He then proceeds with a melting pathos to describe his present in contrast with his former condition, and to give a most beautiful picture of his character and life, very pardonable in one of whom the reader knows what has in the prologue been said by the Governor of the world before the angels of heaven. From this retrospect of his past life, he is led to renewed protestations of his innocence, and of his desire to have his cause tried before the tribunal of his Creator.

In this stage of the discussion, a new disputant is brought forward, probably for the purpose of expressing some thoughts of the author on the design of afflictions, and for the purpose of forming a contrast in respect to style and manner with the manifestation of the Deity which follows. Elihu is represented as a young man coming forward with an air of great confidence, though in words he ascribes the burden with which his breast was laboring to the inspiration of God. He does, indeed, bring forward some thoughts on the moral influence of afflictions which had not been uttered by the friends of Job; maintaining that, though they may not be the punishment of past offences, nor evidence of guilt, they may operate as preventives of those sins which the best of men sometimes commit, and as a salutary discipline for the correction of those faults of which a man may be unconscious until his attention is awakened by adversity. Thus he offers a more rational conjecture than the three friends of Job, in regard to the cause of his afflictions; and, in fact, gives nearly the same account of it which is regarded as true by the writer, and is implied in the prologue and epilogue of the poem. Affliction, according to Elihu, is designed for the moral benefit of the sufferer. His view of the design of human sufferings is, therefore, nearer the Christian doctrine than that of any speaker in the book. Of course, like all others, he fails of completely solving all the difficulties, which, even under the light of the Christian dispensation, are connected with the subject of the amount of evil which exists in the world, and the distribution of good and evil in it, under the government of God. Thus an appropriate place remains for the sublime speech of the Deity relating to the unsearchableness of his counsels and his ways.

Human wisdom, the learned wisdom of age, and the unbiassed genius of youth, having now been exhausted upon the subject, at length the Supreme Being himself is represented as speaking from the midst of a tempest, and putting an end to the controversy; the dignity of his introduction being rendered more impressive by the self-confident egotism with which Elihu had commenced his part in the contest.

The Creator decides the controversy, to a certain extent, in favor of Job. Jehovah does not, however, condescend to explain to him the ways of his providence, or to reveal to him the reasons which influence his conduct; but, in a series of forcible questions relating to the Divine operations in the realms of nature, he convinces him of his inability to fathom the Divine counsels, demonstrates the necessity of faith in a wisdom which he cannot comprehend, produces in him a sense of his weakness and ignorance, and leads him to profound repentance on account of the rashness of his language; and thus prepares the way for the final vindication of his faithful servant. In a strain of sublime irony, he requests him, who had spoken with such confidence and boldness of the ways of God, to give an explanation of some of the phenomena which were constantly presented to his view, — of the nature and structure of the earth, the sea, the light, and the animal kingdom. If he be unable to explain any of the common phenomena of nature, how can he expect to comprehend the secret counsels and moral government of the invisible Author of nature?

But, having shown the reasonableness of entire confidence in his unsearchable wisdom, and of submission to his darkest dispensations, the Supreme Judge does, in the main, decide the controversy in favor of Job. He declares that he had spoken that which was right; that is, in maintaining that his misery was not the consequence of his guilt, or that character is not to be inferred from external condition; and that the friends of Job had not spoken that which was right in condemning him as a wicked man on account of his misery, or in maintaining that suffering always implies guilt. (Chap. xlii. 7, 8.) The cause of Job's afflictions, which was unknown to the disputants, has already been communicated to the reader in the introductory chapters; namely, that they were appointed as a temporary trial of his virtue, in order to vindicate the judgment of Jehovah concerning him, and to prove against all gainsayers the disinterestedness of his piety. Finally, Jehovah is represented as bestowing upon Job double the prosperity which distinguished him before his affliction, and thus as compensating him for the calamities he had suffered; thereby showing, for the consolation of all who endure affliction, that the end of the good man will prove that he was also wise.

If the general design of this wonderful production be such as I have described, the question whether Job was a real or a fictitious character becomes almost too unimportant to be discussed. Truth was illustrated and duty enforced by parable as well as by history, in the teaching of him who spake as never man spake.

Certainly some of the circumstances of the life of Job have the air of fiction, and may have been invented for the promotion of the moral and religious design which we suppose the author to have had chiefly in view.

That the sentiments of Job and of the different disputants, as well as those which are represented as proceeding from the lips of the Creator, must all be regarded as the effusions of the poet's own mind, is also too plain to need argument. The whole structure and arrangement, thoughts and language, form and substance of the work, must all have proceeded from one and the same mind.

The supposition, that so beautiful and harmonious a whole, every part of which bears the stamp of the highest genius, was the casual production of a man brought to the gates of the grave by a loathsome disease, and of three or four friends who had come to comfort him in his affliction, all of them expressing their thoughts in the language of rhythm and poetry; that the Deity was actually heard to speak half an hour from the midst of a violent storm; and that the consultations in the heavenly world were actual occurrences, — is too extravagant to need refutation.

On the other hand, it is against probability and against analogy to suppose that no such person as Job ever existed, and that the work has no foundation in fact. The etymological signification of his name, *persecuted*, has a very slight bearing on the subject. The epic and dramatic poets, ancient and modern, have usually chosen historical rather than fictitious personages as their principal characters, as being better adapted to secure the popular sympathy. It is probable that tradition had handed down the name of such a person as Job, distinguished for his piety and its trials, his virtue and its reward. This tradition the poet used and embellished in a manner adapted to promote the chief object of his work.

A more important question, at the present day, relates to the integrity of the work; whether we have it as it came from the author, or whether various additions have been made to it in later times.

The genuineness of the introductory and concluding chapters

in prose, of chap. xxvii. 7–xxviii., and of the speech of Elihu, has been denied with great confidence by several German scholars, upon what I cannot but regard as very insufficient grounds. Well knowing the array of learned critics from whom I differ on this question, I have some distrust in my own judgment. But I will endeavor to examine with fairness the arguments which have been adduced against the genuineness of the above-mentioned parts of Job.

Against the prologue and epilogue it is urged, "that the perfection of the work requires their rejection, because they solve the problem which is the subject of the work by the idea of trial and compensation; whereas it was the design of the author to solve the question through the idea of entire submission on the part of man to the wisdom and power of God." Thus, from a part of the work it is concluded what was the whole design of the author, and then whatever is inconsistent with this supposed design is rejected. But there is no necessity for the supposition of such an entire unity of purpose as this objection supposes. Much more probable is it, that the author designed not only to establish the necessity of unhesitating faith and unwavering submission, but also to throw all the light in his power upon the subject, considered as a problem for intellectual inquiry. If he has not completely solved the question which forms the principal subject of discussion, it does not follow that he did not undertake to do it; or, at least, to remove from it all the difficulties which he could remove. If it were even admitted, which I do not assert, that there is not a perfect consistency and unity in the views of a poet writing upon a very deep subject, he would not be the only one who has written inconsistently on the origin and design of evil. What author has written with perfect consistency on the principles of the government of the Infinite One? Would it be reasonable to reject as ungenuine all those parts of Soame Jenyns's work on the origin of evil which Dr. Johnson points out as inconsistent with its main design, or with other parts of the composition? It seems, indeed, singular, that a writer who has made such pathetic complaints of human suffering without apparent cause should recur so easily to the doctrine of compensation, which is contained in chap. xlii. But to deny, on this account, that he wrote the latter, is arbitrary and absurd. Perhaps, in the one case, the writer expressed what *he felt* to be true; in the other, what he wished to be true, or what was in conformity with the prevalent Jewish belief respecting Divine retribution. We have a similar phenomenon in the Book of Ecclesiastes. But no one has thought of rejecting large portions of this book.

Far more reasonable is it to gather the author's design from a view of the whole work; especially as there is no inconsistency in the supposition that he endeavored to clear up the difficulties which the subject presents to the human understanding, as well as to illustrate the necessity of the entire submission of the heart to God's will.

Besides, the prologue is important, not only as containing, in part, the writer's solution of the subject, but also as a preparation for the reader in estimating the character and language of Job. We could hardly sympathize with the imprecations with which he commences, or with his irreverent language toward the Deity, or even with his bold assertions of his own innocence, unless we were assured upon higher authority than his own, that he was, what he professed to be, an upright and good man. The whole takes a far deeper hold upon our sympathy, when we know that he who is in a state of such extreme depression, suffering reproach and condemnation from fallible men, has a witness in heaven and a record on high, having received the praise of an upright and good man from the Searcher of hearts before the angels in heaven.

The objection to the genuineness of chap. xxvii. and xxviii. is, that an apparent inconsistency exists between the language here assigned to Job, and what he has uttered in chap. xxi. This inconsistency is obvious, and was long ago observed by Kennicott. See his note on chap. xxvii. 7. And, if the object of the poet was to represent merely a persevering, unbending character like the Prometheus of Æschylus, there might be some force in the objection. But, if the design of the work be, as we have represented it, to throw all possible light upon a moral subject, it is well that Job should be represented as retracting what he had uttered in the heat of passion, and admitting all that he could admit with truth, and consistently with his main position, that he was innocent, or that misery is not always a proof of guilt. The great object of the poem is in fact advanced by such a course, and by Job's anticipating in some measure, in chap. xxviii., the arguments of the Supreme Judge. All that Job admits is not really inconsistent with what he says in chap. xxix., xxx., xxxi., and does not bring the subject to a crisis too soon.

In regard to the speech of Elihu, it is objected, that it differs in style from that of the other speakers; that it is weak, prolix, studied, obscure; that it is distinguished from the genuine parts of the book by the use of favorite expressions, and by reminiscences from the thoughts of some of the other speakers. That there is some difference between the language of Elihu and that of the other speakers is conceded, especially when he is represented as speaking of himself. But, when he has entered upon the subject, his thoughts are as weighty and as well expressed as those of the other speakers. The superiority of other parts of the book to the speech of Elihu appears to me to be stated by Davidson in very extravagant terms. I should be glad to be informed why chap. xxxiv. 16–30, xxxvi. 5–33, and xxxvii. 1–24, are not equal in poetic beauty and sublimity to many other parts of the work. But the true answer is, that this difference was designed; that a different style was assigned to Elihu by the author. There is some difference of manner in the speeches of the other adversaries of Job. It is more marked in the speech of Elihu, because he was a young man. Youthful forwardness was more inconsistent with Eastern feelings and manners than with ours. (See chap. xxix. 8.) And it is not strange that the poet should represent a young man appearing upon such an occasion as giving indications of youthful confidence in matters of theology. The author, however, soon forgets the character in which he is representing Elihu, and speaks in his own vein. It is evident that he had very little power to delineate character, or to go out of himself into the person of another.

It is rather evidence of skill in the poet, that he renders the sublime manifestation and the impressive language of the Deity more striking by contrasting with them the egotistic flourish and self-confidence with which young Elihu commences his discourse, and which he occasionally manifests in other parts of it. In regard to favorite expressions, and the reminiscences of the language of the other speakers, I think they are circumstances of very little importance. They may, at any rate, be the result of design, as part of the manner of Elihu; or they may be the result of inadvertence.

It is objected, secondly, that the speech of Elihu weakens the speeches of Job and of the Deity, in chap. xxix., xxx., xxxi., xxxviii., &c.; obscures the relation in which these stand to each other; and, in part, anticipates the thoughts which that of the Deity contains. We have already made some reply to this by the observation, that the majesty of the Divine appearance is heightened by contrast with the language of Elihu. It may be observed, too, that all the speakers have more or less anticipated the argument of the Deity, and could not well say any thing of the Creator or his works without doing it. But, as a whole, the speech of the Deity is remarkably distinguished from those of the other speakers. As to the interruption of the connection between the speech of Job and that of the Deity, it is not a very important circumstance. Let it be conceded, for the sake of argument, that the omission of the speech of Elihu would contribute to the perfection of the work, or that it is in itself somewhat inferior to other parts of it. What then? Why is it assumed that this poem must be a perfect production? Do not modern critics and reviewers imagine, that they can improve many of the productions of genius by the addition of a part here, or the subtraction of a part there? Some portions of "Paradise Lost" are inferior in strength and majesty to others, and the inferiority of "Paradise Regained" is generally recognized. But no one thinks of doubting their genuineness on this account. Besides, the author does give in Elihu's discourse one view of the cause of human suffering which is not distinctly stated elsewhere. (See chap. xxxiii. 14–28.) He might be expected to give it. For the doctrine of the beneficent design of affliction is found in parts of the Old Testament older than the Book of Job.

It is objected, in the next place, that Elihu perverts the language of Job; a thing which would have been done only by a person who was not the author of the work. To this it may be replied, that though the particular passages, which Elihu pretends to quote, are somewhat misstated, yet he hardly ascribes to Job more objectionable sentiments than he had elsewhere expressed, as in chap. xxi. Besides, it is not unnatural in a disputant, especially a young one, to misapprehend a question, or to misstate the language of an opponent.

It is said, again, that Elihu receives no answer. I apprehend that it was agreeable to Eastern feelings that such a forward young man should receive no answer. At any rate, this objection has little weight. For answers must come to an end at some time or other. It is said also, that Job is mentioned by name in the speech of Elihu, and not elsewhere. But surely so unimportant a circumstance, occurring in a speech where difference of manner was to be expected, affords very slight ground for suspecting its genuineness.

Again, it is said, Elihu is not mentioned in the prologue and epilogue. It is sufficient answer to this to say, that the author thought it proper to have but three speakers in the principal part of the debate, and to give a special introduction to Elihu in chap. xxxii. His judgment on this point may not have been as good as that of his modern critics; but I see not why we should alter the plan of his book on this account. As to the fact that Elihu is not mentioned in the epilogue, it may have been for the reason above assigned for his receiving no reply from Job; or because nothing occurred to the author which was particularly appropriate to be said to him.

Lastly, it is asserted by Davidson, exaggerating what has been adduced by Heiligstedt, that "expressions, word-forms, modes of speech occur, for which others are as uniformly found in the older work." If this broad statement were well supported, it would undoubtedly form a strong argument against the genuineness of Elihu's speech. But the instances which he cites are very far from sustaining it. In the first place, the whole book contains peculiar forms inclining to the Aramæan, as has been remarked by Gesenius,* De Wette,† and others, so that they have referred the whole book to the Chaldee period.‡ In its

* Gesch. d. Heb. Spr., § 33. † Einleit., § 291.

‡ See Int., p. 26.

Aramæan character, generally, the speech of Elihu agrees with the whole book. Secondly, the particular instances adduced by Davidson are of very little weight. Thus דֵּעַ, *knowledge*, instead of דַּעַת. But Elihu uses the latter word in chap. xxxiii. 3, and xxxiv. 35. So that the same argument will prove the speech of Elihu itself to have had two authors. It is not improbable that דֵּעִי, *my knowledge*, was used for דַּעְתִּי, for the sake of euphony.

Another instance is נֹעַר, used in the singular to denote *youth*. But the word is not used in the plural in any part of the book. Of course it proves nothing. It is also found in the singular in Ps. lxxxviii. 15.

Another instance is אָכֵן, *but*, in chap. xxxii. 8. But the word is used in this sense in Ps. xxxi. 23, lxxxii. 7, and Isa. xlix. 4. How this instance proves any thing, I am unable to see.

Another instance is עָוֶל, said to be used for עַוְלָה, in chap. xxxiv. 10. But the same form is found in Ps. vii. 4, liii. 2, and Ezek. iii. 20. So one form of the root denoting *iniquity* is used in Job v. 1, 6; and another, in xi. 29. Thus there is no reason whatever why Elihu should not have used עָוֶל, or עַוְלָה, at pleasure.

Another instance is the use of the singular חַיָּה, to denote *life*, in chap. xxxiii., instead of the plural חַיִּים, which occurs two or three times in other parts of the book. It occurs, however, in Ezek. vii. 13. As this is a familiar word, it must be admitted that its constant use in the singular in the speech of Elihu is something which could hardly be expected from the writer of the other parts of the book. But stranger things than this are found in writings all the parts of which are of undisputed genuineness. I can by no means allow to this instance a conclusive force.

I have examined all the instances brought forward by Davidson, and cannot find any of them to be more conclusive against the genuineness of Elihu's speech than the preceding. It seems to me that they are of no great significance. Generally speaking, an argument of this kind should be founded on very familiar phrases, which a writer has frequent occasion to use, and which he uses from habit. An author may use one word here, and another there, to express the same meaning, either for the sake of variety or of euphony, or without any particular motive.

On the whole, if it were even admitted, what I have no inclination to deny, that the style of Elihu is so diverse from that of the rest of the poem as to be somewhat remarkable, or not wholly explained by what has been said, yet, when we consider the strong presumption that such a work as the Book of Job would not be tampered with by his countrymen, and especially by a poet of no mean pretensions, I cannot help doubting whether there is sufficient reason for rejecting the passages under consideration. I can well conceive of additions being made to annals or history. It is also true that some whole compositions, or independent portions, of the Old Testament are ascribed to those who did not write them. This was the case with many of the Psalms, Ecclesiastes, the Book of Daniel, and with several prophecies in the Book of Isaiah. But this is a very different thing from introducing so large an addition into the midst of one poetical composition. It is easy to conceive that compositions should be ascribed to Homer, Virgil, Milton, Shakspeare, which they did not write. But that one should undertake to make an interpolation of many pages into the very midst of one of the best poems of either of these writers, is much more improbable, both on account of want of sufficient motive, the difficulty of executing the design, and the obstacles in the way of the reception by his contemporaries of such an interpolation. It appears to me that a Jew, and especially a Jewish poet, must have had too great a reverence for this noble production to undertake to improve it by such an addition, and that the early readers of the work would not have given it a universal reception. While, therefore, I readily concede some degree of inferiority, in parts of Elihu's speech, to other portions of the book, in respect to poetic merit, I think it is not of so very extraordinary and marked a nature, so different from what occurs in the works of other poets, as to be unaccountable except on the supposition of the spuriousness of the speech. I well know what a weight of modern critical authority is against me on this point. This consideration, I am free to acknowledge, weakens, in what is partly a matter of taste, my confidence in my own view of the subject, but does not destroy it. At any rate, as the current of modern criticism is against the opinion here expressed, I shall not regret, in a matter of very little moment, to have stated the reasons for holding fast the integrity of the book, even if they should be deemed unsatisfactory.

As to the country of Job, or, in other words, the scene of the poem, there has been a diversity of opinion amongst distinguished scholars. I was formerly inclined to adopt the opinion of those who supposed it to be Idumæa. I now think, that Lam. iv. 21, which at first view seems to favor this supposition, in fact indicates that the land of Uz was not a part of Idumæa, and that the prophet speaks of the Edomites as having gained possession of a country which did not belong to them. It appears to me, too, that Jer. xxv. 20, is also decisive of the question; else why does the prophet speak of the kings of the land of Uz and of Edom, in the next verse, as separate nations, to whom he was to extend the cup of indignation?

I now think it more probable, that the land of Uz was in the north-eastern part of Arabia Deserta, between Palestine, Idumæa, and the Euphrates. Ptolemy speaks of a tribe in this region, called Ἀισαῖται, which may perhaps have been written Ἀυσῖται (see Ros. Com. in Job, p. 30); and the Septuagint renders Uz, Ἀυσῖτις. This country would then be near the Chaldæans and Sabæans, by whose incursions the property of Job is said to have been lost. It is more properly entitled to the appellation of the East than Idumæa, which was nearly south of Palestine. The beautiful valley of Damascus, which Jahn supposes to have been the country of Job, could hardly have been so extensive as to account for the expression, "all the kings of the land of Uz," in Jer. xxv. 20.

A more interesting question remains to be spoken of; namely, in what country and in what age did the author live?

I shall not enter into a discussion of the various conjectures which have been offered in regard to the author of the book. Why should we seek to form an opinion, where there are absolutely no data on which to ground it? To me it seems highly probable, that the author of this incomparable production was one of whom we have no records and no other remains. The opinions of those who have undertaken to name the author are widely diverse. Lowth attributes it to Job himself; Lightfoot and others attribute it to Elihu; some of the Rabbinical writers, as also Kennicott, Michaelis, Dathe, and Good, to Moses; Luther, Grotius, and Döderlein, to Solomon; while Warburton ascribes it to Ezra.

Respecting the age in which the author lived, it might seem, at first view, that some judgment could be formed on internal grounds. But, in consequence of our imperfect acquaintance with the state of civilization, knowledge, opinions, and manners in ancient times, it is difficult to form a satisfactory opinion on the subject.

Some eminent scholars, as Lowth, Eichhorn, and Ilgen, have supposed that the author lived before the settlement of the Israelites in the land of Canaan. The principal argument in favor of this opinion is the absence of allusions to the institutions, rites, and ceremonies introduced by Moses, and to remarkable events in the history of the Jewish nation. This argument would be more satisfactory, if the characters, as well as the author, of the work, had been Hebrews. But as they were Arabians, who had nothing to do with the institutions of Moses, it is plain that a writer of genius would not have been guilty of the absurdity of putting the sentiments of a Jew into the mouth of an Arabian, at least so far as relates to such tangible matters as institutions, positive laws, ceremonies, and history. To me it seems that the author has manifested abundant evidence of genius and skill in the structure and execution of the work, to account for his not having given to Arabians the obvious peculiarities of Hebrews who lived under the institutions of Moses, at whatever period it may have been written. Even if the characters of the book had been Hebrews, the argument under consideration would not have been perfectly conclusive; for, from the nature of the subject, we might have expected as little in it that was Levitical or grossly Jewish as in the Book of Proverbs or of Ecclesiastes, or in several of the Prophets. A poet may nominally belong to a church of forms and ceremonies, and yet give very little evidence of it in his compositions. The argument for the Antemosaic origin of the book seems, therefore, wholly destitute of weight. On the contrary, we find a very strong argument against that opinion in the abstruse nature of its subject, and its speculative and philosophical spirit, which seem to imply a stage of civilization and a state of society different from what we suppose to have existed among the wandering Jews to whom Moses gave the law upon Sinai. It is to be kept in mind that the poet wrote for his contemporaries, and that the spirit of the reader as well as of the writer must be reflected from the work. It was agreeable to the spirit of Moses to say, Thus saith Jehovah, Ye shall do this, and, Ye shall not do that; and to accompany these commands and prohibitions with the most terrible sanctions, rather than to indulge in such bold speculations as are contained in this book.* A very different kind of poetry, if any could have existed at that time, seems also to be proper to the circumstances of the Jews in and before the age of Moses. There is more uncertainty in regard to particular religious conceptions. Those respecting angels, contained in the following verses, are supposed by De Wette to be inconsistent with those of the Mosaic age: iv. 18; v. 1; xv. 15; xxi. 22; xxxiii. 23, &c.; xxxviii. 7, comp. i. 7, ii. 2, &c. But it may be doubted whether this argument is valid. The manners and condition of society referred to or implied in some, at least, of the following passages, adduced by De Wette, seem to point to a much later period of Jewish history than the Antemosaic or the Mosaic age. It strikes me as rather inconsistent with the simplicity of the patriarchal age, that Job should be represented as the ruler or judge of a city, chap. xxix. 7, 8, 9; that there should be an allusion to the *written* sentence of a judge, chap. xiii. 26; to the signing of a bill of defence or complaint, to be brought into court, chap. xxxi. 35; to the recording of facts in a register or book-roll, or upon tablets of stone, chap. xix. 23, 24; to the custom of holding courts in the gates of walled cities, chap. v. 4, xxix. 7; to desolate cities, chap. xv. 28; to cities, chap. xxiv. 12, xxxix. 7; to various kinds of armor, chap. xx. 24, 25, and to the war-horse, chap. xxxix. 21–25; to splendid palaces or tombs, chap. iii. 14; to the deposition of kings, chap. xii. 18; to the laying-up of wealth in

---

* See Exod. xx. 5.

the form of money, chap. xx. 15, xxii. 24, xxiii. 10, xxvii. 16, xxxi, 24; and to mining operations, in chap. xxviii. These allusions may not be perfectly conclusive. Modern discoveries respecting the ancient Egyptian civilization lessen in some degree their conclusiveness; but they certainly do not well harmonize with our notions of the life and manners of the Hebrew patriarchs before the time of Moses. They suggest to us a later age.

In regard to the age of Solomon, or the period which intervenes between Solomon and the captivity at Babylon, which is assigned to it by some writers, there is no very decisive objection. Even if the work is supposed to have a national object, or to have been designed for the encouragement and consolation of the Jewish people as a nation, while in a state of calamity, there are several periods before the captivity when such a work would have been appropriate; for instance, the period of Habakkuk, whose expostulation with the Deity, and what follows in his prophecy, have a resemblance to the subject and sentiments of the Book of Job. There is no necessity, however, for supposing the work to have a national object. If this had been the case, I think it would have been made more distinctly to appear by the author. The subject is one which the vicissitudes of individual experience render as interesting and pertinent in the highest period of national prosperity as at the lowest point of national depression.

There is one consideration, however, which has inclined the best Hebrew scholars, of late, to assign the period of the captivity at Babylon as the age of the author of Job; namely, the Chaldaizing character of the language; for instance, עָנָה, *to answer*, applied to one who begins a discourse. The plural form of מִלָּה, מִלִּין; קְדֹשִׁים, *the holy ones*, applied to angels; שָׂהֵד, xvi. 19; תָּקַף, xiv. 20, xv. 24; חֵפֶץ, xxi. 21, xxii. 3; מִנָּה, vii. 3; מָה, *not*, xvi. 6 (comp. xxxi. 1); קִנְצֵי for קִצֵּי, xviii. 2; חִין for חֵן, xli. 4; שׁ as a prefix, xix. 29, &c.; אָמַר, *to command*. From these and other instances, Gesenius, De Wette, and Umbreit have referred the Book of Job to the time of the captivity; a period assigned to it by Le Clerc, Warburton, Heath, Garnet, and Rabbi Jochanan among the older critics. But from the few remains of Hebrew literature which have come down to us, and our imperfect acquaintance with the history of the language, it follows, that it is by no means certain that the words and forms above mentioned may not have been in use in some parts of Judea before the time of the captivity. שׁ as a prefix occurs in the Book of Judges. (See vi. 17.)

The introduction of Satan, in the historical introduction in prose, is certainly a strong argument against the high antiquity of the work. For there is no mention of such a being, by the name of Satan, in any of the Hebrew writings composed before the exile in Babylon; and there is some reason, though not absolutely conclusive, for believing that it was from the Chaldæans that the Jews derived the conception of such a being. This argument, if founded on correct premises, seems to be conclusive against the high antiquity of the work. For it is hardly credible that the Hebrews should have had the conception of an evil spirit before the time of Moses, and that it should not once occur in the writings which preceded the exile. But it may be doubted whether this argument be conclusive against the supposition that the Book of Job was written a short time before the exile. As to the opinion of Schultens, Herder, Dathe, Eichhorn, and others, that the Satan of the Book of Job was a good angel, it is now universally rejected as untenable.

The question may be asked, whether the perfection of the work is not inconsistent with the state of Hebrew literature during the captivity. Notwithstanding the strong language of Bishop Lowth on this point, I think it may justly be inferred from the psalms composed during this period, and from the ungenuine Isaiah, that this question should be answered in the negative. (See Ps. cxxxvii.; also Isa. xl.–lxvi.)

On the whole, it appears to me that there are no data upon which one can form a very confident opinion in regard to the precise age of the Book of Job. The latest period assigned for it appears to me far more probable than the earliest, and indeed the most probable; but that it may not have been written some time between the age of Solomon and the captivity is more than any one, who has surveyed the subject carefully, will with confidence assert. If a time of national distress is deemed probable, why should not the period of the Assyrian invasion, or that which followed it, have given birth to the work?

One more point remains to be considered; namely, the country of the author of the Book of Job. For it has been maintained that he was not a Hebrew, but an Arabian; and that the work is a translation from the Arabic.

In opposition to this opinion, it is to be observed in the first place, that there is no external evidence in favor of it. The work is now found in Hebrew alone, in the collection of what remains of ancient Hebrew literature; a collection which has been held sacred by the Jews as far back as we can trace their sentiments respecting it. Nor is there any history or tradition which intimates that the work ever existed in a different language.

It is found, too, in the sacred literature of a people peculiarly proud of their religious prerogatives, and regarding with coldness or jealousy, and often with aversion or hatred, all other nations. It is extremely improbable that any Jew would have had the inclination to transfer the production of a heathen into the Jewish literature, or that he would have been permitted to do it.

In the next place, the work is not only in the Hebrew language, but in the best style of Hebrew composition. The parallelism is uniform and well sustained; the sentences are pointed; the style is fresh and vigorous, and bears not, in its general characteristics, the slightest mark of a translation.

In opposition, then, to the external evidence, and to the general style of the composition, what are the reasons which have induced some distinguished men in modern times to regard the work as the production of an Arabian, and as translated from the Arabic?

They are, in the first place, the words, occurring in it more frequently than in other books of the Old Testament, which are regarded as Arabic in a Hebrew dress, or which may be illustrated from the Arabic. But these words are very few in relation to the whole work, and are not the less Hebrew because they may be illustrated from the Arabic. With the exception of the few forms which resemble the Aramæan, the Book of Job is in as pure Hebrew as any other part of the Scriptures. It appears to me that the remark of Jahn is perfectly just and satisfactory in regard to this topic: "It is not at all surprising, that in a lofty poem we find many of the less common words and ideas, which the Hebrew, through the poverty of its literature, has lost; while they have been preserved by the Arabic, the richest of the sister dialects." *

It has been said, that, if the author had been a Hebrew, more of a Levitical or ritual character would have been found in the book. This consideration seems to me to have a satisfactory answer in what has been said in pp. 23–27 against the high antiquity of the poem.

The other argument, in support of the opinion that an Arabian was the author of the poem, is drawn from the various allusions to Arabian manners and customs which are scattered through it. In regard to this argument, there are two things to be observed. First, we have reason to believe that the manners of the Jews, in some parts of Palestine, very much resembled those of the Arabs. As they sprang from the same stock, why should this not be the case, except so far as the Jews were distinguished by their religious institutions?

We are apt to form our conceptions of the whole Jewish nation from what we learn, in the Scriptures, of the inhabitants of cities, of Jerusalem in particular. It is to be recollected that the Hebrews were originally and "essentially a *nomadic* people; their fathers, Abraham, Isaac, and Jacob, had ever been so; they were emphatically Bedouins, removing with their flocks and herds from place to place, as occasion might require. In Egypt they had ever been shepherds, — their province of Goshen was adapted to pasturage, and not to tillage; and now, when they had come out into the deserts, with their flocks and herds, they were still the nomadic race they had ever been, — a people resembling those by whom these desert plains and valleys and mountains are possessed to this day." † It is not singular that the manners of

* Jahn's Introduction, § 196.

† See Biblical Repository, No. VIII. p. 787.

Bedouins should have been in a measure retained by those Hebrews who dwelt out of cities.

It follows from the preceding consideration, that the author of Job, having determined to make his characters Arabians, and to lay the scene of his work in Arabia, would find no difficulty in suiting the manners and sentiments of his characters, and his local allusions, to the scene which he had chosen; so that his only difficulty would be to exclude from his work obvious references to the Jewish history and religion. If, in addition to this, we suppose, what is perfectly reasonable, that the Hebrew philosopher had, like Plato, travelled into Egypt and through Arabia for the purpose of enriching his mind with all the knowledge of those countries, I think we shall find no difficulty in the supposition, that a Hebrew, of such genius and skill as are manifested in this work, might have been the author of it. A recent commentator on Job, Hirzel, has conjectured that the author was a Hebrew captive, carried into Egypt by Pharaoh Necho. (See 2 Kings xxiii. 29, &c.)

But this is not all. It seems to me, that though Arabian manners and scenes are the superficial characteristics of the work, yet, in its general spirit, and in many less obvious characteristics, the author has manifestly shown himself to be a Hebrew poet. The very subject of the work is just what might have been expected to arrest the attention of a Hebrew philosopher, educated in the religion of Moses. It is similar to that of other Hebrew compositions, as has been observed before.* In fact, if we regard the spirit and scope of the work, the remark of De Wette appears not too strong, that it is Hebrew through and through.

There are also many particular sentiments which we know to be appropriate to a Hebrew, possessing an acquaintance with the Hebrew literature and religion, and which we do not know to have been appropriate to an Arabian. Such are the following, which are more or less satisfactory. Chap. ix. 5–9; xii. 10; xv. 7; xxvi. 5, &c.; xxxviii. 4, &c.; — iv. 19; x. 9; xxvii. 3; — iv. 17, &c.; viii. 9; ix. 2; xiii. 26; xiv. 4; xv. 14; xxv. 4, 6; — iv. 18; v. 1; xv. 15; xxi. 22; xxxviii. 7; — xxxi. 26, 27; — vii. 7, &c.;

* Page 8

x. 21, &c.; xiv. 10, &c.; xvi. 22; xxx. 23; xxxviii 17. Add to these the mention of the Jordan as an instance of a great stream (chap. xl. 23), and the use of the name of Jehovah in the introduction and conclusion of the work. The sentiments and some of the expressions which are contained in the preceding references are also common in other parts of the Scriptures. Some of the sentiments may, it is true, have been held by the Arabians in common with the Hebrews; but we do not know it. The presumption, therefore, is, that they proceeded from one who was familiar with Hebrew literature; that is, from a Hebrew.

The following instance of resemblance to passages in the Psalms and Proverbs are also of weight with those who do not believe that the work is of very high antiquity, and translated and incorporated into the Hebrew literature so early that the authors of the Psalms and Proverbs borrowed from it. To me it seems more probable, that these common thoughts and peculiar expressions indicate only that the books in which they occur belong to a common literature, the literature of the same nation. Chap. v. 16, xxii. 19, comp. Ps. cvii. 42. Chap. xii. 21, 24, comp. Ps. cvii. 40. Chap. xiii. 5, comp. Prov. xvii. 28. Chap. xv. 16, xxxiv. 7, comp. Prov. xxvi. 6. Chap. xxii. 29, comp. Prov. xvi. 18, xviii. 12, xxix. 23. Chap. xxvi. 5, comp. Prov. ii. 18, xxi. 16. Chap. xxvi. 6, comp. Prov. xv. 11. Chap. xxvii. 16, &c., comp. Prov. xxviii. 8. Chap. xxviii. 18, comp. Prov. viii. 11. Chap. xxviii. 28, comp. Prov. i. 7. תּוּשִׁיָּה, chap. v. 12, vi. 13, xi. 6, xii. 16, xxvi. 3, xxx. 22, comp. Prov. ii. 7, iii. 21, viii. 14, xviii. 1. הַוָּה, chap. vi. 2, xxx. 13, comp. Prov. xix. 13. תַּחְבֻּלוֹת, chap. xxxvii. 12, comp. Prov. i. 5, xi. 14, and often.

On the whole, it appears to me that the internal evidence alone makes it more probable that the author was a Hebrew than that he was a foreigner; and, when we also add the external evidence in favor of this conclusion, there seems to be very little room for doubt.

It may seem remarkable, that the author of a work, which, for reach of thought, richness of imagination, depth and tenderness of feeling, and skill in its plan and execution, surpasses any production of Hebrew literature which has come down to us, should yet be unknown. But, when we consider the vicissitudes through which the Jewish nation has passed, the wonder is that we retain the work itself.

"But who," says the eloquent Herder, "shall answer our inquiries respecting him to whose meditations we are indebted for this ancient book, this justification of the ways of God to man, and sublime exaltation of humanity; who has exhibited them, too, in this silent picture, in the fortunes of an humble sufferer clothed in sackcloth and sitting in ashes, but fired with the sublime inspirations of his own wisdom? Who shall point us to the grave of him whose soul kindled with these divine conceptions, to whom was vouchsafed such access to the counsels of God, to angels, and the souls of men; who embraced in a single glance the heavens and the earth; and who could send forth his living spirit, his poetic fire, and his human affections, to all that exists, from the land of the shadow of death to the starry firmament, and beyond the stars? No cypress, flourishing in unfading green, marks the place of his rest. With his unuttered name he has consigned to oblivion all that was earthly, and, leaving his book for a memorial below, is engaged in a yet nobler song in that world where the voice of sorrow and mourning is unheard, and where the morning stars sing together.

"Or, if he, the patient sufferer, was here the recorder of his own sufferings and of his own triumph, of his own wisdom, first victorious in conflict, and then humbled in the dust, how blest have been his afflictions, how amply rewarded his pains! Here, in this book, full of imperishable thought, he still lives, gives utterance to the sorrows of his heart, and extends his triumph over centuries and continents. Not only, according to his wish, did he die in his nest, but a phœnix has sprung forth from his ashes; and from his fragrant nest is diffused an incense which gives, and will for ever give, reviving energy to the faint, and strength to the powerless. He has drawn down the heavens to the earth, encamped their hosts invisibly around the bed of languishing, and made the afflictions of the sufferer a spectacle to angels; has taught that God, too, looks with a watchful eye upon his creatures, and exposes them to the trial of their integrity for the maintenance of his own truth, and the promotion of his own glory. 'Behold! we count them happy which endure. Ye have heard of the patience of Job, and have seen the end of the Lord [the happy end which the Lord appointed for him], that the Lord is very pitiful and of tender mercy.'" *

In regard to the use of this book, it is hardly necessary, after what has been said of its character and design, to remind the reader that the instruction which it contains is to be derived from its general spirit and design as a whole, and not from particular verses or passages. Job was censured by the Deity for the rashness of his language; and his friends were condemned by the same unerring Judge, as not having spoken that which was right. If we regard independent sentences or speeches, those uttered by the friends of Job must be regarded as more consistent with the Jewish revelation, and more respectful to God, than much of the language of the afflicted sufferer. It was in the absoluteness of the application of their general maxims that they were wrong; in endeavoring to prove by them that Job was a bad man because he was miserable; or, in general, that misery is a proof of guilt. Perhaps the best lesson to be derived from the book is that which is enforced in the speech of the Deity; namely, humility in view of the limited vision of man, and submission to the will of God in view of the unsearchableness of his wisdom.

CAMBRIDGE, Oct. 14, 1866.

---

* Herder's Spirit of Hebrew Poetry, Marsh's Translation, vol. i. p. 120.

SYNOPSIS.

I. Historical Introduction in Prose. Chap. I., II.

II. Controversy in Verse. Chap. III.–XLII. 7.

The speech of Job, in which he curses his birth-day, is succeeded by—

(1) The First Series of Controversy. Chap. IV.–XIV.

1. Speech of Eliphaz. Chap. IV., V.
2. Answer of Job. Chap. VI., VII.
3. Speech of Bildad. Chap. VIII.
4. Answer of Job. Chap. IX., X.
5. Speech of Zophar. Chap. XI.
6. Answer of Job. Chap. XII., XIV.

(2) Second Series of Controversy. Chap. XV.–XXI.

1. Speech of Eliphaz. Chap. XV.
2. Answer of Job. Chap. XVI., XVII.
3. Speech of Bildad. Chap. XVIII.
4. Answer of Job. Chap. XIX.
5. Speech of Zophar. Chap. XX.
6. Answer of Job. Chap. XXI.

(3) Third Series of Controversy. Chap. XXII.–XXXI.

1. Speech of Eliphaz. Chap. XXII.
2. Answer of Job. Chap. XXIII., XXIV.
3. Speech of Bildad. Chap. XXV.
4. Answer of Job. Chap. XXVI.–XXXI.

(4) Speech of Elihu. Chap. XXXII.–XXXVII.

(5) The Speech of the Deity, which terminates the Discussion. Chap. XXXVIII.–XLII. 7.

III. The Conclusion in Prose. Chap. XLII. 7 to the end

JOB.

I.

Job's trial.—CHAP. I., II.

1 IN the land of Uz lived a man whose name was Job.
He was an upright and good man, fearing God and depart-
2 ing from evil. He had seven sons and three daughters.
3 His substance was seven thousand sheep, three thousand
camels, five hundred yoke of oxen, five hundred she-asses,
and a great number of servants; so that he was the greatest
of all the inhabitants of the East.
4 Now it was the custom of his sons to make a feast in
their houses, each on his day, and to send and invite their
5 three sisters to eat and to drink with them. And when
the days of their feasting had gone round, Job used to
send for them and sanctify them, and to rise up early in the
morning and offer burnt-offerings according to the number
of them all; for Job said, It may be that my sons have
sinned, and have renounced God in their hearts. Thus did
Job continually.
6 Now on a certain day the sons of God came to present
themselves before Jehovah, and Satan also came among
7 them. And Jehovah said to Satan, Whence comest thou?
Then Satan answered Jehovah, and said, From wandering over the earth, and walking up and down in it. And
8 Jehovah said to Satan, Hast thou observed my servant
Job, that there is none like him in the earth, an upright
and good man, fearing God and departing from evil?
9 Then Satan answered Jehovah, Is it for nought that Job
10 feareth God? Hast thou not placed a hedge around him,
and around his house, and around all his possessions?
Thou hast prospered the work of his hands, and his

11 herds are greatly increased in the land But only put
forth thy hand, and touch whatever he possesseth, and
12 to thy face will he renounce thee. And Jehovah said to
Satan, Behold, all that he hath is in thy power; but upon
him lay not thy hand. So Satan went forth from the
presence of Jehovah.
13 Now on a certain day the sons and daughters of Job
were eating and drinking wine in their eldest brother's
14 house, when a messenger came to Job, and said, The oxen
were ploughing, and the asses feeding beside them, and
15 the Sabæans fell upon them, and took them away; the
servants also they slew with the edge of the sword; and
16 I only am escaped alone to tell thee. While he was yet
speaking, there came also another, and said, The fire of
God hath fallen from heaven, and hath burned up the
sheep and the servants, and consumed them; and I only
17 am escaped alone to tell thee. While he was yet speaking, there came also another, and said, The Chaldæans
made out three bands, and fell upon the camels, and
carried them away; the servants also they slew with the
edge of the sword; and I only am escaped alone to tell
18 thee. While he was yet speaking, there came also
another, and said, Thy sons and thy daughters were eating and drinking wine in their eldest brother's house; and,
19 lo! there came a great wind from the desert, and smote
the four corners of the house, and it fell upon the young
men, and they are dead; and I only am escaped alone to
20 tell thee. Then Job arose, and rent his mantle, and
shaved his head, and fell down upon the ground, and wor-
21 shipped; and said, Naked came I forth from my mother's
womb, and naked shall I return thither. Jehovah gave,
and Jehovah hath taken away; blessed be the name of
Jehovah! In all this Job sinned not, nor uttered vain
words against God.
1 Again there was a day when the sons of God came to
present themselves before Jehovah; and Satan came also
among them to present himself before Jehovah. And
2 Jehovah said to Satan, Whence comest thou? And Satan
answered Jehovah, and said, From wandering over the
3 earth, and walking up and down in it. Then said Jehovah to Satan, Hast thou observed my servant Job, that

there is none like him upon the earth, an upright and good
man, fearing God and departing from evil? And still he
holdeth fast his integrity, although thou didst excite me
4 against him to destroy him without a cause. And Satan
answered Jehovah, and said, Skin for skin, yea, all that a
5 man hath will he give for his life. But put forth now
thy hand, and touch his bone and his flesh, and to thy
6 face will he renounce thee. And Jehovah said to Satan,
Behold, he is in thy hand; but spare his life.
7 Then Satan went forth from the presence of Jehovah,
and smote Job with sore boils from the sole of his foot to
8 his crown. And he took a potsherd to scrape himself
withal, and sat down among the ashes.
9 Then said his wife to him, Dost thou still retain thine
10 integrity? Renounce God, and die. But he said to her,
Thou talkest like one of the foolish women. What!
shall we receive good at the hand of God, and shall we
not receive evil? In all this, Job sinned not with his
lips.
11 Now three friends of Job heard of all this evil that
had come upon him, and came each one from his home;
Eliphaz the Temanite, and Bildad the Shuhite, and
Zophar the Naamathite; for they had agreed to come to
12 mourn with him, and to comfort him. And they lifted
up their eyes at a distance, and knew him not; then they
raised their voices and wept, and rent each one his mantle, and sprinkled dust upon their heads toward heaven.
13 And they sat down with him upon the ground seven days
and seven nights, and none spake a word to him; for they
saw that his grief was very great.

II.

Job's complaint. — CHAP. III.

1 AT length Job opened his mouth, and cursed the day
2 of his birth. And Job spake and said:

3 Perish the day in which I was born,
And the night which said, "A man-child is conceived!"

4 Let that day be darkness;
Let not God seek it from above;
Yea, let not the light shine upon it!
5 Let darkness and the shadow of death redeem it;
Let a cloud dwell upon it;
Let whatever darkeneth the day terrify it!

6 As for that night, let darkness seize upon it;
Let it not rejoice among the days of the year;
Let it not come into the number of the months!
7 O let that night be unfruitful!
Let there be in it no voice of joy;
8 Let them that curse the day curse it,
Who are skilful to stir up the leviathan!
9 Let the stars of its twilight be darkened;
Let it long for light, and have none;
Neither let it see the eyelashes of the morning!
10 Because it shut not up the doors of my mother's womb,
And hid not trouble from mine eyes.

11 Why died I not at my birth?
Why did I not expire when I came forth from the womb?
12 Why did the knees receive me,
And why the breasts, that I might suck?
13 For now should I lie down and be quiet;
I should sleep; then should I be at rest,
14 With kings and counsellors of the earth,
Who built up for themselves — ruins!
15 Or with princes that had gold,
And filled their houses with silver;
16 Or, as a hidden untimely birth, I had perished;
As infants which never saw the light.
17 There the wicked cease from troubling;
There the weary are at rest.
18 There the prisoners rest together;
They hear not the voice of the oppressor.
19 The small and the great are there,
And the servant is free from his master.

20 Why giveth He light to him that is in misery,
And life to the bitter in soul,

21 Who long for death, and it cometh not,
And dig for it more than for hid treasures;
22 Who rejoice exceedingly,
Yea, exult, when they can find a grave?
23 Why is light given to a man from whom the way is hid,
And whom God hath hedged in?
24 For my sighing cometh before I eat,
And my groans are poured out like water.
25 For that which I dread overtaketh me;
That at which I shudder cometh upon me.
26 I have no peace, nor quiet, nor respite:
Misery cometh upon me continually.

III.

First speech of Eliphaz. — CHAP. IV., V.

1 THEN spake Eliphaz the Temanite, and said:

2 If one attempt a word with thee, wilt thou be offended?
But who can refrain from speaking?
3 Behold, thou hast admonished many;
Thou hast strengthened feeble hands;
4 Thy words have upheld him that was falling,
And thou hast given strength to feeble knees.
5 But now it is come upon thee, and thou faintest;
It toucheth thee, and thou art confounded!
6 Is not thy fear of God thy hope,
And the uprightness of thy ways thy confidence?
7 Remember, I pray thee, who ever perished being innocent?
Or where have the righteous been cut off?
8 According to what I have seen, they who plough iniquity,
And sow mischief, reap the same.
9 By the blast of God they perish,
And by the breath of his nostrils they are consumed.
10 The roaring of the lion, and the voice of the fierce lion,
And the teeth of the young lions are broken.
11 The fierce lion perisheth for lack of prey,
And the whelps of the lioness are scattered abroad.

12 A word was once secretly brought to me,
And mine ear caught a whisper thereof.
13 Amid thoughts from visions of the night,
When deep sleep falleth upon men,
14 A fear and a horror came upon me,
Which made all my bones to shake.
15 Then a spirit passed before my face,
The hair of my flesh rose on end;
16 It stood still, but its form I could not discern;
An image was before mine eyes;
There was silence, and I heard a voice:
17 "Shall mortal man be more just than God?
Shall man be more pure than his Maker?
18 Behold, he putteth no trust in his ministering spirits,
And his angels he chargeth with frailty.
19 What then are they who dwell in houses of clay,
Whose foundation is in the dust,
Who crumble to pieces, as if moth-eaten!
20 Between morning and evening are they destroyed;
They perish for ever, and none regardeth it.
21 The excellency that is in them is torn away;
They die before they have become wise."

1 Call now, see if any will answer thee!
And to which of the holy ones wilt thou look?
2 Verily grief destroyeth the fool,
And wrath consumeth the weak man.
3 I have seen an impious man taking root,
But soon I cursed his habitation.
4 His children are far from safety;
They are oppressed at the gate, and there is none to deliver them.
5 His harvest the hungry devour,
Carrying it even through the thorns;
And a snare gapeth after his substance.
6 For affliction cometh not from the dust,
Nor doth trouble spring up from the ground;
7 Behold, man is born to trouble,
As the sparks fly upward.

8 I would look to God,
And to God would I commit my cause.

9 Who doeth great things and unsearchable;
Yea, marvellous things without number;
10 Who giveth rain upon the earth,
And sendeth water upon the fields;
11 Who placeth the lowly in high places,
And restoreth the afflicted to prosperity;
12 Who disappointeth the devices of the crafty,
So that their hands cannot perform their enterprises;
13 Who taketh the wise in their own craftiness,
And bringeth to nought the counsel of the artful.
14 They meet with darkness in the daytime;
They grope at noon as if it were night.
15 So he saveth the persecuted from their mouth;
The oppressed from the hand of the mighty.
16 So the poor hath hope,
And iniquity stoppeth her mouth.

17 Behold, happy is the man whom God correcteth;
Therefore despise not thou the chastening of the Almighty
18 For he bruiseth, and bindeth up;
He woundeth, and his hands make whole.
19 In six troubles will he deliver thee;
Yea, in seven shall no evil touch thee.
20 In famine he will redeem thee from death,
And in war from the power of the sword.
21 Thou shalt be safe from the scourge of the tongue,
And shalt not be afraid of destruction, when it cometh.
22 At destruction and famine thou shalt laugh,
And of the wild beasts of the land shalt thou not be afraid.
23 For thou shalt be in league with the stones of the field;
Yea, the beasts of the forest shall be at peace with thee.
24 Thou shalt find that thy tent is in peace;
Thou shalt visit thy dwelling, and not be disappointed.
25 Thou shalt see thy descendants numerous,
And thine offspring as the grass of the earth.
26 Thou shalt come to thy grave in full age,
As a shock of corn gathered in its season.
27 Lo! this we have searched out; so it is:
Hear it, and lay it up in thy mind!

IV.

Answer of Job. — CHAP. VI., VII.

1 THEN Job answered and said:

2 O that my grief were weighed thoroughly!
That my calamities were put together in the balance!
3 Surely they would be heavier than the sand of the sea;
On this account were my words rash.
4 For the arrows of the Almighty have pierced me;
Their poison drinketh up my spirit;
The terrors of God set themselves in array against me.
5 Doth the wild ass bray in the midst of grass?
Or loweth the ox over his fodder?
6 Can that which is unsavory be eaten without salt?
Is there any taste in the white of an egg?
7 That which my soul abhorreth to touch
Hath become my loathsome food.

8 O that I might have my request,
And that God would grant me that which I long for!
9 That it would please God to destroy me;
That he would let loose his hand, and make an end of me!
10 Yet it should still be my consolation,
Yea, in unsparing anguish I would exult,
That I have not denied the commands of the Holy One.
11 What is my strength, that I should hope?
And what mine end, that I should be patient?
12 Is my strength the strength of stones?
Or is my flesh brass?
13 Alas, there is no help within me!
Deliverance is driven from me!
14 To the afflicted, kindness should be shown by a friend;
Else he casteth off the fear of the Almighty.
15 But my brethren are faithless like a brook;
Like streams of the valley that pass away;
16 Which are turbid by reason of the ice,
And the snow, which hideth itself in them.
17 As soon as they flow forth, they vanish;
When the heat cometh, they are dried up from their place.

18 The caravans turn aside to them on their way;
They go up into the desert, and perish.
19 The caravans of Tema look for them;
The companies of Sheba expect to see them;
20 They are ashamed that they have relied on them;
They come to their place, and are confounded.
21 So ye also are nothing;
Ye see a terror, and shrink back.
22 Have I said, Bring me gifts?
Or, Give a present for me out of your substance?
23 Or, Deliver me from the enemy's hand?
Or, Rescue me from the hand of the violent?

24 Convince me, and I will hold my peace;
Cause me to understand wherein I have erred.
25 How powerful are the words of truth!
But what do your reproaches prove?
26 Do ye mean to censure words?
The words of a man in despair are but wind.
27 Truly ye spread a net for the fatherless;
Ye dig a pit for your friend.
28 Look now upon me, I pray you;
For to your very face can I speak falsehood?
29 Return, I pray, and let there be no unfairness;
Yea, return; — still is my cause righteous.
30 Is there iniquity on my tongue?
Cannot my taste discern what is sinful?

1 Is there not a war-service for man on the earth?
Are not his days as the days of a hireling?
2 As a servant panteth for the shade,
And as a hireling looketh for his wages,
3 So am I made to possess months of affliction,
And wearisome nights are appointed for me.
4 If I lie down, I say,
When shall I arise, and the night be gone?
And I am full of restlessness until the dawning of the day.
5 My flesh is clothed with worms, and clods of dust;
My skin is broken and become loathsome.
6 My days are swifter than a weaver's shuttle;
They pass away without hope.

7 O remember that my life is a breath;
That mine eye shall no more see good!
8 The eye of him that hath seen me shall see me no more;
Thine eyes shall look for me, but I shall not be.
9 As the cloud dissolveth and wasteth away,
So he that goeth down to the grave shall arise no more;
10 No more shall he return to his house,
And his dwelling-place shall know him no more.
11 Therefore I will not restrain my mouth;
I will speak in the anguish of my spirit;
I will complain in the bitterness of my soul.

12 Am I a sea, or a sea-monster,
That thou settest a watch over me?
13 When I say, My bed shall relieve me,
My couch shall ease my complaint,
14 Then thou scarest me with dreams,
And terrifiest me with visions;
15 So that my soul chooseth strangling,
Yea, death, rather than these my bones.
16 I am wasting away; I shall not live alway:
Let me alone, for my days are a vapor!
17 What is man, that thou shouldst make great account of him,
And fix thy mind upon him?—
18 That thou shouldst visit him every morning,
And prove him every moment?
19 How long ere thou wilt look away from me,
And let me alone, till I have time to breathe?
20 If I have sinned, what have I done to thee, O thou watcher of men!
Why hast thou set me up as thy mark,
So that I have become a burden to myself?
21 And why dost thou not pardon my transgression,
And take away mine iniquity?
22 For soon shall I sleep in the dust;
And, though thou seek me diligently, I shall not be

V.

First speech of Bildad, the Shuhite. — CHAP. VIII.

1 THEN answered Bildad the Shuhite, and said:

2 How long wilt thou speak such things?
How long shall the words of thy mouth be like a strong wind?
3 Will God pervert judgment?
Or will the Almighty pervert justice?
4 As thy children sinned against him,
He hath given them up to their transgression.
5 But if thou wilt seek early to God,
And make thy supplication to the Almighty, —
6 If thou wilt be pure and upright,
Surely he will yet arise for thee,
And prosper thy righteous habitation;
7 So that thy beginning shall be small,
And thy latter end very great.
8 For inquire, I pray thee, of the former age,
And mark what hath been searched out by their fathers;
9 (For we are of yesterday and know nothing,
Since our days upon the earth are but a shadow;)
10 Will not they instruct thee, and tell thee,
And utter words from their understanding?
11 "Can the paper-reed grow up without mire?
Can the bulrush grow without water?
12 While it is yet in its greenness, and is not cut down,
It withereth before any other herb.
13 Such is the fate of all who forget God;
So perisheth the hope of the ungodly.
14 His confidence shall come to nought,
And his trust shall prove a spider's web.
15 He shall lean upon his house, and it shall not stand;
He shall lay fast hold on it, but it shall not endure.
16 He is in full green before the sun,
And his branches shoot forth over his garden;
17 His roots are entwined about the heap,
And he seeth the place of stones;

18 When he shall be destroyed from his place,
It shall deny him, saying, 'I never saw thee.'
19 Lo! such is the joy of his course!
And others shall spring up from his place."

20 Behold, God will not cast away an upright man;
Nor will he help the evil-doers.
21 While he filleth thy mouth with laughter,
And thy lips with gladness,
22 They that hate thee shall be clothed with shame,
And the dwelling-place of the wicked shall come to nought.

VI.

Answer of Job. — CHAP. IX., X.

1 THEN Job answered and said:

2 Of a truth, I know that it is so:
For how can man be just before God?
3 If he choose to contend with him,
He cannot answer him to one charge of a thousand.
4 He is excellent in wisdom, mighty in strength:
Who hath hardened himself against him, and prospered?
5 He removeth the mountains, and they know it not;
He overturneth them in his anger.
6 He shaketh the earth out of her place,
And the pillars thereof tremble.
7 He commandeth the sun, and it riseth not,
And he sealeth up the stars.
8 He alone spreadeth out the heavens,
And walketh upon the high waves of the sea.
9 He made the Bear, Orion, and the Pleiads,
And the secret chambers of the South.
10 He doeth great things past finding out,
Yea, wonderful things without number.
11 Lo! he goeth by me, but I see him not;
He passeth along, but I do not perceive him.

12 Lo! he seizeth, and who can hinder him?
Who will say to him, What doest thou?
13 God will not turn away his anger;
The proud helpers are brought low before him.
14 How much less shall I answer him,
And choose out words to contend with him?
15 Though I were innocent, I would not answer him;
I would cast myself on the mercy of my judge.
16 Should I call, and he make answer to me,
I could not believe that he listened to my voice, —
17 He who falleth upon me with a tempest,
And multiplieth my wounds without cause!
18 Who will not suffer me to take my breath,
But filleth me with bitterness!
19 If I look to strength, "Lo! here am I!" [saith he,]
If to justice, "Who shall summon me to trial?"
20 Though I were upright, yet must my own mouth condemn me;
Though I were innocent, He would prove me perverse.
21 Though I were innocent, I would not care for myself;
I would despise my life.

22 It is all one; therefore I will affirm,
He destroyeth the righteous and the wicked alike.
23 When the scourge bringeth sudden destruction,
He laugheth at the sufferings of the innocent.
24 The earth is given into the hands of the wicked;
He covereth the face of the judges thereof;
If it be not He, who is it?

25 My days have been swifter than a courier;
They have fled away; they have seen no good.
26 They have gone by like the reed-skiffs;
Like the eagle, darting upon his prey.
27 If I say, I will forget my lamentation,
I will change my countenance, and take courage,
28 Still am I in dread of the multitude of my sorrows;
For I know that thou wilt not hold me innocent.
29 I shall be found guilty;
Why then should I labor in vain?
30 If I wash myself in snow,
And cleanse my hands with lye,

31 Still wilt thou plunge me into the pit,
So that my own clothes will abhor me.
32 For He is not a man, as I am, that I may contend with him,
And that we may go together into judgment;
33 There is no umpire between us,
Who may lay his hand upon us both.
34 Let him take from me his rod,
And not dismay me with his terrors,
35 Then I will speak, and not be afraid of him:
For I am not so at heart.

1 I am weary of my life;
I will let loose within me my complaint;
I will speak in the bitterness of my soul.
2 I will say unto God, Do not condemn me!
Show me wherefore thou contendest with me!
3 Is it a pleasure to thee to oppress,
And to despise the work of thy hands,
And to shine upon the plans of the wicked?
4 Hast thou eyes of flesh,
Or seest thou as man seeth?
5 Are thy days as the days of a man,
Are thy years as the days of a mortal,
6 That thou seekest after my iniquity,
And searchest after my sin,
7 Though thou knowest that I am not guilty,
And that none can deliver from thy hand?

8 Have thy hands completely fashioned and made me
In every part, that thou mightst destroy me?
9 O remember that thou hast moulded me as clay!
And wilt thou bring me again to dust?
10 Thou didst pour me out as milk,
And curdle me as cheese;
11 With skin and flesh didst thou clothe me,
And strengthen me with bones and sinews;
12 Thou didst grant me life and favor,
And thy protection preserved my breath:
13 Yet these things thou didst lay up in thy heart!
I know that this was in thy mind.

14 If I sin, then thou markest me,
And wilt not acquit me of mine iniquity.

15 If I am wicked, — then woe unto me!
Yet if righteous, I dare not lift up my head;
I am full of confusion, beholding my affliction.
16 If I lift it up, like a lion thou huntest me,
And again showest thyself terrible unto me.
17 Thou renewest thy witnesses against me,
And increasest thine anger toward me;
New hosts continually rise up against me.

18 Why then didst thou bring me forth from the womb?
I should have perished, and no eye had seen me;
19 I should be as though I had not been;
I should have been borne from the womb to the grave.
20 Are not my days few? O spare then,
And let me alone, that I may be at ease a little while,
21 Before I go — whence I shall not return —
To the land of darkness and death-shade,
22 The land of darkness like the blackness of death-shade,
Where is no order, and where the light is as darkness.

VII.

First speech of Zophar the Naamathite. — CHAP. XI.

1 THEN answered Zophar the Naamathite, and said:

2 Shall not the multitude of words receive an answer?
Shall the man of words be justified?
3 Shall thy boastings make men hold their peace?
Shalt thou mock, and none put thee to shame?
4 Thou sayest, My speech is pure;
I am clean in thine eyes, [O God!]
5 But O that God would speak,
And open his lips against thee;
6 That he would show thee the secrets of his wisdom, —
His wisdom, which is unsearchable!
Then shouldst thou know that God forgiveth thee many of thine iniquities.

7 Canst thou search out the deep things of God?
Canst thou find out the Almighty to perfection?
8 'Tis high as heaven, what canst thou do?
Deeper than hell, what canst thou know?
9 The measure thereof is longer than the earth,
And broader than the sea.
10 If he apprehend, and bind, and bring to trial,
Who shall oppose him?
11 For he knoweth the unrighteous;
He seeth iniquity, when they do not observe it.
12 But vain man is without understanding;
Yea, man is born a wild ass's colt.

13 If thou direct thy heart,
And stretch out thy hands, toward him;
14 If thou put away iniquity from thy hand,
And let not wickedness dwell in thy habitation, —
15 Then shalt thou lift up thy face without spot;
Yea, thou shalt be steadfast, and have no fear.
16 For thou shalt forget thy misery,
Or remember it as waters that have passed away.
17 Thy life shall be brighter than the noon-day;
Now thou art in darkness, thou shalt then be as the morning.
18 Thou shalt be secure, because there is hope;
Now thou art disappointed, thou shalt then rest in safety.
19 Thou shalt lie down, and none shall make thee afraid;
And many shall make suit unto thee.
20 But the eyes of the wicked shall be wearied out;
They shall find no refuge;
Their hope is — the breathing forth of life.

VIII.

Answer of Job. — CHAP. XII., XIII., XIV.

1 THEN Job answered and said:

2 No doubt ye are the whole people!
And wisdom will die with you!

3 But I have understanding as well as you;
I am not inferior to you:
Yea, who knoweth not such things as these?
4 I am become a laughing-stock to my friend,—
I who call upon God, that he would answer me!
The innocent and upright man is held in derision.
5 To calamity belongeth contempt in the mind of one at
ease;
It is ready for them that slip with the feet.
6 The tents of robbers are in prosperity,
And they who provoke God are secure,
Who carry their God in their hand.
7 For ask now the beasts, and they will teach thee;
Or the fowls of the air, and they will tell thee;
8 Or speak to the earth, and it will instruct thee;
And the fishes of the sea will declare unto thee.
9 Who among all these doth not know
That the hand of Jehovah doeth these things?
10 In whose hand is the soul of every living thing,
And the breath of all mankind.

11 Doth not the ear prove words,
As the mouth tasteth meat?
12 With the aged is wisdom,
And with length of days is understanding.
13 With Him are wisdom and strength;
With Him counsel and understanding.
14 Lo! he pulleth down, and it shall not be rebuilt;
He bindeth a man, and he shall not be set loose.
15 Lo! he withholdeth the waters, and they are dried up;
He sendeth them forth, and they lay waste the earth.
16 With him are strength and wisdom;
The deceived and the deceiver are his.
17 He leadeth counsellors away captive,
And judges he maketh fools.
18 He looseth the authority of kings,
And bindeth their loins with a cord.
19 He leadeth priests away captive,
And overthroweth the mighty.
20 He removeth speech from the trusty,
And taketh away judgment from the elders.

21 He poureth contempt upon princes,
And looseth the girdle of the mighty.
22 He revealeth deep things out of darkness,
And bringeth the shadow of death to light
23 He exalteth nations, and destroyeth them;
He enlargeth nations, and leadeth them captive.
24 He taketh away the understanding of the great men of the land,
And causeth them to wander in a wilderness, where is no path;
25 They grope in the dark without light;
He maketh them stagger like a drunken man.
1 Lo! all this mine eye hath seen;
Mine ear hath heard and understood it.
2 What ye know, I know also;
I am not inferior to you.

3 But O that I might speak with the Almighty!
O that I might reason with God!
4 For ye are forgers of lies;
Physicians of no value, all of you!
5 O that ye would altogether hold your peace!
This, truly, would be wisdom in you.

6 Hear, I pray you, my arguments;
Attend to the pleadings of my lips!
7 Will ye speak falsehood for God?
Will ye utter deceit for him?
8 Will ye be partial to his person?
Will ye contend earnestly for God?
9 Will it be well for you, if he search you thoroughly?
Can ye deceive him, as one may deceive a man?
10 Surely he will rebuke you,
If ye secretly have respect to persons.
11 Doth not his majesty make you afraid,
And his dread fall upon you?
12 Your maxims are words of dust;
Your fortresses are fortresses of clay.
13 Hold your peace, and let me speak:
And then come upon me what will!
14 Why do I take my flesh in my teeth,
And put my life in my hand?

15 Lo! he slayeth me, and I have no hope!
Yet will I justify my ways before him.
16 This also shall be my deliverance;
For no unrighteous man will come before him.
17 Hear attentively my words,
And give ear to my declaration!
18 Behold, I have now set in order my cause;
I know that I am innocent.
19 Who is he that can contend with me?
For then would I hold my peace, and die!

20 Only do not unto me two things,
Then will I not hide myself from thy presence;
21 Let not thy hand be heavy upon me,
And let not thy terrors make me afraid:
22 Then call upon me, and I will answer;
Or I will speak, and answer thou me.
23 How many are my iniquities and sins?
Make me to know my faults and transgressions.
24 Wherefore dost thou hide thy face,
And account me as thine enemy?
25 Wilt thou put in fear the driven leaf?
Wilt thou pursue the dry stubble?
26 For thou writest bitter things against me,
And makest me inherit the sins of my youth.
27 Yea, thou puttest my feet in the stocks,
And watchest all my paths;
Thou hemmest in the soles of my feet.
28 And I, like an abandoned thing, shall waste away;
Like a garment which is moth-eaten.

1 Man, that is born of woman,
Is of few days, and full of trouble.
2 He cometh forth as a flower, and is cut down;
He fleeth also as a shadow, and continueth not.
3 And dost thou fix thine eyes upon such a one?
And dost thou bring me into judgment with thee?
4 Who can produce a clean thing from an unclean?
Not one.
5 Seeing that his days are determined,
And the number of his months, with thee,

And that thou hast appointed him bounds which he cannot pass,
6 O turn thine eyes from him, and let him rest,
That he may enjoy, as a hireling, his day!

7 For there is hope for a tree,
If it be cut down, that it will sprout again,
And that its tender branches will not fail;
8 Though its root may have grown old in the earth,
And though its trunk be dead upon the ground,
9 Through the scent of water it will bud,
And put forth boughs, like a young plant.
10 But man dieth, and he is gone!
Man expireth, and where is he?

11 The waters fail from the lake,
And the stream wasteth and drieth up;
12 So man lieth down, and riseth not;
Till the heavens be no more, he shall not awake,
Nor be roused from his sleep.

13 O that thou wouldst hide me in the under-world!
That thou wouldst conceal me till thy wrath be past!
That thou wouldst appoint me a time, and then remember me!
14 If a man die, can he live again?
All the days of my war-service would I wait,
Till my change should come.

15 Thou wilt call, and I will answer thee;
Thou wilt have compassion upon the work of thy hands!
16 But now thou numberest my steps;
Thou watchest over my sins.
17 My transgression is sealed up in a bag;
Yea, thou addest unto my iniquity.

18 As the mountain falling cometh to nought,
And the rock is removed from its place;
19 As the waters wear away the stones,
And the floods wash away the dust of the earth, —
So thou destroyest the hope of man.

20 Thou prevailest against him continually, and he perisheth;
Thou changest his countenance, and sendest him away.
21 His sons come to honor, but he knoweth it not;
Or they are brought low, but he perceiveth it not.
22 But his flesh shall have pain for itself alone;
For itself alone shall his soul mourn.

IX.

Second speech of Eliphaz the Temanite. — CHAP. XV.

1 THEN answered Eliphaz the Temanite, and said:

2 Should a wise man answer with arguments of wind,
Or fill his bosom with the east wind?
3 Should he argue with speech that helpeth him not,
And with words which do not profit him?
4 Behold, thou makest the fear of God a vain thing,
And discouragest prayer before him.
5 Yea, thy own mouth proclaimeth thy iniquity,
Though thou choosest the tongue of the crafty.
6 Thy own mouth condemneth thee, and not I;
Thy own lips testify against thee.

7 Art thou the first man that was born?
Wast thou formed before the hills?
8 Hast thou listened in the council of God,
And drawn all wisdom to thyself?
9 What dost thou know, that we know not also?
What dost thou understand, that is a secret to us?
10 With us are the aged and hoary-headed;
Much older than thy father.
11 Dost thou despise the consolations of God,
And words so full of kindness to thee?

12 Why hath thy passion taken possession of thee?
And why this winking of thine eyes?
13 For against God hast thou turned thy spirit,
And uttered such words from thy mouth.

14 What is man, that he should be pure,
And he that is born of woman, that he should be innocent?
15 Behold, He putteth no trust in his ministering spirits,
And the heavens are not pure in his sight;
16 Much less, abominable and polluted man,
Who drinketh iniquity as water.

17 Hear me, and I will show thee,
And that which I have seen will I declare;
18 Which the wise men have told,
And not kept concealed, as received from their fathers;
19 To whom alone the land was given,
And among whom not a stranger wandered.
20 "All his days the wicked man is in pain;
Yea, all the years, that are laid up for the oppressor.
21 A fearful sound is in his ears;
In peace the destroyer cometh upon him.
22 He hath no hope that he shall escape from darkness;
He is set apart for the sword.
23 He wandereth about, seeking bread;
He knoweth that a day of darkness is at hand.
24 Distress and anguish fill him with dread;
They prevail against him like a king ready for the battle.
25 Because he stretched forth his hand against God,
And bade defiance to the Almighty,
26 And ran against him with outstretched neck,
With the thick bosses of his bucklers;
27 Because he covered his face with fatness,
And gathered fat upon his loins,
28 And dwelt in desolated cities,
In houses which no man inhabiteth,
That are ready to become heaps.
29 He shall not be rich; his substance shall not endure,
And his possessions shall not be extended upon the earth.
30 He shall not escape from darkness,
And the flame shall dry up his branches;
Yea, by the breath of His mouth shall he be taken away.

31 "Let not man trust in vanity! he will be deceived;
For vanity shall be his recompense.

32 He shall come to his end before his time,
And his branch shall not be green.
33 He shall shake off his unripe fruit like the vine,
And shed his blossoms like the olive-tree.
34 The house of the unrighteous shall be famished,
And fire shall consume the tents of bribery.
35 They conceive mischief, and bring forth misery,
And their breast deviseth deceit."

X.

Answer of Job. — CHAP. XVI., XVII.

1 BUT Job answered and said:

2 Of such things as these I have heard enough!
Miserable comforters are ye all!
3 Will there ever be an end to words of wind?
What stirreth thee up, that thou answerest?
4 I also might speak like you,
If ye were now in my place;
I might string together words against you,
And shake my head at you.
5 But I would strengthen you with my mouth,
And the consolation of my lips should sustain you.

6 If I speak, my grief is not assuaged;
And if I forbear, it doth not leave me.
7 For now He hath quite exhausted me; —
Thou hast desolated all my house!
8 Thou hast seized hold of me, and this is a witness against me;
My leanness riseth up and testifieth against me to my face.
9 His anger teareth my flesh, and pursueth me;
He gnasheth upon me with his teeth;
My adversary sharpeneth his eyes upon me.
10 They gape for me with their mouths;
In scorn they smite me on the cheek;
With one consent they assemble against me.

11 God hath given me a prey to the unrighteous,
And delivered me into the hands of the wicked.
12 I was at ease, but he hath crushed me;
He hath seized me by the neck, and dashed me in pieces;
He hath set me up for his mark.
13 His archers encompass me around;
He pierceth my reins, and doth not spare;
He poureth out my gall upon the ground.
14 He breaketh me with breach upon breach;
He rusheth upon me like a warrior.

15 I have sewed sackcloth upon my skin,
And thrust my horn into the dust.
16 My face is red with weeping,
And upon my eyelids is deathlike darkness.
17 Yet is there no injustice in my hands.
And my prayer hath been pure.
18 O earth! cover not thou my blood,
And let there be no hiding-place for my cry!

19 Yet even now, behold, my witness is in heaven,
And he who knoweth me is on high.
20 My friends have me in derision,
But my eye poureth out tears unto God.
21 O that one might contend for a man with God,
As a man contendeth with his neighbor!
22 For when a few years shall have passed,
I shall go the way whence I shall not return.
1 My breath is exhausted;
My days are at an end;
The grave is ready for me.

2 Are not revilers before me?
And doth not my eye dwell upon their provocations?
3 Give a pledge, I pray thee; be thou a surety for me with thee;
Who is he that will strike hands with me?
4 Behold, thou hast blinded their understanding;
Therefore thou wilt not suffer them to prevail.
5 He who delivereth up his friends as a prey, —
The eyes of his children shall fail.

6 He hath made me the by-word of the people;
Yea, I have become their abhorrence.
7 My eye therefore is dim with sorrow,
And all my limbs are as a shadow.
8 Upright men will be astonished at this,
And the innocent will rouse themselves against the wicked.
9 The righteous will also hold on his way,
And he that hath clean hands will gather strength.
10 But as for you all, return, I pray!
I find not yet among you one wise man.

11 My days are at an end;
My plans are broken off;
Even the treasures of my heart.
12 Night hath become day to me;
The light bordereth on darkness.
13 Yea, I look to the grave as my home;
I have made my bed in darkness.
14 I say to the pit, Thou art my father!
And to the worm, My mother! and, My sister!
15 Where then is my hope?
Yea, my hope, who shall see it?
16 It must go down to the bars of the under-world,
As soon as there is rest for me in the dust.

XI.

Second speech of Bildad the Shuhite. — CHAP. XVIII.

1 THEN Bildad the Shuhite answered and said:

2 How long ere ye make an end of words?
Understand, and then we will speak!
3 Why are we accounted as brutes,
And reputed vile in your sight?
4 Thou that tearest thyself in thine anger!
Must the earth be deserted for thee,
And the rock removed from its place?

5 Behold, the light of the wicked shall be put out,
And the flame of his fire shall not shine.
6 Light shall become darkness in his tent,
And his lamp over him shall go out.
7 His strong steps shall be straitened,
And his own plans shall cast him down.
8 He is brought into the net by his own feet,
And he walketh upon snares.
9 The trap layeth hold of him by the heel,
And the snare holdeth him fast.
10 A net is secretly laid for him on the ground,
And a trap for him in the pathway.
11 Terrors affright him on every side,
And harass him at his heels.
12 His strength is wasted by hunger,
And destruction is ready at his side.
13 His limbs are consumed,
Yea, his limbs are devoured by the first-born of death.
14 He is torn from his tent, which was his confidence,
And is borne away to the king of terrors.
15 They who are none of his shall dwell in his tent;
Brimstone shall be scattered upon his habitation.
16 His roots below shall be dried up,
And his branches above shall be withered.
17 His memory perisheth from the earth,
And no name hath he in the land.
18 He shall be thrust from light into darkness,
And driven out of the world.
19 He hath no son, nor kinsman among his people,
Nor any survivor in his dwelling-place.
20 They that come after him shall be amazed at his fate,
As they that were before them were struck with horror.
21 Yea, such is the dwelling of the unrighteous man;
Such is the place of him who knoweth not God!

XII.

Answer of Job.—Chap. XIX.

1 But Job answered and said:

2 How long will ye vex my soul,
And break me in pieces with words?
3 These ten times have ye reviled me;
Without shame do ye stun me!
4 And be it, indeed, that I have erred,
My error abideth with myself.
5 Since, indeed, ye magnify yourselves against me,
And plead against me my reproach,
6 Know then that it is God who hath brought me low;
He hath encompassed me with his net.

7 Behold, I complain of wrong, but receive no answer;
I cry aloud, but obtain no justice.
8 He hath fenced up my way, so that I cannot pass,
And hath set darkness in my paths.
9 He hath stripped me of my glory,
And taken the crown from my head.
10 He hath destroyed me on every side, and I am gone!
He hath torn up my hope like a tree.
11 He kindleth his anger against me,
And counteth me as his enemy.
12 His troops advance together against me;
They throw up for themselves a way to me,
And encamp around my dwelling.
13 My brethren he hath put far from me,
And my acquaintance are wholly estranged from me.
14 My kinsfolk have forsaken me,
And my bosom friends have forgotten me.
15 The foreigners of my house, yea, my own maid-servants, regard me as a stranger;
I am an alien in their eyes.
16 I call my servant, and he maketh no answer;
With my own mouth do I entreat him.
17 My breath is become strange to my wife,
And my prayers also to my own mother's sons.

18 Even young children despise me;
When I rise up, they speak against me.
19 All my bosom friends abhor me,
And they whom I loved are turned against me.
20 My bones cleave to my flesh and my skin,
And I have scarcely escaped with the skin of my teeth.
21 Have pity upon me, O ye my friends! have pity upon me;
For the hand of God hath smitten me!
22 Why do ye persecute me like God,
And are not satisfied with my flesh?

23 O that my words were now written!
O that they were marked down in a scroll!
24 That with an iron pen, and with lead,
They were engraven upon the rock for ever!
25 Yet I know that my Vindicator liveth,
And will hereafter stand up on the earth;
26 And though with my skin this body be wasted away,
Yet without my flesh shall I see God.
27 Yea, I shall see him my friend;
My eyes shall behold him, and not another:
For this, my soul panteth within me.

28 Since ye say, "How may we persecute him,
And find grounds of accusation against him?"
29 Be ye afraid of the sword!
For malice is a crime for the sword;
That ye may know that judgment cometh.

XIII.

Second speech of Zophar the Naamathite. — CHAP. XX.

1 THEN answered Zophar the Naamathite, and said:

2 For this do my thoughts lead me to reply,
And for this is my ardor within me.
3 I have heard my shameful rebuke;
And the spirit, from my understanding, answereth for me

4 Knowest thou not, that from the days of old,
From the time when man was placed upon the earth,
5 The triumphing of the wicked hath been short,
And the joy of the impious but for a moment?
6 Though his greatness mount up to the heavens,
And his head reach to the clouds,
7 Yet shall he perish for ever, and be mingled with dust;
They who saw him shall say, Where is he?
8 He shall flee away like a dream, and shall not be found;
Yea, he shall disappear like a vision of the night.
9 The eye also which saw him shall see him no more,
And his dwelling-place shall never more behold him.
10 His sons shall seek the favor of the poor,
And their hands shall give back his wealth.
11 His bones are full of his youth,
But they shall lie down with him in the dust.

12 Though wickedness be sweet in his mouth,
Though he hide it under his tongue,
13 Though he cherish it, and will not part with it,
And keep it fast in his mouth,
14 Yet his meat shall be changed within him,
And become to him the poison of asps.
15 He hath glutted himself with riches,
And he shall throw them up again;
Yea, God shall cast them out of his body.

16 He shall suck the poison of asps;
The tongue of the viper shall destroy him.
17 He shall never see the flowing streams,
And the rivers of honey and milk.
18 The fruits of his toil he shall give back, and shall not enjoy them:
It is substance to be restored, and he shall not rejoice therein.
19 Because he hath oppressed and abandoned the poor,
And seized upon the house which he did not build;
20 Because he knew no rest in his bosom,
He shall not save that in which he delighteth.
21 Because nothing escaped his greediness,
His prosperity shall not endure.

22 In the fulness of his abundance he shall be brought low;
Every hand of the wretched shall come upon him.
23 He shall, indeed, have wherewith to fill himself:
God shall send upon him the fury of his anger,
And rain it down upon him for his food.
24 If he fleeth from the iron weapon,
The bow of brass shall pierce him through.
25 He draweth the arrow, and it cometh forth from his body;
Yea, the glittering steel cometh out of his gall.

Terrors are upon him;
26 Calamity of every kind is treasured up for him.
A fire not blown shall consume him;
It shall consume whatever is left in his tent.
27 The heavens shall reveal his iniquity,
And the earth shall rise up against him.
28 The substance of his house shall disappear;
It shall flow away in the day of His wrath.
29 Such is the portion of the wicked man from God,
And the inheritance appointed for him by the Almighty.

XIV.

Answer of Job. — CHAP. XXI.

1 BUT Job answered and said:

2 Hear attentively my words,
And let this be your consolation.
3 Bear with me, that I may speak;
And after I have spoken, mock on!
4 Is my complaint concerning man?
Why then should I not be angry?
5 Look upon me, and be astonished,
And lay your hand upon your mouth!

6 When I think of it, I am confounded;
Trembling taketh hold of my flesh.
7 Why is it that the wicked live,
Grow old, yea, become mighty in substance?

8 Their children are established in their sight with them,
And their offspring before their eyes.
9 Their houses are in peace, without fear,
And the rod of God cometh not upon them.
10 Their bull gendereth, and faileth not;
Their cow calveth, and casteth not her calf.
11 They send forth their little ones like a flock,
And their children dance.
12 They sing to the timbrel and harp,
And rejoice at the sound of the pipe.
13 They spend their days in prosperity,
And in a moment go down to the under-world.
14 And yet they say unto God, "Depart from us!
We desire not the knowledge of thy ways!
15 Who is the Almighty, that we should serve him?
And what will it profit us, if we pray to him?"

16 [Ye say,] "Lo! their prosperity is not secure in their hands!
Far from me be the conduct of the wicked!"
17 How often is it, that the lamp of the wicked is put out,
And that destruction cometh upon them,
And that He dispenseth to them tribulations in his anger?
18 How often are they as stubble before the wind,
Or as chaff, which the whirlwind carrieth away?
19 "But" [say ye] "God layeth up his iniquity for his children."
Let him requite the offender, and let him feel it!
20 Let his own eyes see his destruction,
And let him drink of the wrath of the Almighty!
21 For what concern hath he for his household after him,
When the number of his own months is completed?

22 Who then shall impart knowledge to God,—
To him that judgeth the highest?
23 One dieth in the fulness of his prosperity,
Being wholly at ease and quiet;
24 His sides are full of fat,
And his bones moist with marrow.
25 Another dieth in bitterness of soul,
And hath not tasted pleasure.

26 Alike they lie down in the dust,
And the worms cover them.

27 Behold, I know your thoughts,
And the devices by which ye wrong me.
28 For ye say, "Where is the house of the oppressor,
And where the dwelling-places of the wicked?"
29 Have ye never inquired of travellers,
And do ye not know their tokens,
30 That the wicked is spared in the day of destruction,
And that he is borne to his grave in the day of wrath?
31 Who will charge him with his conduct to his face,
And who will requite him for the evil he hath done?
32 Even this man is borne with honor to the grave;
Yea, he watcheth over his tomb.
33 Sweet to him are the sods of the valley:
And all men move after him,
As multitudes without number before him.
34 Why then do ye offer your vain consolations?
Your answers continue false.

XV.

Third speech of Eliphaz the Temanite. — CHAP. XXII.

1 THEN Eliphaz the Temanite answered and said:

2 Can a man, then, profit God?
Behold, the wise man profiteth himself.
3 Is it a pleasure to the Almighty, that thou art righteous;
Or a gain to him, that thou walkest uprightly?
4 Will he contend with thee because he feareth thee?
Will he enter with thee into judgment?
5 Hath not thy wickedness been great?
Have not thine iniquities been numberless?
6 For thou hast taken a pledge from thy brother unjustly,
And stripped the poor of their clothing.
7 Thou hast given the weary no water to drink,
And withholden bread from the hungry.

8 But the man of power, his was the land,
And the honorable man dwelt in it.
9 Thou hast sent widows away empty,
And broken the arms of the fatherless.
10 Therefore snares are round about thee,
And sudden fear confoundeth thee;
11 Or darkness, through which thou canst not see,
And floods of water cover thee.
12 Is not God in the height of heaven?
And behold the stars, how high they are!
13 Hence thou sayest, "What doth God know?
Can he govern behind the thick darkness?
14 Dark clouds are a veil to him, and he cannot see;
And he walketh upon the arch of heaven."

15 Wilt thou take the old way
Which wicked men have trodden,
16 Who were cut down before their time,
And whose foundations were swept away by a flood?
17 Who said unto God, "Depart from us!"
And, "What can the Almighty do to us?"
18 And yet he filled their houses with good things!—
Far from me be the counsel of the wicked!
19 The righteous see their fate, and rejoice;
And the innocent hold them in derision.
20 "Truly our adversary is destroyed,
And fire hath consumed his abundance!"

21 Acquaint now thyself with him, and be at peace:
Thus shall prosperity return to thee.
22 Receive, I pray thee, instruction from his mouth,
And lay up his words in thy heart.
23 If thou return to the Almighty, thou shalt be built up;
If thou put away iniquity from thy tent.
24 Cast to the dust thy gold,
And the gold of Ophir to the stones of the brook:
25 Then shall the Almighty be thy gold,
Yea, treasures of silver unto thee;
26 For then shalt thou have delight in the Almighty,
And shalt lift up thy face unto God.

27 Thou shalt pray to him, and he shall hear thee,
And thou shalt perform thy vows.
28 The purpose which thou formest shall prosper with thee,
And light shall shine upon thy ways.
29 When men are cast down, thou shalt say, "There is lifting up!"
And the humble person he will save.
30 He will deliver even him that is not innocent.
The purity of thy hands shall save him.

XVI.

Answer of Job. — CHAP. XXIII., XXIV.

1 THEN Job answered and said:

2 Still is my complaint bitter;
But my wound is deeper than my groaning.
3 O that I knew where I might find him!
That I might go before his throne!
4 I would order my cause before him,
And fill my mouth with arguments;
5 I should know what he would answer me,
And understand what he would say to me.
6 Would he contend with me with his mighty power?
No! he would have regard to me.
7 Then would an upright man contend with him,
And I should be fully acquitted by my judge.
8 But, behold, I go eastward, and he is not there;
And westward, but I cannot perceive him;
9 To the north, where he worketh, but I cannot behold him;
He hideth himself on the south, and I cannot see him.
10 But he knoweth the way which is in my heart;
When he trieth me, I shall come forth as gold.
11 My feet have trodden in his steps;
His way I have kept, and have not turned aside from it.

12 I have not neglected the precepts of his lips;
Above my own law have I esteemed the words of his mouth.

13 But he is of one mind, and who can turn him?
And what he desireth, that he doeth.
14 He performeth that which is appointed for me;
And many such things are in his mind!
15 Therefore I am in terror on account of him;
When I consider, I am afraid of him.
16 For God maketh my heart faint;
Yea, the Almighty terrifieth me;
17 Because I was not taken away before darkness came,
And he hath not hidden darkness from mine eyes.

1 Why are not times treasured up by the Almighty?
And why do not they who know him see his days?
2 They remove landmarks;
They take away flocks by violence, and pasture them.
3 They drive away the ass of the fatherless,
And take the widow's ox for a pledge.
4 They push the needy from the way;
All the poor of the land are forced to hide themselves.
5 Behold, like wild asses of the desert, they go forth to their work;
They search for prey;
The wilderness supplieth them food for their children.
6 In the fields they reap the harvest,
And gather the vintage of the oppressor.
7 They lodge naked, without clothing,
And without covering from the cold.
8 They are drenched with the mountain showers,
And embrace the rock for want of shelter.

9 The fatherless are torn from the breast,
And the garment of the needy is taken for a pledge.
10 They go naked, without clothing,
And carry the sheaf hungry.
11 They make oil within their walls,
And tread the wine-vat, yet suffer thirst.

12 From anguish the dying groan,
And the wounded cry aloud;
And God regardeth not their prayer!

13 Others hate the light;
They know not its ways,
And abide not in its paths.
14 With the light ariseth the murderer;
He killeth the poor and needy;
In the night he is as a thief.
15 The eye of the adulterer watcheth for the twilight;
He saith, "No eye will see me,"
And putteth a mask upon his face.
16 In the dark they break into houses;
In the daytime they shut themselves up;
They are strangers to the light.
17 The morning is to them the very shadow of death;
They are familiar with the terrors of the shadow of death.
18 Light are they on the face of the waters;
They have an accursed portion in the earth;
They come not near the vineyards.

19 As drought and heat consume the snow waters,
So doth the grave the wicked.
20 His own mother forgetteth him;
The worm feedeth sweetly on him;
He is no more remembered,
And iniquity is broken like a tree.

21 He oppresseth the barren, that hath not borne,
And doeth not good to the widow.
22 He taketh away the mighty by his power;
He riseth up, and no one is sure of life.
23 God giveth them security, so that they are confident;
His eyes are upon their ways.
24 They are exalted; — in a little while they are gone!
They are brought low, and die, like all others;
And like the topmost ears of corn are they cut off.
25 If it be not so, who will confute me,
And show my discourse to be worthless?

XVII.

Third speech of Bildad the Shuhite. — CHAP. XXV.

1 THEN answered Bildad the Shuhite, and said:

2 Dominion and fear are with Him;
He maintaineth peace in his high places.
3 Is there any numbering of his hosts?
And upon whom doth not his light arise?
4 How then can man be righteous before God?
Or how can he be pure that is born of woman?
5 Behold, even the moon, it shineth not;
And the stars are not pure in his sight.
6 How much less, man, a worm;
And the son of man, a reptile!

XVIII.

Answer of Job. — CHAP. XXVI.

1 THEN Job answered and said:

2 How hast thou helped the weak,
And strengthened the feeble arm!
3 How hast thou counselled the ignorant,
And revealed wisdom in fulness!
4 For whom hast thou uttered these words?
And whose spirit spake through thee?

5 Before Him the shades tremble
Beneath the waters and their inhabitants.
6 The under-world is naked before him,
And destruction is without covering.
7 He stretcheth out the north over empty space,
And hangeth the earth upon nothing.
8 He bindeth up the waters in his thick clouds,
And the cloud is not rent under them.
9 He covereth the face of his throne,
And spreadeth his clouds upon it.

10 He hath drawn a circular bound upon the waters,
To the confines of light and darkness.
11 The pillars of heaven tremble
And are confounded at his rebuke.
12 By his power he stilleth the sea,
Yea, by his wisdom he smiteth its pride.
13 By his spirit he hath garnished the heavens;
His hand hath formed the fleeing Serpent.
14 Lo! these are but the borders of his works;
How faint the whisper we have heard of him!
But the thunder of his power who can understand?

XIX.

Answer of Job to all three of his opponents. — CHAP. XXVII., XXVIII.

1 MOREOVER Job continued his discourse, and said:

2 As God liveth, who hath rejected my cause,
And the Almighty, who hath afflicted my soul;
3 As long as my breath is in me,
And the spirit of God is in my nostrils,
4 Never shall my lips speak falsehood,
Nor my tongue utter deceit.
5 God forbid that I should acknowledge you to be just:
To my last breath will I assert my integrity.
6 I will hold fast my innocence, and not let it go;
My heart reproacheth me for no part of my life.
7 May mine enemy be as the wicked,
And he that riseth up against me as the unrighteous!
8 For what is the hope of the wicked, when God cutteth off
his web,
And taketh away his life?
9 Will he listen to his cry,
When trouble cometh upon him?
10 Can he delight himself in the Almighty,
And call at all times upon God?

11 I will teach you concerning the hand of God;
That which is with the Almighty I will not conceal.

12 Behold, ye yourselves have all seen it;
Why then do ye cherish such vain thoughts?
13 This is the portion of the wicked man from God, —
The inheritance which oppressors receive from the Almighty.
14 If his children be multiplied, it is for the sword;
And his offspring shall not be satisfied with bread.
15 Those of them that escape shall be buried by Death,
And their widows shall not bewail them.
16 Though he heap up silver as dust,
And procure raiment as clay, —
17 He may procure, but the righteous shall wear it,
And the innocent shall share the silver.
18 He buildeth his house like the moth,
Or like the shed which the watchman maketh.
19 The rich man lieth down, and is not buried;
In the twinkling of an eye he is no more.
20 Terrors pursue him like a flood;
A tempest stealeth him away in the night.
21 The east wind carrieth him away, and he perisheth;
Yea, it sweepeth him away from his place.
22 God sendeth his arrows at him, and doth not spare;
He would fain escape from His hand.
23 Men clap their hands at him,
And hiss him away from his place.

1 Truly there is a vein for silver,
And a place for gold, which men refine.
2 Iron is obtained from earth,
And stone is melted into copper.
3 Man putteth an end to darkness;
He searcheth to the lowest depths
For the stone of darkness and the shadow of death.
4 From the place where they dwell they open a shaft;
Forgotten by the feet,
They hang down, they swing away from men.
5 The earth, out of which cometh bread,
Is torn up underneath, as it were by fire.
6 Her stones are the place of sapphires,
And she hath clods of gold for man.

7 The path thereto no bird knoweth,
And the vulture's eye hath not seen it;
8 The fierce wild beast hath not trodden it;
The lion hath not passed over it.
9 Man layeth his hand upon the rock;
He upturneth mountains from their roots;
10 He cleaveth out streams in the rocks,
And his eye seeth every precious thing;
11 He bindeth up the streams, that they trickle not,
And bringeth hidden things to light.

12 But where shall wisdom be found?
And where is the place of understanding?
13 Man knoweth not the price thereof,
Nor can it be found in the land of the living.
14 The deep saith, It is not in me;
And the sea saith, It is not with me.
15 It cannot be gotten for gold,
Nor shall silver be weighed out as the price thereof.
16 It cannot be bought with the gold of Ophir,
With the precious onyx or the sapphire.
17 Gold and crystal are not to be compared with it;
Nor can it be purchased with jewels of fine gold.
18 No mention shall be made of coral or of crystal;
For wisdom is more precious than pearls.
19 The topaz of Ethiopia cannot equal it,
Nor can it be purchased with pure gold.

20 Whence then cometh wisdom?
And where is the place of understanding?
21 Since it is hidden from the eyes of all living,
And kept close from the fowls of the air.
22 Destruction and Death say,
We have heard a rumor of it with our ears.
23 God knoweth the way to it;
He knoweth its dwelling-place.
24 For he seeth to the ends of the earth,
And surveyeth all things under the whole heaven.
25 When he gave the winds their weight,
And meted out the waters by measure;

26 When he prescribed a law to the rain,
And a path to the thunderflash,—
27 Then did he see it, and make it known;
He established it, and searched it out.
28 But he said unto man,
Behold, the fear of the Lord, that is wisdom,
And to depart from evil is understanding.

XX.

Job's review of his past life. — CHAP. XXIX.-XXXI.

1 MOREOVER Job continued his discourse, and said:

2 O that I were as in months past,
In the days when God was my guardian;
3 When his lamp shined over my head,
And when by his light I walked through darkness!
4 As I was in the autumn of my days,
When the friendship of God was over my tent;
5 When the Almighty was yet with me,
And my children were around me;
6 When I bathed my steps in milk,
And the rock poured me out rivers of oil!

7 When I went forth to the gate by the city,
And took my seat in the market-place,
8 The young men saw me and hid themselves,
And the aged arose and stood.
9 The princes refrained from speaking,
And laid their hand upon their mouth.
10 The nobles held their peace,
And their tongue cleaved to the roof of their mouth.
11 When the ear heard me, then it blessed me;
And when the eye saw me, it gave witness to me.
12 For I delivered the poor, when they cried;
And the fatherless, who had none to help him.
13 The blessing of him that was ready to perish came upon me,
And I caused the heart of the widow to sing for joy.

14 I clothed myself with righteousness, and it clothed itself
with me;
And justice was my robe and diadem.
15 I was eyes to the blind,
And feet was I to the lame;
16 I was a father to the poor,
And the cause of him I knew not I searched out;
17 And I broke the teeth of the wicked,
And plucked the spoil from his jaws.
18 Then said I, "I shall die in my nest;
I shall multiply my days as the sand.
19 My root is spread abroad to the waters,
And the dew abideth on my branches.
20 My glory is fresh with me,
And my bow gathereth strength in my hand."

21 To me men gave ear, and waited,
And kept silence for my counsel.
22 To my words they made no reply,
When my speech dropped down upon them.
23 Yea, they waited for me as for the rain;
They opened their mouths wide as for the latter rain.
24 If I smiled upon them, they believed it not;
Nor did they cause the light of my countenance to fall.
25 When I came among them, I sat as chief;
I dwelt as a king in the midst of an army, —
As a comforter among mourners.

1 But now they that are younger than I hold me in derision,
Whose fathers I would have disdained to set with the
dogs of my flock.
2 Of what use to me would be even the strength of their
To whom old age is lost? [hands,
3 By want and hunger they are famished;
They gnaw the dry desert,
The darkness of desolate wastes.
4 They gather purslain among the bushes,
And the root of the broom is their bread.
5 They are driven from the society of men;
There is a cry after them as after a thief.

6 They dwell in gloomy valleys,
In caves of the earth and in rocks.
7 They bray among the bushes;
Under the brambles are they stretched out.
8 An impious and low-born race,
They are beaten out of the land.
9 And now I am become their song;
Yea, I am their by-word!
10 They abhor me, they stand aloof from me;
They forbear not to spit before my face.
11 Yea, they let loose the reins, and humble me;
They cast off the bridle before me.
12 On my right hand riseth up the brood;
They thrust away my feet;
They cast up against me their destructive ways.
13 They break up my path;
They hasten my fall, —
They who have no helper!
14 They come upon me as through a wide breach;
Through the ruins they rush in upon me.
15 Terrors are turned against me;
They pursue my prosperity like the wind,
And my welfare passeth away like a cloud.

16 And now my soul poureth itself out upon me;
Days of affliction have taken hold of me.
17 By night my bones are pierced; they are torn from me,
And my gnawers take no rest.
18 Through the violence of my disease is my garment changed;
It bindeth me about like the collar of my tunic.
19 He hath cast me into the mire,
And I am become like dust and ashes.
20 I call upon Thee, but thou dost not hear me;
I stand up before thee, but thou regardest me not.
21 Thou art become cruel to me;
With thy strong hand dost thou lie in wait for me.
22 Thou liftest me up, and causest me to ride upon the wind;
Thou meltest me away in the storm.
23 I know that thou wilt bring me to death,
To the place of assembly for all the living.

24 When He stretcheth out his hand, prayer availeth nothing;
When He bringeth destruction, vain is the cry for help.
25 Did not I weep for him that was in trouble?
Was not my soul grieved for the poor?
26 But when I looked for good, then evil came;
When I looked for light, then came darkness.
27 My bowels boil, and have no rest;
Days of anguish have come upon me.
28 I am black, but not by the sun;
I stand up, and utter my cries in the congregation.
29 I am become a brother to jackals,
And a companion to ostriches.
30 My skin is black, and falleth from me,
And my bones burn with heat.
31 My harp also is turned to mourning,
And my pipe to notes of grief.

1 I made a covenant with mine eyes;
How then could I gaze upon a maid?
2 For what is the portion appointed by God from above,
And the inheritance allotted by the Almighty from on [high?
3 Is not destruction for the wicked,
And ruin for the workers of iniquity?
4 Doth He not see my ways,
And number all my steps?

5 If I have walked with falsehood,
And if my foot hath hasted to deceit,
6 Let him weigh me in an even balance;
Yea, let God know my integrity!
7 If my steps have turned aside from the way,
And my heart gone after mine eyes,
Or if any stain hath cleaved to my hand,
8 Then I may sow, and another eat;
And what I plant, may it be rooted up!
9 If my heart hath been enticed by a woman,
Or if I have watched at my neighbor's door,
10 Then let my wife grind for another,
And let other men lie with her!
11 For this were a heinous crime,
Even a transgression to be punished by the judges;

12 Yea, it were a fire that would consume to destruction,
And root out all my increase.

13 If I have refused justice to my man-servant or maid-servant,
When they had a controversy with me,
14 Then what shall I do when God riseth up?
And when he visiteth, what shall I answer him?
15 Did not He that made me in the womb make him?
Did not one fashion us in the womb?

16 If I have refused the poor their desire,
And caused the eyes of the widow to fail;
17 If I have eaten my morsel alone,
And the fatherless hath not partaken of it;
18 (Nay, from my youth he grew up with me as with a father,
And I have helped the widow from my mother's womb;)
19 If I have seen any one perishing for want of clothing,
Or any poor man without covering;
20 If his loins have not blessed me,
And he hath not been warmed with the fleece of my sheep;
21 If I have shaken my hand against the fatherless,
Because I saw my help in the gate,—
22 Then may my shoulder fall from its blade,
And my fore-arm be broken from its bone!
23 For destruction from God was a terror to me,
And before his majesty I could do nothing.

24 If I have made gold my trust,
Or said to the fine gold, Thou art my confidence;
25 If I have rejoiced, because my wealth was great,
And my hand had found abundance;
26 If I have beheld the sun in his splendor,
Or the moon advancing in brightness,
27 And my heart hath been secretly enticed,
And my mouth hath kissed my hand,—
28 This also were a crime to be punished by the judge;
For I should have denied the God who is above.
29 If I have rejoiced at the destruction of him that hated me,
And exulted when evil came upon him;

30 (Nay, I have not suffered my mouth to sin,
By asking with curses his life;)
31 If the men of my tent have not exclaimed,
"Who is there that hath not been satisfied with his meat?"
32 The stranger did not lodge in the street;
I opened my doors to the traveller.
33 Have I, after the manner of men, hidden my transgression,
Concealing my iniquity in my bosom,
34 Then let me be confounded before the great multitude!
Let the contempt of families cover me with shame!
Yea, let me keep silence! let me never appear abroad!

35 O that there were one who would hear me!
Behold my signature! let the Almighty answer me.
And let mine adversary write down his charge!
36 Truly I would wear it upon my shoulder;
I would bind it upon me as a crown.
37 I would disclose to him all my steps;
I would approach him like a prince.

38 If my land cry out against me,
And its furrows bewail together;
39 If I have eaten of its fruits without payment,
And wrung out the life of its owners, —
40 Let thorns grow up instead of wheat,
And noxious weeds instead of barley.

The words of Job are ended.

XXI.

Speech of Elihu. — CHAP. XXXII.-XXXVII.

1 So these three men ceased to answer Job, because he
2 was righteous in his own eyes. Then was kindled the
wrath of Elihu, the son of Barachel, the Buzite, of the
family of Ram; against Job was his wrath kindled, because he accounted himself righteous rather than God.
3 Against his three friends also was his wrath kindled, because they had not found an answer, and yet had con-

4 demned Job. Now Elihu had delayed to reply to Job,
5 because they were older than himself. But when Elihu
saw that there was no answer in the mouth of these three
6 men, his wrath was kindled. Then spake Elihu, the son
of Barachel, the Buzite, and said:

I am young, and ye are very old;
Therefore I was afraid,
And durst not make known to you my opinion.
7 I said, "Days should speak,
And the multitude of years should teach wisdom."
8 But it is the spirit in man,
Even the inspiration of the Almighty, that giveth him understanding.
9 Great men are not always wise,
Nor do the aged always understand what is right.
10 Therefore, I pray, listen to me:
I also will declare my opinion.

11 Behold, I have waited for your words,
I have listened to your arguments,
Whilst ye searched out what to say;
12 Yea, I have attended to you;
And behold, none of you hath refuted Job,
Nor answered his words.
13 Say not, then, "We have found out wisdom;
God must conquer him, not man."
14 He hath not directed his discourse against me,
And with speeches like yours will I not answer him.
15 They were confounded! they answered no more!
They could say nothing!
16 I waited, but they spake not;
They stood still; they answered no more!
17 Therefore will I answer, on my part;
I also will show my opinion.
18 For I am full of matter;
The spirit within me constraineth me.
19 Behold, my bosom is as wine that hath no vent;
Like bottles of new wine, which are bursting.
20 I will speak, that I may be relieved;
I will open my lips and answer.

21 I will not be partial to any man's person,
Nor will I flatter any man.
22 For I know not how to flatter;
Soon would my Maker take me away.

1 Hear, therefore, my discourse, I pray thee, O Job
And attend unto all my words!
2 Behold, I am opening my mouth;
My tongue is now speaking in my palate.
3 My words shall be in the uprightness of my heart;
My lips shall utter knowledge purely.
4 The spirit of God made me,
And the breath of the Almighty gave me life.
5 If thou art able, answer me;
Set thyself in array against me; stand up!
6 Behold, I, like thee, am a creature of God;
I also was formed of clay.
7 Behold, my terror cannot dismay thee,
Nor can my greatness be heavy upon thee.

8 Surely thou hast said in my hearing,
I have heard the sound of thy words:
9 "I am pure, and without transgression;
I am clean, and there is no iniquity in me.
10 Behold, He seeketh causes of hostility against me;
He regardeth me as his enemy.
11 He putteth my feet in the stocks;
He watcheth all my paths."
12 Behold, in this thou art not right; I will answer thee;
For God is greater than man.
13 Why dost thou contend with Him?
For he giveth no account of any of his doings.
14 For God speaketh once,
Yea, twice, when man regardeth it not.
15 In a dream, in a vision of the night,
When deep sleep falleth upon men,
In slumber upon the bed;
16 Then openeth he the ears of men,
And sealeth up for them admonition;
17 That he may turn man from his purpose,
And hide pride from man.

18 Thus he saveth him from the pit,
Yea, his life from perishing by the sword.

19 He is chastened also with pain upon his bed,
And with a continual agitation of his bones,
20 So that his mouth abhorreth bread,
And his taste the choicest food;
21 His flesh is consumed, that it cannot be seen,
And his bones, that were invisible, are naked;
22 Yea, his soul draweth near to the pit,
And his life to the destroyers.
23 But if there be with him a messenger,
An interpreter, one of a thousand,
Who may show unto man his duty,
24 Then will God be gracious to him, and say,
"Save him from going down to the pit:
I have found a ransom."
25 His flesh shall became fresher than a child's;
He shall return to the days of his youth.
26 He shall pray to God, and he will be favorable to him,
And permit him to see his face with joy,
And restore unto man his righteousness.
27 He shall sing among men, and say,
"I sinned; I acted perversely;
Yet hath he not requited me for it:
28 He hath delivered me from going down to the pit,
And my life beholdeth the light."

29 Lo! all these things doeth God
Time after time with man,
30 That he may bring him back from the pit,
That he may enjoy the light of the living.

31 Mark well, O Job! hearken to me!
Keep silence, and I will speak.
32 Yet if thou hast any thing to say, answer me!
Speak! for I desire to pronounce thee innocent.
33 But if not, do thou listen to me!
Keep silence, and I will teach thee wisdom!

1 And Elihu proceeded, and said:

2 Hear my words, ye wise men!
Give ear to me, ye that have knowledge!
3 For the ear trieth words,
As the mouth tasteth meat.
4 Let us examine for ourselves what is right;
Let us know among ourselves what is true.

5 Job hath said, "I am righteous,
And God refuseth me justice.
6 Though I am innocent, I am made a liar;
My wound is incurable, though I am free from transgression."
7 Where is the man like Job,
Who drinketh impiety like water;
8 Who goeth in company with evil-doers,
And walketh with wicked men?
9 For he hath said, "A man hath no advantage,
When he delighteth himself in God."
10 Wherefore hearken to me, ye men of understanding!
Far be iniquity from God;
Yea, far be injustice from the Almighty!
11 For what a man hath done he will requite him,
And render to every one according to his deeds.
12 Surely God will not do iniquity,
Nor will the Almighty pervert justice.
13 Who hath given him the charge of the earth?
Or who hath created the whole world?
14 Should he set his heart against man,
Should he take back his spirit and his breath,
15 Then would all flesh expire together;
Yea, man would return to the dust.

16 If thou hast understanding, hear this!
Give ear to the voice of my words!
17 Shall he, that hateth justice, govern?
Wilt thou then condemn the just and mighty One?
18 Is it fit to say to a king, Thou art wicked;
Or to princes, Ye are unrighteous?
19 How much less to him that is not partial to princes,
Nor regardeth the rich more than the poor?
For they are all the work of his hands.

20 In a moment they die; yea, at midnight
Do the people stagger and pass away,
And the mighty are destroyed without hand.
21 For his eyes are upon the ways of man;
He seeth all his steps.
22 There is no darkness, nor shadow of death,
Where evil-doers may hide themselves.
23 He needeth not attend long to a man,
That he may go into judgment before God;
24 He dasheth in pieces the mighty without inquiry,
And setteth up others in their stead.
25 Therefore he knoweth their works,
And in a night he overthroweth them, so that they are destroyed.
26 On account of their wickedness he smiteth them,
In the presence of many beholders;
27 Because they turned away from him,
And had no regard to his ways,
28 And caused the cry of the poor to come before him;
For he heareth the cry of the oppressed.
29 When he giveth rest, who can cause trouble?
And when he hideth his face,
Who can behold him?
30 So is it with nations and individuals alike!
That the wicked may no more rule,
And may not be snares to the people.

31 Surely thou shouldst say unto God,
"I have received chastisement; I will no more offend;
32 What I see not, teach thou me!
If I have done iniquity, I will do it no more."
33 Shall he recompense according to thy mind,
Because thou refusest, or because thou choosest, and not he?
Speak, if thou hast knowledge!
34 Men of understanding,
Wise men, who hear me, will say,
35 "Job hath spoken without knowledge,
And his words are without wisdom."
36 I desire that Job may be tried to the last,
For answering like wicked men.

37 For he addeth impiety to his sin;
He clappeth his hands among us,
And multiplieth words against God.

1 Moreover Elihu proceeded, and said:

2 Dost thou then think this to be right?
Thou hast said, "I am more righteous than God."
3 For thou askest, "What advantage have I?
What have I gained, more than if I had sinned?"
4 I will answer thee,
And thy companions with thee.

5 Look up to the heavens, and see!
And behold the clouds, which are high above thee!
6 If thou sinnest, what doest thou against Him?
If thy transgressions be multiplied, what doest thou to him?
7 If thou art righteous, what dost thou give him?
Or what receiveth he at thy hand?
8 Thy wickedness injureth only a man like thyself,
And thy righteousness profiteth only a son of man.

9 The oppressed cry out on account of the multitude of wrongs;
They cry aloud on account of the arm of the mighty.
10 But none saith, "Where is God, my Maker,
Who giveth songs in the night;
11 Who teacheth us more than the beasts of the earth,
And maketh us wiser than the birds of heaven?"
12 There they cry aloud on account of the pride of the wicked;
But he giveth no answer.
13 For God will not hear the vain supplication,
Nor will the Almighty regard it;
14 Much less when thou sayest thou canst not see him:
Justice is with him, — only wait thou for him!
15 But now, because he hath not visited in his anger,
Nor taken strict note of transgression,
16 Therefore hath Job opened his mouth rashly,
And multiplied words without knowledge.

1 Elihu also proceeded, and said:

2 Bear with me a little while, that I may show thee!
For I have yet words in behalf of God.
3 I will bring my knowledge from afar,
And assert the justice of my Maker.
4 Truly my words shall not be false:
A man of sound knowledge is before thee.

5 Behold, God is great, but despiseth not any;
Great is he in strength of understanding.
6 He suffereth not the wicked to prosper,
But rendereth justice to the oppressed.
7 He withdraweth not his eyes from the righteous;
But establisheth them for ever with kings on the throne,
That they may be exalted.
8 And if they be bound in fetters,
And holden in the cords of affliction,
9 Then showeth he them their deeds,
And how they have set him at defiance by their transgressions;
10 He also openeth their ears to admonition,
And commandeth them to return from iniquity.
11 If they obey and serve him,
They spend their days in prosperity,
And their years in pleasures.
12 But if they obey not, they perish by the sword;
They die in their own folly.

13 The corrupt in heart treasure up wrath;
They cry not to God, when he bindeth them.
14 They die in their youth;
They close their lives with the unclean.
15 But he delivereth the poor in their distress;
He openeth their ears in affliction.
16 He will bring thee also from the jaws of distress
To a broad place, where is no straitness;
And the provision of thy table shall be full of fatness.
17 But if thou art full of the judgment of the wicked,
Judgment and justice shall take hold of thee.
18 For if wrath be with him, beware lest he take thee away by his stroke,
So that a great ransom shall not save thee!

19 Will he esteem thy riches?
No! neither thy gold, nor all the abundance of thy wealth.
20 Long not thou for that night
To which nations are taken away from their place.
21 Take heed, turn not thine eyes to iniquity!
For this hast thou chosen rather than affliction.

22 Behold, God is exalted in his power:
Who is a teacher like him?
23 Who hath prescribed to him his way?
Or who can say to him, "Thou hast done wrong"?
24 Forget not to magnify his work,
Which men celebrate with songs.
25 All mankind gaze upon it;
Mortals behold it from afar.
26 Behold, God is great; we cannot know him,
Nor search out the number of his years.
27 Lo! he draweth up the drops of water,
Which distil rain from his vapor;
28 The clouds pour it down,
And drop it upon man in abundance.
29 Who can understand the spreading of his clouds,
And the rattling of his pavilion?
30 Behold, he spreadeth around himself his light,
And he clotheth himself with the depths of the sea.
31 By these he punisheth nations,
And by these he giveth food in abundance.
32 His hands he covereth with lightning;
He giveth it commandment against an enemy.
33 His thunder maketh him known;
Yea, to the herds, as he ascendeth on high.

1 At this my heart trembleth,
And leapeth out of its place.
2 Hear, O hear, the thunder of his voice,
And the noise which goeth forth from his mouth!
3 He directeth it under the whole heaven,
And his lightning to the ends of the earth.
4 After it the thunder roareth;
He thundereth with his voice of majesty,
And restraineth it not, when his voice is heard.

5 God thundereth with his voice marvellously;
Great things doeth he, which we cannot comprehend.
6 For he saith to the snow, "Be thou on the earth!"
To the shower also, even the showers of his might.
7 He sealeth up the hand of every man,
That all men whom he hath made may acknowledge him.
8 Then the beasts go into dens,
And abide in their caverns.
9 Out of the south cometh the whirlwind,
And cold out of the north.
10 By the breath of God ice is formed,
And the broad waters become narrow.
11 Yea, with moisture he burdeneth the clouds;
He spreadeth abroad his lightning-clouds.
12 They move about by his direction,
To execute all his commands throughout the world;
13 Whether he cause them to come for punishment,
Or for the land, or for mercy.

14 Give ear to this, O Job!
Stand still, and consider the wondrous works of God!
15 Dost thou know when God gave commandment to them,
And caused the lightning of his cloud to flash?
16 Dost thou understand the balancing of the clouds,
The wondrous works of Him that is perfect in knowledge?
17 How thy garments become warm,
When he maketh the earth still by the south wind?
18 Canst thou like him spread out the sky,
Which is firm like a molten mirror?
19 Teach us what we shall say to him!
For we cannot set in order our words by reason of darkness.
20 Shall it be told him that I would speak?
Shall a man speak, that he may be consumed?

21 For now men do not look upon the light,
When it is bright in the skies,
When the wind hath passed over them, and made them clear.
22 From the north cometh gold;
But with God is terrible majesty!

23 The Almighty, we cannot find him out;
Great is he in power and justice,
Abundant in righteousness; he doth not oppress.
24 Therefore let men fear him!
Upon none of the wise in heart will he look.

XXII.

Jehovah's reproof of Job.—Chap. XXXVIII., XXXIX.

1 Then spake Jehovah to Job out of the whirlwind, and said:

2 Who is this that darkeneth counsel by words without knowledge?
3 Gird up thy loins like a man!
I will ask thee, and answer thou me!
4 Where wast thou when I laid the foundations of the earth?
Declare, if thou hast understanding!
5 Who fixed its dimensions, that thou shouldst know it!
Or who stretched out the line upon it?
6 Upon what were its foundations fixed?
And who laid its corner-stone,
7 When the morning stars sang together,
And all the sons of God shouted for joy?

8 And who shut up the sea with doors,
When it burst forth as from the womb?
9 When I made the clouds its mantle,
And thick darkness its swaddling-band;
10 When I appointed for it my bound,
And fixed for it bars and doors;
11 And said, Thus far shalt thou come, and no farther,
And here shall thy proud waves be stayed!

12 Hast thou, in thy life, given charge to the morning,
Or caused the day-spring to know its place,
13 That it should lay hold of the ends of the earth,
And shake the wicked out of it?

14 It is changed as clay by the seal;
And all things stand forth as in rich apparel.
15 But from the wicked their light is withheld,
And the high-raised arm is broken.

16 Hast thou visited the springs of the sea,
And walked through the recesses of the deep?
17 Have the gates of death been disclosed to thee,
And hast thou seen the gates of the shadow of death?
18 Hast thou surveyed the breadth of the earth?
Declare, if thou knowest it all!

19 Where is the way to the abode of light?
And darkness — where is its dwelling-place?
20 That thou shouldst lead it to its boundary,
And that thou shouldst know the paths to its mansion!
21 Surely thou knowest; for thou wast then born!
And the number of thy years is great!

22 Hast thou visited the storehouses of the snow,
Or seen the treasuries of the hail,
23 Which I have reserved against the time of trouble, —
Against the day of battle and war?

24 What is the way to where light is distributed,
And the east wind spread abroad upon the earth?
25 Who hath prepared channels for the rain,
And a path for the thunder-flash,
26 To give rain to the land without an inhabitant,
To the wilderness wherein is no man;
27 To satisfy the desolate and waste ground,
And cause the tender herb to spring forth?

28 Hath the rain a father?
Or who hath begotten the drops of the dew?
29 Out of whose womb came the ice?
And who hath gendered the hoar-frost of heaven?
30 The waters are hid as under stone,
And the face of the deep becometh solid.

31 Canst thou fasten the bands of the Pleiads,
Or loosen the chains of Orion?

32 Canst thou lead forth the Signs in their season,
Or guide the Bear with her sons?
33 Knowest thou the ordinances of the heavens?
Hast thou appointed their dominion over the earth?
34 Canst thou lift up thy voice to the clouds,
So that abundance of waters will cover thee?
35 Canst thou send forth lightnings, so that they will go,
And say to thee, "Here we are"?
36 Who hath put understanding in the reins,
And given intelligence to the mind?
37 Who numbereth the clouds in wisdom?
And who poureth out the bottles of heaven,
38 When the dust floweth into a molten mass,
And the clods cleave fast together?

39 Canst thou hunt prey for the lioness,
Or satisfy the hunger of the young lions,
40 When they couch in their dens,
And lie in wait in the thicket?
41 Who provideth for the raven his food,
When his young ones cry unto God,
While they wander about without food?

1 Knowest thou the time when the wild goats of the rock bring forth?
Or canst thou observe when the hinds are in labor?
2 Canst thou number the months they fulfil,
And know the season when they bring forth?
3 They bow themselves; they bring forth their young;
They cast forth their pains.
4 Their young ones are strong; they grow up in the fields;
They go away, and return not to them.

5 Who hath sent forth the wild ass free?
Who hath loosed the bands of the wild ass,
6 To whom I have given the wilderness for his house,
And the barren land for his dwelling-place?
7 He scorneth the tumult of the city,
And heedeth not the shouting of the driver;
8 The range of the mountains is his pasture;
He seeketh after every green thing.

9 Will the wild-ox consent to serve thee?
Will he pass the night at thy crib?
10 Canst thou bind the wild-ox with the harness to the furrow?
Or will he harrow the valleys after thee?
11 Wilt thou rely upon him because his strength is great,
And commit to him thy labor?
12 Wilt thou trust him to bring home thy grain,
And gather in thy harvest?

13 The wing of the ostrich moveth joyfully;
But is it with loving pinion and feathers?
14 Nay, she layeth her eggs on the ground;
She warmeth them in the dust,
15 And forgetteth that the foot may crush them,
And that the wild beast may break them.
16 She is cruel to her young, as if they were not hers;
Her labor is in vain, yet she feareth not;
17 Because God hath denied her wisdom,
And hath not given her understanding.
18 Yet when she lasheth herself up on high,
She laugheth at the horse and his rider.

19 Hast thou given the horse strength?
Hast thou clothed his neck with his trembling mane?
20 Hast thou taught him to bound like the locust?
How majestic his snorting! how terrible!
21 He paweth in the valley; he exulteth in his strength,
And rusheth into the midst of arms.
22 He laugheth at fear; he trembleth not,
And turneth not back from the sword.
23 Against him rattle the quiver,
The flaming spear, and the lance.
24 With rage and fury he devoureth the ground;
He will not believe that the trumpet soundeth.
25 At every blast of the trumpet, he saith, Aha!
And snuffeth the battle afar off, —
The thunder of the captains, and the war-shout.

26 Is it by thy wisdom that the hawk flieth,
And spreadeth his wings toward the south?

27 Doth the eagle soar at thy command,
And build his nest on high?
28 He dwelleth and lodgeth upon the rock,
Upon the peak of the rock, and the stronghold.
29 From thence he spieth out prey;
His eyes discern it from afar.
30 His young ones suck up blood;
And where the slain are, there is he.

XXIII.

Jehovah's question and Job's reply.—CHAP. XL. 1-5.

1 MOREOVER Jehovah spake to Job, and said:

2 Will the censurer of the Almighty contend with him?
Will the reprover of God answer?

3 Then Job answered Jehovah, and said:

4 Behold, I am vile! what can I answer thee?
I will lay my hand upon my mouth.
5 Once have I spoken, but I will not speak again;
Yea, twice, but I will say no more.

XXIV.

Jehovah's continued reproof of Job.—CHAP. XL. 6-XLI.

6 THEN spake Jehovah to Job out of the whirlwind, and said:

7 Gird up now thy loins like a man!
I will ask thee, and do thou instruct me!
8 Wilt thou even disannul my right?
Wilt thou condemn me, that thou mayst be righteous?
9 Hast thou an arm like God's?
Or canst thou thunder with thy voice like him?
10 Deck thyself with grandeur and majesty,
And array thyself in splendor and glory!

11 Send forth the fury of thy wrath!
Look upon every proud one, and abase him!
12 Look upon every proud one, and bring him low;
Yea, tread down the wicked in their place!
13 Hide them in the dust together;
Shut up their faces in darkness!
14 Then, indeed, will I give thee the praise,
That thine own right hand can save thee.

15 Behold the river-horse, which I have made as well as [thyself;
He feedeth on grass like the ox.
16 Behold, what strength is in his loins!
And what force in the muscles of his belly!
17 He bendeth his tail, like the cedar,
And the sinews of his thighs are twisted together.
18 His bones are pipes of brass,
And his limbs are bars of iron.
19 He is chief among the works of God;
He that made him gave him his sword.
20 For the mountains supply him with food,
Where all the beasts of the field play.
21 He lieth down under the lote-plants,
In the covert of reeds, and in the fens.
22 The lote-plants cover him with their shadow,
And the willows of the brook compass him about.
23 Lo! the stream overfloweth, but he starteth not;
He is unmoved though Jordan rush forth even to his mouth.
24 Can one take him before his eyes,
Or pierce his nose with hooks?

1 Canst thou draw forth the crocodile with a hook,
Or press down his tongue with a cord?
2 Canst thou put a rope into his nose,
Or pierce his cheek with a hook?
3 Will he make many entreaties to thee?
Will he speak soft words to thee?
4 Will he make a covenant with thee?
Canst thou take him for a servant for ever?
5 Canst thou play with him, as with a bird?
Or canst thou bind him for thy maidens?

6 Do men in company lay snares for him?
Do they divide him among the merchants?
7 Canst thou fill his skin with barbed irons,
Or his head with fish-spears?
8 Do but lay thy hand upon him, —
Thou wilt no more think of battle!

9 Behold, his hope is vain!
Is he not cast down at the very sight of him?
10 None is so fierce that he dare stir him up;
Who then is he that can stand before me?
11 Who hath done me a favor, that I must repay him?
Whatever is under the whole heaven is mine.

12 I will not be silent concerning his limbs,
And his strength, and the beauty of his armor.
13 Who can uncover the surface of his garment?
Who will approach his jaws?
14 Who will open the doors of his face?
The rows of his teeth are terrible!
15 His glory is his strong shields,
United with each other, as with a close seal.
16 They are joined one to another,
So that no air can come between them.
17 They cleave fast to each other,
They hold together, and cannot be separated.
18 His sneezing sendeth forth light,
And his eyes are like the eyelashes of the morning.
19 Out of his mouth go flames,
And sparks of fire leap forth.
20 From his nostrils issueth smoke, as from a heated pot, or
caldron.
21 His breath kindleth coals,
And flames issue from his mouth.
22 In his neck dwelleth strength,
And terror danceth before him.
23 The flakes of his flesh cleave fast together;
They are firm upon him, and cannot be moved.
24 His heart is solid like a stone;
Yea, solid like the nether millstone.

25 When he riseth up, the mighty are afraid;
Yea, they lose themselves for terror.
26 The sword of him that assaileth him doth not stand,
The spear, the dart, nor the habergeon.
27 He regardeth iron as straw,
And brass as rotten wood.
28 The arrow cannot make him flee;
Sling-stones to him become stubble;
29 Clubs are accounted by him as straw;
He laugheth at the shaking of the spear.

30 Under him are sharp potsherds;
He spreadeth out a thrashing-sledge upon the mire.
31 He maketh the deep to boil like a caldron;
He maketh the sea like a pot of ointment.
32 Behind him he leaveth a shining path;
One would think the deep to be hoary.
33 Upon the earth there is not his master;
He is made without fear.
34 He looketh down upon all that is high;
He is king over all the sons of pride.

XXV.

Job's entire submission to Jehovah. — CHAP. XLII. 1–6.

1 THEN Job answered Jehovah, and said:

2 I know that thou canst do every thing,
And that no purpose of thine can be hindered.
3 Who is he that darkeneth counsel by words withou knowledge?
Thus have I uttered what I understood not;
Things too wonderful for me, which I knew not:
4 Hear thou, then, I beseech thee, and I will speak!
I will ask thee, and do thou instruct me!
5 I have heard of thee by the hearing of the ear;
But now hath mine eye seen thee.
6 Wherefore I abhor myself,
And repent in dust and ashes.

XXVI.

Jehovah's vindication of Job, and the happy issue of his trials.
CHAP. XLII. 7–17.

7 AND when Jehovah had spoken these words unto Job,
he said to Eliphaz the Temanite: "My wrath is kindled
against thee, and against thy two friends; for ye have not
spoken concerning me that which is right, as hath my ser-
8 vant Job. Take ye, therefore, seven bullocks and seven
rams, and go to my servant Job, and offer for yourselves
a burnt-offering, and my servant Job shall pray for you;
for to him alone will I have regard; that I deal not with
you according to your folly. For ye have not spoken
concerning me that which is right, as hath my servant
Job."

9 So Eliphaz the Temanite, and Bildad the Shuhite, and
Zophar the Naamathite, went and did as Jehovah com-
10 manded them; and Jehovah had regard to Job. And Jehovah turned the captivity of Job, when he prayed for his
friends, and Jehovah gave him twice as much as he had
11 before. Then came to him all his brethren, and all his
sisters, and all his former acquaintances, and ate bread
with him in his house; and condoled with him, and com-
forted him over all the evil which Jehovah had brought
upon him; and every one gave him a piece of money [a
kesita], and every one a ring of gold.

12 Thus Jehovah blessed the latter end of Job more than
the beginning; for he had fourteen thousand sheep, six
thousand camels, a thousand yoke of oxen, and a thousand
13 she-asses. He had also seven sons, and three daughters.
14 And he called the name of the first Jemima, of the second
15 Kezia, and of the third Kerenhappuch. And in all the
land were no women found so fair as the daughters of
Job; and their father gave them an inheritance among
16 their brethren. And Job lived after this a hundred and
forty years, and saw his sons, and his sons' sons, even four
17 generations. Then Job died, being old and satisfied with
days.

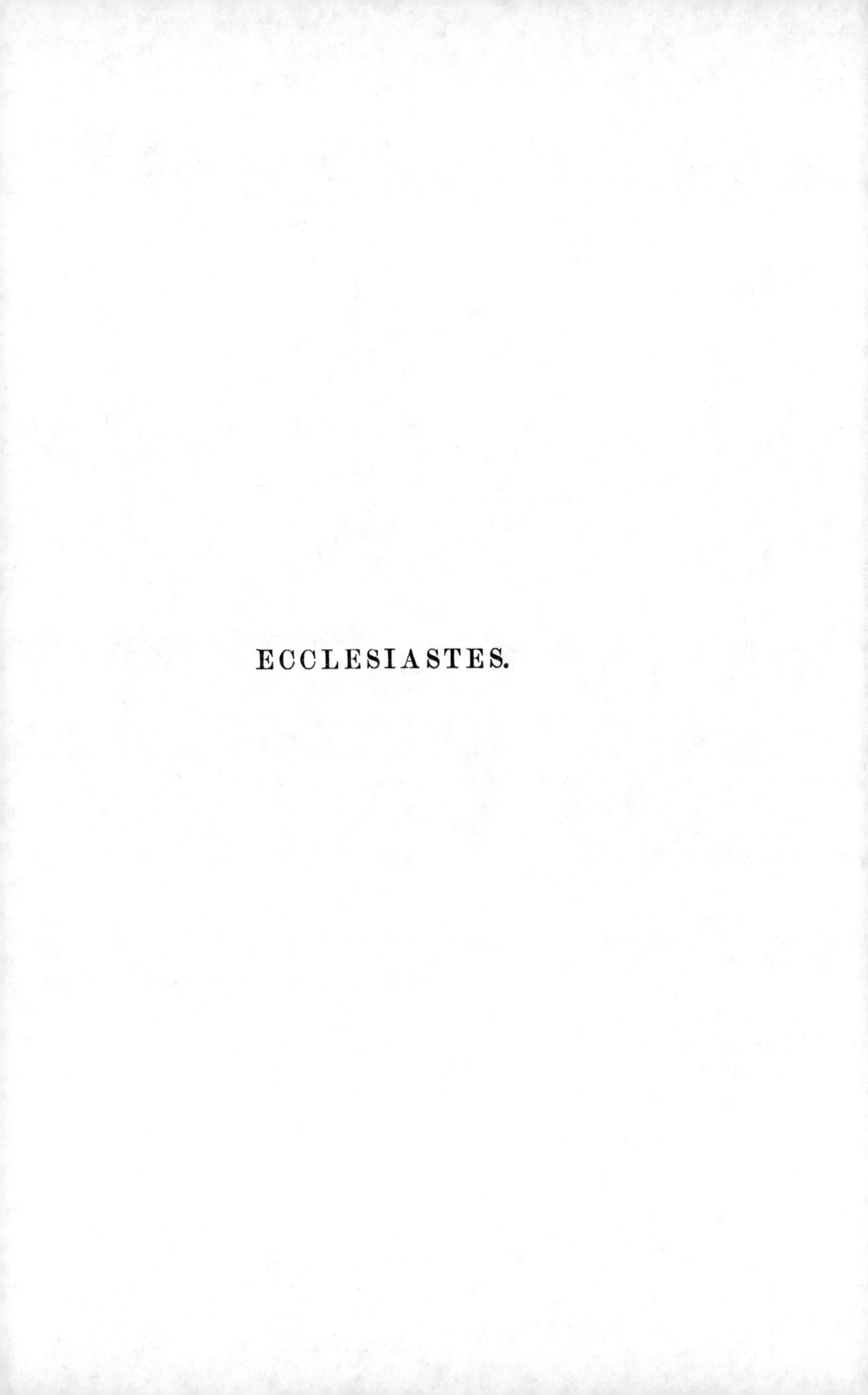

ECCLESIASTES.

INTRODUCTION TO ECCLESIASTES.

FEW books of the Old Testament have given rise to greater diversities of opinion than that which is called Ecclesiastes, or the Preacher. In regard to its form and its spirit, its subject and its meaning, its scope and design, its age and author, widely different opinions have been entertained, and defended with confidence and ingenuity. By different critics the author has been regarded as an Epicurean, a Sadducee, a sceptic, a fatalist. By others his chief aim is supposed to be to prove and maintain the doctrines of the immortality of the human soul, and a future state of retribution. Some of the ancient Jews, according to St. Jerome, entertained objections against this book, saying, that, "as some books, which Solomon wrote, had been lost, this too ought to be obliterated; because it asserted that the creatures of God are vain, and regarded all things as worthless, and preferred meat and drink and delicacies to every thing else; yet they said that the twelfth chapter alone, which summed up all he had written in the precept to fear God and keep his commandments, gave it a sufficient claim to be placed among the sacred books."* So in the Talmud we read, "Some of the wise men desired *to hide*, לִגְנוֹז, that is, to forbid the public reading of, the book Coheleth, because there were found in it words tending to heresy." † Others, because his language was contradictory.

* See Comment. on Eccles. xii. 13, Jerome's Works, vol. ii. p. 787, edit. Martianay.

† See Pesikta Rabbati, fol. 33, c. 1; Midrash, Cohel., fol. 311, c. 1; Vajikra Rab., § 28, fol. 161, c. 2; Tr. Schabb., fol. 30, c. 2.

A consideration of the objections which have been made to the book in ancient and modern times, and of the apparent contradictions which perplex the reader, seems to be demanded as a part of the introduction to this book.

In regard to the class of composition to which the book belongs, it seems to come nearest to what, in modern times, would be called an ethical or moral essay. I do not, with some writers, regard it as a poem, though parts of it run into the region of poetry, and have a degree of rhythm in the construction. It is, however, written with the freedom of poetry, without regard to logical connection of thought, and without any strict and regular plan kept in view throughout. Not that the work is wholly destitute of method. There is, at any rate, a unity of subject pervading it from beginning to end; interrupted, it is true, but not destroyed, by digressions and the introduction of moral maxims. The author evidently throws out freely the thoughts which occur to him on a general subject, rather than undertakes to prove any particular point, or to accomplish any precise plan, to which all the parts should have a definite and intimate relation.

If I were to express the subject of the work in a single sentence, which might serve as a titlepage to it, I should call it "THOUGHTS ON THE VANITY OF HUMAN LIFE, INTERSPERSED WITH SUCH MAXIMS OF PRUDENCE, VIRTUE, AND RELIGION AS WILL HELP A MAN TO CONDUCT HIMSELF IN THE BEST MANNER, AND TO OBTAIN THE GREATEST AMOUNT OF HAPPINESS, IN HIS JOURNEY THROUGH IT." The main doctrine, or speculative view, of the author is the vanity of human things, that is, of human striving, and of human fortunes and experiences; and his most prominent practical precept is, that men should enjoy the present blessings of life as they come, without anxiety and over-strenuous exertions relating to distant and future good. But there are many observations, and many practical precepts of prudence, virtue, and religion, scattered through the work, as having an independent value, and not having a particular and obvious relation to any general plan or design of the author.

In regard to the objectionable sentiments and inconsistencies which have been charged upon the Preacher, it appears to me that much may be said in the way of explanation. One important consideration is the general character of the composition, which does not aim at metaphysical accuracy of expression, or precise statements of doctrine or principles. The writer throws out thoughts and views, which occur to him as the results of his various experience, without making at the time the limitations and qualifications which a more careful and logical writer would have placed in immediate connection with the former. We are not, therefore, to take all the thoughts which he expresses, while contemplating things in certain points of view, as his final and settled convictions. We are to consider whether, in the course of his essay, he has not limited, or modified, former statements, if not formally and expressly, yet by solemn additional declarations, which in fact qualify the former; whether, in the one case, he has not told us what he thought when considering things under certain aspects, and, in the other, what he believed on the whole, and taking all circumstances into the account; whether, in the one case, he has not been stating facts which perplexed his mind, and, in the other, expressed his habitual faith in the religion of the Old Testament, to which he clung notwithstanding these facts. It is very doubtful, however, whether he intends to contradict, or has in fact contradicted, any one proposition which he has laid down, in the same sense and degree in which he asserted it.

It is probable that nothing advanced by the Preacher has given greater occasion for the charge of inconsistency or contradiction, than the sentiments which he expresses in relation to a retribution for sin. The difficulty occasioned by his statements in relation to this subject is the greater, if, as seems to be most probable, he had not attained to faith in a life after death, or a future state of retribution. The doctrine of a retribution after death affords the easy solution of the difficulty, which satisfies many readers. But, if the writer did not believe in the doctrine, we need a different explanation of the facts. Some of the passages relating to this subject are the following: In chap. viii. 14, 15, the Preacher says, "There is a vanity which taketh place upon the earth, that there are righteous men to whom it happeneth according to the work of the wicked, and that there are wicked men to whom it happeneth according to the work of the righteous. I said, This also is vanity. Then I commended joy; because nothing is good for a man, except to eat, and to drink, and to be joyful; for it is this that abideth with him for his labor during the days of his life which God giveth him under the sun." So, chap. ix. 2–5, "All things [come to them] as to all. There is one event to the righteous and to the wicked; to the good, to the clean, and to the unclean; to him that sacrificeth, and to him that sacrificeth not; as is the good, so is the sinner; he that sweareth [falsely], as he that fears an oath. This is an evil among all things which take place under the sun, that there is one event to all; therefore also the heart of the sons of men is full of evil, and madness is in their heart while they live, and afterward they go down to the dead. For who is there that is excepted? With all the living there is hope; for a living dog is better than a dead lion. For the living know that they must die; but the dead know not any thing, and there is no more to them any advantage; for their memory is forgotten. . . . Go thy way, eat thy bread with joy, and drink thy wine with a cheerful heart." Other passages of similar import might be quoted; but these are sufficient.

On the other hand, we read, in chap. iii. 17, "Then I said in my heart, God will judge the righteous and the wicked. For there shall be a time for every employment and for every work [to be judged]." And in chap. viii. 12, 13, "But though a sinner do evil a hundred times, and have his days prolonged, yet surely I know that it shall be well with them that fear God, that fear before him. But it shall not be well with the wicked; he shall be like a shadow, and shall not prolong his days; because he feareth not before God." And in chap. xi. 9, "Know that for these things God will bring thee into judgment." And in chap. xii. 14, "For God will bring every work into judgment, with every secret thing, whether it be good, or whether it be evil." (See also chap. v. 3–7; vii. 17, 18; viii. 8.)

Now, the first remark, which may be made upon these seeming inconsistencies respecting the doctrine of retribution for sin is, that they are not peculiar to the Book of Ecclesiastes. We find similar representations in the Psalms, in the Book of Job, and in Habakkuk. (See Ps. lxxiii.; Hab. i. 12–17.) The Book of Job contains strong representations of the prosperity of the wicked, and the misery of the righteous; which representations the writer reconciles with faith in a righteous retribution for sin, and that, too, in the present world. That these representations are generally put into the mouths of different speakers is a mere matter of form, adopted by the author in order to present different views of the subject. But this is not always the case. Job himself is made to utter sentiments apparently so diverse in chap. xxiv. and xxvii., that some critics have made arbitrary alterations in the text to meet the supposed difficulty. It is probable, therefore, that the alleged inconsistency in the case of the Preacher is to be explained in the same way as the passages referred to in the Psalms, Job, and Habakkuk.

2. It is to be remarked, that the facts asserted by the Preacher are, to a considerable extent at least, what we all know to be true. Physical events do take place according to physical laws. The sun rises on the evil and the good, and the rain descends on the just and the unjust. When a tempest rages, it does not spare the fields and dwellings of the righteous. When the pestilence lays waste, it does not pass by the innocent and devout. If there be any exaggeration in the Preacher's statements, if he places the difficulties which occur to his mind respecting the moral government of God in a very strong light, this is to be referred to the bold, unqualified way in which he expresses all his thoughts, and to his desire to give a striking illustration of the vanity of human things. He does not make his statements as deciding the question against a retribution for sin, but only as presenting difficulties. He is expressing thoughts which occurred to his mind at the time, not giving his view on the whole. He is complaining that the wicked escape for a long time, though he may yet have believed, as he has expressly asserted, that judgment would at some time overtake them. Notwithstanding the extent to which all things happen alike to all, he may have believed in the doctrine of a righteous retribution, as established by the general consequences of human actions, as required by the justice of God, and as certainly contained in the religious books of his nation.

For it will be conceded by all, that the doctrine of a righteous retribution in the present life is the doctrine of the Old Testament. It is found throughout the Pentateuch and the Book of Proverbs. It was firmly held by the Psalmists, by Habakkuk, and the author of Job, notwithstanding the difficulties presented by the prosperity of the wicked, and the sufferings of the righteous. Their faith in retribution was not shaken by their observation, that "the ungodly prospered in the world, and increased in riches," while the righteous "have been smitten every day, and chastened every morning." They had faith, that, though "judgment against an evil work was not executed speedily," the wicked "stood in slippery places;" and that in some way, and at some time, the ways of transgressors would be found to be hard, and that, too, in this world. Why, then, should we seek a solution of the difficulty in Ecclesiastes different from that which is applicable to other writers of the Old Testament? What more is necessary than to suppose, that, in the one class of passages, the Preacher states his faith, and the faith of his nation, in the doctrine of temporal retribution; whilst, in the other class, he only states facts in regard to the temporary distribution of good and evil in the world, especially in regard to the occurrence of the same physical events to all without distinction of character, which, though they perplex his mind and occasion embarrassment, and impress it with the vanity of human things, yet do not shake his faith. In the one case, he declares what is true on the whole, in the long-run, and all things considered, and what may be expected from the eternal justice of the Almighty. In the other, he is stating what fell under his own observation and experience in a given time, and which occasioned him so much embarrassment, that he exclaims, "Then I saw the whole work of God, that a man cannot comprehend that which is done under the sun; how much soever he may labor to search it out, yet shall he not comprehend it; yea, though a wise man resolve to know it, yet shall he not be able to comprehend it."

We Christians believe in the moral government of God, and in a retribution for sin to a certain extent in the present world, though we are sometimes inclined to wonder that a surer and a swifter punishment does not overtake evil-doers. We cannot deny the facts which the Preacher has stated, and which, at first view, seem inconsistent with his doctrines, however we might qualify the statement of them. We think we bring those facts into more perfect harmony with our faith in the moral government of God by extending the retributions of sin into the future world. The mind of the Preacher may have been more embarrassed than that of the Christian. It would be strange if it were not. He may not have been so able to account for the phenomena of human life, as the Christian, to whom life and immortality have been brought to light. But his faith was not shaken, though his understanding was perplexed. He admits, like an honest man, all the difficulties of the subject, and believes still, that though for a time the sinner goes unpunished, yet that at some time, and in some way, he is brought into judgment by the Supreme Ruler.

It is true that the Preacher does not limit and qualify all his statements, like one who weighs all his words with the accuracy of Bishop Butler. It is rather his manner to give bold, unqualified, and, as it were, paradoxical statements of the results of his experience and observation, as well as of the course of conduct which he thinks it advisable to pursue. But if we make due allowance for the style of the writer in this respect, and for his use of figurative and hyperbolical language, we are not compelled to believe, notwithstanding his strong statements respecting the equal condition of the righteous and the wicked, that doubt on the subject of retribution was the prevailing habit of his mind.

It may appear singular to some readers that I have spent so much time on this topic, when the supposition, that the writer believed in a state of retribution after death, would afford so obvious a solution of the difficulty in question. But, in several notes on various passages in the book, I have given reasons which make it appear to my mind most probable that the Preacher had not faith in a desirable future life, much less in a future state of retribution. It appears to me, that he has himself intimated that this was not the way in which he viewed the subject. Thus, in chap. viii. 13, he says, "But it shall not be well with the wicked, neither shall he prolong his days, which are as a shadow; because he feareth not before God." I think, too, that if he had had faith in the doctrine of a retribution after death, it would have pervaded the whole book, and given an entirely different complexion to it. The practical inferences, or recommendations, especially, which the Preacher makes in view of the vanity, perplexities, and shortness of life, would, it seems to me, have been entirely different, if he had entertained the Christian faith in immortality and retribution. (See chap. ii. 24; iii. 12, 13, 22; v. 18–20; vii. 14; viii. 15; ix. 7–10, &c.) I have already mentioned the probability, that no other solution of the difficulties in Ecclesiastes is to be sought, than that which applies to the Book of Job, to Habakkuk, and to the Psalms.

With regard to the Preacher's alleged tendency to fatalism, it may be admitted that the sentiments of chapters first and second, and of such passages as chap. iii. 14, vi. 10, vii. 13, if taken by themselves, and pursued to their consequences, without regard to other statements and sentiments contained in the book, may seem to give some plausibility to the charge. But what author is not liable to the same charge, if treated in the same way? Calvin, Dr. Priestley, Dr. Emmons, might receive the same appellation. Would not even the doctrine of our Saviour and of the Apostle Paul, respecting the dependence of all things upon God and the unlimited extent of the Divine providence, be liable to the same charge? The Preacher has amply qualified his statements respecting the impotency of human exertion, and the inevitable course of events, and the dependence of all things upon God, by the doctrine of a righteous retribution, and by various passages, which imply faith in human freedom and accountableness. In respect to this point, as to others, we must keep in mind the characteristic of the writer to give a strong, I might almost say paradoxical, view of the condition of human things, which is immediately before his mind. The necessary limitations and qualifications are not given at the time. At any rate, if some expressions indicate a tendency to fatalism, it is certain that the Preacher was not a fatalist.

It may, however, be admitted, that the author gives a stronger view than any other Biblical writer of the circumscribed limits of human efforts, and their subjection to a higher, established, inevitable course of things, or ordination of Divine providence, which man can neither resist nor control. (See chap. iii. 1–15, especially 14, 15; vi. 10; vii. 13; ix. 1, 11.) The great theme of the book, the vanity of human things, is made to consist chiefly of the vanity of human effort or striving, as being either wholly fruitless, or fruitless in relation to its express object. But, if we interpret the language of the author by other parts of the book, we must come to the conclusion, that he by no means designs to encourage inactivity or neglect of our powers, but only an anxious, ambitious, and over-strenuous pursuit of future and distant good. If, in one passage, he asks, "What profit hath a man of all his labor?" he says, in another, "Whatever thy hand findeth to do, do it with thy might." However strong is the writer's representation of the influence of a higher power over his concerns and actions, he has enforced doctrines and duties which imply faith in human freedom and accountableness. Nor has any one a right to charge him with inconsistency, unless he is able to prove that the doctrines of the Divine foreknowledge, providence, and government are inconsistent with human freedom and accountableness.

As to the opinion, that the author of Ecclesiastes was a Sadducee or sceptic, in the sense of settled unbeliever, it appears to me to be unfounded. He had doubts, indeed; but he did not abandon himself to them. He goes on with his speculations, till he clears some of them up. It is true that he has not faith in a future life of retribution. But this doctrine, it must be remembered, formed no part of the Jewish religion. In this respect, the Preacher does not differ essentially from the author of the Book of Job, and other writers of the Old Testament. He lived, indeed, as is probable, at a later period, when the faith in a future life of retribution may have begun to prevail; but he had had no authoritative assurance of it. It was a mere question of speculative philosophy, when speculation on the subject commenced. (See the note on chap. iii. 17, 19, 21; xii. 7.) As to the charge of Sadduceeism, it is at least inconsistent with the author's alleged tendency to fatalism. For the Sadducees, according to Josephus, "take away fate, and say there is no such thing, and that the events of human affairs are not at its disposal; but they suppose that all our actions are in our own power, so that we are ourselves the causes of what is good, and receive what is evil from our own folly."*

As to the charge of Epicurism, if by this is meant that the Preacher recommends self-indulgence, — that is, the pleasures of sense, or pleasures of any kind, without regard to the obligations

* Whiston's Josephus, Antiq., xiii. 5, 9.

of duty and religion, — it appears to me that it is entirely false, as I shall show in the notes upon those passages which have been supposed to justify it. The foundation of this opinion is a too literal interpretation of certain figurative and pointed expressions, in which the author recommends a quiet enjoyment of the good that one possesses, in contradistinction from excessive earnestness, anxiety, and exertion after distant and future good. No sound moralist will maintain, that the pleasures derived from the eye, the ear, or even the palate, are to be regarded as sinful, and denounced as Epicurean. The Preacher is careful to tell us, that a man cannot have the quiet enjoyment of life, namely, "wisdom and knowledge and joy," except by "the gift of God to those who are good in his sight," that is, who discharge the duties of morality and religion. (Chap. ii. 26.) It is idle to say that he recommends the pleasures of sense as constituting a happy life without "wisdom and knowledge and joy."

There are some other topics on which the Preacher has been supposed to utter sentiments irreconcilable with each other, when he is, in fact, only giving the results of his various experience, and speaking of the subject in different relations. Thus, he often speaks in praise of wisdom, and of the advantages which it confers on its possessor; whilst, in other passages, he gives an impressive view of its insufficiency to guard its possessor from many of the calamities and trials which flesh is heir to. There is no inconsistency here. He also uses the word in different senses. When he says that "in much wisdom is much vexation, and he that increases knowledge increases sorrow," he is speaking of mere speculative knowledge. His meaning is, that the more one knows of the world, the more he knows of its vanity, and that mere speculative knowledge cannot confer true satisfaction or happiness. In other passages, he commends that practical wisdom which enables its possessor to avoid the consequences of folly.

In order to explain the seeming inconsistencies which have been considered, the hypothesis has been advanced by some critics, such as Herder and Eichhorn, who were never at a loss for an hypothesis on any subject, that the Book of Ecclesiastes consists of a dialogue, in which the speakers offer different sentiments on the subject under discussion. If our views are correct, such an hypothesis is unnecessary. But if the exigency for it were ten times greater than it is, the difficulty of dividing and arranging the book, so as to make it form a natural dialogue, is such, that the hypothesis must be regarded as forced and arbitrary in the highest degree. It has met with very little favor, and is too improbable to deserve a particular examination.

The great fault of the interpreters of this book has been that of ascribing to it more depth of thought, more logic, more method, more consistency, greater definiteness of statement, and greater particularity of design, than really belong to it. Stuart, though not consistent, is liable to this charge. (See his Introduction, p. 34.) The bold, indefinite, unprecise language of the author has given great opportunity to the commentators of attaching their thoughts to the writer's language, instead of extracting from it his own thoughts. Thus, Desvoeux, in his Commentary, makes the book contain a logical and well-arranged argument to prove the immortality of the soul and a future state of retribution. Umbreit regards it as a philosophical inquiry relating to the *summum bonum*, or chief good.* Martin Luther says: "The nature and design of this book is to teach us that we should with thankfulness enjoy present things, and the creatures which God has abundantly bestowed upon us, and not be anxious about the future; keeping a tranquil, quiet spirit, and a mind full of joy, being contented with the word and works of God."† Jahn coincides in opinion with Luther. "The author," says he, "does not dwell upon the vanity and vexatiousness of human affairs more than upon an agreeable use of the pleasures of life; and therefore his intention evidently was to repress the restless and eager efforts of men, which hurry them on in heaping up wealth, in securing pleasures, and acquiring honors; and, at the same time, to instruct them not to increase the troubles of life by denying themselves the enjoyment of harmless, though uncertain and fleeting, pleasures."‡ On this opinion of Luther and Jahn, the remark may be made, that it is just to a certain extent. The practical design which they

---

* Koheleth Scepticus de Summo Bono. Commentatio philosophicocritica. Gotting., 1820.

† Pref. in Ecclesiastem, in Opp. Lat., edit. Wittenb., tom. iv. p. 2.

‡ Jahn's Introd. to O. T., § 212.

ascribe to the author was, without doubt, entertained by him; but whether it ought to be regarded as the chief and special design of the whole book may be doubted. On the contrary, the practical recommendation of the Preacher, as stated by Luther and Jahn, occurs in the book as an inference from the general view of the vanity of human things which he undertook to illustrate.

Various other designs have been assigned to the author; among which is that of Kaiser, who supposes the work to be an historico-didactic poem, in which the characters of the Jewish kings, from Solomon to Zedekiah, are set forth and censured, so as to show what was the cause of the ruin of the Jewish nation.* The chief objection to this theory is, that the author of the work has given no intimation, directly or indirectly, of any such design.

There is also the theory of Ewald, who supposes the book to have been written when Palestine had become a province of Persia, and the Jews were suffering under the tyranny and violence of the Persian satraps. In this state of things, some of them had become weary of life and indifferent to all things; some plunged themselves into pleasures; and some openly inveighed against their oppressors, and thus exasperated their minds the more against them. In such times, says Ewald,† the Preacher undertook to compose a book in which he exhorts his countrymen "to bear present evils with patience, to be cautious and circumspect in speech, and, above all, to fear God, who would at some time bring all things into judgment and set all things right. He exhorts them, therefore, not to sink under their calamities, but to enjoy, with a grateful and cheerful mind, the goods which had been placed within their reach."

The objection to this theory, too, is, that it is mere theory; that, even if the book was written in the circumstances of national distress which the writer supposes, of which, however, there is no evidence, there is no such necessary allusion to national affairs as this theory implies. There are no sentiments in the book which

* Koheleth, das Collectivum der Davidischen Könige in Jerusalem, ein historisches Lehrgedicht über den Umsturtz des Judischen Staates. Erlangen, 1823.

† In his remarks on Ecclesiastes, appended to his work, Das Hohelied Salomo's, übersetzt, &c. Götting., 1826.

the vicissitudes of human life may not have led the author to express in any circumstances of the Jewish nation. A similar theory was proposed by Warburton, with reference to the Book of Job, and with as little foundation.

The only proper way of coming at the truth in relation to this subject is to consider the author as having designed to do what he has actually done; not to ascribe to him any greater unity or speciality of purpose than appears in his work; not to make the thoughts on various topics, thrown off as they arose freely in the mind of the author and connected by casual associations, the parts of a logical argument, or the means of accomplishing an elaborate plan, which may never have existed in his mind.

If we gather the design of the author from what he has done, we must conclude that his purpose was to please, to instruct, and to improve his readers, by making known to them his thoughts on the vanity of human life. The illustration of this topic is, and is regarded by the common reader, the prominent aim of the author. "Vanity of vanities, vanity of vanities, all is vanity," is the beginning, the middle, and the end of the essay. It is the chain which binds the whole together. And yet all parts of it do not conspire merely to illustrate this one topic. Throughout the work are interspersed advice and proverbial maxims respecting the conduct of life and the discharge of duty in relation to man and God. The author springs from one topic to another, to which he is drawn by some casual association, pursues the latter for a time, and then returns to the former. The vanity of human things being regarded as the main doctrinal view of the author, the general subject of the book, what Luther maintains to be its chief design, may be regarded as his prominent practical inference; namely, that men should, in the discharge of duty, enjoy with gratitude the blessings of life as they come, without distressing anxiety and over-strenuous exertions after distant and future good. Yet the practice of virtue and the fear of God are enjoined as of the first importance in regard to the enjoyment of such happiness as may be attained in a world of vanity; and while the young and the old are encouraged to enjoy life as it passes, and to lose none of its pleasures through a spirit of asceticism, or of anxiety and ambition about the distant and the future, yet only such an enjoyment of the good things of life is recommended as is consistent with the constant remembrance of the Creator, and of the judgment which is appointed for all.

That the preceding account of the subject and design of the book is correct, may appear from a more particular analysis of it, and from the commentary which follows it.

The principal thought is first laid down, that all is vain and unprofitable. (Chap. i. 1, 2.) This view the Preacher illustrates, —

1. By the wearisome, ever-recurring changes which are taking place without bringing to pass any thing new, or leading to any new result which is adapted to give satisfaction to the mind of man. (Ver. 4–11.)
2. By the dissatisfaction attending the pursuit of wisdom or knowledge. (Ver. 12–18.)
3. By the unsatisfactoriness of the pleasures of life and of strivings after them, even when united with the pursuit of knowledge and philosophy. (Chap. ii. 1–11.)
4. The author then compares the pleasures of knowledge and the pleasures of sense with one another, and passes judgment on them; and recommends it as the best course which a man can pursue, in order to make the best of a vain world, to give up anxious cares about distant objects and perplexing subjects, and to enjoy with a tranquil, contented, cheerful mind the blessings of life, as he goes along in its paths. (Chap. ii. 12–26.)
5. The vanity of human things is illustrated by their established changes and periods, their fixed course, all things having their limits and time appointed by a higher power than man's. Hence the folly of anxiety, and the vanity of over-strenuous exertion, since man cannot alter the fixed and established course of things; and hence the wisdom of taking things as they come, and making the best of them, in obedience and submission to the Divine will, which controls and disposes all things. (Chap. iii. 1–15.)
6. The vanity of human things is illustrated by the prevalence of injustice and violence among men, and the resemblance

of man to brutes in respect to hardships and death. Hence, too, the Preacher derives the conclusion, that it is best to take a cheerful enjoyment of the good things of life, without anxious cares respecting the future. (Chap. iii. 16–22.)

7. The vanity of human things is next illustrated by reference to the sufferings of the oppressed; the envy which is excited toward the prosperous; the evils of avarice and of solitude; the evils attendant on royalty, arising from the infirmities of its possessor and the fickleness of the people. (Chap. iv.) Then follow some proverbial maxims respecting the worship of God (chap. v. 1–7); then proverbs recommending the quiet pursuit of agriculture, in preference to the agitating, avaricious pursuit of wealth (8–17). These are followed by the advice before given; namely, to enjoy the good things of life as they come, without anxiety or wearisome efforts after distant and future good (18–20).

8. The vanity of human things connected with wealth hoarded up without being enjoyed or used (chap. vi. 1–6), and with insatiable desires (7–9). Then follows an obscure passage, apparently intended to illustrate the vanity of human things (10–12).

9. Then follows a series of maxims and precepts respecting the guidance, support, and consolation of men in their passage through life, recommending righteousness and piety, with occasional remarks on the vanity of human things, such as the vanity of striving after wisdom, the certainty of death, &c. (Chap. vii. 1 – viii. 13.)

10. Then follows a new illustration of the vanity of human things, drawn from the prosperity of the wicked and the sufferings of the righteous, and the impossibility of comprehending the ways of Providence; closing with the practical exhortation, which he has given so many times before, to a quiet and cheerful enjoyment of life, while life lasts, as "his portion," as "all that abideth with him of his labor," without indulging in vain grief for what cannot be helped, or in the anxious, restless pursuit of that which cannot be attained, or which, when attained, yields no satisfaction. "Go thy way," says he, after giving the most melancholy picture of life which he

has yet presented, "eat thy bread with joy, and drink thy wine with a cheerful heart; for now is God pleased with thy works. Let thy garments be always white, and let not fragrant oil be wanting upon thy head. Enjoy life with the wife whom thou lovest, all the days of thy vain life, which he hath given thee under the sun, all thy vain days."—(Chap. viii. 14-ix. 10.)

11. A new illustration of the vanity of human life, drawn from the circumstances, that success does not always answer to a man's strength, wisdom, or other advantages; and that wisdom, with all its benefits to the public, often brings but little consideration to its possessor. Then follow various proverbial maxims, showing the advantages of wisdom and prudence, and the evil of rulers unfit for their station; and designed to regulate the conduct in private and public. This section closes with a recommendation of liberality to the poor, and of diligent exertion in our appropriate pursuits, without an over-anxious solicitude respecting the issue of our labors. (Chap. ix. 11-xi. 6.)

12. The Preacher now exhorts to a cheerful enjoyment of life as it passes, and the putting away of care and sorrow, in view of that portion of life's vanity which consists in the evil days of old age, and of the long period of darkness in prospect. (Chap. xi. 7-xii. 8.) Then follows a repetition of the chief truth which has been illustrated in the work, namely, the vanity of human things; and the final recommendation of the Preacher, as the conclusion of the whole discourse, and the duty of every man; namely, "to fear God and keep his commandments." (Chap. xii. 9-14.)

From this view of the contents of the Book of Ecclesiastes, it may be inferred that the author was a man of wisdom, virtue, and religion, according to the light which he had. He was not a fatalist, or a sceptic, or an Epicurean, in any offensive sense of those terms. He may be regarded as of a free, speculative, and somewhat sceptical turn of mind, but still holding fast the fundamental principles of the Jewish faith. If he had doubts, they related to subjects upon which he found no certain light in the religion of his fathers and his country. If he recommended the enjoyment of life, it was such an enjoyment as was consistent with virtue and religion. A deep sense of religion is evidently habitual to him, notwithstanding the difficulties which perplexed his understanding. He has a living faith in a wise and benevolent God, and a righteous government of the world, though the principles of this government are regarded by him as being beyond the comprehension of man.

On the other hand, it may be conceded that he has given a more melancholy view of human life than is consistent with the spirit of Christianity, or of a comprehensive philosophy. Many Christians have taken just such a melancholy view of human life, and like no hymn better than the one beginning, "I would not live alway." But the Preacher had never heard the glad tidings of great joy to all people. The light of the Sun of Righteousness had not arisen upon his mind.

It may be admitted, too, that the subject of enjoyment occupied a more prominent place in the mind of the author than in the mind of Jesus Christ. A higher, more disinterested, more devoted spirit pervades the teachings of Him who spake as never man spake than we can find in any of the writings of the Old Testament. The Christian is taught to do his duty, and let enjoyment take care of itself. "Seek first the kingdom of God and his righteousness, and all these things shall be added unto you," is the language of him who came to perfect the law. I do not mean that the Book of Ecclesiastes contains any particular precept absolutely inconsistent with the Sermon on the Mount. But in respect to its tone, spirit, and the prominence it gives to certain topics, it must be allowed to be far behind it. A spirit of self-sacrifice for the good of others is certainly not so congenial to the mind of the author as to the mind of Christ.

Finally, if it be conceded that the Preacher expresses occasional doubts, where Paul or John would be rejoicing in hope and confidence, this should not lead us to give the ancient Hebrew essayist the name of Sadducee, sceptic, or Epicurean, but rather to thank God, who has raised up Jesus to show us the nature and design of our present existence, and "to bring life and immortality to light."

Perhaps it may be well to say a few words on the authorship of Ecclesiastes, though, in a work of its didactic character, this is not a very important question. That by "the Preacher, the son of David," in chap. i. 1, is denoted Solomon, there can be no doubt. But this by no means proves that Solomon was the author of the composition; but only that the author, whoever he was, adopted the plan of introducing into the book one so celebrated throughout the East for wisdom and for prosperity as Solomon, for the purpose of giving weight to the sentiments which are put into his mouth. In adopting this plan, it is not probable that he intended to deceive his contemporaries, but only to make use of a literary fiction, such as is common in modern times; a fiction which is not very carefully supported. The prevalent belief, it is true, has been that Solomon was the author of the book. The first commentator, so far as I know, who called the received opinion in question, was the accomplished scholar and jurist, Hugo Grotius. "I think," says he, "the work is not a production of Solomon, but one written in the name of that king, as being led by repentance to the composition of it. It contains many words which cannot be found, except in Ezra, Daniel, and the Chaldee paraphrasts." In expressing his opinion, Grotius, with his usual sagacity, has mentioned by far the strongest argument in its support; namely, the characteristics of the language of Ecclesiastes, especially those which give it an Aramæan complexion. These are so scattered throughout the work, that it is sufficient to refer the Hebrew scholar to the whole Hebrew original. He cannot read the first chapter of it, without having strong doubts whether it was written by the principal author of the Book of Proverbs.*

The Book of Proverbs, if not wholly composed by Solomon, must be regarded, to a great extent, as his production, and undoubtedly belongs to his age, to the flourishing period of the Hebrew language and literature. But whoever will proceed from

* For an enumeration of the peculiarities of the language of Ecclesiastes, the critical reader is referred to De Wette's Introduction to the Old Testament, or to a still more complete view of them in Knobel's German Commentary, pp. 60–75.

the perusal of the Proverbs of Solomon to that of the Book of Ecclesiastes must receive from the diction of the latter a strong conviction that it is not only the production of a different author, but of a later age. In fact, there has been no greater opposition to this opinion than was to be expected from the natural prejudice in favor of the received tradition. The best scholars since the time of Grotius, who have given attention to the subject, have adopted his opinion. Even the Romanist, Jahn, who is very slow to adopt an opinion not in accordance with the tradition of the church, is unable to resist the evidence against the opinion that Solomon was the author of Ecclesiastes. Such critics as Dathe, Döderlein, and Pareau are of the same opinion. Dathe observes, that "Döderlein and Eichhorn have established their point by arguments so weighty, that none except very stubborn defenders of ancient traditions can deny it." *

Even Professor Stuart, in his recent work on the canon of the Old Testament (p. 139), admits, though the admission is hardly consistent with the general argument of his book, that "the diction of this book differs so widely from that of Solomon in the Book of Proverbs, that it is difficult to believe that both came from the same pen. Chaucer does not differ more from Pope, than Ecclesiastes from Proverbs. It appears to me, when I read Coheleth, that it presents one of those cases which leave no room for doubt, so striking and prominent is the discrepancy."

Knobel, the author of one of the best critical commentaries on Ecclesiastes with which we are acquainted, says, "No point in the criticism of the Old Testament is better established than that Ecclesiastes was not written by Solomon, but in a later age." More recently, Hitzig and Heiligstedt agree in the same conclusion. It ought to be mentioned, however, that there are those who maintain a different opinion. Whoever wishes to see the arguments on the other side of the question may find them well stated in a preliminary dissertation to Ecclesiastes, by George Holden, London, 1822. They will not pass for much with those who are in the habit of weighing, rather than of counting, arguments.

* Jobus, Ecclesiastes, &c., a Dathio, p. 358.

There are also other considerations, which, though they may not be in the highest degree conclusive when standing alone, yet confirm the conclusion drawn from the diction of Ecclesiastes. It appears to me, that the English reader may perceive, in the general style, character, and topics of the book, reasons for supposing that it came from another author than that of the Book of Proverbs. The style of the latter is concise, terse, elevated; that of the former is quite diffuse, vague, prosaic. The instruction of the one is preceptive and positive, having no reference to speculative doubts; that of the other is in the way of philosophic discussion, presenting the different aspects in which a subject may be viewed, and what, on the whole, is to be regarded as the truth.

There are several topics, introduced into the book, which seem not very appropriate to the reign of Solomon, and which, if they had been so, that wise monarch might have been expected to pass over in silence. Among these are the complaints of the oppression of unjust rulers (chap. iii. 16; iv. 1), of the extortions of provincial magistrates (chap. v. 8), and of the elevation of inferior men to high stations (chap. x. 5–7). In fact, whenever the author speaks of kings and governors, he speaks in the tone of a subject rather than a king; of an observer, rather than of a holder, of kingly power. (See iv. 13–16; v. 8, 9; viii. 2–5; ix. 13–18; x. 4–7, 16–20.)

The fiction, according to which the sentiments of the book are put into the mouth of Solomon, is so unskilfully sustained, that it appears to be only a fiction. If the book were written by Solomon, why does he say, "I *was* king"? A living king would be more likely to say, "I, the king," &c. Why should Solomon say to his contemporaries that he was king *in Jerusalem?* Before the separation of the ten tribes, it was a superfluous expression. No one had been king in Samaria. Especially, why should he say that he had gained greater wisdom than *all* his predecessors at Jerusalem (chap. i. 16), when he had only one predecessor in that city; namely, David. All these expressions, however, might easily have escaped from an author not careful to maintain a literary fiction. In chap. i. 16, ii. 9, 15, 19, Solomon is represented as praising his own wisdom, and relating his own experience in a manner not very natural to a real, living person. Finally, the author, in chap. xii. 9, seems to drop the fiction, and to speak of Solomon in the third person.

It is much more difficult to form a confident opinion as to the time when the Book of Ecclesiastes was written, than it is to decide that it belongs to a much later age than that of Solomon. From the Aramæan complexion of the language, from the religious and literary character of the book, and from its spirit and tone, as being suited to times of calamity and oppression, one may feel considerable confidence that it was written after the return of the Jews from the exile at Babylon; and there seems to be nothing to object to the prevalent opinion of the German critics, such as De Wette, Knobel, and Ewald, who date the composition of it near the fall of the Persian monarchy, or at the beginning of the Macedonian domination under Alexander; that is, about three hundred and thirty years before the Christian era. But it may have been written somewhat later. The occurrence of two words of Persian origin, פַּרְדֵּס and פִּתְגָם, in chap. ii. 5, viii. 11, in connection with the arguments which have been mentioned for the late origin of the book, seems to favor this supposition. There are no reasons of any weight for supposing the Jewish canon of Scripture to have closed before this period. We are inclined, however, to adopt the date above mentioned, rather from the absence of more valid arguments in favor of any other opinion, than from the conclusiveness of the reasons urged in its support.* As to the opinion which has been advanced, that traces of an acquaintance with Grecian philosophy are found in Ecclesiastes, we can only say that we have not been able to discern them.

Whoever wishes for a list of the commentators on Ecclesiastes will find one long enough to satisfy him in Rosenmüller's Introduction to this book. Of those which he has not mentioned, I have seen—An Attempt to illustrate the Book of Ecclesiastes, by the Rev. George Holden, M.A., London, 1822; Uebersetzung des Koheleth nebst grammatisch exegetischem Commentar, von Moses Heinemann, Berlin, 1831; and Commentar über das Buch Kohe-

---

* See Davidson's Int. to O. T., ii. p. 356, &c.

leth, von August Knobel, Leipzig, 1836. In preparing this edition, I have also, on the more important passages, consulted the Commentaries of Hitzig, Heiligstedt, Stuart, and Ginsburg (London, 1861). A few changes in the version, and some additional notes, have been made.

CAMBRIDGE, Nov. 14, 1866.

ECCLESIASTES.

---

1 The words of the Preacher, the son of David, king in
Jerusalem.

2 Vanity of vanities, saith the Preacher, vanity of vani-
3 ties, all is vanity. What profit hath a man by all his labor
4 with which he wearieth himself under the sun? One
generation passeth away, and another generation cometh;
5 while the earth abideth for ever. The sun riseth, and the
sun goeth down, and hasteneth to the place whence it
6 arose. The wind goeth toward the south, and turneth
about to the north; round and round goeth the wind, and
7 returneth to its circuits. All the rivers run into the sea,
yet the sea is not full; to the place whence the rivers
8 come, thither they return. All words become weary; man
cannot express it; the eye is not satisfied with seeing, nor
the ear filled with hearing.
9 The thing that hath been is that which shall be, and
that which hath been done is that which shall be done;
10 and there is no new thing under the sun. Is there any
thing of which one may say, "Behold, this is new"?
11 It was long ago, in the times which were before us. There
is no remembrance of former things, and of things that
are to come there shall be no remembrance to those who
live afterwards.

12 I, the Preacher, was king over Israel at Jerusalem.
13 And I gave my mind to seek and to search out with wisdom concerning all things which are done under heaven;
an evil business, which God hath given to the sons of

14 men, in which to employ themselves. I saw all the
things which are done under the sun; and, behold, it was
15 all vanity, and striving after wind. That which is crooked
cannot be made straight, and that which is wanting cannot
16 be numbered. I communed with my heart, saying, "Behold, I have gained more and greater wisdom than all who
have been before me at Jerusalem; yea, my mind hath
17 seen much wisdom and knowledge." And I gave my
mind to know wisdom, and to know senselessness and folly;
18 I perceived that this also is striving after wind. For in
much wisdom is much vexation, and he that increaseth
knowledge increaseth sorrow.

1 I said in my heart, "Come, now, I will try thee with
mirth; therefore enjoy pleasure!" But, lo! this also
2 was vanity. I said of laughter, "It is mad;" and of mirth,
3 "What availeth it?" I thought in my heart to strengthen
my body with wine, and, while my heart cleaved to wisdom, to lay hold on folly, till I should see what was good
for the sons of men, which they should do under heaven
4 all the days of their life. I made me great works. I
5 builded me houses; I planted me vineyards. I made me
gardens and parks, and planted in them fruit-trees of every
6 kind. I made me pools of water, with which to water the
7 grove shooting up trees. I got me men-servants and
maid-servants, and had servants born in my house. I had
also great possessions of herds and flocks, more than all
8 who were in Jerusalem before me. I heaped me up also
silver and gold, and the wealth of kings and of provinces.
I got me men-singers and women-singers, and the delight
of the sons of men, a chosen woman and chosen women.
9 So I became greater than all that were before me in Jeru-
10 salem. My wisdom also remained with me. And whatever mine eyes desired I kept not from them; I withheld
not my heart from any joy. For my heart rejoiced by
means of all my labor, and this was my portion from all
11 my labor. Then I looked upon all the works which my
hands had wrought, and upon all the labor which I had
toiled in performing; and, behold, it was all vanity, and
striving after wind, and there was no profit under the
sun.

12 Then I turned myself to behold wisdom and senselessness and folly. For what can the man do that cometh
after the king? even that which hath been already done.
13 I saw, indeed, that wisdom excelleth folly, as far as light
14 excelleth darkness. The wise man's eyes are in his head,
but the fool walketh in darkness; yet I perceived also that
15 one event happeneth to them all. Then I said in my heart,
"As it happeneth to the fool, so it happeneth to me.
Why, then, became I wiser than others?" Then I said in
16 my heart, "This also is vanity." For there is no remembrance of the wise man more than of the fool for ever;
for in the days to come shall all have long been forgotten;
17 and, alas! the wise man dieth, as well as the fool. Therefore I hated life, because what is done under the sun
appeared evil to me. For all is vanity, and striving after
18 wind. Yea, I hated all my labor which I had performed
under the sun, because I must leave it to the man that
19 shall be after me. And who knoweth whether he shall
be a wise man or a fool? Yet shall he be lord of all
the labor with which I have wearied myself, and in which
I have shown myself wise under the sun. This also is
vanity.

20 Therefore I turned to give up my heart to despair in
regard to all the labor with which I had wearied myself
21 under the sun. For there is a man whose labor has been
with wisdom and knowledge and skill; yet to a man who
hath not labored for it must he leave it as his portion.
22 This also is vanity and a great evil. For what hath man
of all his labor, and the striving of his spirit, with which
23 he wearieth himself under the sun? For all his days are
grief, and his occupation trouble; even in the night his
24 heart taketh no rest. This also is vanity. There is nothing better for a man than to eat and drink, and let his soul
enjoy good in his labor. But this, as I have seen, cometh
25 from the hand of God. For who can eat, or hasten there-
26 unto, more than I? For to a man who is good in his sight
God giveth wisdom and knowledge and joy; but to the
sinner he giveth the wearisome business of gathering and
heaping up, to give it to him who is good before God.
This also is vanity, and striving after wind.

1 For every thing there is a fixed period, and an appointed
2 time to every thing under heaven:—A time to be born,
and a time to die. A time to plant, and a time to pluck up
3 what is planted. A time to kill, and a time to heal A time
4 to breaking down, and a time to build up. A time to weep,
and a time to laugh. A time to mourn, and a time to
5 dance. A time to cast stones asunder, and a time to gather
stones together. A time to embrace, and a time to refrain
6 from embracing. A time to seek, and a time to lose. A
7 time to keep, and a time to cast away. A time to rend,
and a time to sew. A time to keep silence, and a time to
8 speak. A time to love, and a time to hate. A time of
9 war, and a time of peace.—What profit hath he who la-
boreth from that with which he wearieth himself?
10 I have seen the business which God hath given to the
11 sons of men to exercise themselves therewith. God maketh
every thing good in its time; but he hath put the world
into the heart of man, so that he understandeth not the
work which God doeth, from the beginning to the end.
12 I know that there is nothing better for a man than that
13 he should rejoice and enjoy good his life long. But when
a man eateth and drinketh, and enjoyeth good through all
14 his labor, this is the gift of God. I know that whatever
God doeth, that shall be for ever. Nothing can be added
to it, and nothing taken from it; and God doeth it that
15 men may fear before him. That which is, was long ago;
and that which is to be, hath already been; and God recalleth that which is past.

16 Moreover, I saw under the sun that in the place of justice there was iniquity; and in the place of righteousness,
17 iniquity. Then said I in my heart, "God will judge the
righteous and the wicked For there shall be a time for
every matter and for every work.
18 I said in my heart concerning the sons of men, that God
will prove them, in order that they may see that they are
19 like the beasts. For that which befalleth the sons of men
befalleth beasts: one lot befalleth both. As the one dieth,
so dieth the other. Yea, there is one spirit in them, and
a man hath no pre-eminence above a beast; for all is van-
20 ity. All go to one place; all are from the dust, and all

21 turn to dust again. Who knoweth the spirit of man,
whether it goeth upward, and the spirit of a beast, whether
22 it goeth downward to the earth? And so I saw that there
is nothing better than that a man should rejoice in his
labors; for that is his portion. For who shall bring him
to see what shall be after him?

1 Then I turned and saw all the oppressions which take
place under the sun; and, behold, there were the tears
of the oppressed, and they had no comforter; and from
the hand of their oppressors there was violence, and they
2 had no comforter. Therefore I praised the dead, who
have been long ago dead, more than the living, who are
3 yet alive. Yea, better than both of them is he who hath
not yet been, who hath not seen the evil work which is
done under the sun.
4 And I saw all labor, and all success in work, that for
this a man is envied by his neighbor. This also is van-
5 ity, and striving after wind. The fool foldeth his hands
6 together and eateth his own flesh. Better is a hand full
of quietness, than both hands full of weariness and striving after wind.
7 Then I turned and saw other vanity under the sun.
8 There is one who is alone, and no one with him; yea, he
hath neither son nor brother; yet is there no end to all his
labor, and his eye is not satisfied with riches. "For whom,
then [saith he], do I labor and deprive myself of good?"
9 This also is vanity; yea, it is an evil thing! Two are
better than one, because they have a good reward for
10 their labor. For if they fall, the one will lift his fellow
up; but woe to him who is alone when he falleth, and hath
11 not another to help him up! Again, if two lie together,
then they have heat; but how can one be warm alone?
12 And if an enemy prevail against one, two shall withstand
him; and a threefold cord is not quickly broken.
13 Better is a child poor but wise, than a king old and
14 foolish, who will no more be admonished. For out of prison
cometh forth such a one to reign; for in his own kingdom
15 he was born a poor man. I saw that all the living, who
walk under the sun, were with the child who stood up in
16 his stead. There was no end to all the people before

whom he went forth; yet they that come afterwards shall not rejoice in him. This also is vanity, and striving after wind.

1 Look well to thy feet, when thou goest to the house of
God, and draw nigh to hear, rather than to offer sacrifice
2 as fools. For they consider not that they do evil. Be
not hasty with thy mouth, and let not thy heart be swift
to utter any thing before God. For God is in heaven,
and thou upon earth. Therefore let thy words be few.
3 For a dream cometh with much bustle, and a fool's voice
4 with a multitude of words. When thou vowest a vow to
God, delay not to pay it; for he hath no pleasure in fools.
5 Pay that which thou hast vowed. Better is it that thou
shouldst not vow than that thou shouldst vow and not pay.
6 Suffer not thy mouth to bring punishment on thy flesh, and
say not before the angel, "It was a mistake." Wherefore should God be angry on account of thy voice, and
7 destroy the work of thy hands? For in a multitude of
dreams is a multitude of vanities; so also in a multitude
of words; but fear thou God!
8 If thou seest oppression of the poor, and justice and
equity perverted in a province, be not alarmed at the matter. For over the high there is a higher, who watcheth,
9 and there is one higher than they all. An advantage to a
10 land in all respects is a king over cultivated ground. He
that loveth silver shall not be satisfied with silver; and
he that loveth riches shall have no profit from them.
11 This also is vanity. When goods increase, they are increased that eat them; and what advantage hath the owner
12 thereof, save the beholding of them with his eyes? Sweet
is the sleep of a laboring man, whether he have eaten little
or much; but the repletion of the rich will not suffer him
13 to sleep. There is a sore evil which I have seen under the
14 sun, — riches kept by the owner thereof to his hurt. For
those riches perish by some calamity, and, if he have a
15 son, there is nothing in his hand. As he came forth from
his mother's womb naked, so shall he go away again, as
he came, and shall take away nothing of his labor which
16 he may carry in his hand. This is also a sore evil, that,
in all points as he came, so shall he go. And what profit

17 is there to him who toileth for wind? Also all his days
he ate in darkness, and had much grief and anxiety and
18 vexation. Behold, what I have seen is, that it is good and
proper for one to eat and drink, and to enjoy the good of
all his labor which he taketh under the sun all the days
19 of his life, which God giveth him; for it is his portion. To
whatever man also God hath given riches and wealth, and
hath given him to enjoy them, and to take his portion, and
20 to rejoice in his labor; this is the gift of God. For he
will not much remember the days of his life; for God
answereth him with the joy of his heart.

1 There is an evil which I have seen under the sun, and
2 it lieth heavy upon men; a man to whom God hath given
riches, wealth, and honor, and nothing is wanting to him
of all which he desireth, yet God giveth him not to taste
thereof; but a stranger enjoyeth it. This is vanity, yea,
3 a grievous evil. Though a man have a hundred children,
and live many years, and though the days of his years be
many, if his soul be not satisfied with good, and he have
no burial, I say that an untimely birth is better than he.
4 This, indeed, cometh in nothingness, and goeth down into
5 darkness, and its name is covered with darkness; it hath not
seen the sun, nor known it; yet hath it rest rather than
6 the other. Yea, though he live a thousand years twice
told, and see no good, — do not all go to one place?
7 All the labor of man is for his mouth, and yet his de-
8 sires are not satisfied. For what advantage hath the wise
man over the fool? What advantage hath the poor, who
9 knoweth how to walk before the living? Better is the
sight of the eyes than the wandering of the desire. This
also is vanity, and striving after wind.
10 That which is was long ago called by name; and it was
known that he is a man, and that he cannot contend with
11 Him who is mightier than he. Seeing there are many
things which increase vanity, what advantage hath man
12 [from them]? For who knoweth what is good for man in
life, in all the days of his vain life, which he spendeth as a
shadow? For who can tell a man what shall be after him
under the sun?

1 A good name is better than precious perfume, and the
2 day of one's death than the day of his birth. It is better
to go to the house of mourning than to go to the house of
feasting; for that is the end of all men; and the living
3 will lay it to heart. Sorrow is better than laughter; for
by the sadness of the countenance the heart is made better.
4 The heart of the wise is in the house of mourning; but
5 the heart of fools is in the house of mirth. It is better
for a man to hear the rebuke of the wise than to hear the
6 song of fools. For as the crackling of thorns under a pot,
7 so is the laughter of a fool. This also is vanity. Surely
the gain of oppression maketh a wise man foolish, and
8 a gift corrupteth the understanding. Better is the end of a
thing than its beginning. Better is the patient in spirit than
9 the proud in spirit. Be not hasty in thy spirit to be angry;
10 for anger resteth in the bosom of fools. Say not, "What
is the cause that the former days were better than these?"
11 For thou dost not inquire wisely concerning this. Wisdom
is as good as an estate? yea, it hath an advantage over it
12 for them that see the sun. For wisdom is a defence, and
money is a defence. But knowledge hath the advantage.
13 For wisdom giveth life to them that have it. Consider
the work of God! Who can make straight that which
14 he hath made crooked? In the day of prosperity be joyful; but look for a day of adversity! for this also, as well
as the other, hath God appointed, to the end that a man
should not find out any thing which shall be after him.
15 All this have I seen in my days of vanity. There are
righteous men who perish in their righteousness, and there
16 are wicked men who live long in their wickedness. Be
not righteous overmuch; neither make thyself over-wise!
17 Why shouldst thou destroy thyself? Be not overmuch
wicked; neither be thou a fool! Why shouldst thou die
18 before thy time? It is good that thou shouldst take hold
of this; yea, also, from that withdraw not thy hand. For
19 he that feareth God shall escape all those things. Wisdom strengtheneth the wise more than ten mighty men
20 who are in the city. Truly there is not a righteous man
21 upon the earth who doeth good and sinneth not. Give no
heed to all the words which are spoken, lest thou hear thy
22 servant curse thee! For many times thine own heart

knoweth also that even thou thyself hast cursed others.
23 All this have I tried by wisdom. I said, "I will be
24 wise;" but it was far from me. That which is far off
and exceeding deep, who can find it out?
25 I applied my mind earnestly to know, and to search,
and to seek out wisdom and intelligence, and to know
26 wickedness and folly, yea, foolishness and madness. And
I found more bitter than death the woman whose heart is
snares and nets, and her hands bands. He that pleaseth
God shall escape from her; but the sinner shall be caught
27 by her. Behold, this have I found, saith the Preacher,
28 putting one thing to another to find knowledge. That
which my soul hath hitherto sought, and I have not found,
is this: a man among a thousand I have found, but a
29 woman among a thousand have I not found. Lo, this only
have I found, that God made man upright, but they have
sought out many devices.
1 Who is like the wise man, and who knoweth the explanation of a thing? A man's wisdom brighteneth his
countenance, and the harshness of his face is changed.
2 I counsel thee to keep the king's commandment, and that
3 on account of the oath of God. Be not in haste to depart
from his presence; persist not in an evil thing; for what-
4 ever pleaseth him, that he doeth. For the word of the
king is powerful; and who can say to him, "What doest
5 thou?" He that keepeth the commandment shall experience no evil; and the heart of the wise man hath regard
6 to time and judgment. For to every thing there is a time
and judgment. For the misery of man is great upon him.
7 For no one knoweth what shall be; for who can tell him
8 how it shall be? No man hath power over the spirit to
retain the spirit, and no man hath power over the day of
death; and there is no discharge in that war; and wickedness shall not deliver those that are guilty of it.
9 All this have I seen, and I have given heed to all things
that are done under the sun. There is a time when man
10 ruleth over man to his hurt. And so I saw the wicked
buried, while the righteous came and went from the holy
place, and were forgotten in the city. This also is vanity.
11 Because sentence against an evil work is not executed

speedily, therefore doth the heart of the sons of men be-
12 come bold within them to do evil. But though a sinner
do evil a hundred times, and have his days prolonged, yet
surely I know that it shall be well with them that fear
13 God, that fear before him. But it shall not be well with
the wicked: he shall be like a shadow, and shall not prolong his days, because he feareth not before God.

14 There is a vanity which taketh place upon the earth,
that there are righteous men to whom it happeneth according to the work of the wicked, and that there are
wicked men to whom it happeneth according to the work
15 of the righteous. I said, "This also is vanity!" Then
I commended joy; because nothing is good for a man
under the sun, except to eat and to drink and to be joyful; for it is this that abideth with him for his labor
during the days of his life which God giveth him under
the sun.
16 When I applied my mind to know wisdom, and to see
the business which is done upon the earth, — that one
17 seeth no sleep with his eyes by day or by night, — then I
saw the whole work of God, that a man cannot comprehend that which is done under the sun; how much soever
he labor to search it out, yet shall he not comprehend it;
yea, though a wise man resolve to know it, yet shall he
not be able to comprehend it.
1 For I gave my mind to all this, even to search out all
this, that the righteous and the wise and their works are
in the hand of God, and yet neither his love nor hatred
2 doth any man know. All is before them. All [cometh to
them] as to all. There is one event to the righteous and to
the wicked; to the good, to the clean, and to the unclean;
to him that sacrificeth, and to him that sacrificeth not; as
is the good, so is the sinner; he that sweareth, as he that
3 feareth an oath. This is an evil among all things which
take place under the sun, that there is one event to all;
therefore also the heart of the sons of men is full of evil,
and madness is in their heart while they live, and after-
4 ward they go down to the dead. For who is there that is
excepted? With all the living there is hope; for a living
5 dog is better than a dead lion. For the living know that

they shall die; but the dead know not any thing, and
there is no more to them any advantage, for their memory
6 is forgotten. Their love also, and their hatred, and their
envy, is now perished; neither have they a portion any
more for ever in any thing which taketh place under the
sun.
7 Go thy way, eat thy bread with joy, and drink thy wine
with a cheerful heart; for long since hath God been
8 pleased with thy works. Let thy garments be always
white, and let not fragrant oil be wanting upon thy head.
9 Enjoy life with the wife whom thou lovest, all the days
of thy vain life which he hath given thee under the sun,
all thy vain days. For this is thy portion in life, and in
thy labor with which thou weariest thyself under the sun.
10 Whatever thy hand findeth to do, do it with thy might!
For there is no work nor device nor knowledge nor wisdom in the under-world, whither thou goest.

11 I turned and saw under the sun, that the race is not to
the swift, nor the battle to the strong, nor yet bread to the
wise, nor riches to men of understanding, nor favor to men
of knowledge; but time and chance happen to them all.
12 For man knoweth not his time. As fishes that are taken
in a destructive net, and as birds that are caught in a
snare, so are the sons of men snared in a time of distress,
when it falleth suddenly upon them.
13 This also have I seen; even wisdom under the sun, and
14 it seemed great to me. There was a little city, and few
men within it; and a great king came against it, and
15 besieged it, and built great bulwarks against it. Now
there was found within it a wise poor man; and he, by
his wisdom, delivered the city; yet no man remembered
16 that same poor man. Then said I, "Wisdom is better
than strength;" and yet the poor man's wisdom is des-
17 pised, and his words are not heard. The quiet words of
the wise are sooner heard than the shouting of a foolish
18 ruler. Wisdom is better than weapons of war. But one
1 offender destroyeth much good. Dead flies make the oil
of the perfumer loathsome and corrupt; thus doth a little
2 folly weigh down wisdom and honor. A wise man's mind
3 is at his right hand; but a fool's mind is at his left. Yea,

even when the fool walketh in the way, his understanding
faileth him, and he saith to every one that he is a fool.
4 If the anger of a ruler rise up against thee, leave not
5 thy place! for gentleness pacifieth great offences. There
is an evil which I have seen under the sun; an error
6 which proceedeth from a ruler. Folly is set in many high
7 stations, and the noble sit in a low place. I have seen
servants upon horses, and princes walking as servants on
8 foot. He that diggeth a pit shall fall into it; and whoso
9 breaketh down a wall, a serpent shall bite him. Whoso
removeth stones shall be hurt therewith, and he that
10 cleaveth wood shall be endangered thereby. If the iron
be blunt, and one do not whet the edge, then must he put
forth more strength; but an advantage for giving success
11 hath wisdom. If a serpent bite before he is charmed, then
12 there is no advantage to the charmer. The words of a
wise man's mouth are gracious; but the lips of a fool are
13 his destruction. The beginning of the words of his mouth
is folly, and the end of his talk is mischievous madness.
14 A fool also multiplieth words, though no man knoweth
what shall be; and who can tell him what shall be after
15 him? The labor of the foolish man wearieth him, because
16 he knoweth not how to go to the city. Woe to thee, O
land, when thy king is a child, and thy princes feast in the
17 morning! Happy thou, O land, when thy king is a noble,
and thy princes eat in due season, for strength, and not for
18 drunkenness! By much slothfulness the building decay-
eth; and by the slackness of the hands the house leaketh.
19 A feast is made for laughter, and wine makes merry; but
20 money answereth all things. Curse not the king; no, not
in thy thought; and curse not the rich in thy bed-chamber!
for a bird of the air shall carry the voice; and that which
hath wings shall tell the matter.
1 Cast thy bread upon the waters; for after many days
2 thou shalt find it. Give a portion to seven, yea, to eight;
for thou knowest not what evil shall be upon the earth.
3 When the clouds are full of rain, they empty upon the
earth; and when a tree falleth to the south or the north,
4 in the place where the tree falleth, there it shall be. He
that watcheth the wind will not sow, and he that gazeth
5 upon the clouds will not reap. As thou knowest not the

way of the wind, nor how the bones are formed in the
womb of her that is with child, so thou canst not know
6 the work of God, who doeth all things. In the morning
sow thy seed, and in the evening withhold not thy hand!
For thou knowest not whether this shall prosper, or that,
or whether both of them shall be alike good.
7 Truly the light is sweet, and a pleasant thing it is for
8 the eyes to behold the sun. Yea, though a man live many
years, let him rejoice in them all, and let him think of
the days of darkness; for they shall be many. All that
9 cometh is vanity. Rejoice, O young man, in thy youth,
and let thy heart cheer thee in the days of thy youth, and
walk in the ways of thy heart, and in the sight of thine
eyes! but know thou, that for all these things God will
10 bring thee into judgment. Therefore remove sorrow from
thy heart, and put away evil from thy body! for childhood
and youth are vanity.
1 Remember, also, thy Creator in the days of thy youth,
before the evil days come, and the years draw nigh, of
which thou shalt say, "I have no pleasure in them;"
2 before the sun, and the light, and the moon, and the stars
3 become dark, and the clouds return after the rain; at the
time when the keepers of the house tremble, and the
strong men bow themselves, and the grinders cease because they are few, and those that look out of the windows
4 are darkened; when the doors are shut in the streets,
while the sound of the mill is low; when they rise up at
the voice of the bird, and all the daughters of music are
5 brought low; when also they are afraid of that which is
high, and terrors are in the way, and the almond is despised, and the locust is a burden, and the caper-berry is
powerless; since man goeth to his eternal home, and the
6 mourners go about the streets; — before the silver cord
be snapped asunder, and the golden bowl be crushed, or
the bucket broken at the fountain, or the wheel shattered
7 at the well, and the dust return to the earth as it was, and
the spirit return to God who gave it.
8 Vanity of vanities, saith the Preacher; all is vanity!
9 Moreover, because the Preacher was wise, he still
taught the people knowledge; yea, he considered, and
10 sought out, and set in order, many proverbs. The

Preacher sought to find out acceptable words, and to write
11 correctly words of truth. The words of the wise are
as goads; yea, as nails driven in are the words of mem-
12 bers of assemblies, given by one shepherd. And, moreover, by these, my son, be warned! To the multiplying
of books there is no end, and much study wearieth the
13 flesh. Let us hear the end of the whole discourse! Fear
God and keep his commandments! For this is the duty
14 of every man. For God will bring every work into the
judgment which there is upon every secret thing, whether
it be good, or whether it be evil.

THE CANTICLES,

OR

THE SONG OF SONGS,

BY SOLOMON.

INTRODUCTION TO THE CANTICLES.

THE title of this book could not have been prefixed to it by its author. The Song of Songs is undoubtedly an instance of the Hebrew superlative, meaning the finest or most beautiful of songs. It is, moreover, improbable that the title implies a comparison of the work with other poetry written by Solomon. The meaning of the person who gave the book its title was, that it contained the most beautiful of songs, and that Solomon was its author.

The first and most interesting question that presents itself in relation to this work is, What is its subject? If the Song of Songs had been found in any book except the Bible, I presume there would have been great unanimity in answering the question. It would be said that few compositions existed, every line of which revealed so fully the subject occupying the mind of the author. It would be said that one sentiment pervaded the whole, and that that sentiment was love. In fact, there is now no dispute respecting the subject of the book, so far as it can be expressed in a single word. It is allowed by all to be love, reciprocal love. The question is, What kind of love is here represented? Is it spiritual, or is it sentimental love; that is, the love of the sexes, as represented in poetry? Is it that love which exists between God and man, or Christ and the Church; or that which exists between man and woman?

Since the time of Origen, the opinion has prevailed, that the work is designed to set forth the mutual love of Christ and the Church. This distinguished allegorist exerted his great talents, as we are informed by St. Jerome,* in illustrating the book. In his other works, says he, Origen surpassed other men; in this he

* Opera, tom. ii. p. 807, edit. Martianay.

surpassed himself; so that in him may seem to have been fulfilled that which is said, "The king has led me to his chamber." The unbounded influence of Origen gave the allegorical interpretation prevalence in the Church; so that, when Theodore of Mopsuestia, a man of great learning and talent, defended the literal sense of the Canticles, he was excommunicated for this and other causes after his death, by an assembly of fanatical bishops and monks, the second council of Constantinople, in the year 553.*

Since the time of the condemnation of Theodore, the prevalent belief of Christendom has been, that the book contains a representation of the mutual love of Christ and the Church. This would seem to be the most general view at the present day, if we may judge of the opinion of the Christian Church by what is expressed in the popular commentaries. It is contained in the captions to the chapters in the common version.

Among the modern Jews, too, the allegorical sense of the book has prevailed, according to which it has been supposed to set forth the dealings of God with the Jewish people. Thus, the Targumist on this book applies it to Jehovah and the Jewish nation, in their journeyings from Egypt to the land of Canaan.

As the mystical interpretation of this book commenced and advanced with the general prevalence and progress of the allegorical mode of interpretation, so it has declined in proportion as that mode of interpretation has been understood to be without foundation. Since the time of Grotius, the prevailing opinion of the learned critics who have examined the work has been, that the subject of it is not spiritual or religious love, but that which exists between man and woman.

The peculiar view of Grotius has found few supporters. He supposes the book to contain a dialogue between newly married persons, in which very gross ideas are veiled by decent expressions.† But since his time,—that is, since the principle of inter-

* See Rosenmülleri Historia Interpretationis, vol. iii. pp. 251 and 262.

† "Est ὀαριστὺς (i.e. garritus conjugum inter se) inter Salomonem et filiam regis Egypti, interloquentibus etiam choris duobus, tum juvenum tum virginum, qui in proximis thalamo locis excubabant. Nuptiarum arcana sub honestis verborum involucris hic latent; quæ etiam causa est cur Hebræi veteres hunc librum legi noluerint, nisi a jam conjugio proximis."

pretation has been generally acknowledged, that language can have no other meaning than that which exists in the mind of the writer, — the mystical sense has been given up by most critics on the Continent, and by many in England; such as Michaelis, Herder, Eichhorn, Döderlein, Dathe, Seiler, Jahn, De Wette, Umbreit, Ewald, Heiligstedt, Hitzig, and many others. In England, the distinguished Methodist, Adam Clarke; the Calvinistic dissenter, John Pye Smith; and the Biblical translator, Dr. Boothroyd, who is also an Orthodox dissenter, — have also abandoned the mystical explanation.

There are those, however, in modern times, who yet hold fast the allegorical interpretation. Among these is the Romanist Hug, who supposes the book to be of a political nature. Under the image of a spouse, as he thinks, is set forth a part of the ten tribes, which, being left in their country after the destruction of Samaria, sought to be re-united to the Jewish nation under the reign of Hezekiah. The Jews, represented by the brothers of the Shulamite, are unwilling that the union should take place.

Rosenmüller adopts the theory, that the work sets forth the love of Solomon for wisdom. It is not a little remarkable, however, that while Rosenmüller avows this to be his view in the introduction to his commentary on the book, he makes not the slightest allusion to it in the commentary itself, extensive as it is.

In England, Bishop Percy and John Mason Good avow their belief in the mystical interpretation. Like Rosenmüller, however, they do not apply their theory to the interpretation of the book, but comment upon it as if the literal were the only sense.

In this country, the old notion, that the book sets forth the mutual love of Christ and the Church, is probably the most prevalent. But Professor Robinson, in his Bible Dictionary, adopts the view, that the subject of the book is the mutual love of Jehovah and the Jewish nation.

Professor Stuart, of Andover, has also avowed his faith in the mystical exposition of the Canticles, in his hasty work on the canon of the Old Testament. He has adopted the view, that the subject of the book is the relation of God to the individual soul, and the aspirations of the soul to be united to the Creator.

I might mention several other theories. But it would answer no good purpose, as I do not intend to examine them one by one, in order to show which is the most, or the least, tenable. I believe that there is not the slightest foundation for any one of them; that not one of them can be accepted, without setting at defiance all just views of the nature of language, and all solid principles of interpretation.

The decisive objection, which applies in nearly an equal degree to all these theories, is, that there is no mention, or even intimation, in the work itself, of that which they make its great and principal subject. These interpreters tell us, that the work expresses the mutual love of Jehovah and the Hebrew nation, or of Christ and the Church, or of God and the individual soul. In opposition to this, it is enough to say, that it is mere fancy; that there is not the slightest allusion to God, to Christ, to the Church, or to the soul of man as related to God, in the whole book. The only persons introduced into it are human. There is not a sentence, or part of a sentence, which, according to the common use of language, expresses any religious idea. This with me is the decisive consideration. The author has in no way indicated that he uses language in any but the obvious and usual sense. In all allegory, it is necessary that the principal subject should be in some way indicated. If allegory is a long-continued comparison, it is necessary that the author should decidedly make known to us the subject compared. But in the Book of Canticles this is not the case. The principal subject, as understood by the allegorists, does not appear in it. The book is all comparison, and nothing to be compared; all illustration, and nothing to be illustrated. The thing to be illustrated comes from without, — from the mind of the interpreter, arbitrarily imposing a sense on the author's words in consequence of some imagined necessity, which is wholly independent of any thing in the work itself. In the parable of the Prodigal Son, who would have known that it was intended to illustrate the disposition of God towards men, unless our Saviour had indicated such an application of it? So in the allegory of the Vine which came out of Egypt, it is expressly stated, "The vineyard of the Lord of hosts is the house of Israel." So every writer of common sense, who makes use of metaphor, comparison, or allegory, will in some way indicate the principal subject to be illustrated. But it is not pretended that the author of the Canticles has done this. The only just conclusion, then, is, that he has not made use of allegory; that he designed his language to be understood in its common and obvious sense.

It has been said, in favor of the mystical interpretation, that in other writers of the Scriptures language similar to that in the Canticles is used; that Jehovah is called the husband of his people, and the people represented as a faithless wife. Now, without stating at present how small is the resemblance between the Canticles and the comparisons just referred to, there is one obvious difference which deprives this reference to such comparisons of any force as an argument. It is, that the subject compared is always prominent in those illustrations of the Hebrew prophets. Thus, in Isa. liv. 5, "Thy Maker is thy husband; Jehovah of hosts is his name." Such illustrations, therefore, if they resembled the language in the Canticles much more than they do, would only show how its language *might have been*, not how it *is*, used. Because an adulterous woman, in the writings of the prophets, represents the Jewish people in their rebellion against Jehovah, it surely does not follow that every woman or maiden in the Scriptures does, or may, denote the Jewish people. Because a tender husband sometimes denotes a compassionate God in relation to his people, it surely does not follow that every husband or lover in the Scriptures denotes the Supreme Being. Because the Church is compared to a chaste virgin, it does not follow that every virgin denotes the Church. Before we can admit that any writer intends to denote the Supreme Being by such expressions, he must himself indicate it by express declaration or intelligible implication, as the prophets have done in the cases to which reference has been made. Now, the author of the Canticles has not intimated to us in any way, that in his songs he had in view any other characters than man and woman, or any other kind of love than human or sentimental love. We have no right, then, to go beyond this meaning. Those who have adduced this illustration from the prophets have at best only shown what *might be*, not what *is*. There is no part of the Old Testament, or at least no difficult part, which may not be allegorized with as much reason as the Canticles.

But, in the second place, I deny that the language of the prophets, in the cases referred to, is at all analogous to that of the Canticles. Those passages in the prophets which set forth the ingratitude of the house of Israel to Jehovah under the image of a wife faithless to a tender husband, are wholly unlike any thing in the Book of Canticles. In the former, the Supreme Being always appears as Jehovah, the most holy governor of the world, the comparison being used incidentally to illustrate his own conduct or that of his people. In the latter, we find only lovers and maidens; the praise of personal beauty and passionate expressions of love; lovers conversing with each other, placed in different scenes, eating, drinking, sleeping, embracing, running, climbing, visiting gardens, feeding flocks; in fine, all that is usually found in erotic poetry. Who can fail to perceive the difference between such representations and any views which the sublime Hebrew prophets give of the character and conduct of God?

It seems to me wholly inconsistent with the reverence for Jehovah which existed in the Hebrew mind, that one of their writers should compose such a book as Canticles to illustrate the feelings which should exist between man and his Creator. It is a monstrous supposition. There is nothing in the Hebrew literature to justify it. Who is there among us that would dare to use much of the language of the Canticles in reference to the high and lofty One that inhabiteth eternity? Had not the Jews as great a reverence for the venerable name as Christians? Let us conceive of the author of the fortieth chapter of Isaiah — after he had spoken of the Supreme Being as having "measured the waters in the hollow of his hand, and meted out the heavens with his span, and gathered the dust of the earth into a measure, and weighed the mountains in scales, and the hills in a balance," as the Being "before whom all nations are nothing, and accounted less than nothing and vanity" — as addressing himself to his devotions. Would he have commenced with, "Let him kiss me with one of the kisses of his mouth; for thy caresses are better than wine"? Would he have applied to the Supreme Being the language, "My beloved spake and said unto me, 'Rise up, my love, my fair one, and come away' "? Would Solomon, who, in his prayer at the dedication of the temple, used the sublime language, "Behold, the heaven, even the heaven of heavens, cannot contain thee," have addressed his Creator in the language, "The voice of my beloved! Behold, he cometh, leaping upon the mountains, bounding over the hills. Like a gazelle is my beloved, or a young hind," &c.? I might proceed with interrogations of this kind; but there is language in the Canticles which I could not apply to the Infinite Spirit in the manner required by the mystical theory, without feeling guilty of blasphemy.

In support of the mystical interpretation of the Canticles, reference has been made to the pantheistic mysticism of the religious sect called Sufis, which has long existed in the East, and especially to the songs of Hafiz, a Persian writer of the fourteenth century, who has been supposed to teach mystic religious doctrines under the images of love, wine, &c. But it is doubtful whether Hafiz himself attached a religious meaning to many of his songs. It is certain, that most of them relate only to sentimental love. Umbreit, who appears to have given considerable attention to the subject, says, "The love-poems of Nisami, Leila and Medschnun, and Jussuf and Suleicha, have been explained allegorically, although, according to the evident intention of the poet, they require a literal interpretation."* Sir William Jones observes, "It has been made a question, whether the poems of Hafiz must be taken in a literal or in a figurative sense; but the question does not admit of a general and direct answer: for even the most enthusiastic of his commentators allow that some of them are to be taken literally."† The "Conversations-Lexicon," or "Encyclopædia Americana," which may be supposed to represent the opinion of the learned in Germany, says, "The songs of Hafiz were collected into a *divan*, after his death, which was published complete (Calcutta, 1791) and translated into German by the celebrated Orientalist, Von Hammer (2 vols. Stuttgard, 1812–1815). The poems of Hafiz are distinguished for

* See Umbreit's Lied der Liebe, p. 5.

† Asiatic Researches, vol. iii. p. 172.

sprightliness and Anacreontic festivity. He is not unfrequently loud in praise of wine, love, and pleasure. *Some writers have sought a mystic meaning in these verses.* Feridoun, Sururi, Sadi, and others, have attempted to explain what they supposed to be the hidden sense."

Before what appear to be love-songs in any nation can afford any confirmation of a mystical sense in the Canticles, it must be shown that there are some intimations in them that their sensual expressions are designed as images of spiritual things. If this cannot be shown, it is reasonable to conclude that they have no allegoric meaning. But if there are in them decided intimations of a spiritual meaning, then they are unlike the Song of Solomon.

In the literature of several nations, an allegorical sense has been given to the productions of distinguished poets by their admirers. The Iliad of Homer, the songs of Hafiz, and the Canticles ascribed to Solomon, have met with the same fortune. From the allegorical use of them made in an age subsequent to that in which they were written, we cannot infer what was the original design and meaning of either.

I have no disposition to deny, however, that among the productions of the Sufi poets are found poems in which sensual images are used for the purpose of expressing devotional feelings. This might be expected from the obscene symbols of the Sufi religion, as described by Tholuck. "Voluptatem ex unione [i.e. cum Deo] captam, turpem adsciscentes figuram, assimilaverunt cum coitu maris et feminæ, præeuntibus Indis quorum in Upnekhato, t. i. p. 241, conjunctio mystica cum Deo comparatur cum concubitu mulieris prædilectæ, inter quem nulla in mariti animo firma cogitatio permaneat aut imaginationis species, sed universæ sensuum animique vires immersæ sint in suavissimam jucunditatis commotionem."*

I do not profess a thorough acquaintance with these writings. But, having examined the specimens found in the writings of Sir William Jones, and in Tholuck's Selections† from the mystic poets

* Tholuck's Ssufismus, p. 94.

† Blüthensammlung aus der Morgenländischen Mystik, von F. A. G. Tholuck. Berlin, 1825.

of the East, I am convinced that none of them bear much resemblance to the Canticles. They are evidently productions of a different nature, and connected with a religion as different from the Jewish as darkness from light.

Among the specimens most favorable to the opinion of those who form their judgment of the nature of a Hebrew poem from the productions of mystic Sufi pantheists or the songs of Mahometan dervishes, are the two given by Mr. Lane in his work on the "Modern Egyptians," contained in the Library of Entertaining Knowledge. These specimens I shall quote entire for the satisfaction of the reader, the more especially because they appear to have had great influence on the mind of Professor Stuart, and are quoted by him as the principal support of the opinion which he adopts, that the Canticles "express the warm and earnest desire of the soul after God, in language borrowed from that which characterizes chaste affection between the sexes."

"The durweesh," says Mr. Lane,* "pointed out the following poem as one of those most common at zikrs, and as one which was sung at the zikr, which I have begun to describe. I translate it verse for verse, and imitate the measure and system of rhyme of the original, with this difference only, that the first, third, and fifth lines of each stanza rhyme with each other in the original, but not in my translation:—

"'With love my heart is troubled,
  And mine eyelid hindereth sleep:
My vitals are dissevered,
  While with streaming tears I weep.
My union seems far distant:
  Will my love e'er meet my eye?
Alas! did not estrangement
  Draw my tears, I would not sigh.

By dreary nights I 'm wasted:
  Absence makes my hope expire:
My tears, like pearls, are dropping;
  And my heart is wrapt in fire.
Whose is like my condition?
  Scarcely know I remedy.
Alas! did not estrangement
  Draw my tears, I would not sigh.

* Modern Egyptians, vol. ii. p. 195.

O turtle-dove! acquaint me,
  Wherefore thus dost thou lament?
Art thou so stung by absence?
  Of thy wings deprived and pent?
He saith, "Our griefs are equal;
  Worn away with love, I lie."
Alas! did not estrangement
  Draw my tears, I would not sigh.

O First and Everlasting!
  Show thy favor yet to me;
Thy slave, Ahh'mad El-Bek'ree*
  Hath no Lord excepting thee.
By Ta′-ha′,† the great prophet!
  Do thou not his wish deny.
Alas! did not estrangement
  Draw my tears, I would not sigh.'"

"I must translate a few more lines," says Mr. Lane, "to show more strongly the similarity of these songs to that of Solomon; and, lest it should be thought that I have varied the expressions, I shall not attempt to render them into verse. In the same collection of poems sung at zikrs is one which begins with these lines: —

"'O gazelle from among the gazelles of El-Yem′en!
I am thy slave without cost:
O thou small of age, and fresh of skin!
O thou who art scarce past the time of drinking milk!'

"In the first of these verses, we have a comparison exactly agreeing with that in the concluding verse of Solomon's Song; for the word which, in our Bible, is translated a 'roe' is used in Arabic as synonymous with ghaza'l (or a gazelle); and the mountains of El-Yem'en are 'the mountains of spices.' This poem ends with the following lines: —

"'The phantom of thy form visited me in slumber;
I said, "O phantom of slumber! who sent thee?"
He said, "He sent me whom thou knowest;
He whose love occupies thee."

* The author of the poem. † A name of Mahomet.

The beloved of my heart visited me in the darkness of night;
I stood, to show him honor, until he sat down.
I said, "O thou my petition, and all my desire!
Hast thou come at midnight, and not feared the watchmen?"
He said to me, "I feared; but, however, love
Had taken from me my soul and my breath."'

Compare the above with the second and five following verses of the fifth chapter of Solomon's Song."

Now, as to the first of these religious love-songs of the Mahometan dervishes, whatever slight resemblance it may have to any part of the Canticles, it differs essentially from any of them in the circumstance, that the Supreme Being is expressly introduced as the object of worship. Without this essential circumstance, no one could tell whether it were originally composed for a love-song, or a religious hymn expressing a longing for a union of the soul with God, according to the Sufi philosophy and religion.

In the second poem, quoted by Mr. Lane, it is to be regretted that he did not quote the whole of it. For I can by no means admit the circumstance that it was sung by the dervishes in their morning devotions to be conclusive in regard to the original design of the hymn. Mr. Lane expressly tells us, in a note, that he found the last six lines inserted, with some slight alterations, as a common love-song, in a portion of the "Thousand and One Nights," printed at Calcutta, vol. i. p. 425; Lane's Translation, ii. p. 349. Whether the whole was originally composed as a love-song or a devotional hymn does not appear from the parts of it which Mr. Lane gives us. If, in the parts omitted, there is any clear reference to the Deity, it is unlike any of the Canticles. If there is no such reference, the meaning of the hymn is too doubtful to allow any inference to be drawn from it. For we might as well allow the singing of Dr. Watts's version of the Canticles to be an argument for their original design, as to admit the singing of the mystic dervishes to be an evidence of the original design of the hymns, which they sung.

Before making some general remarks on this whole subject of attempting to show the character of the Canticles by reference to the pantheistic poetry of the Mahometan Sufis, it may be well to mention that reference has been made even to the poets of Hindostan for the same purpose; especially to the Gitagovinda,* the production of a celebrated Hindoo poet, named Jayadeva. This appears to be a mystical poem, designed to celebrate the loves of Crishna and Radha, or the reciprocal attraction between the Divine goodness and the human soul. Now, whatever may be the resemblance between the Gitagovinda and the Canticles in some of their imagery, there is this essential difference, that, in the former, Crishna was the chief incarnated god of the Hindoos; † and that there are in it references to other gods, and to various superstitions of the Hindoo mythology, whilst in the Canticles there is no reference to any but human characters. Besides, the author of the Gitagovinda clearly intimates its religious character in the conclusion of the poem.

We have seen, then, that there are material differences between the Canticles and the religious love-songs to which reference has been made. But, supposing the resemblance to be much greater than it is, those mystical songs do not in any essential respect resemble the Canticles more than they do the odes of Anacreon, or some of the eclogues of Virgil, and the idyls of Theocritus. And it is not easy to see why the resemblance does not prove the religious character of the odes of Anacreon as much as that of the Canticles.

But, after all, the great objection remains to any conclusion drawn from the pantheistic mystic poets, whether of Persia or India, whether Mahometans or Hindoos; namely, that their productions are founded on a religion and philosophy entirely different from the Jewish. The Canticles are productions of a different country, and separated from any of the songs of the Sufi poets by an interval of nearly two thousand years. The Jewish religion

---

* It may be found appended to Dr. Adam Clarke's Commentary on the Canticles. Also in the Asiatic Researches, vol. iii.

† "Crishna continues to this hour the darling god of the Indian women. The sect of Hindoos, who adore him with enthusiastic and almost exclusive devotion, have broached a doctrine which they maintain with eagerness, and which seems general in these provinces; that he was distinct from all the *Avatars*, who had only an *ansa* or portion of his divinity; while Crishna was the person of Vishnu himself in a human form." — Sir W. Jones, in Asiatic Researches, vol. i. p. 260.

has nothing in common with the pantheistic mysticism on which those songs are founded. There is nothing in the Old Testament of a similar character. If any productions similar to those mystical love-songs had existed in the religious literature of the Hebrews, undoubtedly we should have found some of them in the Book of Psalms, which comprises compositions from the age preceding that of David to a period long after the return of the Jews from the captivity at Babylon. But in the most fervent psalms, the forty-second for instance, nothing of the kind is found. Neither is any thing similar to these mystic songs ascribed to the Jewish sects, as described by Josephus and Philo. Nothing of the kind is laid to the charge of the Essenes. It is needless to say that nothing approaching to a like character is found in the New Testament. Nothing similar is discovered even in the allegorical paraphrase of the Targumist* on the Canticles. All those religious love-songs are founded on the Sufi religion, or rather religious philosophy, which, whether it was borrowed from India, as Von Hammer supposes, or arose independently among the Mahometans, according to the opinion of Tholuck,† has no connection with, or resemblance to, the Jewish. It is as different from the latter as darkness from light. The argument, therefore, which is drawn from the mystical songs of the Mahometan devotees for ascribing a mystical character to the Canticles is without foundation.

To me also it appears singular, that any one should think it to be for the honor of the book, or of the Jewish religion, or of the Bible, to regard the Canticles as designed to be a book of devotion, a guide to the Jews in the expression of their religious feelings to their Creator. If it be regarded as a specimen of the erotic poetry of the Hebrews, it will be treated with indifference by most readers, and consequently do them no harm. But, if regarded as an inspired model and help for devotion, its direct tendency is injurious to morals and religion. That such is its tendency, when so understood, is too plain to need argument. Even Professor Stuart, who professes to believe it an inspired composition, de-

* The Targum on Solomon's Song may be found translated, appended to Dr. Adam Clarke's Commentary on the Canticles.

† Tholuck's Ssufismus, etc., cap. ii.

signed "to express the warm and ardent desire of the soul after God," is compelled by his moral feelings to express the strangely inconsistent opinion, that "it is the safer and better course to place the Canticles, as the Jews did, among the גְּנוּזִים, or books withdrawn from ordinary use;" and, again, that those who neglect to read the book "are to be commended rather than blamed."* He attempts, indeed, to show that what would be dangerous to us in the Western world might be safe for the Orientals, on account of the secluded state in which females were kept among them. But it is not easy to see why sensual imagery should have less influence on the imagination and feelings of an Oriental on account of any difference between Eastern and Western society, or why the language of love-songs, used as the vehicle of devotion, should have less influence to corrupt and debase the religion of an Asiatic than of an American. It seems to be at least probable, that what could not with decency be sung in a mixed assembly in this country was never designed by Heaven to be sung or said as a religious exercise in any country. On general principles, I should suppose that the safety was on the side of the colder temperament of the Western world, and that the freer social intercourse between the sexes in the West was less likely to inflame the imagination and the passions than that guarded seclusion of females through which they are presented to the mind only as objects of sensual love.

It may be that some of the Sufi devotees sing their religious love-songs with devotional feelings. But that the tendency of such a mode of worship is bad is almost self-evident. No one can be surprised when Professor Tholuck, who in general gives the most favorable aspect of the Oriental mysticism, informs us concerning the dissoluteness and sensuality of the dervishes and Sufis, whose devotional exercises consist of language and images borrowed from sensual love, "Proinde, si quæ dissolutioris vitæ, quin etiam veneris promiscuæ criminationes adversus Derwischios et Ssufios factæ sunt, earum me repellendarum equidem haud parem crederem."†

---

* Stuart on the Canon, &c., p. 381.

† See Tholuck's Ssufismus, sive Theosophia Persarum Pantheistica, etc., Berlin, 1821. p. 88.

On the injurious effect of a religious use of the Canticles, the testimony of Dr. Adam Clarke, who as a travelling Methodist preacher had great opportunities for observation relating to the subject, is as follows. Speaking of those who attach a spiritual meaning to the book, he says: "Their conduct is dangerous; and the result of their well-intentioned labors has been of very little service to the cause of Christianity in general, or to the interests of true morality in particular. By their mode of interpretation, an undignified, not to say mean and carnal, language has been propagated among many well-meaning religious people, that has associated itself too much with selfish and animal affections, and created feelings that accorded little with the dignified spirituality of the religion of the Lord Jesus. I speak not from report; I speak from observation and experience, and observation not hastily made. The conviction on my mind, and the conclusion to which I have conscientiously arrived, are the result of frequent examination, careful reading, and close thinking at intervals, for nearly fifty years; and, however I may be blamed by some and pitied by others, I must say, and I say it as fearlessly as I do conscientiously, that in this inimitably fine, elegant Hebrew ode I see nothing of Christ and his Church, and nothing that appears to have been intended to be thus understood; and nothing, if applied in this way, that, *per se*, can promote the interests of vital godliness, or cause the simple and sincere not to know Christ after the flesh. Here I conscientiously stand: may God help me."*

Indeed, the history of religion in all ages and in all countries is full of examples of the danger that excited religious feeling may unite itself with sensual feelings, and express itself in sensual images. Witness the representations of some of the Hindoo gods, and the religious rites of various heathen nations. Even in Christendom, hymns have been sung as religious, which fall below any heathen addresses to Phallus or Priapus. In proof of this may be adduced the obscene language used by the early Moravians, in their hymns and other acts of worship. Examples of language of this kind, indecent beyond conception, are quoted

* See his Introduction to the Song of Solomon.

by Rimius,* in his writings relating to the Moravians. Fortunately, these sincere but misguided Christians were taught by their assailants to correct their dangerous error. But let it be generally believed that the Canticles were inspired and designed "to express the warm and earnest desire of the soul after God," and we shall be likely to have the error of the early Moravians repeated in all its disgusting offensiveness. Its direct influence will be to debase religion and promote immorality. Let it not be said there is no danger, in a community in which Millerism and Mormonism have found so many proselytes.

The opinion, then, that the Canticles were designed as helps to the soul in its devotions, is more discreditable to the book itself, to the Scriptures, and to the Jewish religion, than that which regards them as relics of the amatory poetry of the Hebrews. That which is noxious is more discreditable than that which is merely indifferent. The odes of Anacreon, while they are read in our schools as amatory poetry, have but little influence of any kind. But if they were taught as helps to devotion, to be repeated day after day as religious exercises during one's whole life, the effect would be very different.

One other argument has been urged of late in favor of the mystical interpretation of the Canticles, which I should think unworthy of notice, were it not for the respectability of those who offer it. It is drawn from the difference of opinion, in regard to the object, plan, and design of the Canticles, among those who reject the allegorical interpretation. But this difference of opinion relates not to the general character of the book, or to the meaning of its language, but to the author's special plan and design. It is not strange that there should have been a difference of opinion on these points, since no special object or plan may have existed in the author's mind. But, after all, there is no greater difference of opinion in regard to the Canticles than in regard to Ecclesiastes, Job, and some other books of the Old Testament. And this argument, if it proves any thing, proves that we may fasten an allegorical sense upon any difficult passage or book of the Bible.

---

* See Rimius's History of the Moravians, &c., Tracts, vols. i. and ii. (London, 1754). See also Southey's Life of Wesley, vol. i. pp. 188 and 387.

Besides, for every two different opinions expressed by those who reject the mystical sense of the Canticles, it will be very easy to find four expressed by those who hold it.

Why, then, says the friend of the allegorical interpretation of the Canticles, is the book found in the Scriptures, if it has not a religious meaning or a moral value? This, after all, is, I apprehend, the only argument which has much real weight even with the allegorists. The book is found in the Scriptures; therefore it cannot be understood in its obvious sense; therefore it must have an allegorical sense; and, since the author has not said or intimated what the religious sense of his words is, the reader must supply it for him.

Now, suppose that we were wholly unable to answer the question, how an amatory poem, or a collection of amatory poetry, came into the Jewish canon of the Scriptures. Is our ignorance on a point like this a reason for assigning to a man's words a sense which was never in his mind, and which, according to the usage of the language in which he wrote, and of the authors of the same nation, in his own age, or before or after his time, his words are not adapted to express?

No one knows, or has good reason to believe, what individuals or body of men made the collection of the writings of the Old Testament. Of course, we do not know on what judgment, if any, the admission of a writing into this collection rests. For aught we know, all the Hebrew works extant at a particular time may have been included in the collection. The incredible and contradictory Jewish traditions on the subject all go to show that absolutely nothing is known respecting it.* One may find abundance of conjecture and of strained inferences relating to it, but no genuine history. The Book of Canticles, then, if placed in the collection of Hebrew literature by an act of judgment, may have been placed there by those who supposed it a production, possessing much poetic beauty, of a person so celebrated throughout the East as Solomon. Much uncertainty exists in regard to the time when the books of the Old Testament began to be

---

* See De Wette's Introduction to the Old Testament, § 14, and his references.

regarded as holy writings. That they were so regarded when this book was added to the number cannot be proved. It may then have been regarded as only a collection of national writings; of all that was esteemed valuable in Hebrew literature. That a great part of the Old Testament has a religious character may be accounted for by the predominant religious spirit of the Jews, and the existence of their theocratic institutions.

Or, if we suppose the collector or collectors to have regarded the collection of the Hebrew writings as possessing a moral or religious character when the Canticles were introduced into it, why may not the book have been regarded by them as having a good moral tendency in its literal sense; as designed to recommend monogamy, as some modern expositors suppose; or as designed to show "the reward of fidelity and constancy in affairs of the heart," as others imagine; or that its object was to prove "that love, as the freest and fairest gift of the heart, can no more be destroyed than called forth by outward power," as a third class has maintained; or that the author's design was the general one of setting forth "the pleasures of virtuous love"? These or other reasons may have influenced the collector or collectors in giving it a place in the volume afterwards held sacred by the Jews, without supposing that it possessed a religious or mystical character.

But, even supposing that the allegorical interpretation prevailed at so early a period as that of the completion of the canon of the Jewish Scriptures, and that the Canticles were admitted into it by those who regarded it as an allegory expressive of religious ideas, it by no means follows that such is the fact. There is abundant reason for distrusting the judgment as well as the information of the collectors of the books of the Old Testament. Witness the false captions to many of the Psalms, the confused state of the prophecies of Jeremiah, the mode in which the prophets were arranged, the ascription to Isaiah of much which he could not have written, in the judgment not merely of rationalists, but of the most Orthodox critics. If he or they who placed the Canticles in the Old Testament, hundreds of years after it was written, regarded it as a religious or even an inspired book, this is not a sufficient reason why we should so regard it.

In respect to the mere question, whether the book was contained in the Jewish canon, that is, whether it was generally received by the Jews as a part of their sacred writings for nearly two hundred years before the Christian era, I entirely agree with those who regard it as canonical. But whether any book has in reality a claim on my faith or practice depends on very different considerations from that of its general reception, whether by the Jewish nation or the Christian Church. I must satisfy myself, first, whether the writer ever laid claim to Divine authority; and, if he did, whether he gave any proof of his claim, internal or external. If I admit the authority of the Church, that is, of a majority of it, as settling conclusively what I am to receive as of Divine authority, I must admit the authority of the Church in other matters, and adopt the creed of Romanism at once. The Church, that is, the majority of the Church, the Roman Church, regards the books commonly called apocryphal as canonical. Such is the decree of the Council of Trent.

The only way in which a critical and historical inquirer can satisfy himself as to the Divine authority of any book of the Old or the New Testament is to take it up separately, and consider what it claims to be, and how far its claims are supported by internal and external evidence, and then accept it for what it is. If in the Canticles, for instance, we find no mention of God, of duty, or of the destination of man, no doctrine of any kind requiring the faith, or duty requiring the practice, of mankind, let us take the book for what, according to the received use of language, it purports to be, — a collection of amatory songs; and award to it, as a work of taste, that portion of praise to which we consider it entitled. This would seem to be all that duty requires of us.

There are some, it is true, who maintain that Jesus Christ and his apostles have given the sanction of Divine authority to the genuineness and inspiration of all the books contained in the Jewish canon. In regard to the particular question which I have been discussing, I might urge that the Canticles are nowhere alluded to in the New Testament, as would naturally have been the case if they had been regarded as setting forth the mutual love of Christ and the Church, or of Jehovah and the Jewish people, or of God and the human soul. But I have no faith in the proposition, that Jesus Christ meant to extend his authority and approbation to all that was contained in the Jewish canon in his time. I do not believe that it was a part of his mission, even if it were within the compass of his knowledge, to decide questions of criticism and interpretation more than of astronomy or geology, or the causes of disease. He referred to the books of the Old Testament, just as he used the phraseology concerning demoniacs, according to the received opinions of the Jews. If he held these opinions himself, he did not inculcate them upon others. He had ample work to employ all his time during his short ministry on earth, in establishing, as God's prophet, the fundamental doctrines of his religion, without entering into controversy with the Jews on matters of criticism and interpretation. If his mission was to settle, by Divine authority, all the various questions which have arisen in regard to the character, criticism, and meaning of the Old Testament, then one object of his coming into the world was to set bounds to criticism, the inevitable consequence of which would be to put a stop to that mental improvement and that exact knowledge which are the result of criticism. For it is idle to pretend that we have a right to study the Old Testament critically, unless we have a right to judge of its contents according to the laws of critical and historical investigation. I cannot believe that the design of Christ's coming into the world was to put a stop to any scientific investigation. Nothing, it appears to me, is more likely to promote the cause of scepticism than attempts to restrain historical and critical inquiry by dint of authority, whatever the authority may be.

From the references made by our Saviour to the Old Testament, we may conclude that in his view it contained much that is Divine. But that he intended to sanction all that is contained in it, or to settle critical questions in regard to the genuineness and authority of every book in it, is in the highest degree improbable. The arguments which have been adduced to support such a proposition fall very far short of their aim. How could he who gave the command, "Love your enemies, bless them that curse you, and pray for them that despitefully use you and persecute you," have supposed that the barbarous extermination of the Canaanites was by express Divine command? Or how could he who died praying for his enemies, "Father, forgive them, for they know not what they do!" have sanctioned the horrible imprecations in the hundred and ninth Psalm, or other passages of the Old Testament having a similar character? (See also Matt. xix. 8, 9; vii. 31–34, 38, 39.)

These views, or those which have a similar bearing on the Old Testament, have been expressed by divines of different denominations. The late Dr. Arnold, of the Church of England, whose praise as a scholar and a Christian is high wherever the English language is spoken, regarded it as perfectly consistent with the acknowledgment of the Divine authority of Christ to pronounce the Book of Daniel a forgery.* One of the most distinguished orthodox dissenting divines in England, after expressing the opinion that the Song of Songs is "a pastoral eclogue, or a succession of eclogues, representing, in the vivid colors of Asiastic rural scenery, with a splendor of artificial decoration, the honorable loves of a newly-married bride and bridegroom, with some other interlocutors," writes thus: "It is, I deeply feel and acknowledge, an awful thing to appear to go in contravention to the generally assumed position, that our Lord and his apostles recognized the writings received as sacred by the Jews at that time as the exclusive and entire canon. But I humbly request that it may be considered what is meant by the term canon or rule; and whether that meaning can be attached to a composition which has not in it a sentence, or a single word, possessing the nature of a rule, directory, standard, or prescription whatsoever, in reference to facts or doctrines or precepts, or any thing at all of a religious kind, *except upon a plan of translating its terms and ideas into another kind of subjects*, of which not the shadow of intimation is given in the composition itself, and against which I am bound to protest, as destructive of the certainty of language, and by inevitable consequence inflicting a deep injury upon the records of revealed truth. If we cannot depend upon the definite and constant meaning of words and references of sentences as drawn out by honest philology, we may as well shut our books, resign ourselves to impious indifference, or fall back into the bosom of

* See Arnold's Life and Writings, Letter 218, p. 369, Amer. edit.

the pretended infallible Church. When I reflect upon the difficulties, using the mildest term, which arise from an endeavor to convert passages containing matter merely genealogical, topographical, numerical, civil, military, — fragments of antiquity, domestic or national, presenting no character whatever of religious matter, — into a rule of faith and manners, I feel it impossible to accept the conclusion; I can find no end to my anxiety, no rest for my faith, no satisfaction for my understanding, till I embrace the sentiment, that the qualities of sanctity and inspiration belong only to the *religious and theological element*, which is *diffused through* the Old Testament; and that, where this element is absent, where there is nothing adapted to communicate 'doctrine, reproof, correction, or instruction in righteousness,' nothing fitted 'to make the man of God perfect, thoroughly furnished unto every good work,' — there we are not called to acknowledge any inspiration, nor warranted to assume it. Thus, I regard as inspired Scripture all that refers to *holy things*, all that can bear the character of 'oracles of God;' and admit the rest as appendages, of the nature of private memoirs or public records, useful to the antiquary and the philologist, but which belong not to the rule of faith or the directory of practice. To this extent, and to this only, can I regard the sanction of the New Testament as given to the *inspiration* of the Old. In other words, the quality of inspiration, forming the ground of faith and obedience, inheres in every sentence, paragraph, or book, which, either directly or by implication, contains religious truth, precept, or expectation. This, I humbly think, leaves us every thing that a Christian can wish for; and it liberates us from the pressure of difficulties which have often furnished the enemies of revealed truth with pretexts for serious objections. Inspiration belongs to religious objects; and to attach it to other things is to lose sight of its nature, and misapply its design."*

To other theories, which assign a mystical meaning to the Canticles, some of the arguments which I have used against the view adopted by Professor Stuart apply with equal, others with less,

* Scripture Testimony to the Messiah, by John Pye Smith, D.D. London, 1837. p. 53, &c.

force. All of them are liable to the decisive objection, that they are in opposition to the received use of language. At a time when all the books of the Scriptures were interpreted in the allegorical mode, as by the Church fathers, it was a matter of course that the Canticles should be treated in the same way. But now that just principles of interpretation have been applied to the explanation of most parts of the Bible, it is time to give up attempts to allegorize the Canticles. To the popular theory, that Christ and the Church are denoted, may be urged the additional objection, that there is not in the book the least appearance of prediction. It implies throughout a state of things then existing or past. This theory is also, if possible, more arbitrary, and more completely destitute of support from the use of language and the state of religious knowledge among the contemporaries of the writer, or among the Jews before the time of Christ, than any one of the principal theories which have been mentioned. Against this view, too, it may be justly urged that the book is nowhere alluded to in the New Testament. If the subject of it had been supposed to be Christ and the Church, it is reasonable to suppose that allusions to it would have been very frequent, both in the Gospels and Epistles.

Since, then, there is no reason for supposing a mystical religious meaning in the Canticles, and since their whole tenor and complexion are in opposition to such a meaning, the book must be interpreted according to the received use of language. Thus interpreted, its principal subject, as all will admit, is the reciprocal affection between the sexes, as set forth in poetical representation. There may be some doubt as to the relation in which the parties stood to each other, whether in that of lovers before marriage, or in that of the head of the harem to one of its members, or in that of husband and wife. That the last supposition is not true throughout seems to be obvious from the general character of the representation, as well as from particular passages. It is also not analogous to similar compositions by writers of other countries to suppose the affection of married life to be the subject of the work.

We have, then, in the Canticles the remains of the amatory or erotic poetry of the Hebrews. Whether the book is to be regarded as one whole, a regular dramatic poem, or as a collection of several amatory songs or idyls, is a question which may be considered as somewhat doubtful. Without going into a full discussion of the subject, I adopt the latter opinion, which was the opinion of Richard Simon, Herder, Döderlein, Eichhorn, De Wette, Sir William Jones, and Dr. Good, — for the reason that there is not sufficient evidence in favor of a general plan or course of dramatic action. Those who have maintained the other opinion have been obliged to make some very arbitrary suppositions, and to draw largely on their own imaginations, in order to make out any plausible course of action, or any general design which the writer intended to accomplish, or has accomplished. I have supposed the book to consist of twelve songs.

Thus, while Bossuet and Percy suppose the work to be a pastoral drama, designed to celebrate the marriage of Solomon with the daughter of the king of Egypt, several of the most recent of the German writers* on the book suppose that it is designed to set forth the praise of true love in humble life, and how an innocent country maiden resisted all the arts of King Solomon to seduce her from her faith to her shepherd lover. Respecting the first of these theories, it may be remarked that there is very little in the book which seems suited to the occasion of royal nuptials; that there are no allusions to Solomon which imply that he was the subject of the composition, except in chap. iii. 6–11, and perhaps chap. i. 9–ii. 7; and that there is too much of rural life in it to be suited to the scene of a royal court. The objection to the second theory is, that it comes more from the imagination of the interpreter than from the language of the author. Dr. Good remarks: "The Song of Songs cannot be one connected epithalamium, since the transitions are too abrupt for the wildest flights of the Oriental muse, and evidently imply a variety of openings and conclusions; while, as a regular drama, it is deficient in almost every requisite that could give it such a classification: it has neither dramatic

---

* Lied der Liebe, das älteste und schönste aus dem Morgenlande. Uebersetzt und ästhetisch erklärt von Friedrich Wilhelm Carl Umbreit. Heidelberg, 1828.

Das Hohelied Salomo's übersetzt, etc., von Dr. Georg Heinrich August Ewald. Göttingen, 1826.

fable nor action, neither involution nor catastrophe; it is without a beginning, a middle, or an end. To call it such is to injure it essentially; it is to raise expectations which can never be gratified, and to force parts upon parts which have no possible connection."*

Having thus given the view which seems to me most probable, I admit that there are some indications of unity in the Canticles, such as the refrains in chap. ii. 7; iii. 5; viii. 4; and the recurrence of similar thoughts or expressions in various parts of the book. There are also some indications that the work possesses a dramatic character, being designed, however, only to be read, not to be acted. This is undoubtedly the most prevalent opinion in regard to the book. The subject and design of it, according to most of those writers who adopt this opinion, may be stated as follows: A country maiden, called the Shulamite, who had engaged her affections to a shepherd lover, and who was perhaps betrothed to him, has been carried to the interior of Solomon's palace. This monarch tries to win her affections by praises, blandishments, and entreaties, but without success. She is constant and faithful to her lover in humble life, and rejects all the overtures of royalty. She is constantly thinking of her beloved, declaring her attachment to him, and desiring to return to the place where he is. After Solomon had tried in vain to alienate her affection from the shepherd and fix it upon himself, she is set free from the harem, and hastens to rejoin her beloved shepherd in the country. The design is said to be, to set forth the praises of fidelity in love, or the praises of that love which is only to be preserved by innocence and virtue.

Respecting the number of sections, or acts, scenes, and speakers, there has been, as might be expected, a wide difference of opinion among those who assign to the whole book a dramatic form, as one poem. Renan has gone farthest in reducing it to the form of a modern drama in five acts, and the appropriate scenes. Dr. Davidson's analysis of the book,† which, considered as a mere theory, is as satisfactory as any which has been given, is, with a few slight abbreviations, as follows: —

* See Preface to his Translation of the Canticles.

† Introduction to the O. T., vol. ii. p. 389–392.

"The poem may be divided into six sections: —

"1. (Chap. i. 2–ii. 7.) — After the inscription, the Shulamite appears in the royal tent in the country into which she had been carried, still clothed in her rustic robes, but thinking only of her absent shepherd-lover. The court ladies attendant on the king look curiously at her, on account of the swarthy color of her face; but she informs them that it was caused by exposure to the sun; for her brothers had obliged her to keep their vineyards. Continuing her soliloquy after this, she asks her lover, as if she were already free, where she may find him. The ladies bid her go and feed her sheep (i. 1–8). Solomon now steps forward, praising her beauty, and promising to adorn her with a beautiful chain (i. 9–11). But she praises her beloved, and is insensible to the monarch's words. She then implores the women around her to grant her leisure to think of her friend (i. 12–14, Shulamite; 15, Solomon; 16, 17–ii. 1, Shulamite; ii. 2, Solomon; ii. 3–7, Shulamite).

"2. (ii. 8–iii. 5.) — Here the place is not changed; but the time is supposed to be considerably prior to that in ii. 7. The Shulamite refers to the occasion of her being first separated from her beloved, who invited her out into the fields in the spring. The fifteenth verse gives the words of her brothers, which led to the separation. She consoles herself, however, with the inseparableness of their hearts, bidding him hasten to her side (ii. 8–17).

"The espoused one now relates a dream which she had respecting her lover, saying that she had sought but did not find him; that she had risen up and gone through the streets (of Shunem); and when she met with the watchmen of the city, and asked them if they had seen her beloved, they had hardly passed by her when she laid hold of him, and took him to the house of her mother (iii. 1–5).

"3. (iii. 6–v. 1.) — Solomon is now described returning to Jerusalem from his royal castle in the country, with great pomp and splendor. The people admire the magnificent palanquin in which the Shulamite is conveyed (iii. 6–11). Wishing to procure her favor by his flatteries, the monarch praises her gracefulness, and greatly desires to gain the love of one so beautiful (iv. 1–7). In iii. 6–11, spectators looking at the procession from the country are supposed to speak. Solomon is represented as having all preparations made for his marriage. He is crowned, but she is not. He appears resolved to overcome her inclination.

"The language of iv. 1–7 is sufficient to show that Solomon is the speaker here, not the shepherd-lover. The latter, who is suddenly introduced, assures her that he would attempt every thing to rescue her from her perilous position. He then praises her chastity, fidelity, and modesty; employing the figure of an enclosed garden (iv. 8–15).

"The Shulamite replies in iv. 16; and the shepherd responds in v. 1, giving utterance to his delight in her charms. The poet addresses them both: 'Eat, O friends! Drink, yea, drink abundantly, O beloved!'

"4. (v. 2–vi. 3.) — The Shulamite relates a dream she saw respecting her shepherd to the court ladies. The purport of this was, that he came to her dwelling at night, and asked her to let him in. At first she was reluctant to do so; but when he put his hand through the window, and begged more earnestly that he might be admitted, she rose up and opened the door, but found him gone, and called him in vain. In seeking him, she met with the watchmen of the city, who wounded and shamefully treated her. She then beseeches these ladies, that, if they found her friend, they would tell him how sick of love she was. When they ask what his attractions are more than those of an ordinary lover (v. 9), the Shulamite describes his personal appearance and beauty. After the description, the daughters of Jerusalem inquire whither he is gone (vi. 1), professing their willingness to go with her to seek him out. She answers that he has gone to his garden, and declares that their affection is mutual and inseparable.

"5. (vi. 4-viii. 4.) — Solomon now appears and addresses the Shulamite in flattering terms, affirming that he prefers her to all his wives and concubines. In vi. 10 he cites the encomium of the court ladies upon her. The Shulamite explains how she had fallen in with the royal cortege; at the sight of which she was at first frightened, and hastened away, till by the advice of the court ladies she remained (vi. 13), and so came to be seen by the king, who tries to induce her to love him, and therefore celebrates her beauty (vi. 4-vii. 9).

"The Shulamite declaring that she is wholly devoted to her bridegroom, and so showing that she steadfastly resists all the arts of Solomon, speaks to her shepherd as if she were already free, inviting him to go to the country with her, and enjoy the pleasures of life there. She wishes that he were a brother to her, that she might manifest her attachment to him in public, introduce him into her mother's house, and give him the most delicious drinks. Then, exhausted with the strength of her affection, she wishes for the presence and embraces of her lover, and beseeches the court ladies not to attempt to turn away her affection from him (vii. 10-viii. 4).

"6. (viii. 5-14.) — The shepherd is supposed to have been at the palace; and Solomon, finding her proof against his allurements, had set her free. In company with the bridegroom, she returns to her native place, and visits the apple-trees where they had first pledged their vows. Speaking of her virtue and innocence as things invincible to temptation, she reminds her brothers of what they had said about her preserving or losing her chastity before she was marriageable. In alluding to her temptations, she says, that though Solomon was a very rich man, having a most valuable vineyard, yet that she despised all his possessions, content to preserve her innocence. In conclusion, the shepherd, with his companions, requests of her a song. With this she complies, as she sits in her garden invisible, and repeats the words she had already sung (ii. 17): 'Make haste, my beloved; and be thou like to a roe, or to a young hart, upon the mountains of spices.' The mountains of separation exist no longer: mountains, fragrant with spices, take their place."

Parts of this theory appear to me to imply immense improbabilities; as seems to be conceded by Dr. Davidson, if the existing arrangement of the Hebrew text came from the author. How incongruous, for instance, is chap. viii. 8–10, in its present position, with a dramatic plot of which the sister there mentioned is the heroine! It is like laying the foundation after the house is built.

As to the number of speakers in the Canticles, regarded as consisting of separate songs, I have indicated in the margin those which seemed to me to be required. If any reader thinks that more speakers are necessary, he can supply them according to his taste.

That this book, whether consisting of one dramatic poem or of several separate songs or poems, proceeded from one author, is now so general an opinion of the best critics, that it is not necessary to discuss the subject. Whether this author were Solomon admits of greater doubt. When we consider how many of the inscriptions in the Book of Psalms are at variance with their contents, we cannot attach much importance to the title of this book. The diction,* in its Aramæan character, varies so much from that of the Proverbs, that many modern critics have, with great reason, concluded that it proceeded from a different author. There are also passages which do not well harmonize with the supposition that Solomon was the author; such as chap. i. 4, 5; iii. 6–11; vii. 5; viii. 11, 12. If Solomon is censured in the book, according to the dramatic theory, of course he could not have been the author. On the other hand, there seem to be several allusions to the circumstances and historical relations of the age of Solomon, or that immediately succeeding it. (See i. 4, 5, 9, 12; iii. 7, &c.; iv. 4; vi. 4, 8, 9; viii. 11, 12.) The spirit and character of the poetry seem also to agree well with the most flourishing period of Hebrew literature. The peculiar diction is supposed by De Wette to be susceptible of explanation by maintaining that these songs were preserved orally in the mouths of the people, and were thus in some measure altered. Others seek an explanation of this peculiarity in the province of Palestine, to which the writer may have

* On this topic, see the Introductions of Jahn, De Wette, or Davidson.

belonged. Either of these suppositions appears to me more probable than that the author wrote long after the Captivity, and transferred himself back to the age of Solomon. I therefore suppose the Canticles to have been written by some Jewish poet, either in the reign of Solomon or soon after it.

For a list of interpreters of the Canticles, see the introduction to this book in Rosenmüller's Scholia. Of those which he has not mentioned, I have seen the translations and notes of Bishop Percy, Thomas Williams, and John Mason Good. In this edition, I have also had access to the translations and commentaries of Heiligstedt, Hitzig, and Renan.

CAMBRIDGE, Jan. 10, 1867.

THE SONG OF SONGS.

1 *The Song of Songs, which is by Solomon.*

I.

An innocent country maiden, in a company of ladies of Jerusalem, is anxious to see her lover. — CHAP. I. 2–8.

2 [*M.*] O THAT he would kiss me with one of the kisses
of his mouth!
For thy love is better than wine.
3 Because of the savor of thy precious perfumes,
(Thy name is like fragrant oil poured forth,)
Therefore do the virgins love thee.
4 Draw me after thee; let us run!
The king hath led me to his chambers!
We will be glad and rejoice in thee;
We will praise thy love more than wine.
Justly do they love thee!

5 I am black, but comely, O ye daughters of Jerusalem,
As the tents of Kedar, as the curtains of Solomon.
6 Gaze not upon me because I am black,
Because the sun hath looked upon me!
My mother's sons were angry with me;
They made me keeper of the vineyards;
My vineyard, my own, have I not kept.
7 Tell me, thou whom my soul loveth, where thou feedest
thy flock,
Where thou leadest it to rest at noon;
For why should I be like a veiled one by the flocks of thy
companions?

8 [*Lad.*] If thou know not, O thou fairest among women,
Trace thou thy way by the tracks of the flock,
And feed thy kids beside the shepherds' tents!

II.

Conversation between a lover and maiden. — Chap. I. 9.–II. 7.

9 [*Lov.*] To the horses in the chariots of Pharaoh
Do I compare thee, my love!
10 Comely are thy cheeks with rows of jewels,
Thy neck with strings of pearls.
11 Golden chains will we make for thee,
With studs of silver.

12 [*M.*] While the king reclineth at his table,
My spikenard sendeth forth its fragrance.
13 A bunch of myrrh is my beloved to me;
He shall abide between my breasts.
14 My beloved is to me a cluster of henna-flowers
From the gardens of Engedi.

15 [*Lov.*] Behold, thou art fair, my love; behold, thou art fair!
Thine eyes are doves.

16 [*M.*] Behold, thou art fair, my beloved, yea, lovely;
And green is our bed.
17 The cedars are the beams of our house,
And its roof the cypresses.
1 I am a rose of Sharon,
A lily of the valleys.

2 [*Lov.*] As the lily among thorns,
So is my love among the daughters.

3 [*M.*] As the apple-tree among the trees of the forest,
So is my beloved among the sons.
In his shadow I love to sit down,
And his fruit is sweet to my taste.

4 He hath brought me to his banqueting-house,
And his banner over me is love.
Strengthen me with raisins,
5 Refresh me with apples!
For I am sick with love.
6 His left hand is under my head,
And his right hand embraceth me!

7 [*Lov.*] I charge you, O ye daughters of Jerusalem,
By the gazelles, and by the hinds of the field,
That ye stir not up, nor awake my love, till she please!

III.

The maiden's meeting with her lover in the vineyard. — **CHAP. II. 8–17.**

8 [*M.*] THE voice of my beloved!
Behold, he cometh,
Leaping upon the mountains,
Bounding upon the hills.
9 Like a gazelle is my beloved,
Or a young hind.
Behold, he standeth behind our wall;
He is looking through the windows;
He glanceth through the lattice.
10 My beloved speaketh, and saith to me,
"Rise up, my love, my fair one, and come away!
11 For, lo, the winter is past,
The rain is over and gone;
12 The flowers appear on the earth;
The time of the singing of birds is come,
And the voice of the turtle is heard in our land;
13 The fig-tree is spicing its green fruit;
The vines in blossom give forth fragrance.
Arise, my love, my fair one, and come away!
14 O my dove, that art in the recesses of the rock,
In the hiding-places of the steep craggy mountain,
Let me see thy face,
Let me hear thy voice!
For sweet is thy voice,
And thy face lovely."

15 Take ye for us the foxes,
The little foxes that spoil the vines;
For our vines are now in blossom.
16 My beloved is mine, and I am his;
He feedeth among the lilies.
17 When the day breathes, and the shadows flee away,
Come again, my beloved, like a gazelle, or a young hind,
Upon the craggy mountains.

IV.

The maiden's search for her lover. — CHAP. III. 1–5.

1 [*M.*] UPON my bed, in the night,
I sought him whom my soul loveth;
I sought him, but found him not.
2 I will arise now [said I], and go about the city;
In the streets and the broad ways will I seek him whom my soul loveth;
I sought him, but found him not.
3 The watchmen who go about the city found me;
"Have you seen [said I] him whom my soul loveth?"
4 I had but just passed them,
When I found him whom my soul loveth;
I held him, and would not let him go,
Till I had brought him into my mother's house,
Into the apartment of her that bore me.

5 [*Lov.*] I charge you, O ye daughters of Jerusalem!
By the gazelles, and by the hinds of the field,
That ye stir not up, nor awake my love, till she please.

V.

A song relating to Solomon; or, The conducting of a spouse of Solomon, or of a maiden beloved by him, to his palace. — CHAP. III. 6–11.

6 WHO is this that cometh up from the wilderness,
Like pillars of smoke,
Perfumed with myrrh and frankincense,
With all the powders of the merchant?

7 Behold, the carriage of Solomon!
Threescore valiant men are around it,
Of the valiant men of Israel.
8 They all wear swords,
Being skilled in war.
Every one hath his sword girt upon his thigh,
On account of danger in the night.
9 King Solomon made for himself a carriage
Of the wood of Lebanon.
10 The pillars thereof he made of silver,
The railing of gold,
The seat of purple,
Its interior curiously wrought by a lovely one of the daughters of Jerusalem.
11 Go forth, O ye daughters of Zion!
And behold King Solomon
In the crown with which his mother crowned him,
In the day of his espousals,
In the day of the gladness of his heart.

VI.

Conversation between a lover and maiden. — CHAP. IV. - V. 1.

1 [*Lov.*] BEHOLD, thou art fair, my love! behold, thou art fair!
Thine eyes are doves behind thy veil;
Thy locks are like a flock of goats
Which lie down on mount Gilead;
2 Thy teeth are like a flock of shorn sheep,
Which come up from the washing-place,
Of which every one beareth twins,
And none is barren among them;
3 Thy lips are like a thread of scarlet,
And thy mouth comely;
Thy cheeks are like a divided pomegranate behind thy veil;
4 Thy neck is like the tower of David,
Built for an armory,
In which there hang a thousand bucklers,
All shields of mighty men;

5 Thy two breasts are like two young twin gazelles,
That feed among the lilies.
6 When the day breathes, and the shadows flee away,
I will betake me to the mountain of myrrh
And the hill of frankincense.
7 Thou art all fair, my love;
There is no spot in thee!
8 Come with me from Lebanon, my spouse,
With me from Lebanon!
Look from the top of Amana,
From the top of Senir and Hermon,
From the dens of the lions,
From the mountains of the leopards.
9 Thou hast taken captive my heart, my sister, my spouse;
Thou hast taken captive my heart with one of thine eyes,
With one chain of thy neck.
10 How sweet is thy love, my sister, my spouse!
How much more precious thy caresses than wine,
And the fragrance of thy perfumes than all spices!
11 Thy lips, O my spouse! drop the honeycomb;
Honey and milk are under thy tongue,
And the fragrance of thy garments is as the fragrance of Lebanon.
12 A garden inclosed is my sister, my spouse;
A spring shut up, a fountain sealed;
13 Thy plants are an orchard of pomegranates, with choicest fruits,
Henna and spikenard,
14 Spikenard and saffron,
Sweet cane and cinnamon,
With all trees of frankincense;
Myrrh and aloes,
With all the chief spices;
15 A fountain of the gardens,
A well of living water,
A stream that floweth from Lebanon!

16 [*M.*] Awake, O north wind, and come, thou south!
Blow upon my garden,
That its spices may flow out!
May my beloved come to his garden,
And eat his pleasant fruits.

1 [*Lov.*] I am come to my garden, my sister, my spouse!
I gather my myrrh with my balsam,
I eat my honeycomb with my honey,
I drink my wine with my milk.
Eat, O friends!
Drink, yea, drink abundantly, my loved companions!

VII.

The maiden's search for her lover by night, and praise of his beauty.
CHAP. V. 2.–VI. 3.

2 [*M.*] I SLEPT, but my heart was awake;
It was the voice of my beloved, who was knocking:
"Open to me, my sister, my love,
My dove, my perfect one!
For my head is filled with dew,
And my locks with the drops of the night."
3 "I have taken off my vest [said I];
How shall I put it on?
I have washed my feet;
How shall I soil them?"
4 My beloved put in his hand by the hole of the door,
And my heart was moved for him.
5 I rose up to open to my beloved,
And my hands dropped with myrrh,
And my fingers with self-flowing myrrh, upon the handles
of the bolt.
6 I opened to my beloved;
But my beloved had withdrawn himself, and was gone.
I was not in my senses while he spake with me!
I sought him, but could not find him;
I called him, but he gave me no answer.
7 The watchmen that go about the city found me;
They smote me, they wounded me;
The keepers of the walls took away from me my veil.
8 I charge you, O ye daughters of Jerusalem!
If ye should find my beloved, —
What will ye tell him? —
That I am sick with love.

9 [*Lad.*] What is thy beloved more than another beloved,
O thou fairest among women!
What is thy beloved more than another beloved,
That thus thou dost charge us?

10 [*M.*] My beloved is white and ruddy,
The chief among ten thousand.
11 His head is as the most fine gold;
His locks waving palm-branches,
Black as a raven;
12 His eyes are doves by streams of water,
Washed with milk, dwelling in fulness;
13 His cheeks are like a bed of balsam,
Like beds of spices;
His lips are lilies
Dropping self-flowing myrrh;
14 His hands are gold rings set with chrysolite;
His body is wrought-work of ivory, overlaid with sapphires;
15 His legs are marble pillars, resting on pedestals of fine gold;
His aspect is like Lebanon,
Majestic like the cedars;
16 His mouth is sweetness;
His whole being, loveliness.
This is my beloved,
This my friend,
O ye daughters of Jerusalem!

1 [*Lad.*] Whither is thy beloved gone, thou fairest among women?
Whither hath thy beloved betaken himself?
That we may seek him with thee.

2 [*M.*] My beloved is gone down to his garden,
To the beds of balsam,
To feed in the gardens,
And to gather lilies.
3 I am my beloved's, and my beloved is mine;
He feedeth among the lilies.

VIII.

The lover's praise of the object of his attachment. — CHAP. VI. 4-9.

4 BEAUTIFUL art thou, my love, as Tirzah,
Lovely as Jerusalem;
But terrible as an army with banners.
5 Turn away thine eyes from me!
They overpower me!
Thy locks are like a flock of goats,
Which lie down upon Gilead.
6 Thy teeth are like a flock of sheep,
Which come up from the washing-place,
Of which every one hath twins,
And none is barren among them.
7 As a divided pomegranate
Are thy cheeks behind thy veil.
8 Threescore are the queens, and fourscore the concubines,
And the maidens without number.
9 But my dove, my undefiled, is the one;
She is the incomparable one of her mother,
The darling of her that bore her.
The daughters saw her, and blessed her;
The queens and concubines, and they praised her.

IX.

Conversation between a lover and maiden. — CHAP. VI. 10 – VIII. 4.

10 [*Lov.*] WHO is this that looketh forth like the morning,
Fair as the moon, bright as the sun,
And terrible as an army with banners?

11 [*M.*] I went down into the garden of nuts,
To see the green plants of the valley,
To see whether the vine blossomed,
And the pomegranates budded.

12 Or ever I was aware,
My soul had made me like the chariots of the prince's [train.

13 [*Lad.*] Return, return, O Shulamite!
Return, return, that we may look upon thee!

[*M.*] Why should ye look upon the Shulamite,
As upon a dance of the hosts?

1 [*Lov.*] How beautiful are thy feet in sandals, O prince's daughter!
The roundings of thy hips are like neck ornaments,
The work of the hands of the artificer;
2 Thy navel is like a round goblet, that wanteth not the spiced wine;
Thy belly like a heap of wheat, inclosed with lilies;
3 Thy two breasts are like two young twin gazelles;
4 Thy neck is as a tower of ivory;
Thine eyes are like the pools at Heshbon, by the gate of Bath-rabbim;
Thy nose is as the tower of Lebanon, which looketh toward Damascus;
5 Thy head upon thee is like Carmel,
And the hair of thy head like purple;
The king is captivated by thy locks.
6 How fair, how pleasant art thou, love, in delights!
7 This thy stature is like the palm-tree,
And thy breasts like clusters of dates.
8 I will go up, say I to myself, upon the palm-tree;
I will take hold of its boughs,
And thy breasts shall be as clusters of the vine,
And the fragrance of thy nose like apples,
9 And thy mouth like the best wine —

[*M.*] — that goeth down smoothly for my beloved,
Flowing over the lips of them that sleep.
10 I am my beloved's,
And his desire is toward me.

11 Come, my beloved, let us go forth into the country;
Let us lodge in the villages!

12 Then will we go early to the vineyards,
To see whether the vine putteth forth,
Whether its blossom openeth,
And the pomegranates bud forth;
There will I give thee my love!
13 The love-apples give forth fragrance;
And at our doors are all kinds of precious fruits, new and old:
I have kept them for thee, my beloved!

1 O that thou wert as my brother,
That sucked the breast of my mother!
When I found thee abroad, I might kiss thee;
And for it no one would deride me.
2 I will lead thee, and bring thee into my mother's house, that thou mayst teach me;
I will give thee spiced wine to drink, and the juice of my pomegranates.
3 His left hand is under my head,
And his right hand embraceth me.

4 [*Lov.*] I charge you, O ye daughters of Jerusalem!
That ye stir not up, nor awake my love,
Till she please!

X.

Chorus of ladies, maiden, and lover. — CHAP. VIII. 5-7.

5 [*Lad.*] WHO is this that cometh up from the wilderness,
Leaning upon her beloved?

[*M.*] Under the apple-tree I awakened thee;
There thy mother brought thee forth;
There she that bore thee brought thee forth!
6 O set me as a seal upon thy heart,
As a seal upon thine arm!
For love is strong as death;
True love is firm as the grave:

Its flames are flames of fire,
The fire of Jehovah.
7 Many waters cannot quench love,
Nor can floods drown it.
Would a man give all the wealth of his house for love,
It would be utterly contemned.

XI.

A conversation of two brothers about their sister, with her remarks.
CHAP. VIII. 8–12.

8 [*Br.*] WE have a sister who is yet young;
She is yet without breasts.
What shall we do with our sister,
When she shall be spoken for?
9 If she be a wall,
We will build upon it a silver tower;
If she be an open gate,
We will inclose her with planks of cedar.

10 [*Sis.*] I am a wall, and my breasts like towers;
Therefore am I become in his eyes as one that findeth [peace.
11 Solomon had a vineyard at Baal-hamon;
He let out the vineyard to keepers;
Every one was to bring a thousand shekels of silver for its fruit.
12 My vineyard is before my eyes.
Be thine the thousand, O Solomon!
And two hundred to the keepers of its fruit!

XII.

The lover sent away. A fragment.—CHAP. VIII. 13, 14.

13 [*Lov.*] THOU that dwellest in the gardens!
Friends listen to thy voice;
Let me hear thee!

14 Fly, my beloved! like a gazelle, or a young hind,
Upon the mountains of spices.

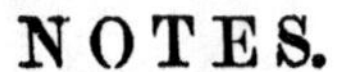

NOTES.

NOTES ON JOB.

I.

In the first two chapters is contained a brief account of the excellent character and flourishing condition of Job; — of the afflictions decreed in heaven to be sent upon him, and the design of those afflictions, namely, to prove the disinterestedness and firmness of his integrity and piety; — of the actual occurrence of these afflictions, and of Job's conduct under them; — and of the visit of three of his friends to mourn with him and comfort him.

The character of this introduction, so far as it relates to the upper world, is thus given by Scott: " This is not history, but a piece of allegorical scenery. The noble instruction which it veileth is, that God governs the world by the instrumentality of second causes, that the evils of human life are under his direction, and that the afflictions of good men are appointed by him for the illustration of their virtue, and for advancing, by that means, the honor of religion." The learned Mr. Poole also observes: " You must not think that these things were really done; . . . but it is only a parabolical representation of that great truth, that God, by his wise and holy providence, doth govern all the actions of men and devils to his own ends." Considered as a part of the whole work, the design of these chapters is to suggest the subject of discussion, and, in part, to illustrate it; and also to dispose the reader to a favorable opinion of Job See introduction, p. 18.

Ch. I. 1. — *Job.* The most probable meaning of the name is *persecuted, harassed.* See Ges. ad verb.

3. — *three thousand camels.* The Arabs used these animals in war, in their caravans, and for food. One of their ancient poets, whose hospitality grew into a proverb, is reported to have killed yearly, in a certain month, ten camels every day, for the entertainment of his friends. *Scott*, from Schultens and Pococke. We have here the description of the wealth of an Arab ruler, or chief, similar to those who at the present day are called Emirs.

4. — *each on his day:* i e. on the day in which it fell to him in course to give a feast.

5. — *sanctify:* by ablutions and other observances. See Exod. xix. 10, 14; Josh. vii. 13. — *renounced God in their hearts:* i. e. been unmindful of him, dismissed him from their thoughts, or withheld the reverence and homage which are his due. It is hardly credible that Job suspected his children of *cursing* God. He was only apprehensive lest the gayety of a festival had made them forget God, and neglect his service and worship. The term ברך generally signifies to *bless*. It was the term of salutation between friends at meeting and parting. See Gen. xxviii. 3, xlvii. 10. In the latter use of it, it corresponded to the English phrase *to bid farewell to*, and like that, came to be used in a bad sense for *to renounce, to abandon, to dismiss from the mind, to disregard.* It may imply *disregard, neglect, renunciation*, or *abhorrence*, according to the connection in which it is used. *Χαίρειν* in Greek, and *valere* in Latin, are used in the same way. Thus Eurip. Med. 1044.: Οὐ δῆτ᾽ ἔγωγε· χαιρέτω βουλεύματα. And Cicero, in a letter to Atticus (VIII. 8.), in which he complains of the disgraceful flight of Pompey, applies to him a quotation from Aristophanes: πολλὰ χαίρειν εἰπὼν τῷ καλῷ, *bidding farewell to honor*, he fled to Brundusium. Another instance of this use of *valere* is in Ter. And. IV. 2. 14.: *Valeant*, qui inter nos dissidium volunt. Also in Cic. de Nat. Deor. 1. 44. near the end: Deinde si maxime talis est Deus, ut nullâ gratiâ, nullâ hominum caritate teneatur, *valeat!*

6. — *sons of God:* i. e. the angels. See ch. xxxviii. 7; Dan. iii. 25, 28. — *Satan.* There has been a question whether by the person denominated Satan in this chapter is denoted the malignant spirit, the enemy of God and man, otherwise called the Devil; or one of the sons of God, a faithful, but too suspicious, servant of Jehovah.

This latter opinion has been defended by some critics, because they could not easily account for the presence of the Devil in heaven amongst the angels of God, and for his free conversation with Jehovah; by others, because they regarded the belief in the Devil as having had no existence amongst the Jews until their return from the Babylonish captivity, and, consequently, as inconsistent with their opinion of the high antiquity of the book. But the disposition ascribed to Satan in the narrative is not very consistent with this view. Nor is there any strong argument to show that a belief in evil spirits may not have arisen among the Jews at least a short time before the captivity, in consequence of their intercourse with foreigners. Satan appears, in this passage, in the office indicated by his name, that of the *adversary, the accuser*, the office uniformly ascribed to him by the later Jews. See Zech. iii. 1 2; Rev. xii. 10. See also Christian Examiner, for May, 1836, p. 236. It is observed by Rosenmüller, that in the life of Zoroaster, (see Zendavesta, by J. G. Kleukner, vol. iii. p. 11,) the prince of the evil demons, the angel of death, called *Engremeniosh*, is said to go about the earth for the purpose of opposing and injuring good men.

11. — *will he renounce thee.* The phrase is stronger here than in verse 5. It imports an utter and public renunciation of religion as a vain thing. *Scott.*

15. — *Sabeans:* inhabitants of Sheba, a country of Arabia Felix, abound ing in spices, gold, and precious stones. 1 Kings x. 1, &c.; Is. lx. 6; Ps. lxxii. 10, 15.

16. — *fire of God:* i. e. *lightning;* which has a similar appellation in Eurip. Med. 144:

> Αἶ, αἶ· διά μου κεφαλᾶς φλὸξ οὐρανία
> Βαίη.
> Alas! alas! May the fire of heaven
> Strike through my head!

17. — *Chaldeans:* a fierce and warlike people, who originally inhabited the Carduchian mountains, north of Assyria, and the northern part of Mesopotamia, portions of whom settled in Babylonia and founded a mighty empire. They are described in Hab. i. 6 – 11.

20. — *rent his mantle, and shaved his head.* The custom of rending the mantle, as an expression of grief, is said to prevail at the present day in Persia, and, like that of shaving the head, to have been common amongst several nations of antiquity. Herodotus (II. 26) remarks, that the latter was the practice of all nations except the Egyptians, in cases of mourning.

21. — *my mother's womb:* i. e. the womb of the earth, the universal mother; for he speaks of returning *thither*. The same figure is found in several languages. See Cic. de Nat. Deor. II. 26. — *blessed be the name, &c.* Here the contrast is observable between the object of Satan, which was to induce Job to *renounce* God, and the issue of the temptation, in which Job *blesses* God.

Ch. II. 4. *Skin for skin, &c.* This is a proverbial expression, importing, as is generally supposed, that any man will give the skin or life of another, whether animal or man, to save his own. The observation of Satan will then imply that Job gave up all, without complaint, from the selfish fear of exposing his own life to danger. Others understand the term "skin" to denote "the life." The proverb will then be, "Life for life"; i. e. Nothing is so precious as life. All other calamities are light, compared with those which threaten one's own life. Others, *like for like*, i. e. what a man holds as dear as *his skin*, i. e. his life, he will give for his life.

7. It is generally supposed that Job was afflicted with that species of leprosy called elephantiasis, the elephant disease; so called from its covering the skin with dark scales, and swelling the mouth, legs, and feet to

an enormous size, although the body at the same time is emaciated. See Deut. xxviii. 35. The pain is said not to be very great, but there is a great debility of the system, and great uneasiness and grief. See Jahn's Archaeology, § 189.

9. *Renounce God, and die:* i. e. since you must die. Since your exemplary piety has been of no use to you, give it up; renounce God; desist from your idle prayers and praises, and look to death as the only termination of your miseries, the only fruit of your virtue which you will ever receive. *Schultens.* See i. 5, and the note.

But, perhaps, the common meaning of the verb בָּרֵךְ, *to bless*, has some claim to consideration. According to this rendering, Job's wife ironically exhorts him to go on blessing God, since he received such precious returns for it. *Bless God, and die:* i. e. Bless God ever so much, thou wilt die after all. I am inclined to believe, however, that the term means here what it does in the nearly connected passages, ver. 5 and 11.

10. *In all this Job sinned not with his lips.* The author repeats this circumstance a second time, in order to excite the attention of the reader to what follows, viz., the conduct of Job with respect to his reverence for the Deity, and the changes which accumulated misery might produce in his temper and behavior. Accordingly we find that another still more severe trial of his patience yet awaits him, and which, indeed, as the writer seems to intimate, he scarcely appears to have sustained with equal firmness; namely, the unjust suspicions, the bitter reproaches, and the violent altercations of his friends. *Lowth.*

11. — *Temanite.* Teman was one of the principal cities of Edom, or Idumea, distinguished for its wise men. See Jer. xlix. 7; Obad. 8, 9. Amos. i. 12. — *Shuhite.* Shuah, a son of Abraham by Keturah, was sent by him into the East country. Gen. xxv. 2, 6. From him may have descended the Shuhites. Gesenius observes that the country of the Shuhites was not improbably the same with the Σακκαία of Ptolemy, 5, 15, eastward of Batanea. — *Naamathite* an inhabitant of Naamah, a place whose situation is unknown. It could not be the same which is mentioned in Josh. xv. 41.

12, 13. When they saw him, at the distance at which they could formerly recognize him without difficulty, disease had so altered his appearance, that at first sight they knew him not. The expression of his grief resembles, in several circumstances, that of Achilles, when informed of the death of Patroclus. Iliad, xviii. 21 – 27.

Seven days was the customary time of mourning among the Orientals. See Gen. l. 10; 1 Sam. xxxi. 13; and Ecclesiasticus, xxii. 13. "Seven days do men mourn for him that is dead." It is not meant that they remained in the same place and posture for the space of seven days, but that they mourned with him during that time, in the usual way. — *and none spake a word to him.* Poole remarks that the meaning probably is, that no one spake a word to him about his afflictions, and the causes of them. But as this is not in the text, it seems more probable that the seven days' silence is only a poetical or oriental exaggeration, designed to express the profound amazement of the friends of Job, on account of the condition in which they found him. It may be compared with Ch. xlii. 12, 13, 14.

II.

At the end of the seven days of mourning, when no hopes of recovery from his afflicted condition were entertained by Job, and not a word of consolation had been offered by his friends, he unburdens his heart in the strongest language of complaint, lamentation, and despair. He curses the day of his birth, and longs for death, as the only refuge from his miseries.

The poet has secured the sympathy of the reader in favor of Job by the introductory chapters upon the cause of his afflictions, and by the declaration of Jehovah, that he was "an upright and good man;" so that in this place, and throughout the poem, we are more inclined to pity him for his afflictions than to censure him for his irreverent language.

Ch. III. 2.—*spake.* The verb עָנָה, used of a person beginning to speak, appears, says Gesenius, to be peculiar to the later Hebrew.

3.—*the day, &c.* The birth of a son was one of three great occasions of festivity among the Arabians. The other two were the birth of a foal of a valued race, and the rising up of a poetical genius in any of their tribes. When an Arabian gave his daughter in marriage to a person whom he approved, he used the benediction, "Facilis sit tibi partus, et masculos parias, non fœminas!" *Pococke.* Spec. Hist. Arab. pp. 160, 337. —*And the night, &c.:* i. e. which was privy to my conception; a bold personification, as in verse 10, and xxx. 17. The Arabic poets delight to personify the day and the night in this way, as is shown by various quotations in Schultens ad loc. See also Burder's Oriental Customs, No. 490.

4.—*seek it.* This is the primary meaning of the word דָּרַשׁ, and admits of a good explanation. The poet seems to conceive of the day as sunk beneath the horizon, or in the deep waters by which he supposed the earth to be surrounded. He prays that God may not seek it, and bring it from its dark abode. The secondary meaning, *regard, care for,* though perfectly allowable, is less poetic.

5.—*shadow of death:* i. e. *thick darkness;* or, a black and dark shadow, like that of the dead. —*redeem it:* i. e. resume their dominion over it, excluding the light. Thus the common meaning of גָּאַל gives a highly poetical sense to the line. —*whatever darkens the day:* lit. *obscurations of the day.* By *obscurations of the day,* I suppose he understands eclipses, dreadful storms, &c. Less probably, *deadly heats of the day:* i. e. intolerable sultriness, which causes pestilence. Some writers suppose that there is a reference here to the poisonous wind Samum, or Samiel, which is feared in the hottest months of summer. But it appears from the testimony of modern travellers that the injurious effects of this wind have been very much exaggerated. See Robinson's Calmet, Art. *Wind.* Otherwise, *the bitterness,* or *the misfortunes of the day;* כ being considered only as the particle of emphasis, as it is often used.

7. *O let that night be unfruitful!* i. e. May there be no births in that night! See Ch. xxx. 3, and the note. —*no voice of joy:* i. e. on account of the birth of a son. See note on verse 8.

8. *Who are skilful to stir up the leviathan!* In all other parts of the sacred writings, in which the word לִוְיָתָן occurs, it denotes an animal. Nearly all the ancient versions, and nearly all the modern critics, consider it as the name of an animal here. It seems to be a common name to denote monstrous animals of different kinds, as a huge serpent, the crocodile, &c. Here it may denote a monstrous serpent. In Ch. xli. 1, the crocodile. See Ges. ad verb. The verse probably refers to a class of persons who were supposed to have the power of making any day fortunate or unfortunate, to control future events, and even to call forth the most terrific monsters from impenetrable forests, or from the deep, for the gratification of their own malice, or that of others. Balaam, whom Balak sent for to curse Israel, affords evidence of the existence of a class of persons who were supposed to be capable of producing evil by their imprecations. See Numb. xxii. 10, 11. Job calls upon the most powerful of these sorcerers to assist him in cursing the day of his birth.

9. *Neither let it see the eyelashes of the morning!* This is the literal version, and contains an image too beautiful to be thrown away. So Soph. Antig. 104.:

> ἐφάνθης πότ᾽, ὦ χρυσέας
> ἁμέρας βλέφαρον, Διρκαί-
> ων ὕπερ ῥέεθρων μολοῦσα.

So in Milton's Lycidas:

> ——"ere the high lawns appeared
> Under the opening eyelids of the dawn,
> We drove afield."

The sun, when above the horizon, is called by the poets the eye of day: hence his earliest beams, before he is risen, are the eyelids, or eyelashes, of the morning. Schultens observes, that the Arabian poets compare the sun to an eye, and attribute eyelashes to it. See ad loc.

12. *Why did the knees receive me?* Why did the officious midwife receive me, and lay me upon her lap, and not suffer me to fall to the ground and perish? Or it may refer to the father, as it was usual for him to take the child upon his knees as soon as it was born, and thus to declare that it was his own, and that he intended to bring it up. Gen. l. 23. See Jahn's Archaeol. § 161.

14. *Who built up for themselves — ruins!* i. e. splendid palaces, or, perhaps, tombs, destined soon to fall into ruins. See Is. xliv. 26. In the form of expression, the line is similar to Hab. ii. 13; Jer. li. 58.

> That nations shall labor for fire,
> And kingdoms weary themselves for nought.

i. e. for that which shall be burnt up, &c. Otherwise, *The repairers of desolated places;* a circumstance mentioned to show their wealth, grandeur and glory. See Is. lviii. 12, lxi. 4; Ezek. xxxvi. 10.

20. The name of the Supreme Being is often omitted in this book, and the pronoun made to supply its place. In such cases the pronoun is printed, in this version, with a capital letter. This corresponds to the custom in Scotland, where they say, "May His will be done!" "May His name be praised!" without an antecedent to the pronoun. So in Scott's Black Dwarf, near the end of Chap. VII.:

"O, my child, before you run on danger let me hear you but say, 'His will be done!'"

"Urge me not, mother — not now." He was rushing out, when, looking back, he observed his grandmother make a mute attitude of affliction. He returned hastily, threw himself into her arms, and said, "Yes, mother, I can say, 'His will be done!' since it will comfort you."

"May He go forth — may He go forth with you, my dear bairn: and O, may He give you cause to say, on your return, 'His name be praised!'"

23. —*from whom the way is hid, &c.:* i. e. who knows not which way to turn himself; who can see no way of escape from the miseries, which, in the latter clause of the verse, are represented as surrounding him, as with a high wall or hedge.

24. — *my sighing cometh before I eat:* i. e. it cometh on when I begin to eat, and prevents my taking my necessary nourishment. So Juv. Sat. xiii. 211.:

> Perpetua anxietas, nec mensæ tempore cessat.

25. *for that which I dread, &c.* I understand this as referring to continual fears caused by the disease, which fears are said not to be greater than his actual miseries. See note on ii. 7, where uneasiness and grief are said to be caused by the disease.

III

In the fourth and fifth chapters, Eliphaz, one of the three friends who had come to comfort Job, is represented as constrained by his intemperate language to express those sentiments, and vent those suspicions, which the view of his miserable condition had suggested, and which, from pity and delicacy, had been hitherto suppressed. The inhumanity of Eliphaz and the other friends of Job, which by many is thought unnatural, serves to introduce and help forward the discussion of the moral question which it was the main design of the poem to illustrate.

He reproves Job's impatience, and exhorts him not to give way to grief and despondency, but to put in practice those lessons which he had so often recommended to others. He then advances the doctrine which he and his friends maintain throughout the poem, that misery implies guilt ; and insinuates that the wickedness of Job was the cause of his present afflictions. Ch. iv. 2 – 11. In support of his views he brings forward a revelation which he professes to have formerly received in a vision. This revelation asserts the exceeding imperfection of human virtue, the absolute rectitude of God, and the impiety of arraigning the justice of his moral government. The oracle itself is therefore excellent. It is the application of it in which Eliphaz is mistaken. He has erroneous notions of what the justice of God requires. He supposes that it implies that all suffering must be the punishment of sin ; and he seems to condemn Job not only for his actual complaints, but also for not regarding and acknowledging his afflictions to be the merited punishment of his transgressions. 12 – 21.

In the fifth chapter he is more direct, as well as more severe, in his censures, and exhorts Job to humble himself before God, and repent of his sins. He assures him that, by such a course, he may regain his former prosperity.

Ch. IV. 5. *But now it*, i. e. *calamity, &c.*

6. *Is not thy fear, &c.* These words may be understood as a friendly admonition to Job to recollect his religious principles, and to support himself by the clearness of his conscience. On the other hand, they may import that no good man would fall into *despair* under affliction, as he had done. There is an appearance of art in this ambiguity. *Scott.*

As the substantive verb is understood, some critics prefer to render it thus :

Was not thy fear of God thy hope ?
And the uprightness of thy ways thine expectation ?

i. e. Did not thy piety and integrity spring from the hope of reward, from a regard to thine own interest, rather than from the love of God ? So Mercier, and Castalio, whose version is,

Nimirum tantum religionis, quantum expectationis;
Quantum spei, tantum habebas integritatis morum.

This corresponds with the question of Satan, " *Is it for nought that Job feareth God?* "

7, 8. These expressions, also, may be understood as a consolatory argument to confirm the hope which conscious integrity should inspire : " Good men are sometimes chastised severely for their crimes, but not destroyed; calamities which end in *destruction* are the portion of the wicked only." On the other hand, his meaning may be : " Calamities like yours being the lot of wicked men only, some wickedness of yours must needs have brought these calamities upon you." Here, then, we have another instance of artful ambiguity. *Scott.*

10. Unjust and rapacious men are in Scripture frequently called *lions.* See Ps. xxxiv. 10; lviii. 6.

19. *Who crumble to pieces, as if moth-eaten!* Lit. *They crumble them to pieces, as the moth* a garment. So Ros., who remarks, after Schultens and Noldius, that the particle לִפְנֵי often has the meaning, *as, like, tanquam.* Thus, 1 Sam. i. 16, " Regard not thy servant *as* a daughter of Belial." The Sept. has it, σητὸς τρόπον, and the old Vulg., *tanquam tinea;* the Vulg., *sicut a tinea.* Comp. ch. xiii. 28; Is. i. 9, li. 8.

20. *Between morning and evening, &c.* The meaning is, They live scarcely a single day. See Ex. xviii. 14; Isa. xxxviii. 12. It is not the frequent occurrence of death in the course of a day, but the shortness of man's life, that is meant to be expressed. So Pindar, Pyth. viii. 135. :

Ἐπάμεροι. τί δέ τις; τί δ' οὔ τις;
Σκιᾶς ὄναρ ἄνθρωποι.

Beings of a day! What is man? What is he not?
He 's the dream of a shadow!

— *and none regardeth it.* The destruction of mankind by death is not regarded, or minded, by the rest of the creation. This is only a rhetorical way of representing how insignificant a creature man is, compared with the higher orders of beings.

Ch. V. 1. *See if any one, &c.* i. e. will take thy part, and advocate thy cause.

— *to which of the holy ones wilt thou look?* i. e. whom amongst the heavenly host wilt thou persuade to be thine advocate, or to take thy part, in a controversy with the Almighty? The words *call* and *answer* are used in this judicial sense in ch. xiii. 22, xiv. 15, and in other places. Another less probable meaning is that of Grotius and others, who suppose that Eliphaz, having triumphantly produced a divine revelation in support of his views respecting the conduct of Job, calls upon him to bring forward something of the same kind in his defence, if he could, — to call and see if any of the heavenly spirits would answer *him*, and give a revelation in *his* favor.

2. *Verily grief destroyeth the fool.* Grief and wrath hasten the destruction of the foolish man, either by preying upon his spirits, or by drawing down upon him severe punishment from the Almighty. His sufferings are the fruit of his own criminal passions. The terms *foolish* and *weak* are often, in Scripture, applied to impious and wicked men.

3. — *I cursed his habitation.* This may mean, I predicted his downfall See Gerard's Inst., § 882. Or, I actually witnessed the sudden ruin of his fortunes, and pronounced his habitation accursed.

4. — *at the gate:* i. e. in the courts of justice, which used to be held at the gates of cities. See Jahn's Archæol., § 247.

5. — *the thorns* : i. e. the hedge of thorns.

6. *For affliction cometh not, &c.* The meaning appears to be, The afflictions of life are not to be ascribed to chance, or to merely natural causes, but to the will of Heaven.

7. *Behold, man is born to trouble:* i. e. men are born under a law, or with a constitution, which subjects them to sorrow as soon as they become transgressors. Bishop Patrick's paraphrase is, "God hath made it as natural for man to suffer, (having offended him,) as it is for the sparks to fly upward." בְּנֵי רֶשֶׁף, *sons of flame*, or *of lightning*, may denote *sparks*, or *birds* swift as lightning. As birds have not been mentioned, the former seems the closest rendering.

15. — *oppressed.* This version is obtained by altering the points מֵחֶרֶב (*from the sword*) to מָחֳרָב, hophal participle from חָרַב. This amendment of the text is adopted by Durell, Michaelis, Dathe, Doederlein, Eichhorn, and others.

16. — *iniquity stoppeth her mouth:* i. e. unrighteous and insidious oppressors are confounded and struck dumb, when they see their schemes frustrated, and find themselves entangled in the snares which they have laid for others. See Ps. cvii. 41, 42.

23. *For thou shalt be in league with the stones of the field:* i. e. thou shalt be secure from injury from the stones in walking, journeying, &c See Ps. xci. 11, 12. Dr. Shaw observes: "The custom, which still continues, of walking either barefoot or with slippers, requires the ancient compliment of bringing water, upon the arrival of a stranger, to wash his feet." — "The feet, being thus unguarded, were every moment liable to be hurt and injured; and from thence perhaps the danger, without the divine assistance, which ever protects us from the smallest misfortunes, *of dashing them against a stone*, Ps. xci. 12, which perhaps may further illustrate that difficult text, Job v. 23, of *being in league with the stones*

of the field." Shaw's Travels, &c. Vol. 1. p. 428. Or, Thy field shall be free from stones, which would make it barren.

24.—*tent.* There is some doubt whether אֹהֶל should be rendered *tent,* according to its primary meaning, or *house, habitation,* its secondary meaning. For in ch. xxix. 7, and other passages, Job is represented as dwelling in a city. —*and not be disappointed.* Lit. *miss;* used of slingers, Judg. xx. 16: i. e. thou shalt find all thy household affairs in such a condition as meets thy best wishes and expectations. נָוֶךָ here rendered *thy dwelling,* may denote *thy fold* or *pasture.* It occurs in the Scriptures in both senses. But as it is parallel with *tent,* and occurs in verse third of this chapter in the sense of *habitation,* I prefer the latter sense here.

IV.

In reply to the harsh censures and insinuations of Eliphaz, Job justifies the boldness of his complaints by the severity of the afflictions which extorted them from him. Ch. vi. 2–13. He complains of the unkindness of his friends in pronouncing him guilty because he was miserable, and in coming to him with reproaches instead of consolations. 14–23. He requests them to treat him with fairness; to examine his case, and not to condemn him on account of his miserable condition. 24–30. He proceeds to speak of the miseries and of the shortness of human life, from which he passes to his own condition, and expostulates with the Deity upon the greatness of his afflictions, and their long continuance. Ch. vii.

Ch. VI. 2.—*my grief:* i. e. *my distress* or *my affliction.* He wishes that his afflictions, together with the distress of mind caused by them, might be put into one scale, and weighed against the sand of the sea in the other. This is only a poetical way of saying that they were insupportable.

3.—*rash.* See Ges. Lexicon, upon לָעָה.

4. *For the arrows.* His distress, arising from his other afflictions as well as his disease, is compared to that of a person shot with poisoned arrows. He exaggerates his distress by the circumstance that these arrows are hurled by the arm of the Almighty.

5. *Doth the wild ass bray, &c.* As the lower animals do not complain by braying and lowing, when they have plenty of food, so neither should I complain, were it not for the insupportable weight of my afflictions.

6. *Can that which is unsavory, &c.* Men usually complain of their food, when it is unsavory; but how much greater reason have I to complain, when I am obliged to bear those afflictions at the very thought of which I used to shudder! Some critics, however, suppose that he here lashes Eliphaz for his harangue on the blessings of patience, and characterizes his discourse as insipid, impertinent, and disgusting. — *white of an egg.* It may be that the term חַלָּמוּת, which occurs not elsewhere in the Scriptures, rather denotes *purslain*, an herb which was proverbial for its insipidity among the Arabs, Greeks, and Romans. The literal meaning will then be, *Is there any taste in purslain saliva?* a contemptuous expression for *purslain broth.* But as the comparison is more expressive to the English reader according to the common version, and has the support of the Rabbins and Targums, I retain it.

7. *What my soul, &c.* In order to justify this rendering, which in sense is that of the Common Version, it is not necessary to decide whether there is an ellipsis of the relative אֲשֶׁר or not; or whether such an ellipsis is an allowable idiom of Hebrew Grammar, or not. It is certainly most probable that הֵמָּה refers to the calamities or sufferings, expressed in verses 2–4. My version sufficiently expresses this reference without adding anything which is not implied in the connection.

9. — *let loose his hand.* Lit. *loosen his hand*, which, when inactive, is figuratively regarded as *bound*, and when exerted, as *set free.* — *make an end of me!* a metaphor, which seems to be borrowed from the practice of a weaver, who cuts off the web, when it is finished, from the thrum, by which it was fastened to the beam.

10. — *I would exult:* lit. *leap.* סָלַד occurs only once in the Scriptures, except as a proper name. I now prefer the rendering *exult*, as better supported by tradition, and rather better suited to the parallelism and the connection, than the former rendering, *be consumed*, lit. *burn.* The Sept. has it ἡλλόμην; the old Latin, *saliebam*; the Chald. *exultarem.* It is also supported by a similar word in the Arabic. See Ges. Lex. in verb.

11. — *And what mine end, that I should be patient?* i. e. How distant mine end? How long have I to live? Or, since my end, threatened by my disease, is so near, why should I not prefer to die at once, and invoke destruction, rather than bear continued calamities with patience? Am I not so much exhausted, and brought so near my end, as to have reason to be impatient?

13. הַאִם is used as an adverb of exclamation in this and other passages. See Ges. In the Vulg. *ecce!* For the rendering *deliverance*, see Ges So the Sept., βοήθεια δὲ ἀπ' ἐμοῦ ἄπεστιν. Arab. *salus.*

14. *Else:* The particle וְ is so rendered in the common version, in

Ps. li. 16 : Thou desirest not sacrifice, *else* would I give it. — *he :* i. e. the friend who does not show kindness to the afflicted.

15–20. *But my brethren, &c.* This simile is exquisitely beautiful, considered as a description of a scene of nature in the deserts of Arabia. But its principal beauty lies in the exact correspondence of all its parts to the thing it is intended to represent. The fulness, strength, and noise of these temporary streams in winter answer to the large professions made to Job in his prosperity by his friends. The drying up of the waters, at the approach of summer, resembles the failure of their friendship in his affliction. And the confusion of the thirsty caravans, on finding the streams vanished, strongly illustrates his feelings, disappointed as he was of the relief he expected in these men's friendly counsels. *Scott.* Schultens observes that the Arabs compare a treacherous friend to one of these torrents, and hence say, "I put no trust in the flowing of thy torrent ;" and, "O torrent, thy flowing subsides." —*that pass away ;* Com. xi. 16.

16. — *the ice :* i. e. which melts on the hills and flows into them. — *hides itself in them :* i. e. melts and flows into them. Scott observes that these streams are first formed by the *autumnal* rains. The warmth and rains of the *spring*, melting the ice and snow on the mountains, increase them. They then rush down into the valleys, in a large body of turbid water, and assume the appearance of deep rivers. The *beds* of these winter rivers are also called *torrents.* Bishop Pococke saw several of them perfectly dry, in his journey to Mount Sinai in the month of April. See Pococke's *Description of the East*, Vol. I. pp. 139–141.

17. —*flow forth :* i. e. as soon as the snowwater is exhausted, the streams disappear. The contrast is between streams from natural perennial fountains, and those which proceed from torrents of melted snow and ice.

18. *The caravans, &c. :* i. e. The caravans turn aside to them with the expectation of finding a supply of water, but are disappointed, and obliged to pursue their journey without a supply in the desert, where they perish with thirst. Thus it agrees, in its general meaning, with the following verses — *go up into the desert :* which, like the sea, seems to rise to him that beholds it.

20. — *their place :* i. e. the place or channel of the streams, where they flowed before they were dried up.

21. — *terror ;* i. e. my terrible sufferings.

22. — *a present :* i. e. to the judge, to secure his good-will by a bribe.

25. — *what do your reproaches prove ?* i. e. what guilt do they convict me of ?

26. *Do ye mean to censure words ?* i. e. Do ye think it reasonable to carp at mere words, extorted from me by extreme misery ? You ought to

consider that a man in the extremity of misery utters many inconsiderate expressions, which ought not to be severely censured, but rather laid to the account of human infirmity, and regarded as idle wind.

27. *Truly ye spread, &c.* The expressions in this verse are proverbial, and refer to the cruelty of his friends in bringing unfounded charges against his moral character.

28. *Look now upon me, I pray you.* He may be understood literally, as requesting them to look in his face, and see if he betrayed any signs of falsehood or guilt; or figuratively, as requesting them to be more favorable to him, and to give him a hearing; to judge from his appearance whether he was false or guilty.

29. *Return, &c.*: i. e. to the discussion.

30. *Is there iniquity, &c.*: i. e. Is there any falsehood or wickedness in what I have said, or am about to say? Have not I the capacity of distinguishing right from wrong, and truth from falsehood, as well as yourselves; and if I had said or done anything wrong, should I not be conscious of it?

Ch. VII. 1. *Is there not a war-service.* The word צָבָא is rendered *warfare*, in Is. xl. 2, in the common version. The Vulg., Syr., and Arab. render it so in this verse. But the expression has particular reference to the hard and wearisome service which the military life required, and to the longing of the soldier to see the end of it.

5. *My flesh, &c.* Maundrell, describing ten lepers whom he saw in Palestine, says: "The whole distemper, indeed, as it there appeared, was so noisome, that it might well pass for the utmost corruption of the human body on this side the grave." Maundrell's Journey, p. 252, &c. Amer. edit.

7. *O remember, &c.* He here turns to the Deity, and pleads the shortness of life as a reason why he should be relieved from his sufferings. In ver. 9, 10, he urges, for the same reason, the certainty that he should not return to life.

8. *Thine eyes shall look for me.* See note on ver. 22.

9. *—the grave.* Lit. *to sheol, the underworld.*

12. *Am I a sea, &c.* He complains that God treated him as though he were some furious tyrant, whom only the most severe inflictions could restrain from exceeding the bounds of justice, and spreading destruction among mankind. "Am I as fierce and dangerous as the raging sea, or as some strong and ungovernable sea-monster, both of which must be restrained by great exertions, and watched with unceasing vigilance, lest they should spread destruction and death?" Michaelis thinks that by *the sea* Job meant the Nile, which, when it rises beyond a certain height,

becomes an inundation, and causes immense damage. Schultens quotes Arabsjah, an Arabic poet, who calls Tamerlane "a vast sea, swallowing up everything." Burder observes: "Crocodiles are very terrible to the inhabitants of Egypt; when, therefore, they appear, they watch them with great attention, and take proper precautions to secure them, so that they may not be able to avoid the deadly weapons afterwards used to kill them. To these watchings and those deadly after-assaults I apprehend Job refers."

15. — *rather than these my bones.* Lit. *rather than my bones*; i. e. than the wretched skeleton, which is nearly all that is left of me.

16. *I am wasting away.* The Hebrew word, thus rendered, is translated *melt away*, in the common version, in Ps. lviii. 7. The Arab., according to Walton, is, *Jam viribus defectus sum.*

17, 18. Job suggests that it was beneath the character of the infinite God to bestow so much time and attention, and such vigilant inspection, upon so insignificant a being as man; and this for no other purpose than to mark and punish all his defects and failures.

19. — *look away from me:* i. e. turn away thine angry countenance from me, or cease to afflict me. So xiv. 6. "This is a metaphor drawn from combatants, who never take their eyes off from their antagonists." *Schultens.* — *till I have time to breathe.* I have substituted this for the proverb, which is literally rendered in the common version, and which has been retained in Arabia to the present day, by which they understand, "Give me leave to rest after my fatigue." There are two instances (quoted by Schult. in loc.) in Hariri's *Narratives*, entitled the Assembly. One is of a person who, when eagerly pressed to give an account of his travels, answered with impatience, "Let me swallow down my spittle, for my journey hath fatigued me." The other instance is of a quick return made to one who used that proverb; "Suffer me," said the person importuned, "to swallow down my spittle;" to which his friend replied, "You may, if you please, swallow down even the Tigris and Euphrates;" that is, You may take what time you please. *Burder.*

20. *If I have sinned, &c.:* i. e. "Suppose, for a moment, that I have sinned, yet as I can have done thee no injury, as my sins cannot have affected thy safety or happiness, I see not why I should be treated with such severity, and even set up for a mark at which thou mayst shoot thine arrows." The particle אִם, *if*, is often understood. The Sept. has supplied it here: εἰ ἐγὼ ἥμαρτον. So the Arab. and Syr. See Ges. Gram. § 152. 4. — *what have I done to thee?* i. e. *what injury have I done to thee?* The verb עָשָׂה signifies *to do an injury*, in Exod. xiv. 11; Gen. xix. 8, xxii. 12. This sentiment agrees better with the context, and is also found in ch. xxxv. 6. — *O thou watcher of men!* i. e. O thou that watchest men strictly, and markest

all their sins. The word is undoubtedly used in an invidious sense, and not merely to express the general truth that God takes notice of human actions. See ver. 12, and xiv. 16. Dr. Kennicott renders it, *O thou spy upon men!* The word נֹצֵר, *inspector*, is rendered *watchman*, in 2 Kings xvii. 9, in the common version; and in ch. xxvii. 18, of this poem, it denotes *the watchman* of a vineyard. The Sept. has it, ὁ ἐπιστάμενος τὸν νοῦν τῶν ἀνθρώπων. The same sentiment is expressed in ch. x. 6, xiii. 27, and elsewhere. The word might be rendered *preserver*, in another connection, since a person sometimes *watches* a thing for its preservation; but not properly here, where the Deity is represented as the avenger of sin. — *So that I have become a burden to myself?* The Sept. renders the two last lines,

> Why hast thou set me up for thy mark,
> And why have I become a burden to thee?

The Hebrew copy, from which they translated, had עָלֶיךָ instead of עָלַי. The Masorites also place this amongst the eighteen passages which they say were *altered by transcribers*. In this case the reading preserved by the Sept. may have been altered by some transcriber who supposed the sentiment which it conveyed to be irreverent to the Deity. But, as the received text is supported by all the versions except the Sept., and by all the Hebrew manuscripts hitherto examined, it may be retained, notwithstanding the intrinsic probability that the Sept. has preserved the true reading.

22. *Soon shall I sleep in the dust.* He urges the shortness of the term of life which yet remained to him, as a reason why he should be relieved from his afflictions; and he intimates, in the latter clause of the verse, that death would, as it were, put it out of the power of the Deity to favor him, should he relent and be inclined to mercy, since he should be no longer in existence. So Castalio explains it: "Nisi mihi in hâc vitâ benefacias et condones, non erit post mortem locus." So Poole: "When thou shalt diligently seek for me, that thou mayst show favor to me, thou wilt find that I am dead and gone, and so wilt lose thy opportunity. Help, therefore, speedily."

V.

In chapter eighth, Bildad, another of Job's professed friends, comes forward as a disputant, interrupting him in his discourse, and reproving him with severity for the boldness of his language in regard to his afflictions, and for his firm protestations of his innocence, as if he had thereby called in question the justice of the Deity. He holds the opinion that, under the government of a being infinitely wise and good, afflictions cannot take place, unless for the purposes of vindictive justice. Hence he asserts that the children of Job had perished on account of their wickedness; although he had no grounds for the assertion, but that of their ruin. He tells Job that if he were in reality the devout and upright man he professed to be, he would again be restored to prosperity. He quotes a passage from an ancient poem, representing by striking images the miserable condition of the wicked, and holds out to Job the hope of the renewed favor of God, as the reward of repentance.

These exhortations to repentance, addressed, as they were, to one whom Jehovah had pronounced an upright and good man, are to be regarded as an indirect mode of charging him with perverseness and guilt. Thus it appears that Bildad agrees with Eliphaz in the opinion that misery is a decisive proof of wickedness.

Ch. VIII. 2. — *like a strong wind?* The same figure is found in Aristoph. Ran. 872.: Τυφὼς γὰρ ἐκβαίνειν παρασκευάζεται· *A tempest of words is preparing to burst forth.* So in Sil. Italicus, XI. 581.:

— qui tanta superbo
Facta sonas ore, et spumanti turbine perflas
Ignorantum aures.

6. — *thy righteous habitation:* i. e. the abode where thou shalt dwell, a righteous man. Bildad insinuates, says Schultens, that the dwelling of Job had hitherto been the abode of wickedness.

7. *So that thy beginning shall be small*: i. e. thy former prosperity shall *appear* small, compared with that which thou shalt hereafter enjoy, if thou art pure and righteous. So the Sept., Ἔσται τὰ μὲν πρῶτα σου ὀλίγα. So Castalio, *Adeo ut fuerit tua prior conditio tenuis, præ ut posterior amplificabitur.* Thus the poet puts into the mouth of Bildad a reference, undesigned on his part, to what is afterwards recorded to have taken place in the fortunes of Job: "*Jehovah blessed the latter end of Job more than the beginning.*" xlii. 12. Bildad had no prophetic anticipation of this, but merely utters a general promise, naturally suggested by the subject; while the writer intended that it should refer to the subsequent history of Job. The skill of the poet is manifested in this way in several passages, and reminds one of the admirable use made of this expedient to give interest and pathos to their compositions by the most celebrated Greek dramatists, as by Sophocles, for instance, in his Œdipus Tyrannus.

11. — *paper-reed:* πάπυρος, Sept. See Ges. We are entertained here, says Mr. Scott, with a specimen of the manner of conveying moral instructions in the oldest times of the world. They couched their observations in pithy sentences, or wrapped them in concise similitudes; and cast them into metre to fix them in the memory. Bp. Lowth mentions the words of Lamech to his two wives, (Gen. iv. 23, 24,) as the oldest example of this kind on record.

17. —*heap.* I now prefer this rendering, as favored by the parallelism, and by its connection with the verb *entwined.* —*And he seeth the place of stones:* i. e. taketh deep root in the earth. Thus the verse denotes the flourishing, and apparently durable, condition of the wicked man. So Mercier, Doed., Ges. See Ps. i. 3, xxxvii. 35; Jer. xvii. 8.

18. The particle אִם, translated *if* in the common version, is often used for emphasis, or asseveration, and, according to the connection, may be rendered, *truly, indeed, yea, yet, behold! lo!* &c., or occasionally omitted. See Noldius in verb.

19. —*from his place.* Lit. *from the earth* or *soil* from which the tree was removed. Thus others shall fill the place and enjoy the wealth of the wicked man who is taken away. See xxvii. 16, 17, and Eccles. ii. 18. So Merc., Ros. But Dathe and Eichhorn, *and another shall spring up in his place!* i. e. other wicked men, not deterred by his dreadful fate, shall take his place, and follow his example.

21. Instead of עַד, it is better to alter the point, and read עֹד. So Houb., Michaelis, De Wette.

VI.

In reply to Bildad, who had charged him with virtually denying the justice of God, Job remarks that he knows full well the greatness and holiness of God, and the weakness and sinfulness of man; intimating that he does not pretend to be free from the infirmities and sins which are common to the human race. But these, in his view, are incident to the best of men, so that no one can answer to one charge of a thousand in a controversy with God. Admitting this, however, it by no means follows that one whom God pleases to afflict is a wicked man; or, that he is a great sinner who suffers great affliction. Ch. ix. 1–3. He maintains that in the distribution of happiness and misery God is an absolute sovereign, influenced by no consideration but that of his own inscrutable and irresistible will; that his afflictions, therefore, ought not to be attributed to the justice of God, but rather to be ranked with those acts of Providence which confound all our reasonings. 4–14. He says, that though he is conscious of no guilt which should draw down upon him the afflictions which he suffered, yet he will not attempt to defend himself before the majesty of God; that he is weak; that the contest is unequal; that, were his cause ever so just, he could not hope to prevail; that, though he is conscious of innocence, he would not enter into a controversy with God in order to save his life. 15–21. (It may be observed here, that, when Job asserts his innocence, he does not lay claim to entire freedom from fault. He means only that he is innocent of the charges of secret crimes brought against him by his friends; that he is free from uncommon guilt, which his friends held to be the cause of his great misery; that he is, in fine, a sincere, upright man.) He affirms that misery, far from being a proof of uncommon guilt, is equally the portion of the righteous and of the wicked. 22 – 24. Passing to the contemplation of his own misery, he asserts that his righteousness avails him nothing; that his cause cannot be brought to a fair trial; and that the majesty and power of God reduce him to silence. 25 – 35. Then with great earnestness and pathos he expostulates with the Deity on account of his severity to the work of his own hands, continues to assert his innocence, and urges the shortness of the term of life which yet remained to him, as a reason why he should be relieved from his miseries. Ch. x.

In regard to apparent inconsistencies in the language of Job, it may be observed here that he is represented as agitated by various contending emotions. Fear and hope, despair and confidence, the spirit of submission and of bold complaint, by turns have possession of his mind; and, as either predominates, it gives, of course, a character to his language. Truth in the exhibition of opposite feelings and passions requires some inconsistency in language and sentiment. Disregard of this obvious truth led Dr. Kennicott to propose some alterations of the text, which, if adopted, would greatly injure the poem.

Ch. IX. 3. *If he choose :* i. e. If God choose to mark strictly the sins of which all men are guilty, and accuse them of these sins; or, if man choose to enter into controversy with God.

5. *He removeth the mountains, and they know it not.* This is a Heb. idiom, meaning, *He removeth them suddenly* or *unexpectedly ;* as it were, before they, i. e. the mountains, are aware of it. So in Ps. xxxv. 8, where, in the Hebrew, the expression "*at unawares*" is "*let him not know.*" Schultens remarks that the same idiom occurs frequently in the Koran.

6. —*the pillars thereof.* The earth is represented as an edifice, supported by pillars, resting on foundations, having a corner-stone, &c. See ch. xxxviii. 4 – 6. Earthquakes seem to make these pillars tremble. According to the same mode of conception respecting the earth, it is represented as *standing* forever, Ecc. i. 4, and as reeling like a drunkard, and moving like a hammock, in Is. xxiv. 20.

7. *He commandeth, &c.* Some suppose the allusion is to the effects of an eclipse ; others, to those of a continued storm, as in Acts xxvii. 20; and others, that he asserts that light and darkness depend upon God; that, if he forbid, the sun and the stars cease to shine. *To seal up*, or to shut up as with a seal, I suppose to be a figurative expression, denoting great or total obscuration. The expression to *seal up* is used with great latitude of signification. See ch. xxxiii. 16, xxxvii. 7.

8. — *spreadeth out, &c.* Comp. Is. xl. 22. Otherwise, *boweth down the heavens.* See Ps. xviii. 9–15. This latter version would denote the descent of black, heavy clouds, in a great storm. — *walketh upon the high waves.* The Egyptian hieroglyphic for what was not possible to be done was a man walking on the water. *Burder.*

9. — *the Bear, Orion, and the Pleïads.* The Hebrew names are Ash, Chesil, and Chimah. See note upon ch. xxxviii. 31, 32. — *secret chambers of the South:* i. e. the remotest regions of the South, the constellations of which are invisible to the inhabitants of the northern hemisphere.

12. *seizeth:* as a lion his prey.

13. *God will not turn away his anger:* i. e. on account of any opposition which may be made to it. *Dei irrevocabilis ira est. Castalio.*

15. — *I would not answer him.* The word is used in a judicial sense, and means, I would not undertake to make my defence.

16. *Should I call, and he make answer to me.* The words קָרָא and עָנָה are supposed by Schultens, and by most critics since his time, to be used in a judicial sense. *Si in jus vocarem,* ut actor, *et responderet mihi* compellatus, seque sisteret. If, as plaintiff, I should summon him to trial, and he should make answer, and consent to stand as defendant, I could scarcely believe it; for although I am conscious of uprightness, yet, from the severe afflictions under which I suffer, I have reason to conclude that he will act no other part towards me than that of an absolute sovereign who will give no account of his doings.

19. *If I look to strength.* Lit. *If to, or concerning, the strength of the mighty:* i. e. if it be a question of strength, &c. See Jer. xlix. 19, l. 44. If we adopt the various reading, found in the Sept. and Syr., ו instead of י, we may translate,

> If I look to strength, lo, he is strong!
> If to justice, who shall summon him to trial?

Thus Dathe and Eichhorn render the verse.

20, 21. *Though I were upright, &c.* The meaning probably is, Though I am conscious of no guilt, and though my cause is just, yet were I as pure as an angel, I should not be able to sustain myself, and make good my defence before the brightness of the divine majesty; notwithstanding the testimony of my conscience, I would give up all care for myself, every effort to preserve my life, rather than enter into a vain controversy with a Being infinitely above me, so superior in strength.

22. *It is all one.* The meaning may be either, All things are now alike to me; I am indifferent as to what may happen to me; or, It is all one whether a person be righteous or wicked, so far as his fortune is concerned. Some suppose, however, that אַחַת־הִיא should be rendered, *He is*

the one; unicus est: i. e. He is unlike all others; he stands alone; he is bound by no rules, and gives no account of his matters. Comp. ver. 32.

24. — *covereth the face of the judges.* Either, God treats them as condemned malefactors, overwhelming them with calamities, disgrace, and ruin, Job himself being one example of this melancholy truth. *Scott.* See 2 Sam. xv. 30; Esth. vii. 8; Jer. xiv. 3. Is. xxii. 17; Mark xiv. 65. Thus the meaning of the verse will be, God commonly advances wicked men to honor and power, and casts down men of true worth and virtue from their seats. Or, *to cover the face of the judges* may have the same meaning as the phrase, *to blind their eyes*, so that they are partial, unjust, and oppressive. — *If it be not he, who is it?* So the Sept., *εἰ δὲ μὴ αὐτός ἐστι, τίς ἐστιν;* If it be not God who doeth the strange things which I have mentioned, who is it that doeth them?

25. *My days have been swifter than a courier, &c.* Time and enjoyment, that are succeeded by great misery, appear as an instant that is past. The depth of his present affliction makes him forget his former prosperity, and to say that he had seen no good during his life. "The common pace of travelling in the East is very slow. Camels go little more than two miles an hour. Those who carried messages in haste moved very differently. Dromedaries, a sort of camel which is exceedingly swift, are used for this purpose; and Lady M. W. Montague asserts that they far outrun the swiftest horses. Lett. II. 65. There are also messengers who run on foot, and who sometimes go an hundred and fifty miles in less than twenty-four hours; with what energy then might Job say, '*My days are swifter than a courier!*' Instead of passing away with a slowness of motion like that of a caravan, my days of prosperity have disappeared with a swiftness like that of a messenger carrying dispatches." *Harmer.*

26. — *reed-skiffs:* i. e. "boats or skiffs made of the papyrus of the Nile, in common use among the Egyptians and Ethiopians, and famous for their lightness and swiftness. Thus Pliny, xiii. 11, Ex ipso quidem papyro navigia texunt; vi. 56, Etiam nunc [naves] in Britannico oceano vitiles corio circumsutæ sunt; in Nilo ex papyro, et scirpo, et arundine. And Lucan. Pharsal. iv. 136, Conseritur bibula Memphitis cymba papyro. Heliodorus, Æthiop. x. 460, speaks of such boats, *πορθμείοις ἐκ καλάμων πεποιημένοις*, as having been very swift, *ὀξυδρομώτατα*. They may be compared in this respect to Indian canoes."

27, 28. *If I say, &c.:* i. e. If I resolve within myself that I will cease complaining, and endeavor to be more cheerful, I find all such endeavors vain; for if my griefs be suspended for a short time, yet my fears continue, for thou, O God, wilt not clear my innocence, by removing those afflictions which make them judge me guilty of some great crime. *Poole.*

29. *I shall be found guilty, &c.:* i. e. Whether I be holy or wicked, if I dispute with thee, I shall be found guilty. Why then should I trouble

myself with clearing mine innocency? *Poole.* Or, I must pass for a wicked person; I am treated as such by God, and condemned by man. All my labor, therefore, to clear myself will be to no purpose.

30. *If I wash, &c.* By *washing himself, &c.*, and *cleansing his hands, &c.*, he asserts the purity of his heart, and innocence of his life. Thus Zophar understood him: "*Thou sayest, 'My speech is pure; I am clean in thine eyes.'*" The Psalmist also declares his own integrity in terms somewhat similar: "I have cleansed my heart in vain, and washed my hands in innocency." Ps. lxxiii. 13.

31. *Still wilt thou plunge me, &c.* The meaning is, that his calamities would cause him to be looked upon by all his intimate friends as an abominable wretch, smitten of God, and accursed. No protestations of innocence, no appeals, no defence whatever, could overcome that prejudice against him. — *my own clothes.* This circumstance is added, I imagine, as a heightening of the image of impurity; to represent more strongly the infamy with which his character was blackened by his overthrow. *Scott.*

32. *For He is not, &c.*: i. e. He is infinitely superior to me in majesty and power, so that I cannot venture to *contend with him*: i. e. to debate my cause with him, or to answer his allegations against me; neither can we *go together into judgment*: i. e. meet each other face to face, and plead upon equal terms before a superior and indifferent judge.

33. *Who may lay his hand upon us both*: i. e. who may have authority and power to control either of us who shall exceed the limits of propriety in the controversy, and also to oblige us to stand to his decision.

34. —*his rod*: i. e. my present afflictions. —*his terrors*: i. e. the terror of his majesty and power.

35. —*and not be afraid of him*: i. e. as an opponent in a judicial controversy. I should not fear but that I should be able to make good my cause, and prove my innocence. — *For I am not so at heart*: i. e. as to have any reason to fear the result of debating my cause with him upon equal terms. So Schult., Le Clerc, Ros. *Οὐ γὰρ συνεπίσταμαι ἐμαυτῷ ἄδικον·* Sept.: *I am not conscious to myself of unrighteousness.* But this is paraphrastic.

Ch. X. 2. — *Do not condemn me*: i. e. Do not pronounce me guilty and punish me with such severity, without showing me wherein I have offended, and what I have done to deserve my sufferings.

4-7. *Hast thou eyes, &c.*: i. e. Seest thou as imperfectly as man? or does thy life pass away as swiftly as that of a man? One might suspect this from thy searching after sins in me so thoroughly and so suddenly; i. e. from thy inflicting upon me such heavy blows and in such quick succession, to bring me to a confession of sin. *Umbreit.*

8. *Have thy hands completely fashioned, &c.* His argument now is, that it looks like caprice to bestow great skill and labor on a work, and then on a sudden, and without just cause, dash it in pieces. This is what he meant also in verse 3, "*Is it a pleasure to thee . . . to despise the work of thy hands?*" *Scott.*

9. *O remember, &c.* Here he pleads the common mortality. He must soon die, as all other men; what occasion then for so much torture to dispatch him? *Scott.*

10–12. The argument in these verses is taken from God's creating and providential goodness towards him, as not being consistent with his present treatment of him. *Scott.*

13. *Yet these things thou didst lay up in thy heart.* By *these things* he means his calamities; and insinuates that God had given him being with a secret purpose to make him miserable; and had advanced him so high in order to render his fall the more terrible. *Scott.* —*in thy mind:* lit. *with thee;* a phrase repeatedly used in this book, and in other parts of Scripture, to denote what was in the mind of God, i. e. what was his intention, or purpose. See ch. xiv. 5, xxiii. 14; Ps. l. 11; John xvii. 5.

15. If I am wicked, as my friends suppose me, then am I indeed undone! yet though I am righteous, I derive no benefit from it. It is all one, whether I am good or bad.

16. —*like a lion thou huntest me.* The allusion, in this and the following verse, is to that manner of hunting the lion, wherein the hunters, armed with spears and javelins, formed themselves in a ring about the beast, and threw their weapons at him one after another. By this image Job represents, in lively colors, the violent and rapid succession of his calamities. *Scott.* Another explanation, and perhaps the best, is, Thou huntest me, as a furious lion pursues his prey; but, whereas the lion tears his prey speedily, and so ends its torments, thou renewest my calamities again and again.

17. *Thou renewest thy witnesses:* i. e. thy judgments — my afflictions, which my friends regard as an evidence of wickedness. —*New hosts:* lit. *changes and a host,* by the figure hendiadys, for *hosts constantly recruited.* Or, *changes* may mean *afflictions;* and the sense may be, *a host of afflictions.* According to the former rendering, *new hosts* figuratively denote miseries constantly succeeding each other. *Exercitus immutas contra me.* Arab. and Syr.

18, 19. *Why then, &c.* But for thine agency I should have perished, unseen and unknown, and have avoided my present misery and disgrace. So in Euripides, Troad. 637, Andromache utters similar sentiments.

20. *Are not my days few? &c.:* i. e. My life is short, and hastens apace to an end. Do not then continue my afflictions to the last moment

of my existence. Let the very short term of life, which remains to me, be a season of rest and enjoyment.

21, 22. *Before I go — whence I shall not return, — &c.* These verses contain a description of sheol, or hades, the under-world, the place of all the dead. So Sen. Herc. Furens, 861. :

Stat chaos densum, tenebræque turpes,
Et color noctis malus, ac silentis
Otium mundi, vacuæque nubes.
Sera nos illo referat senectus !
Nemo ad id sero venit, unde nunquam,
Cum semel venit, potuit reverti.

VII.

In the eleventh chapter, Zophar the Naamathite, the third of Job's friends, comes forward in reply to him. He censures him with severity, as guilty of using vain, arrogant, and irreverent language in his bold protestations of his innocence, and in his loud complaints of unkind treatment from the Almighty. 1-4. He speaks of the unfathomable counsels and infinite knowledge of the Deity, and, like his predecessors in the controversy, intimates plainly that the sufferings of Job were the punishment of wickedness which the Deity had seen in him, and of which he might easily convict him. 5-12. He assures him that, if he would put away his wickedness, he might hope to regain his former prosperity ; at the same time threatening him with severe judgments if he should continue in his sins. 13-20.

Ch. XI. 3. *Shall thy boastings:* i. e. thy false assertions respecting thine innocence, and concerning the ways of Providence.

4. *Thou sayest, My speech,* or discourse, *is pure:* For thou pretendest not to have offended in word or deed, and that God himself can find no reason to condemn thee. *Patrick.* See ch. x. 7.

6. *His wisdom, which is unsearchable!* This rendering expresses the sense, whether we regard כִּפְלַיִם as signifying *complicated, intricate,* or *double,* i. e. manifold. See Ges. in verb. — *God forgiveth thee many of thine iniquities.* With Ros. and Ges., I take נָשָׁה in the sense *to forget. God causeth thee to forget of thine iniquities,* i. e. forgiveth a part of them,

7. — *the deep things of God?* See חֵקֶר in Ges. *Secretum Dei,* Arab. *Inquisitionem Dei,* Syr.

8. *Deeper than hell:* i. e. than sheol or hades, the place of the dead without distinction of character. See note upon ch. xxvi. 6.

10. *If he apprehend, and bring to trial.* The judgments of God upon the wicked are here represented by figurative language drawn from the arrest, imprisonment, and trial of a criminal. The word וְיַקְהִיל, rendered *and bring to trial*, means, literally, *and gather together*, as in the common version; it refers to the ancient custom of gathering an assembly of the people for the trial of a criminal. See Prov. v. 14; Ezek. xvi. 39, 40, xxiii. 46. — *Who shall oppose him?* i. e. Who shall, by entering into an argument with the All-wise, defend the criminal with any prospect of delivering him? or, Who shall by force deliver a criminal from his hands?

11. *He seeth iniquity, when they do not observe it.* The words וְלֹא יִתְבּוֹנָן have been explained in a great variety of ways. I suppose the verb to refer, by an enallage of number, to *the unrighteous*, in the preceding line, or to *man* understood; and that the meaning is, that God sees iniquities of which the thoughtless and wicked person who commits them has no knowledge. In this, as in the next verse, I suppose Zophar to make general remarks with particular reference to the case of Job, who had so boldly asserted his innocence. Another mode of understanding the line, which has perhaps equal claims with that which I have adopted, is that of Cocceius: *He seeth iniquity, though he attend not to it:* i. e. without an effort of attention; without looking carefully for it.

12. *But vain man is without understanding, &c.* יִלָּבֵב seems to be used in a privative sense, as the word is used in Piel in Cant. iv. 9: "Thou hast deprived me of my heart;" as it were *Thou hast hearted me.* It has been said that there is no instance in which the privative signification of Piel is transferred to Niphal. But, in the last edition of his lexicon, Gesenius observes that in Arabic there are instances in which other forms of the verb are used in the same way. It is therefore probable that a similar usage prevailed in the Hebrew, although from the paucity of its remains no other instance occurs. Schultens and Dathe render,

Let then vain man be wise,
And the wild ass's colt become a man.

According to this version, *the wild ass's colt* is used figuratively for *a perverse and obstinate man.*

15. *Then shalt thou lift up thy face without spot.* He describes the happy change of his condition by its effects in his countenance; contrasting his present dejected face, sullied and disfigured by terror, grief, and tears, with the look he shall then assume, erect, firm, and clear as the

polished mirror. He may refer to the words of Job, x. 15, "*I dare not lift up my head.*" *Scott.*

17. *Now thou art in darkness.* So Merc., Schult., Ges. Ch. x. 22; Amos iv. 13. The Chald. has it, *Obscuritas tenebrarum quasi lux matutina erit.* The Syr., *Et caligo sicut aurora erit.*

18. *Thou shalt be secure, &c.:* i. e. Thou shalt feel secure that thy prosperity will be permanent, on account of the bright hopes which present themselves. —*Now thou art disappointed, &c.* The Sept. has it, ἐκ δὲ μερίμνης καὶ φροντίδος ἀναφανεῖται εἰρήνη.

19. *Thou shalt lie down, &c.* A metaphor borrowed from flocks lying down in the pastures. As in Ps. xxiii. 2, "He maketh me to lie down in green pastures."

20. *But the eyes of the wicked shall be wearied out:* i. e. by anxiously looking for relief from their miseries. — *Their hope is — the breathing forth of life:* i. e. They expect no deliverance from their miseries, but in death. Or, Death shall be the issue of their hopes.

VIII.

Job begins his reply to Zophar, and his other friends, with a severe sarcasm upon the airs of superiority which they had assumed; and complains that he had become the object of their contempt, for no other reason than his miserable condition. Ch. xii. 1 – 5. He reasserts his opinion respecting the point in dispute, maintaining that the worst of men, far from receiving the punishment which they deserve, often live in the enjoyment of ease and prosperity. 6. They had spoken to him of the wisdom and power of God, as if he were entirely ignorant on the subject. Hence he is led to say that what they had advanced on this topic is trite and obvious; and to discourse upon the power and providence of God, in a style of eloquence well suited to make them ashamed of their pretensions to superior intelligence. This discourse may be designed to illustrate generally the power and wisdom of God, as contrasted with the weakness of man; and also to show that, in the distribution of good and evil, God acts from his sovereign will and pleasure alone, and not, as the opponents of Job contended, from a regard to the merit or demerit of men; that he treats the righteous and the wicked alike; and consequently, that nothing which he or they might advance on the subject of the wisdom and power of God could prove him guilty, or that his misery was the punishment of his sins. 7 – xiii. 2. He longs to transfer his cause from partial and misjudging man to the omniscient and righteous Judge, confident that, if he could have an opportunity of pleading his cause before him, he should not fail to vindicate his innocence. 3. He accuses his friends of partiality and injustice; of taking part against him from selfish motives and a slavish fear of God's power, rather than from honest conviction and a disinterested regard to God's honor. 4 – 11. With the most earnest protestations of innocence, the most fervent appeals to the Deity in regard to the justice of his cause, and the most pathetic description of his sufferings, he closes ch. xiii. He then proceeds to give an affecting view of the miseries of human life, especially insisting upon the shortness of it, as a reason why man should be exempted from constant and extraordinary sufferings. xiv. 1 – 6. He complains that man's condition is worse than that of the vegetable creation; since the plants, when the hand of death has apparently been upon them, come forth again with renovated beauty; but that to pass from a life of wretchedness to the never-ending sleep of death is a condition too hard to be borne. He intimates that, if he had the hope of a second life, he might be encouraged to bear with patience his heavy load of afflictions, in the hope that, at some future time, a favorable change in his condition might take place. But not entertaining this hope, he implores the Deity to grant him a trial, so that his true character may appear before he dies; and earnestly expostulates with the Deity on account of his dealings towards him. 7 – 22.

This chapter, as well as many passages scattered through the poem, renders it highly probable, either that Job had no belief in the resurrection of the dead, or in a future state of existence equally desirable with the present life; or that the author of the poem excluded from it all regard to a future state, as inconsistent with its general plan and design. It contains several assertions of man's ceasing to exist, so far as real desirable life is concerned. It is true, that, if we make some allowance for the language of strong emotion in which he expresses himself, we may suppose that he had some vague notions of the existence of the disembodied spirit, in a half-conscious, inactive state, in the interior of the earth, such, for instance, as prevailed among the ancient Greeks, but more gloomy and less definite; an existence wholly undesirable, and offering no equivalent for the loss of present enjoyments and of the present life. See ch. x. 21, 22, and the note. It is almost impossible for the human soul to conceive that its consciousness will be wholly lost. See note on xiv. 22. The separate existence of the soul seems also to be implied in the distinction which is made between *sheol* and *the grave;* the former being represented as a vast subterraneous cavern, where all the spirits of the dead dwell together. The belief in some sort of existence of the soul after death seems also to be implied in the credit which the ancient Hebrews gave to the art of necromancy. See 1 Sam. xxviii. 3 – 10. But the language of this chapter appears to be wholly inconsistent with the supposition that Job had any expectation of a *desirable* existence after death. It was reserved for the

Prince of life, the author and finisher of our faith, to bring the glad tidings of great joy to the aching hearts of men — to bring life and immortality to light.

Some critics have endeavored to lessen the force of Job's express denials of a future life, in this chapter, by the remark that he only meant that he could not hope to live again *in the present world;* but that he might still have believed that he should exist hereafter in a better world. I admit that a second life in this world was what he intended to deny ; but I think it was because he was sceptical in regard to a happy state of existence after death. Heaven he evidently regards as the abode of Jehovah and his angels alone ; and hades, or the under-world, as a place of gloom and horror. If, as he asserts, the hope of living again in this world would have afforded him consolation and comfort under his afflictions, then surely the hope of a happier state of being than the present life might have afforded him still greater comfort and consolation. How can it possibly be accounted for that he should sink into despair, because he could not hope to enjoy the doubtful good of living again in this world of sin and misery, whilst at the same time he believed in the existence of a world of happiness and purity, to which the righteous were to be admitted? See note upon ch. xix. 25. In ch. x. 21, 22, we have a description of the place where Job expected to be after death.

Ch. XII. 2. — *the whole people?* i. e. ye have engrossed all the wisdom in the world, and all others are mere brutes or fools !

4. *I, who call upon God, that he would answer me?* i. e. I, who am so conscious of my uprightness, that I am not afraid to appeal to God, and to desire that my cause may be brought to trial, and that the Deity would bring his charges against me, and show me the reasons of my afflictions ; the words *call* and *answer,* or at least the latter, being used in a judicial sense, as in ix. 16, xiii. 22, xxiii. 5, xxxi 35. Castalio and Dathe, however, give the same translation as the preceding, but understand the words in their common acceptation, which is less suited to the connexion.

6. *Who carry their God in their hand:* i. e. Who trust to their strength nd their weapons, and have no regard to the Supreme Being. See Hab. i. 11, and note.

7-9. These verses are probably to be regarded as a continuation of verse 3 ; the intermediate verses being parenthetical. In reference to the discourse of Zophar, who had spoken, with considerable parade, of the wisdom of God, and had affected to consider Job as ignorant of it, or as having called it in question, he remarks that what Zophar wished to teach him was so obvious that it might be learned from the lower animals. They made it evident, by their properties, actions, and modes of life, that God created the world by his wisdom, and that he governed it with absolute dominion ; so that it was not necessary to ascend to heaven, or to go down to the under-world, to obtain such knowledge. See xi. 7–9. Others suppose the meaning to be, that, in the distribution of happiness and misery, God is so far from having a regard to moral distinctions, that even of the lower animals the mischievous and rapacious fare well, while the useful and gentle meet with harsh treatment from man, or are the prey of the rapacious of their own kind.

9. — *among all these :* i. e. these irrational creatures, which are represented in the preceding verses as *teaching, declaring, &c.*, and in this verse in the way of poetical exaggeration, as *knowing* the wisdom and power of the Deity, which they so plainly declare. It is said that "with the Hindoos, he who refuses instruction, and will not be convinced, is told to ask the cattle." Or, in reference to the second exposition of verses 7–9, *these things* may refer to such things as are referred to in ver. 6. See Is. xxii. 11. Otherwise — *hath made these things :* i. e. the heaven and earth and all things therein, to which Job may be supposed to have directed the attention of his hearers by the motions of his hands, or of his eyes. So Schult. and Cocc. Thus Job declares that the wisdom of God is so plain, that all nature, as it were, feels and acknowledges it ; but he means to deny that this has anything to do with the question of his guilt or innocence.

11, 12. *Doth not the ear, &c. :* i. e. As the palate distinguishes the sweet from the bitter, so the ear, or rather the mind by the ear, discerns truth and falsehood in discourse ; and wisdom is the attribute of age and experience. The connection and application of these proverbial maxims are by no means so clear as their general meaning. It is probable that he means by them to censure his friends for not hearing and weighing his observations with more attention, candor, and impartiality, instead of despising and rejecting them at once.

14. *Lo! he pulleth down, &c.* None can repair what He tears down, whether houses, castles, or cities. — *He bindeth, &c :* i. e. None can extricate the man whom he casts into difficulties and straits. *Patrick.* See ch. xxxvi. 8.

15. *Lo! he withholdeth the waters :* whether from the clouds or springs. — *and they are dried up.* The waters may be said, in a popular sense, to be dried up, when they cease to exist in their fountains, and when the heavens seem to be changed into brass, and the earth into iron, according to the expression in Deut. xxviii. 23. — *He sendeth them forth.* This clause describes an inundation, such as might happen, in Job's country, from the torrents caused by too great an abundance of rain. *Scott.*

16. *The deceived and the deceiver.* A proverbial expression, says Gesenius, denoting *every description of men.* — *are his :* i. e. all alike depend upon him for their powers ; the subtle and the weak are alike subject to his control, and subservient to the purposes of his providence.

17. *He leadeth counsellors away captive.* Statesmen, who promised themselves success and victory, as the result of their plans, he disappoints and leads into captivity; and *judges* he deprives of their peculiar attribute, reason or discernment. Or *judges* may denote rulers, whom he infatuates, and leads to the adoption of measures which end in their own ruin.

18. *He looseth, &c.:* i. e. He dethroneth kings, and leadeth them, bound in chains, into servitude. So Mer., Schult., Ges. But Dathe renders the verse,

> He looseth the girdle of kings,
> And he encircleth their loins with a belt:

i. e. He takes away their authority, and he invests them with it. But usage does not favor this explanation, as Ros. observes. See Gen. xlii 24; Judg. xv. 13; Ps. cxlix. 8.

19. *And overthroweth the mighty:* i. e. the mighty men of war, in battle.

20. *He sealeth up the lips:* lit. *He taketh away the lips.* — *the trusty:* i. e. persons of tried wisdom and long experience, to whom the people are wont to repair for advice.

21. *And looseth the girdle of the mighty.* As the Orientals wore long and flowing robes, they were unfit for fighting, or for any kind of active service, until they had girded up their loins. Hence *to loose the girdle* of a person is to take away his strength, or power of resisting an enemy. Schultens and others suppose the girdle to be a badge of office, and that to loose it means to deprive those who wore it of their dignity and honors.

22. *He revealeth deep things out of darkness.* Some understand this as a general remark, setting forth the infinite knowledge and power of God, who can bring to light the most secret things; as in Matt. x. 26. So Merc. Others suppose particular secrets are referred to, such as plots, conspiracies, or the deep-laid plans of princes. Others, the hidden designs of God himself, which in course of time are brought to light.

24, 25. *He taketh away, &c.* Divine infatuation of the governing powers is here described in forcible language and striking resemblances. In their confusion, mistakes, perplexity, and distress, they resemble persons who have lost themselves in the Arabian solitudes, without a path, without a waymark, without a light to guide them; and their irresolution and unstable counsels are like the reeling motions of a drunken man. *Scott.*

Ch. XIII. 4. —*forgers of lies:* i. e. in maintaining that great afflictions are peculiar to the wicked; and that I am guilty because I am miserable.

8. *Will ye be partial to his person?* i. e. Will ye utter falsehoods from partiality to him? The phrase *to receive or accept persons* was probably borrowed from the practice of corrupt rulers or judges, who received or admitted to their presence those who came with gifts, and favored their cause.

9. *Will it be well for you, if he search you thoroughly?* i. e. If he search you thoroughly, will he not find that your condemnation of me has sprung not so much from honest conviction, as from the selfish desire of winning his favor?

11. *Doth not his majesty make you afraid?* i. e. Is it not a slavish fear of what God can do to you that induces you to condemn me without proof?

14. *Why do I take my flesh in my teeth?* עַל־מָה. "To take the flesh in the teeth," and "to put the life in the hand," evidently mean "to risk the life," as what is carried in the teeth or the hand is liable to be dropped. See 1 Sam. xxviii. 21; Ps. cxix. 109. The meaning is, Why do I risk my life by asserting my integrity before God, unless because I am fully conscious of it?

15. —*I have no hope!* This is the literal rendering of the received text. The common version adopts the various reading לוֹ, *in him*, instead of that of the text לֹא, *not*. I prefer the latter, as the more difficult reading, and yet quite as well suited to the context, and to the general plan of the book.

16. *This also shall be my deliverance.* An opportunity of appearing before God, and pleading my cause, will lead to my deliverance, i. e. to my vindication from the charges of wickedness and guilt which have been brought against me. —*For no unrighteous man will come before him:* i. e. For I shall not go before him an unrighteous man. Others suppose the meaning to be, My readiness to appear before God, and to plead my cause before him, ought to be considered a proof of my innocence; for no unrighteous man would dare to do it.

18. —*that I am innocent:* i. e. that my cause is just; or, that I am innocent of the charge of gross wickedness, which is alleged against me as the cause of my calamities.

19. —*contend with me:* i. e. maintain the cause successfully against me.

22. *Then call upon me, &c.* These expressions import that he aimed to dispute his cause, not merely *before* God as a judge, but *with* God as a party. *Scott.*

26 *For thou writest:* A judicial term, referring to the custom of writing the sentence of a person condemned, i. e. decreeing his punishment. See Ps. cxlix. 9; Jer. xxii. 30; John xix. 22. So the Greeks used the ex-

pression γράφεσθαι δίκην; and amongst the Arabs *a writing* is a term commonly used for a *judicial sentence.*

27. *Thou watchest all my paths:* i. e. all the paths by which I might escape. The allusion is to a prisoner who is not only fettered, or in the stocks, but closely watched by sentinels. — *Thou hemmest in the soles of my feet:* i. e. by a trench, beyond which thou wilt not suffer me to pass; i. e. thou hast stopped my way. See xix. 8; Lam. iii. 8, 9.

28. *And I:* lit. *And he.* Upon this change of persons in the Hebrew, see Ges. Heb. Gram. § 217.; Storr's Observ. § 23. The Greek idiom, by which τῷδε ἀνδρὶ is used for ἐμοί, has some resemblance to it.

Ch. XIV. 1. — *born of woman:* This is said in conformity with the Oriental sentiments in regard to the inferiority of the female sex, in ancient and modern times. See ch. xv. 14, xxv. 4.

3. *And dost thou fix thine eyes upon such an one?* This expression denotes, in Zech. xii. 4, *to look angrily* at another. *Scott.* It refers here probably, to *vigilant inspection* for the sake of discovering faults. — *And dost thou bring me into judgment with thee?* i. e. Dost thou treat me as a criminal, and decree against me severe punishments?

4. *Who can produce a clean thing from an unclean?* He now pleads for lenity on account of the natural weakness of man's moral powers. Who can expect so frail and weak a being as man to be without faults? Who can expect frail man to be as pure as an angel? Vitiis sine nemo nascitur.

6. *That he may enjoy, as a hireling, his day!* i. e. That he may enjoy his term of life, at least to that degree in which the hireling enjoys his term of service. The Sept. favors this mode of translating the verse: Ἀπόστα ἀπ' αὐτοῦ, ἵνα ἡσυχάσῃ, καὶ εὐδοκήσῃ αὐτοῦ τὸν βίον, ὥσπερ ὁ μισθωτός. Otherwise, *Until he shall, as a hireling, have completed his day. To complete* or *accomplish* is a less common meaning of רָצָה, but not without support. See Lev. xxvi. 34, 41, 43; 2 Chron. xxxvi. 21; Is. xl. 2. Others render, *Until, as a hireling, he shall rejoice in his day:* i. e. the day of his death. Let him be exempt from afflictions during the common short term of human life, until, weary and worn with service, he shall rejoice in the day of his death, as a hireling rejoices in the day of his release from service.

7–12. Compare the well-known passage of Moschus. Epitaph. Bion. 105.

The meanest herb we trample in the field,
Or in the garden nurture, when its leaf,
At Winter's touch, is blasted, and its place
Forgotten, soon its vernal buds renews,

And, from short slumber, wakes to life again.
Man wakes no more! — man, valiant, glorious, wise,
When death once chills him, sinks in sleep profound,
A long, unconscious, never-ending sleep. *Gisborne*

See also in Dr. Beattie's Hermit:

'T is night, and the landscape is lovely no more;
I mourn, but, ye woodlands, I mourn not for you;
For morn is approaching, your charms to restore,
Perfumed with fresh fragrance, and glittering with dew.
Nor yet for the ravage of winter I mourn;
Kind nature the embryo blossom will save;
But when shall spring visit the mouldering urn?
O when shall it dawn on the night of the grave?

10. —*and he is gone!* וַיֶּחֱלָשׁ. This word means *to be so entirely prostrated, overthrown,* or *weakened,* as not to be able to recover. Man, when dead, has no strength or vital principle remaining in him, by which he can, like a tree that is felled, return to life. A more literal rendering, such as *pass away, waste away,* is, by English usage, synonymous with death. Gesenius renders it, *dahin ist, it is all over with him.*

12. *Till the heavens be no more:* i. e. Never. For things unchangeable and eternal are in Scripture compared in duration to the heavens. See Ps. lxxii. 5, 17, lxxxix. 29, 36, 37, cxlviii. 6; Jer. xxxi. 35, 36. Dr. Good supposes that the phrase refers to a definite period, that of the general resurrection. But this supposition is inconsistent with Scripture usage and with the context, and is not countenanced by the most respectable of those critics who suppose the general resurrection to be referred to in ch. xix. 25.

13. *O that thou wouldst hide me in the under-world!* i. e. *in sheol* or *hades.* Schultens takes great pains to show that Job, by this expression, does not wish for death, but only to be shut up alive in hades. But if we understand him to wish for a temporary death, the connection of this verse with the 14th will be closer. Under the influence of passionate emotion he expresses the thought, that, if he were by death removed out of the sight of the Deity for a time, his wrath might subside, like man's resentment, which time and the absence of the object of it weaken or extinguish.

14. *If a man die, can he live again?* Here he checks his wish for death by a question which is equivalent to a negation. A man once dead cannot live again. Else, or if it were so, I might have strength and patience to endure all my present afflictions, *until my change should come,* i. e. until I should be relieved from my hard service by new recruits, or from my wearisome station by a fresh guard; i. e. until a favorable

change in my condition should take place. Or, *war-service* may relate to his wished-for residence in the lower world, ver. 13, and *his change* to his restoration to the upper world, when his character should be vindicated, and his happiness restored. The poet probably means here to make another allusion to the actual history of Job in the close of the poem.

15. *Call upon me, and I will answer thee!* So Le Clerc, Schultens, Ros., De Wette. Unable to bear the thought of going out of the world under such a load of infamy, and having no hope of coming back into it again to clear his innocence, he earnestly begs of God to relent towards his creature, and to bring him to immediate trial. The terms *call* and *answer* ought surely to be taken in the same judicial sense as in ch. ix. 16, xiii. 22, xxxi. 14; the former denoting the action of bringing the complaint; the latter, the part of the defendant in replying to it. *Scott.*

16, 17. As a contrast to the regard which he pleaded for in the foregoing verse, and as a reason for his urging an immediate trial, he here sets forth the severity with which God treats him now.

16. —*thou numberest my steps:* i. e. thou makest strict inquiry into my actions, that thou mayst find out all my errors, and punish them. — *Thou watchest over my sins:* i. e. Thou watchest for my haltings or miscarriages, as if thou wert glad of an occasion to punish me. *Poole.*

17. *My transgression is sealed up in a bag:* i. e. as writings, money, or other choice things, that they may be safely kept, and brought forth upon occasion, and that not one of them may be forgotten or lost. See Hos. xiii. 12. "The money, that is collected together in the treasuries of eastern princes, is told up in certain equal sums, put into bags, and sealed." *Chardin.* —*thou addest unto my iniquity.* Either, thou addest one sin to another, the sins of my youth to those of my riper age, so as to swell the number laid up against me, and thus to increase my punishment; or, thou makest my iniquity greater than it is. Gesenius renders it, perhaps correctly, (see in the Hebrew, xiii. 4; Ps. cxix. 69,) *thou inventest* (falsehood) *unto mine iniquity:* i. e. *thou chargest me with iniquity falsely.* The rendering which I have adopted may be considered as a milder way of expressing the same idea. It is that of the old Geneva version, i. e. the English version made in the time of queen Elizabeth; which, in several passages of this poem, is more correct than the common version. The Chald. has it, *accumulas super iniquitates meas.*

19. *So thou destroyest the hope of man:* i. e. the hope of living again after death.

22. *But his flesh shall have pain, &c.* By a bold, but not unnatural personification, the dead man in his grave is represented as conscious of his own miserable condition, and of that alone. He knows not of the miseries of his living relatives, but his body consumed by worms feels its own pain, and the soul in the underworld mourns its own sad condition.

IX.

Eliphaz begins his reply to Job with bitter sarcasms and reproaches. He censures particularly the assertions of Job respecting the indiscriminate distribution of happiness and misery, as tending to undermine religion, and to encourage men in the neglect of prayer. He says that the assertion of such opinions is sufficient evidence of his guilt. Ch. xv. 1 – 6. He then lashes him severely for pretending to understand the ways of God better than those who were his elders ; and for his passionate complaints concerning God's dealings toward him. He repeats, for his admonition, the substance of the oracle which he had brought forward in his former discourse. 7 – 16. He proceeds to give, as a quotation from an ancient poem, a highly wrought description of the misery which in various ways pursues the wicked man. The drift of the whole is to vindicate Providence, to condemn Job as an object of divine wrath on account of his wickedness, and to terrify him, if possible, into a confession of his guilt. 17 – 35.

Ch. XV. 4. *And discouragest prayer before him.* Literally, *lessenest prayer.* The meaning is, that Job, by maintaining that God treated the righteous and the wicked alike, sapped the very foundations of religion ; since, in that case, the wicked would have nothing to fear, and the righteous nothing to expect from him.

5. *Though thou choosest the tongue of the crafty.* He gives this invidious turn to Job's protestations of innocence, prayers, and appeals to God ; which he represents as an artful address to the passions of his hearers, in order to blind their judgment, and deceive them into a favorable opinion of his piety.

7. *Art thou the first man, &c.:* i. e. Hast thou lived ever since the creation of the world, and treasured up the experience of all ages in th own breast, that thou speakest so arrogantly, and with such contempt o other men ? *Poole.*

8. *Hast thou listened in the council of God:* i. e. in such a council as is described in the first and second chapters of this poem, where the angels are represented as assembled around Jehovah for the purpose o giving an account of their ministry, and of receiving orders respecting the government of the world. Eliphaz sarcastically inquires, whether, in consequence of being admitted into God's council, he, of all men in the world, is acquainted with his purposes. For *wisdom* seems here, as in ch. xxviii., to have special, though not exclusive, reference to the wisdom or purposes of God, by which he governs the world. For the rendering *drawn all wisdom*, see Ges. Thes. ad גָּרַע.

11. —*consolations of God.* Eliphaz may here refer to the oracle, ch. iv. 17–21. —*words so full of kindness:* So Cocc., Schult., Ges. By their *consolations,* and *words of kindness,* he means their distant intimations of his guilt, their warnings insinuated in the way of examples, and their exhortations to confession and amendment. *Scott.*

12. —*winking of thine eyes.* *To wink with the eyes,* according to Hebrew usage, denoted arrogance, haughtiness, and contempt. See Ps. xxxv. 19; Prov. vi. 13.

19. *To whom alone, &c.:* i. e. the ancient inhabitants of Arabia, who had not been corrupted by intercourse with foreigners. It was no modern or imported doctrine, but that which prevailed amongst the earliest and best inhabitants of the country. *Le Clerc.* Eliphaz here speaks like a genuine Arab, whose pride is in his tongue, his sword, and his pure blood. *Umbreit.*

20. *Yea, all the years that are laid up for the oppressor:* i. e. he is in constant fear of death. He is not secure of his life for a moment, his guilty conscience continually conjuring up fears of assassination or violence of some kind. He is in the situation of Dionysius of Sicily:

> Districtus ensis cui super impiâ
> Cervice pendet, non Siculæ dapes
> Dulcem elaborabunt saporem;
> Non avium citharæque cantus
> Somnum reducent.
>
> *Hor.* Carm. III. i. 17.

With this description of the condition of the wicked compare that of Juvenal, Sat. xiii. 192.

21. *In peace the destroyer cometh upon him.* Schultens and others understand this, When there are no signs of invasions, insurrections, or plots against him, his disturbed imagination is continually presenting destruction to him. Post equitem sedet atra cura.

22. —*darkness:* a common metaphorical expression for *calamity.* His despair of escaping some unhappy end, assassination for instance, is described here. *Schult.* —*set apart, &c.:* i. e. destined to a violent death. So, in substance, the Sept., ἐντέτακται γὰρ ἤδη εἰς χεῖρας σιδήρου.

26. *And ran against him with outstretched neck:* i. e. with his neck stooping and stretched out, the attitude of a combatant running upon his adversary. —*With the thick bosses of his bucklers.* Schultens has shown that *to turn the boss of one's buckler* against a person is a proverbial expression among the Arabs, meaning *to become his deadly enemy.* These metaphors drawn from the single combat, which was much in practice in the ancient wars, are intended to express the most daring impiety, atrocious violation of God's laws, and contempt of his vindictive justice.

27. *Because he covered his face with fatness.* This is a graphical description of a luxurious and licentious person.

30. —*darkness:* i. e. ruin, destruction. —*his branches:* i. e. his wealth, power, glory, all with which he was adorned, as a tree with its branches. —*by the breath of His mouth:* i. e. of God's mouth. The destruction of the wicked man seems to be represented under the image of a tree destroyed by a burning wind, (see note upon ch. iii. 5,) or by lightning; or torn up by a tempest sent by the Deity. See ch. iv. 9; Ps. xviii. 15; Is. xi. 4.

31. —*vanity.* The term *vanity* has two meanings, and therefore well represents the original. In the first line of the verse it denotes *wickedness;* in the second, the consequences of wickedness, or *misery.*

X.

The speech of Eliphaz was admirably fitted to carry on the design of the poem, by irritating the passions of Job, and inflaming his discontent with the ways of Providence. In his reply he gives a pathetic representation of the inhumanity of his friends, and of his other severe afflictions. He then makes the most solemn protestations of innocence, and expresses an earnest desire that his cause may be tried, and his innocence vindicated, before he goes the way whence he shall not return. Ch. xvi. He dwells upon nearly the same topics in ch. xvii., and ends his reply with the strongest expressions of grief and despair.

Ch. XVI. 4. — *string together:* lit. *tie together; nectere verba.* Some prefer the rendering, *make a league with words:* i. e. raise a host of words.

7. *For now He, &c.:* i. e. God, whom he addresses in the next line.

8. *Thou hast seized hold of me:* תִּקְמְטֵנִי. See ch. xxii. 16, and Ges. Lex. The meaning of both clauses of the verse is, that the afflictions of Job made his friends believe that he was a bad man.

9. *His anger:* i. e. God's. The image is drawn from a wild beast tearing the flesh of a person whom he is pursuing. —*My adversary:* i. e. God. See ch. xiii. 24, xix. 11. — *sharpeneth his eyes:* i. e. darts piercing looks at me, or looks upon me with fierce and sparkling eyes.

10. *They gape:* i. e. My friends, the instruments of God's anger. - *they assemble:* i. e. like conspirators, to effect my ruin.

15. *And thrust my horn.* See Ges. Rosenmüller supposes the metaphor to be borrowed from some strong and noble animal lying dead, with

its horn thrust into the ground; and that the meaning is, My wealth, power, and glory are prostrate in the dust. See Deut. xxxiii. 17; Ps. lxxv. 5.

16. —*deathlike darkness.* See note on ch. iii. 5.

18. *O earth, cover not thou my blood.* He compares his accumulated miseries to blood unjustly shed, and prays that his injuries may not be concealed from man or Heaven, nor remain unavenged. —*And let there be no hiding-place for my cry?* i. e. May nothing hinder my cry for redress from ascending to heaven! See ch. xix. 7. In the height of his emotion he forgets that it is God who hath laid him low.

19. *And he that knoweth me:* שָׂהֲדִי, lit. *my witness:* I paraphrase it to avoid repetition. The Sept. has it, ὁ συνίστωρ μου, probably for the same reason. Cranmer's Bible, *And he that knoweth me is above in the height.*

21. *O that one might contend:* i. e. in a judicial controversy. His meaning is, that if the Deity would bring his charges against him, he should be able to clear himself, and vindicate his integrity. See ch. xvii. 3.

Ch. XVII. 3. *Give a pledge, &c.* The terms in this verse are obscure, on account of our ignorance of the ancient forms of trial. Job seems again to challenge the Deity to enter into a judicial contest with him in regard to the uprightness of his character; and desires the Deity *to give a pledge* that he would not avail himself of his almighty power in the contest, but deal with him upon fair and equal terms, so that the cause might be decided according to strict justice, and without regard to the rank of the parties concerned. — *Who is he that will strike hands with me?* i. e. Who, by the usual form of striking hands, will agree with me to be surety for thee? See Prov. vi. 1, xvii. 18, xxii. 26. This challenge, says Mr. Poole, savors of too much boldness and irreverence to God; yet seeing Job expresses the same desire, almost in the same manner, in ch. ix. 32, 33, and is sharply reproved by God for contending with him, in xl. 2, I see no inconvenience in ascribing the same thing to him here.

4. *Therefore thou wilt not suffer them to prevail:* i. e. to gain the victory in this contest. Thou wilt rather pronounce me innocent, and censure them.

5. *He that delivers up his friend as a prey.* לְחֵלֶק, *for a prey.* So used in Gen. xiv. 24; 1 Sam. xxx. 24.

6. —*their abhorrence;* תֹּפֶת, from the Chald. תּוּף, *to spit out.* καὶ ἀπέβην αὐτοῖς γέλως. Sept.

8. — *at this:* i. e. at seeing so good a man oppressed with such a heavy load of afflictions. —*And the innocent, &c.:* i. e. the innocent will

resolutely oppose the wicked, when he judges the worse of piety because of my afflictions. *Patrick.*

10. —*return:* i. e. to the debate.

11. *Even the treasures of my heart:* i. e. what most occupied my heart.

12. *Night hath become day to me:* i. e. I have sleepless nights. I am as much awake by night as by day. — *The light bordereth on darkness:* i. e. The day seems very short. The daylight seems to go as soon as it is come.

13. *Yea:* אִם, a particle of asseveration. Hos. xii. 11; Prov. xxiii. 18. See Ges. ad verb. —*I have made my bed in darkness:* i. e. the darkness of the grave. I shall soon lie down in the grave, the only place in which I can expect repose.

14. *I say to the pit, &c.* By these strong expressions he intimates how near he believed himself to be to death. I have already made so near an alliance with death, that my father and mother and nearest kindred are nothing so near to me as the grave and worms. Others suppose him to express a strong desire of death in this verse.

16. —*bars of the under-world:* Sheol, the gates of which are fastened by massive bars, so that those who have entered it cannot return. See ch. xxxviii. 17; Is. xxxviii. 10; Ps. ix. 13, cvii. 18. Some render בַּדֵּי *solitudes* or *wastes*, with less probability. See Hos. xi. 6. *When together there is rest, &c.* Otherwise, *Yea, we shall descend together into the dust!* i. e. I and my hopes shall be buried in the same grave. So the Sept., ἢ ὁμοθυμαδὸν ἐπὶ χώματος καταβησόμεθα. This is a figurative way of saying that all his expectations would end in misery, death, and corruption; or that these were all he had to expect.

XI.

In the eighteenth chapter Bildad again comes forward, full of resentment against Job, on account of the low estimation in which he held their discourses. He accuses him of pride and arrogance. He reasserts the general doctrine, maintained by the friends of Job, that misery implies guilt, by giving a highly wrought description of the calamities which, as he contends, are the portion of the wicked. This description contains some particulars closely adapted to the circumstances of Job, and was, without doubt, designed to intimate that Job must resemble in character those whom he so much resembled in condition.

Ch. XVIII. 2. *How long ere ye make, &c.* Though the pronoun is in the plural, there can be little doubt that Job is the person addressed. — *Understand:* i. e. Consider and weigh our arguments.

3. He refers to what Job had said in ch. xvii. 4, 10.

4. *Thou that tearest thyself:* lit. *He teareth, &c.* This is a common Hebrew idiom. See ch. xii. 4, xvi. 7, xvii. 10, xxxii. 15, xli. 9.—*Must the earth be deserted for thee? &c.* When the Orientals would reprove the pride or arrogance of any person, it is common for them to desire him to call to mind how little and contemptible he and every mortal is, in these or similar apophthegms:

> What though Mohammed were dead?
> His Imams (or ministers) conducted the affairs of the nation.
> The universe shall not fall for his sake;
> The world does not subsist for one man alone.
>
> *Lowth*, Lect. 34.

Most critics, however, suppose the verse to have a more definite meaning. "These are proverbial forms of speech for altering what is fixed and unchangeable. The meaning is, if I mistake not, that God must give up his moral kingdom among men, or violate the immutable laws of justice by which it is administered, if such a man as Job escaped punishment. This interpretation makes an easy transition to the other part of the discourse, which is designed to prove that, by an unchangeable rule of Providence, the signally wicked shall signally perish." *Scott.*

5. *Behold, the light: — the flame, &c.* These metaphors denote, in general, splendor, prosperity, glory, or festivity. There is an allusion, in the latter clause of the verse, to what the Arabian poet calls *the fires of hospitality;* these were beacons lighted upon the tops of hills by persons of distinction among the Arabs, to direct and invite travellers to their houses and tables. Hospitality was their national glory; and the loftier and larger these fires were, the greater was the magnificence thought to be. See Pococke in Carm. Tograi, p. iii. A wicked rich man, therefore, would affect this piece of state from vanity and ostentation. Another Arabian poet expresses the permanent prosperity of his family almost in the very words of our author: "Neither is our fire, lighted for the benefit of the night-stranger, extinguished." Hamasa, p. 473. *Scott.* See also the note on ch. xxxi. 17.

6. — *lamp:* He refers to the lamp which hung from the ceiling of the apartment. The Arabs are fond of this image. Thus they say: "Bad fortune hath extinguished my lamp;" and concerning a man whose hopes are remarkably blasted; "He is like a lamp, which is immediately extinguished if you let it sink into the oil." See Schult.

7. *His strong steps shall be straitened:* i. e. Instead of advancing freely and firmly, in a wide path, he shall be reduced to the necessity of going timidly, in a narrow way, full of obstacles, where there is great danger of stumbling. This is a very common metaphor in Oriental poetry to denote the loss of power, prosperity, &c., as Schultens has shown by numerous quotations. *Strong steps* are free, firm, unimpeded steps.

11. *Terrors* are here represented as allegorical persons, like the Furies in the Greek poets.

13. *His limbs:* בַּדֵּי עוֹרוֹ : lit. *The limbs of his skin:* i. e. of his body. — *the first-born of death:* i. e. the most terrible death.

14. — *the king of terrors.* This is probably to be regarded as a poetical personification of death, considered as a resident of the underworld, comp. xxx. 23. It is not to be considered as a mythical person. For there are in the Hebrew writings no clear traces of a king of Hades, corresponding to the king of the infernal regions in Grecian and Roman mythology. — Otherwise, *Terror pursueth him like a king.* But the rendering "pursueth" does not appear to have sufficient support from usage.

15. *Brimstone is scattered upon his habitation:* i. e. it is destroyed, like Sodom and Gomorrha, by fire and brimstone from heaven. Grotius, Le Clere, Schult., and Ros. think that lightning is referred to both in this passage and in Gen. xix. 24; Deut. xxix. 23; Ps. xi. 6. Pliny says, (Hist. Nat. xxxv. 15,) Fulmina et fulgura quoque sulphuris odorem habent ac lux ipsa eorum sulphurea est. And Persius, Sat. ii. 24, 25.:

—— At sese non clamet Jupiter ipse?
Ignovisse putas, quia, cum tonat, ocyus ilex
Sulphure discutitur sacro, quam tuque domusque?

—— graves halantes sulphuris auras.

Lucret. VI. 222.

Bildad may refer to the circumstance that a part of Job's property was consumed by lightning. Ch. i. 16.

18. *And driven out of the world:* i. e. He is not conducted out of life, as Plato expresses it, with funeral pomp, by a numerous train of relatives and citizens, but is cast out of human society like a malefactor, and thrown under ground with infamy and execration. *Scott.*

XII.

Job begins his reply to the harsh and passionate invective of Bildad with pathetic complaints of the inhumanity of his friends, in regarding his afflicted condition as unquestionable evidence of guilt. He maintains that his sufferings are not to be charged upon himself, but upon God, who had overwhelmed him with calamities, though he had done nothing to deserve them, and though he had often desired to be brought to trial. Perceiving that the representation of his misery had no effect upon his hard-hearted friends, he suddenly turns from them, and expresses the earnest desire that all which he had said in his defence might be recorded upon some lasting monument, so that posterity, at least, might do him justice ; or that it might remain uneffaced till the event should justify it. But his consciousness of innocence does not allow him to stop here. He is not satisfied with the tardy justice which posterity may render to his memory ; and he gives utterance to the firm and triumphant conviction, that, low as he is reduced by sorrow and disease, he shall yet live to see the Deity stand up in his favor, and vindicate him from the unfounded charges which have been brought against him. He also warns his friends that the time will come, when they shall be put to shame for their injustice and cruelty toward him.

Ch. XIX. 2. — *break me in pieces:* a metaphor drawn from the pounding of kernels in a mortar, or from breaking rocks in pieces by repeated blows of the hammer.

4. *My error abideth with myself:* i. e. I alone shall bear the consequences of my error.

Mihi dolebit, non tibi, siquid stultè fecero.

Plaut. Menæch. ii. 3.

5 — *my reproach:* i. e. my calamities, which bring reproach and disgrace upon me.

7. *Behold, I complain of wrong.* He certainly means wrong or violence done to him by God. This language is extremely harsh, and utterly inexcusable. It is, however, nothing more than what he had already said in effect, in ch. ix. 17, x. 3, xvi. 18. Indeed if such rash speeches as these had not come from his lips, what ground would there have been for

those cutting reproaches in xl. 8: "*Wilt thou even disannul my judgment? Wilt thou condemn me, that thou mayst appear righteous?*" *Scott.*

9. *And taken the crown from my head:* i. e. deprived me of all my dignity and honors. See Prov. iv. 9.

10. —*I am gone:* i. e. I am near death. See x. 21, xiv. 20; Gen. xv. 2; Ps. xxxix. 13. —*like a tree:* which, being plucked up by the roots, does not grow again.

12. *His troops, &c.* He represents his calamities by metaphors drawn from the siege of a city.

15. —*foreigners, &c.:* or *sojourners:* i. e. servants not born in his house; or, perhaps, clients, persons who looked to him for protection; persons connected with his family, but not residing under his roof. Schultens says that the same word is used by the Arabian poets to denote the dependents of a great man, who are adopted into his family and taken under his protection. But the first meaning seems to agree better with the connection.

17. *My breath is become strange, &c.* i. e. My wife denies me her company on account of my offensive breath and sores. Otherwise, *My spirit is become a stranger:* i. e. *I am become a stranger.* —*children of my own mother:* lit. *children of my womb:* i. e. of the same womb from which I came.

20. *And I have scarcely escaped with the skin of my teeth.* A proverbial expression, denoting the utmost emaciation from disease.

22. *Why do ye persecute me like God?* i. e. without giving any reason or account of your conduct, accusing me of crimes without proof, and condemning me without trial. —*And not rest satisfied with my flesh:* i. e. with the consumption and torment of my whole body, but add to it the vexation of my spirit, by your grievous reproaches and calumnies. Or, according to Schultens, Why are ye not satisfied with the reproaches and slanders with which ye have already tormented me? Schultens remarks that *to eat the flesh* of another is an Arabian phrase for *calumniating* him. One of their poets has the line, "I am not addicted to slander, nor am I one who devours the flesh of his friend." Another, speaking of his calumniator, says, "Who worries my flesh, and yet has not satisfied his avidity." The phraseology is taken from a wild beast rending his prey.

23. *O that my words:* i. e. all my discourses, all that I have said in my defence, my protestations of innocence, my appeals to God, &c., so that all ages may be able to judge between me and my accusers, and to know the justice of my cause.

24. —*and with lead:* i. e. infused into the letters engraven in the rock, in order to make them plain and legible. See Jer. xvii. 1.

25 - 27. The design of this passage appears to be the same with that of xvi. 19, where Job exclaims, "*My witness is in heaven, and he that knoweth me is on high;*" and of the numerous passages in which he desires and prays that his cause may be brought to trial, and that the Deity may pronounce judgment respecting the integrity of his character. This design is, to express, in a striking manner, the depth and sincerity of Job's conviction of his own innocence. So strong and clear is the testimony of his conscience in his favor, that what has heretofore been the object of his ardent wishes and prayers is now become the object of his confident expectation; and he expresses the firm persuasion that God will be the *vindicator* of his integrity from the charges of his friends; that he *will stand up on the earth*, as a judge, and decide the cause in his favor; that *though his body be wasted away* to a mere skeleton, *yet without his flesh*, i. e. in his emaciated state, *he shall see God*, interposing in his favor and taking his side in the controversy. I have, in this edition, preferred to give the sense *without* to מִן, as the particle is used in xi. 15, xxi. 9. The rendering of the Common Version "*in* my flesh" may be defended, as to its sense, by taken מִן in its usual meaning of *from*, and understanding Job to say that he, looking out from his flesh, should see God. Whichever rendering be preferred, the expectation of Job refers to a time before his death.

It appears more consistent with Job's character, and with the design of the poem, to suppose that the main object of his confident expectation was, not restoration to general prosperity, but the vindication of his character from false imputations. He has the conviction that a just and good God will yet make it appear that his misery is no proof of his guilt. Throughout the poem he seems to regard all other evils light, in comparison with the loss of character; and to desire not so much deliverance from misery, as from the imputation of guilt; and thus he refutes the insinuation of Satan, that his piety was founded in selfish motives.

Whether Job connected the recovery of his health, and his restoration to general prosperity, with the vindication of his character by the Deity, it is not very important to decide. One objection to this supposition appears to be very futile. Job could not have hoped for recovery from his disease, or for restoration to prosperity, say some critics; for he had said, more than once, that he had no hope, and that he was near his grave. As if a person, who is represented as agitated by the most violent and opposite emotions, could be expected to be consistent in his sentiments and language. What can be more natural than that Job, in a state of extreme depression, arising from the thought of his wrongs, the severity of his afflictions, and the natural tendency of his disease, should express himself in the language of despair, and yet that he should be animated, soon after, by conscious innocence, and the thought of God's justice, goodness, and power, to break forth into the language of hope and confidence?

But, for the reasons before mentioned, it is probable that the main, if not the sole, object of Job's confident expectation was *the vindication of his character by the Deity.* The writer, however, without doubt, intended that the whole passage should have relation to the concluding part of the poem, where the Deity is represented as appearing and vindicating the character of Job by calling him four times his servant; by rebuking his calumniators, and pardoning them through his intercession; by declaring that he, and not his friends, had spoken that which was right, i. e. in regard to the question whether misery was a proof of guilt; and by giving him temporal blessings in two-fold greater abundance than before his affliction. This interposition of the Deity appears to have been kept in view by the writer throughout the poem, and thus the mind of the reader is prepared for it.

Of the objections to the supposition that Job here expresses his confident expectation of a resurrection to a life of happiness, a few will be briefly mentioned. They are entirely independent of the question, what was the general belief of the Hebrews in regard to the state of the soul after death. The author of the poem may have been more sceptical than others.

1. The supposition is inconsistent with the general design of the poem, and with the course of argument. The belief in a future state of retribution would have, in some measure, solved the difficulty respecting the afflictions of the good, and the prosperity of the wicked. But no one of the speakers alludes to it in the course of the poem. If it be a declaration of that doctrine, it is a single independent declaration of it, in a work, in which, from the nature of the subject, it might have been expected to occur upon every page.

2. It is inconsistent with the connection of the discourse. Zophar, who replies to Job, makes no allusion to it, but goes on to assert the temporal miseries which are the portion of the wicked and of their children. So, too, verses 23 and 24 lose their force, if we suppose the state after death to be referred to in the passage.

3. It is inconsistent with several express declarations of Job in other parts of the poem. See ch. vii. 7, 8, x. 20 – 22, xiv. throughout, and xvii. 11 – 16. When he wishes for death, he speaks of it as the termination of his miseries, and not as the introduction to a life of happiness. Ch. iii. It is, moreover, too much to suppose that the influence of feeling would have led him to deny so important a doctrine, had he believed in it. Under the influence of opposite emotions, one may be expected to express different opinions respecting his condition, prospects, &c, but not to deny so important an article of his faith. So good a man as Job would naturally

have been led, in his affliction, to cling the more closely to the doctrine of a future life of happiness, had he believed in it; or rather, had he been represented by the poet as believing in it.

4. It is not urged as a topic of consolation by either of the three friends of Job, nor even by Elihu, who acts the part of an umpire in the controversy, and who gives a more philosophical account than either of the speakers of the design of afflictions. Nor is it alluded to by God himself in the decision of the controversy.

5. The Jewish commentators, who sought for every shadow of proof of the doctrine of a future life in the Old Testament, do not consider this as one of the passages by which it is supported. The same remark applies to most of the Greek fathers. Chrysostom speaks expressly of Job as "a righteous man, who knew nothing of the resurrection." Ep. ii. ad Olymp., &c. The supposition that this doctrine is contained in the passage derives its chief support from the mistranslation or misapplication of certain expressions in it. See also the prefatory remarks to ch. xii., xiii., xiv.

6. Ewald, in his notes on the passage, being convinced that it cannot refer to the *resurrection* of the dead, brings forward a new hypothesis, namely, that Job's hope is in the happy existence of the disembodied spirit after death; the immortality of his soul in Sheol, the underworld. To us this view seems still more contrary to the expressed opinions of the whole book, than that which supposes a reference to a resurrection of the body. It is liable to the preceding objections to a bodily resurrection, and is more specially contradicted by the author's representation of the state of the disembodied soul in Sheol. We have already stated, p. 123, that the author of Job entertained the common belief of the Hebrews in a certain future existence of the soul in Sheol. But it was as a mere *shade* of its former existence in the upper world. It was without hope. xiv. 19, xvii. 11–16, xxi. 26, and had a mere consciousness of existence, without activity or enjoyment. x. 21, 22, xiv. 11–14. So in Ps. vi. 5. "In Sheol, who can give thee thanks?" Is. xiv. 10. "Art thou also become weak as we?"

No doubt it would be agreeable to every Christian interpreter to find the doctrine of a blessed immortality beyond the grave in every ancient book. But why believers in Christ should wish to force it into books where it does not exist, it is not easy to perceive.

25. —*my Vindicator:* גֹּאֲלִי. This term, in its primitive sense, was applied to the person whose duty it was to maintain the rights, interests, and reputation of a near relative, either by repurchasing his mortgaged inheritance, by marrying his widow, and saving his family from extinction, by redeeming him from servitude, or by avenging his blood. In this passage it is figuratively applied to the Deity, as taking the part and

vindicating the character of Job against the cruel treatment and false accusations of his friends. It is elsewhere applied to the Deity in the more general sense of *a deliverer* from calamities of any kind. The term *redeemer* might be retained, as a figurative expression for *a deliverer from reproach and calumny*; but it would be less intelligible than the term *vindicator*, and more likely to be misapplied. That there is no allusion to Christ in the term, nor to the resurrection to a life of happiness in the passage, has been the opinion of the most judicious and learned critics for these last three hundred years; such as Calvin, Mercier, Grotius, Le Clerc, Patrick, Warburton, Durell, Heath, Kennicott, Doederlein, Dathe, Eichhorn, Jahn, De Wette, Heiligstedt, Hirzel, and many others. — *And will stand up:* i. e. appear or interpose to decide the controversy. Ps. xii. 5, "For the sighing of the needy now will I arise, (or *stand up*,) said the Lord." xliv. 26, "Arise, (or *stand up*,) for our help, and redeem us." xciv. 16; Jer. ii. 27. — *hereafter*, or, *at last*; or, *at length; tandem*, Dathe; *postremo*, Cast.; *posthæc*, Doed. אַחֲרוֹן is used adverbially, בְּ or לְ being omitted. See Is. viii. 23, xxx. 8; Numb. ii. 31; 1 Sam. xxix. 2; Prov. xxix. 11, xxxi. 25. The rendering of the common version is entirely unsupported by usage. — *on the earth*. עַל-עָפָר. See ch. xxxix. 14, xli. 25. Lit. *upon dust*. Possibly the expression *dust* is emphatic, as contrasted with heaven, the usual residence of the Creator.

26. *And though with my skin this body be wasted away*. So Ros., Eich., and De Wette. Or, the pronoun זֹאת may agree with עוֹרִי, and the line be rendered, *And after this skin*, or *body*, *of mine is wasted away*. According to either rendering, the meaning will be, Although I should be reduced by disease and sorrow to a still lower condition than I am at present. The rendering which Gesenius adopts in his Thesaurus does not strike me favorably: *And after my body is wasted away, this* — supply *shall happen*. The expression *wasted away* does not imply the death of Job, but only that he should be extremely reduced by disease; — *without my flesh*, i. e. reduced to a skeleton.

27. — *my friend:* לִי, lit. *for me*, or *on my side*. It is so rendered in Ps. cxxiv. 1, "If it had not been the Lord, who was on our side," &c. — *and not another, &c.* i. e. in my absence, after I am dead. An emphatic expression of Job's confidence that before his death he should see the favor of God. — *For this my soul panteth within me:* lit. *my reins are consumed:* i. e. with desire to see that happy day. So Patrick, Dathe, Ros., De Wette, Ges. See Ps. lxxxiv. 2, cxix. 81, 82, cxliii. 7.

28. *And find grounds of accusation against him?* So the Sept. and Vulg. So Ros. and Ges.

XIII.

ZOPHAR, not softened by the earnest and pathetic appeals of Job, nor convinced by his solemn protestations of innocence, but rather provoked by the impressive warning with which he had closed his last discourse, proceeds to portray, by new images and striking examples, the calamities which in all ages had been the lot of the wicked. He infers that Job resembles those in character whom he resembles in condition.

Ch. XX. 10. *His sons shall seek the favor of the poor:* i. e. the poor whom their father had plundered, and who may require satisfaction or reparation. Or it may mean, generally, that they shall be so much reduced as to seek the good-will and assistance of the most destitute and abject; a stronger expression than if he had merely said that they should become poor. It is placing them below poverty itself. — *And their hands:* i. e. the hands of the children of the oppressor: lit. *his hands.* The singular pronoun is in Hebrew not unfrequently thus used. So Deut. xxi. 10, "When thou goest forth against thine enemies, and God gives *him* into thine hand." See Gesenius' Gram. § 143.

11. *His bones are full of youth:* i. e. of youthful vigor. So Ges. The same word is used in ch. xxxiii. 25; Ps.lxxxix. 45. The meaning is, He shall be cut off in his youth — in the fulness of his strength. So the Sept. The Syr. and Arab. have it *marrow.* The Chald., *strength.*

12. *Though wickedness, &c.* The wickedness in which he takes so much pleasure is avarice, with its accompanying crimes, oppression, injustice, and cruelty. The pleasure which a depraved mind has in the indulgence of its criminal inclination is compared to an epicure's enjoyment of some delicious morsel.

14. *Yet his meat shall be changed within him:* i. e. changed into something of an opposite nature, as from sweet to bitter, from nutritious to poisonous. *His meat* is riches acquired by oppression; but it is poisoned. A curse is connected with iniquitous acquisition. This is *the poison of asps* to him, even the Divine vengeance. *Scott.*

15. *He hath glutted, &c.* The original word is very forcible. The metaphor included in it is drawn from a ravenous beast devouring his prey, denoting great voracity. — *And he shall throw them up again:* as an epicure does that which he has drunk or swallowed with greediness and delight. The sudden loss of his ill-gotten wealth, and the intolerable anguish of his mind in suffering such loss, are involved in this strong

metaphor. The curse or vengeance of God will bring this punishment; *God shall cast them out of him.*

16. *He shall suck the poison of asps.* That which he greedily swallowed, as pleasant nutriment, shall be as destructive to him as the poison of asps.

17. —*rivers of honey and milk.* These are Oriental emblems of abundance and felicity. The wicked man shall not have that secure and permanent enjoyment of the good things of this life which he expected, or which is promised to the good.

18. *It is substance to be restored.* See Ges. upon תְּמוּרָה. So De Wette.

20. *Because he knew no rest, &c*: i. e. because his cupidity was insatiable.

21. *Because nothing escaped his greediness*: i. e. his rapacity. So Heath, Ros., and De Wette. —*His prosperity shall not endure.* *Non durabit bonum ejus.* Syr. *Nihil permanebit de bonis ejus.* Vulg. οὐκ ἀνθήσει αὐτοῦ τὰ ἀγαθά. Sept.

22. *Every hand of the wretched*: i. e. Every blow or wound which cometh upon the wretched. So in ch. xxiii. 2, "*My wound is deeper,*" *&c.*, is, in the original, *My hand is deeper, &c.*; the instrument being used for the effect. *Omnis dolor.* Vulg. πᾶσα ἀνάγκη· Sept.

23. *He shall, indeed, have wherewith to fill himself.* This is said sarcastically. The next line shows what sort of food he was to have. —*for his food.* בִּלְחוּמוֹ. So Schult., Ges., and Ros. See Ps. xi. 6. Similar images occur in the Koran. Thus: Qui occultant quod Deus revelavit, illi non edent in ventribus suis nisi ignem.

24. *He fleeth, &c.* This was probably a proverbial expression, like that in Latin, Incidit in Scyllam, cupiens vitare Charybdim.

26. —*is treasured up for him*: lit. *is hidden*, or *laid up*, *for his treasures.* See Rom. ii. 5.—*A fire, not blown*: i. e. not kindled by man, but sent from heaven: i. e. lightning.

27. *The heavens shall reveal his iniquity*: i. e. by lightning, for instance, such as destroyed the herds of Job, or by storms of wind, such as destroyed his children. —*And the earth shall rise up against him*: i. e. when wild beasts, venomous serpents, or bands of robbers shall destroy his substance.

XIV.

The opponents of Job had persisted in maintaining that great calamities were a proof of uncommon guilt; that they were the portion of the wicked, and of them only. This position Job overthrows, by adducing instances of impious men who pass their lives in ease and prosperity, enjoy a comfortable old age, and are favored with an easy death. Ch. xxi. 6 – 15. They might object, that the fear of reverses must mar the enjoyment of the guilty; but he contends that such reverses happen so seldom, that the bad have not more reason to fear them than the good. 16 – 18. They might say that the children of the impious man suffered, if he did not; but he asserts, with justice, that this is no punishment to the offender who is numbered with the dead. 19 – 21 He maintains, that, of two persons of the same character, one might be seen enjoying uninterrupted prosperity, and the other suffering misery without cessation; and that both came to the same end. 22 – 26. Perceiving by their looks that they were not satisfied, but still regarded his miserable condition as evidence of his guilt, he appeals to the testimony of travellers, who would mention instances of great oppressors who had escaped in a time of general destruction, and died a peaceful death; who had been buried with great pomp, and had had so splendid a monument erected to their memory that they almost seemed to flourish and live again in their very tombs. 27 – 34.

Ch. XXI. 2. *And let this be your consolation:* i. e. I will regard your candid attention as an equivalent for those consolations which I had reason to expect from you.

4. *Is my complaint concerning man?* The preposition ל means *of* or *concerning*, in Gen. xx. 13, and elsewhere. See Ges. He seems to intimate that he had not so much reason to complain of man or of his friends, as of the severe afflictions which he received from God, whilst so many wicked men enjoyed prosperity. — *Why then should I not be angry?* διατί οὐ θυμωθήσομαι; Sept. He seems to consider the fact that his misery was sent upon him by God, notwithstanding his endeavors to please him, as a sufficient reason for his impatience and complaints.

5. *Look upon me, &c.* Silent astonishment, instead of censure, should be the effect of beholding a man of integrity and piety in my afflicted condition, while so many contemners of God, and oppressors of his creatures, are happy in life and fortunate in death.

6. *When I think of it:* i. e. of what follows, viz., the prosperous condition of the wicked.

12. *They sing, &c.* יִשְׂאוּ, scil. קוֹל, *attollunt vocem.* See Is. xlii. 2.

13. *And in a moment, &c.* This assertion is opposed to Zophar's representation of the terrible death of such men, in ch. xx. 24, 25. See also ch. xviii. 12, 13. This is that sudden and easy death, in a green old age, without pain, without lingering sickness, and while their families are flourishing around them, which Tiresias predicts to Ulysses in the shades: "Death shall come to thee from the sea. It shall be a gentle death. It shall come when thou art subdued by a happy old age, and thy people about thee are happy." Odyss. xi. 133, &c. *Scott.* So Suetonius, after describing the death of Augustus, says: Sortitus est exitum facilem, et qualem semper optaverat. Nam ferè, quoties audisset cito ac nullo cruciatu defunctum quempiam, sibi et suis εὐθανασίαν similem (hoc enim et verbo uti solebat) precabatur. Life of Augustus, § 99.

16. *Thou sayest, &c.* There can be no doubt that, in the first line, at least, of this verse, Job refers to the sentiments advanced by his opponents, and probably in both. Some suppose that the first line is ironical; and that, in the second, Job expresses his abhorrence of wickedness, notwithstanding the prosperity which often accompanies it.

17. *How often happens it, &c.* This question is equivalent to the assertion that the wicked are seldom in adversity and misery. It is thus an answer to the assertion in the preceding verse.

21. *—is completed:* i. e. according to Cocceius, *is reckoned in full tale:* i. e. when he has lived out the whole term of human life.

22. *Who then shall impart knowledge to God, &c.* Shall we be so bold as to instruct God how to govern the world, and to tell him that he is not just, unless he punish the wicked when we expect it? He judges the highest beings, and therefore surely knows how to govern us. He that rules the world of spirits surely knows how to manage the little concerns of mankind.

24. *His sides, &c.* Otherwise, *His pastures are full of milk.* See Ges. upon עֲטִין. *Latera ejus plena adipe.* Arab. and Syr. τὰ δὲ ἔγκατα αὐτοῦ πλήρη στέατος. Sept. *Viscera ejus plena sunt adipe.* Vulg.

28. *For ye say, &c.* Although these questions relate to tyrannical princes in general, and to other wicked men in high stations, they are intended to be applied to Job's overthrow in particular. His adversaries still insisted that destructive calamities are the usual portion of the wicked; and that, such calamities being his portion, there was wanting no other evidence of his guilt. But the testimony of travellers, as he tells them, shows the falsity of their premises, and therefore of the conclusion drawn from them. *Scott.*

30. *That the wicked is spared in the day of destruction:* i. e. when destruction comes upon other men. So Merc., Schult., Pat., Ros., and

Ges. — *And that he is borne to his grave in the day of wrath.* See ver. 32, and x. 19. He dies a natural, peaceful death.

32. *Even this man, &c.* He is too powerful to be called to account by man, and, not meeting with chastisement from God, he goes to the grave with all the honors of interment usually paid to personages of the highest rank. *Scott.* — *Yea, he still watches over his tomb.* So Dathe, Ros., Eichhorn, and De Wette. He enjoys, as it were, a second life upon his tomb, in the honors paid to his memory, his splendid monument, and the fame he leaves behind him. *καὶ αὐτὸς ἐπὶ σωρῶν ἠγρύπνησεν.* Sept. *Et super congeriem vigilabit.* Chald. *Et in congerie mortuorum vigilabit.* Vulg.

33. — *the sods of the valley, &c.* These words also seem to suppose that the person who is buried may partake, in some respects, of the prosperous state of the tomb which contains him. See the note on ch. xiv. 22. Such an idea seems to have been indulged by Sultan Amurath the Great, who died in 1450. "Presently after his death, Mahomet his sonne, for feare of some innovation to be made at home, raised the siege, and returned to Hadrianople: and afterwards with great solemnitie buried his dead body at the west side of Prusa, in the suburbs of the citie, where he now lieth, in a chappell without any roofe, his grave nothing differing from the manner of the common Turks; which, they say, he commanded to be done, in his last will, that the mercie and blessing of God (as he termed it) might come unto him by the shining of the sunne and moone and falling of the reine and dew of heaven upon his grave." *Knolles'* Hist. of the Turks, p. 332. *Burder's* Oriental Customs, No. 507. — *And all men, &c.* In going down to the grave, he does but share the common lot of mortals. Innumerable multitudes have gone thither before him, and the succeeding generations of men shall follow him to the same place of assembly for all the living. Others suppose a funeral procession to be referred to.

XV.

Here begins the third series of controversy. Eliphaz, unable to refute the reasoning in Job's last discourse, founded as it was on undeniable facts, proceeds to misrepresent his sentiments, and even to charge him with particular crimes. He begins with an attempt to expose to ridicule Job's complaints respecting his afflictions, his assertions of his innocence, and his appeals to the Deity, as if he had set up arrogant claims upon the divine justice, and had demanded a reward for his goodness. Ch. xxii. 1–5. He goes on to assert that Job's wickedness, and not injustice on the part of the Deity, was the cause of his misery, and charges him with a variety of enormous crimes. 6–11. He also accuses him of having adopted the corrupt principles of those impious men, who, in former times, had perished by a flood, and warns him not to pursue their course, and thus incur their punishment. 12–20. In conclusion, he exhorts him to repentance, and gives a splendid picture of the prosperity to which he might look as a reward. 21–30.

Ch. XXII. 2. *Behold, the wise man profiteth himself.* Comp. xxxv. 7. Prov. ix. 12. Whatever wisdom or goodness a man has, he has the benefit of it, not God.

4. *Will he contend, &c.?* i. e. in a judicial controversy. Is he afraid that his character will suffer by thy complaints, unless, in obedience to thy citation, he submit to a trial, and argue his cause before some tribunal?

7. *Thou hast given, &c.* Among the Eastern nations hospitality was, and still is, regarded as a duty of the most sacred obligation.

8. *But the man of power had the land:* i. e. The rich were always welcome to Job; his house was open to them, and his land before them, while the poor were driven away from his house and territories. Or perhaps it is a more general proverbial expression, denoting the partiality and honor with which Job regarded the great and powerful. Or the meaning may be, Through your connivance, or influence, the great were sure to gain their cause, when they set up a claim to the land of the poor.

9. *And broken the arms:* i. e. thou hast taken away all their support. All the ancient versions render יְדֻכָּא in the second pers. sing., which makes it probable that תְּדַכֵּא was formerly in the text.

10, 11. — *snares.* This was a common metaphor for danger and destructive calamities; as *darkness* and *floods of water* for overwhelming misery.

12–20. What Job had said, in the preceding chapter, of the general impunity and prosperity of the wicked, was matter of fact. But this calumniator misrepresents his discourse, as a denial of a divine providence grounded on most absurd notions of the Supreme Being, as though he were limited in his presence, and could not see what passeth in our world. — The immense distance of heaven, the habitation of God, is represented by its being far above the stars. *Scott.*

13. *Can he govern behind the thick darkness?* Can he see, through the thick clouds, the crimes that are committed on earth, and thus inflict the punishment which they merit?

14. *And he walketh upon the arch of heaven :* i. e. He is at an immense distance from the earth, and wholly occupied in the concerns of the heavenly world. So Lucretius, Lib. II. 646.

15. *Wilt thou take the old way, &c. :* i. e. Are you willing to adopt the principles of those impious men who lived in the time of the deluge ?

16. *— cut down.* Lit. *seized, hurried away.*

17. By describing the impiety of these men in the very terms used by Job in ch. xxi. 14, 15, he confronts their exemplary destruction to Job's assertion of the impunity and felicity of such characters. *Scott.*

18. — *counsel :* i. e. purposes, plans, &c.

24. *Cast to the dust thy gold, &c. :* i. e. When thou shalt regard gold as of no account, and cease to place thy dependance upon earthly treasure, as thou hast done, and shalt place thy trust upon God alone, then, &c.

27. *And thou shalt perform thy vows :* i. e. Thou shalt obtain those blessings for which thou didst make thy vows, and accordingly perform them.

28. *And light shall shine upon thy ways :* i. e. Thou shalt have success and prosperity in all thy pursuits.

29. *When men are cast down, &c.* The meaning probably is, When men are in affliction, or in low circumstances, such shall be the efficacy of thy prayers, that God will raise them up.

30. *— him that is not innocent.* The particle אִי, rendered *island* in the common version, is used as a negative in 1 Sam. iv. 21. It is so rendered here, in the Chald., and by Le Clerc, Ros., Ges., and De Wette. The same sentiment is found in Gen. xviii. 24 ; Ezek. xxii. 30 ; Jer. v. 1. Ros. also observes, that it may be designed to refer to ch. xlii. 8, &c., where it appears that Jehovah forgave the friends of Job on account of his intercession. See the note on ch. viii. 7.

XVI.

This reply of Job is the effusion of a mind agitated by various strong emotions ; by deep grief, ch. xxiii. 2 ; by an earnest desire to argue his cause with God, since he could obtain neither justice nor mercy from his friends, 3 – 7 ; by distress, that he could not obtain his desire, 8, 9 ; by consolation in the testimony of his conscience, 10 – 12 ; and by consternation and despair, arising from the thought of God's absolute dominion, and the immutability of his designs, 13 – 17. Having in some measure relieved his mind by the foregoing effusions, he makes one effort more to convince his adversaries by reasoning with them. He denies the constancy, and even the frequency, of the judgments of God upon wicked men. He produces a catalogue of enormous crimes, such as theft, oppression of the poor, murder, adultery, and tyranny, at which, as he thinks, the Governor of the world seems to connive, by forbearing to punish the authors of them ; by suffering them to flourish during life, and to be fortunate and happy in the time and circumstances of their death. Ch. xxiv.

Ch. XXIII. 2. — *my wound:* lit. *my hand:* i. e. the hand of God upon me.

3. *O that I knew, &c.* He desires to go before the tribunal of God, as a man, whose character has been assailed, may demand a trial at an earthly bar.

6 *Would he contend, &c.?* i. e. He would not overawe me, or put me down, by his superior power, but would rather listen to what I might offer in my defence. — *would have regard:* לִבּוֹ, יָשִׂם being understood. See iv. 20, xxxiv. 23.

7. *Then would an upright man, &c.* He speaks of himself in the third person.

8, 9. These words are designed to express, not the mere invisibility of the Deity, but the earnest desire of Job, conscious, as he was, of his innocence, to obtain some visible manifestation of the Deity, and to expostulate with him, face to face, upon his unmerited sufferings. *Scott.* The Hebrews, like some other of the Oriental nations, in speaking of the different quarters of the heavens, regarded themselves as facing the East, the rising sun. Backward would then be West ; the left, North ; and the right, South. See Ges. Thes. ad אָחוֹר. — *where he worketh:* Some suppose that God is represented as working in the places northward from Job, because mankind were there most numerous, and most attentive in observing the works of God. But may there not here be an allusion to an opinion, which is known to have prevailed amongst the ancient eastern nations, that in the farthest regions of the north was a high mountain, corresponding to the Olympus of the Greeks, where was the seat or peculiar residence of God, or the Gods? See Is. xiv. 13 ; Ezek. i. 4, and the notes, and the dissertation on the subject of the Oriental opinion above referred to, appended to Gesenius's Comment. on Isaiah, vol. III. p. 316.

10. *But he knoweth, &c.* But my consolation is, that God seeth my heart and my conduct. — *he trieth me:* i. e. he examineth and proveth my character.

12. *Above my own law:* i. e. above what my own desires dictated.

14. *He performeth, &c.:* i. e. without regard to my expostulations,

pleadings, and protestations, he proceeds to inflict upon me what he had purposed to inflict. Comp. ch. x. 13, 14. — *such things:* i. e. proceedings of God's providence, as dark and unaccountable as his dealings toward me.

17. — *darkness:* i. e. affliction, misery.

Ch. XXIV. 1. *Why are not times, &c.* — *days:* i. e. such as those of the deluge, the destruction of Sodom, &c. *days* of God are days when he manifests himself in retribution or judgment for sin. Why are not the wicked visited with signal punishments, which the righteous may recognise as such? For the meaning given to עֵת, see Is. xiii. 22; Jer. xxvii. 7; Ezek. xxx. 3; Ecc. ix. 11, 12.

2. — *and pasture them.* They are so shameless, that they pasture, in public view, the flocks which they have stolen from the helpless.

4. —*from the way.* The proud rich men push the poor from the way, when they meet, and oblige them to retreat, as it were to hide themselves.

5. — *they go forth to their work:* i. e. the poor and needy, of the preceding verse, who go forth to their daily toil of seeking such roots and vegetables as the woods and mountains afford for their miserable subsistence. So Cocceius and Schultens, who refer to Ecclesiasticus xiii. 19.

6. — *the harvest:* lit. *his harvest,* referring to *oppressor*, in the next line.

7. Dr. Shaw tells us that in Arabia Petræa the day is intensely hot, and the night intensely cold. *Travels;* p. 438. 4to. *Scott.*

8. *And embrace the rock.* This exactly agrees with what Niebuhr says of the modern wandering Arabs, near Mount Sinai, *Voyage en Arabie,* tom. I. p. 187.: "Those who cannot afford a tent spread out a cloth upon four or six stakes; and others spread their cloth near a tree, or endeavor to shelter themselves from the heat and the rain in the cavities of the rocks." *Burder.*

10, 11. So *Addison*, in his Letter from Italy:

> The poor inhabitant beholds in vain
> The reddening orange and the swelling grain;
> Joyless he sees the growing oils and wines,
> And in the myrtle's fragrant shade repines;
> Starves, in the midst of nature's bounty curst,
> And in the loaden vineyard dies for thirst.

12. *And God regardeth not their prayer!* יָשִׂים, for יָשִׂים עַל לֵב, *to lay to heart, to regard.* Ps. l. 23. And, by altering the points, תִּפְלָה, *folly,*

becomes תְּפִלָּה, *a prayer;* which is the reading of two manuscripts, and of the Syriac version. So Doed. and Dathe. Others, *And God regarded not the wickedness.*

13. *Others hate the light, &c.:* lit. *These*, i. e. the following, *are among those who hate, &c.* So Merc. This is a description of criminals who practise their deeds of violence and injustice under the protection of darkness.

14. *With the light, &c.:* i. e. Very early, by day-break. Micah ii. 1, "Wo to them that devise iniquity, and work evil upon their beds! in the light of the morning they practise it."

15. *And putteth a mask upon his face.* So Juv. Sat. viii. 144.:

——— si nocturnus adulter
Tempora Santonico velas adoperta cucullo.

16. *In the daytime they shut themselves up.* See Ges. upon חָתַם. ἐσφράγισαν ἑαυτούς. Sept.

17. *The morning*, which discovers their evil deeds, is as terrible and hateful to these criminals as *the shadow of death*, or *the grossest darkness*, is to other people. — *They are familiar with:* i. e. They like and desire *the terrors of midnight darkness:* i. e. midnight darkness which is terrible to others. So Merc., Poole and Ros.

18. *Light are they, &c.:* This line expresses the speed with which he is hurried away as a retribution for his crimes, like a light substance, or a stream; or the speed with which the person escapes after the commission of a crime. —*accursed portion, &c.:* i. e. They dwell in desert and uncultivated places. —*the vineyards:* i. e. the abodes of civilized men, lest they be apprehended. The explanation of this and the following difficult verses is that adopted by Mercier, Patrick, and Ros.

20. *And iniquity, &c.* i. e. The unrighteous man is destroyed as completely as a tree, which, once broken or cut down, cannot grow again.

21. *He oppresseth the barren, &c.* He adds affliction to one who has no children to help her, and who is already afflicted with that which in those days was regarded as a curse and reproach.

22. *He taketh away:* i. e. destroyeth. See Ps. xxviii. 3; Ezek. xxxii. 20. *He riseth up:* i. e. against the mighty, and every one of them fears for his life. *Ros.*

23. *God giveth:* lit. *He giveth.* See note on ch. iii. 20. — *And his eyes are upon their ways:* i. e. God seems to smile upon them and prosper them in all their enterprises.

24. *They are exalted, &c.* The complaint is, 1. that the wicked are

advanced to great preëminence ; 2. that they are favored with a death quick and easy, which is preceded by no reverse of their prosperity, is brought on by no disease, and is embittered by no sharp and lingering pains. This indulgent circumstance is happily illustrated by the beautiful simile which closes the period. *Scott.*

XVII.

The short reply of Bildad, in the twenty-fifth chapter, asserts, in a lofty strain, the awful majesty, supreme dominion, and infinite perfection of the Deity. Hence he infers the excessive arrogance of justifying one's self before God, and impeaching the rectitude of his government. His remarks are directed against the conduct of Job in calling upon God for a trial, and in using arguments which seemed to call in question God's justice. He does not attempt to answer the assertions of Job, in the last chapter, respecting the prosperity of the wicked. These were founded on facts which could not be denied, and which could not be explained on the principles of Job's opponents. It is, therefore, probable that the poet assigned this last feeble effort to Bildad, merely in order to give occasion to the triumph of Job in the chapter following.

Ch. XXV. 2. *He maintaineth peace in his high places:* i. e. He ruleth all the inhabitants of heaven in peace and harmony. Ch. xxi. 22.

3. — *his hosts?* i. e. the stars, as is probable from the parallel line ; or his angels. See Dan. iv. 35. — *And upon whom doth not his light arise?* Some suppose that this line is intended to set forth the glory of God in general, as manifested in the universal diffusion of light ; as, in ch. xxxvi. 30, he is said *to spread around himself his light*, and, elsewhere, *to cover himself with light, as with a garment,* and *to dwell in the light which no man can approach unto.* Others, that it expresses the omniscience of God ; that it represents his light as penetrating everything, and making everything known. Others, that *his light* here denotes *his sun.*

5. *Behold, even the moon, &c.* So the Vulg., *Ecce, luna etiam non splendet.* Comp. Is. xxiv. 23.

XVIII.

Job begins his reply with sarcasms upon his last opponent, as having offered nothing relevant to the subject in dispute. He then endeavors to show that, if the question related to the power and perfections of the Deity, he could speak in as lofty a style as his opponents of the effects of the divine power in heaven, earth, and the regions under the earth. His purpose is to show that his confident assertions of his innocence are by no means inconsistent with the most exalted views of the wisdom and power of the Governor of the world; that he adores the perfections of God, and yet denies that his misery is a proof of his guilt.

Ch. XXVI. 2. —*the weak.* There has been a doubt to whom this ironical expression is to be applied; whether to Job, to the other two opponents of Job, or to the Deity. From the connection, verse 4, and from the design and tenor of the whole chapter, it seems most probable that Job refers to himself.

4. *For whom, &c.:* i. e. Do you think me ignorant of the perfections of God, that you address me on the subject with such a magisterial air? or *By whom,* i. e. by whose aid, &c. —*And whose spirit spake through thee?* i. e. To what extraordinary inspiration canst thou pretend?

5. —*the shades:* i. e. ghosts, departed spirits, the inhabitants of Hades, or the under-world, whom the ancient Hebrews conceived of as without strength and with little sensation, mere shadows of what they once were · εἴδωλα καμόντων. See Ps. lxxxviii. 10; Prov. ii. 18, ix. 18, xxi. 16; Is xiv. 9, 10, xxvi. 14, 19. —*tremble:* i. e. at the majesty and power of God. The verb חול is often used in this sense, and is so rendered in the common version, in Hab. iii. 10. — *the waters, &c.:* i. e. the seas and all the monsters that inhabit their lowest depths.

6. *The under-world — Destruction.* These are different words, expressing the same thing, viz. the abode of departed spirits, which was supposed to be a vast cavern, far in the interior of the earth. See the passages referred to in the preceding note, and Jahn's Archæology, §§ 203 and 207. With this description of the Hebrew poet, compare the passage on the same topic, quoted by Longinus from Homer, as one of unrivalled sublimity. Iliad, xx. 61.

7 *He stretcheth out the North* · i. e. the northern hemisphere, or the

whole visible heaven, like a canopy or tent. Is. xl. 22. — *upon no hing:* i. e. without anything to support it.

And earth self-balanced from her centre hung.

8. *He bindeth, &c.:* i. e. He collecteth the waters into the clouds, as it were, in bottles or vessels, which do not let them fall until he is pleased to send them, drop by drop, upon the earth.

9. — *the face of his throne:* i. e. the clear sky, which is sometimes covered with clouds. Is. lxvi. 1, "The heaven is my throne."

10. *He hath drawn a circular bound, &c.* The ancients seem to have believed that only the northern hemisphere enjoyed the light of the sun, and that all below the horizon was in perpetual darkness. They also supposed that the earth was surrounded by water, upon which the concave of heaven seemed to rest, and hence the idea of a circular bound, drawn, as it were, by compasses at the extreme verge of the celestial hemisphere, where the light was supposed to end, and the darkness to begin. See Virg. Georg. I. 247.

11. *The pillars of heaven tremble.* Some suppose that the mountains of the earth, upon which the sky seems to rest, are intended; but it is more probable that the vault of heaven is represented as an immense edifice, supported on lofty columns, like a temple. — *his rebuke:* i. e. thunder, lightning, and tempestuous winds, which were supposed to be tokens of God's displeasure.

12. — *he smiteth its pride:* i. e. he restrains its rage, and turns a storm into a calm. So Is. li. 15.

13. — *the fleeing Serpent:* i. e. *the fugacious, fugitive serpent;* an epithet borrowed from the living serpent, but referring to the constellation of the great Serpent or Dragon in the Northern hemisphere. The reader will remark the coincidence of this epithet with the word *elabitur* in Virgil, Georg. I. 244.

14. *Lo! these are but the borders of his works:* i. e. We are acquainted only with the surface and outlines of the works of God. — *How faint the whisper, &c.:* i. e. How very little do we know concerning the divine operations! — *But the thunder of his power.* By this expression I understand *the higher exertions of his power*, as opposed to its ordinary operations, with which we are in some measure acquainted. The meaning thus will be, that what is known of God's works is to that which is unknown as a whisper to a peal of thunder. Others suppose that *the thunder of his power* means *the loudest and most terrible thunder.* But it is not probable that he referred to literal thunder, as a special mystery among the works of God.

XIX.

The three friends of Job now give up the discussion. Bildad, his last opponent, had said but a few words, and those in the manner of a retreating adversary. He had also been triumphantly driven, as it were, from his ground by Job. Zophar, therefore, is represented as thinking it prudent to make no reply. From this discomfiture of his opponents, Job, taking courage, goes on to express his feelings and views, in a more calm, but not less decided manner than before. He begins with a renewed and solemn declaration of his innocence, and expresses the most resolute determination to assert it against all who may call it in question, to the very last moment of his life. Ch. xxvii. 2–7. On account of what he had said of the prosperity of the wicked, his opponents had accused him of approving them, and of envying their condition. He therefore expresses his abhorrence of a vicious character, and speaks of the satisfactions arising from virtue and piety, to which the wicked man is a stranger. 8–10. He had all along maintained, in opposition to his friends, that this world is not the scene of a regular distribution of good and evil; that virtue is often oppressed, and vice triumphant; and that the greater part of wicked men go unpunished, grow old in ease and affluence, and at length die in peace. But now, having reduced his opponents to silence, he frankly owns that there are some examples of divine vengeance, such as they had asserted; that the evils which *sometimes*, though not *always*, as they contended, are the consequences of guilt, are sufficient to deter him from envying the condition of the wicked, and from following their evil courses. 11–23. The inconsistency of Job is only apparent, proper allowance being made for strong expressions elicited by the heat of controversy. He concedes not his main position, viz., that the innocent often suffer. He holds fast his innocence, and will not let it go. He admits not the main conclusion of his opponents, viz., that human suffering always implies guilt, or that he is wicked because he is a sufferer. His present deliberate position is, that, as the virtuous do suffer, there is some mysterious cause of human suffering besides the vices of men, while he admits the correctness of the representations of his opponents respecting the ordinary consequences of sin. Thus the dispute is brought to a crisis. Without this concession, compromise, or apparent inconsistency in the language of Job, there could have been no end to discourses on the miseries of sin, on the one hand, and the prosperity of the wicked, on the other.

The difficulty, therefore, which has puzzled so many critics, and led Dr. Kennicott to propose an important alteration in the text, proves to be a necessary part of the plan of the profound and ingenious author of the book.

The subject of the next chapter is wisdom : i. e. that high, absolute Divine wisdom, which formed the plan, and directs all the concerns, of the Universe. Job had allowed, in the former chapter, that God makes examples of some wicked men. He had maintained, in ch. xxi., that others equally guilty escape with impunity. He had also asserted, in ch. ix. 22, that general calamities involve the best and the worst men in one common destruction. These are perplexing appearances. Hence his thoughts are naturally led up to those impenetrable counsels which direct all this seeming confusion. The powers of the human mind have made surprising discoveries in natural things. Man has penetrated the bowels of the earth, and surmounted the greatest obstacles for the purpose of obtaining the treasures hidden in those regions of darkness. But all the riches of the world cannot purchase, nor the highest genius and industry of man attain, the knowledge of the whole plan of Providence in the administration of the world, or the reasons for which he sometimes sends calamities upon individuals. Only He can comprehend the whole to whom are known all his works from the beginning. The inference is, that instead of prying into mysteries which he cannot understand, the duty of man is to adore his Maker, and obey his commandments. This is the wisdom proper to man.

Ch. XXVII. 2. —*who hath rejected my cause :* i. e. who hath refused me justice.

4. —*deceit :* i. e. the deceit of confessing guilt, of which he is not conscious.

6. *I will hold fast, &c.* I will continue to assert it, or I will not acknowledge that I am guilty. I will be as tenacious of it as a good soldier is of his shield. The original term for *hold fast* is the same as that used in Ps. xxxv. 2, in connection with a shield. —*My heart, &c.* *οὐ γὰρ σύνοιδα ἐμαυτῷ ἄτοπα πράξας.* Sept. *Neque enim reprehendit me cor meum in omni vitâ meâ.* Vulg.

8. —*cutteth off his web, &c.* This metaphor seems to be drawn from the weaver, who, when his web is finished, cuts it off from the thrum by which it was fastened to the beam. See vi. 9 ; and Is. xxxviii. 12. Otherwise, *when he hath gotten plunder.* —*taketh away his life.* lit. *draweth out his life :* i. e. as a sword from its sheath. Schnurrer conjectures that יֵשֶׁל is contracted for יִשְׁאַל, in which case the meaning will be, *demandeth his life.*

12. — *vain thoughts :* i. e. such as they had expressed, when they maintained that suffering was a sure proof of guilt, or that Job was suffering the punishment of a grossly wicked man, such as he goes on to describe. See the introductory remarks to this chapter.

13. The passage from this verse to the end of the chapter presents a difficulty ; since, at first view, Job seems to renounce his former sentiments, and to adopt those of his opponents. One method of explaining it, satisfactory to me, is given in the introduction to this chapter.

14. — *it is for the sword :* i. e. they shall be slain in war.

15. — *shall be buried by Death :* i. e. they shall have no grave-digger but Death; or, they shall be unburied. See Jer. xvi. 4. Others render it, *shall be brought to the grave by the pestilence.* θάνατος sometimes has this meaning in the Apocalypse.

16. *And procure raiment as clay.* It was the custom of the ancients to lay up raiment in their treasuries as well as gold and silver. So Virgil of Messapus, Æn. ix. 26. :

Dives equûm, dives pictaï vestis et auri.

It is customary through all the East, says Sir J. Chardin, to gather together immense quantities of furniture and clothes ; for their fashions never alter.

18. — *like the moth.* The house and family of the oppressor shall not be more durable than the slight fabric which the moth makes in a garment, and which is destroyed when the garment is moved or shaken. See Dr. Harris's Nat. Hist. of the Bible, p. 297. — *Or like the shed, &c. :* which was made for the watchman of a garden, whose business it was to defend the fruit from birds and beasts while it was ripening, and which was taken down when the fruit was gathered. See Is. i. 8. Niebuhr, in his Description of Arabia, p. 139, says, " In the mountains of Yemen they have a sort of nest in the trees, where the Arabs sit to watch their fields after they have been planted. But in the Kehama, where there are but few trees, they build a light kind of scaffolding for this purpose." Mr. Southey opens the fifth part of his Curse of Kehama with a similar allusion, quoted by Dr. Good :

Evening comes on : arising from the stream,
Homeward the tall flamingo wings his flight ;
And where he sails athwart the setting beam,
His scarlet plumage glows with deeper light.
The watchman, at the wished approach of night,
Gladly forsakes the field, where he, all day,
To scare the winged plunderers from their prey,
With shout and sling, on yonder clay-built height,
Hath borne the sultry ray.

19. *The rich man lieth down:* i. e. dies. —*and is not buried:* lit. *not gathered:* i. e. as the slain are gathered in battle for burial. —*In the twinkling of an eye he is no more:* lit. *He openeth his eyes, and is no more.* So Merc., Ges., and Ros.

Ch. XXVIII. 2. *And stone is melted into copper.* So Pliny, Nat. Hist. xxxiv. 1, 22, and xxxvi. 27, 66: Æs fit ex lapide æroso, quem vocant Cadmiam; et igne lapides in æs solvuntur.

3. *Man putteth an end to darkness:* i. e. The darkest recesses of the earth are made light by torches, carried thither by man. —*For the stone of darkness.* Schultens supposes the centre of the earth to be denoted by this expression. Others, the metallic ore in the darkest parts of the earth.

4. *From the place where they dwell:* מֵעִם גָּר. Following Schultens, who assigns to גָּר a meaning from the Arabic, I formerly rendered these words, *From the foot of the mountain.* The present rendering is according to the common meaning of the Hebrew terms. Gesenius supposes the expression to be elliptical for מֵעִם אֲשֶׁר גָּר שָׁם, lit. *From there where one dwells:* i. e From the surface of the earth, the abode of man. This corresponds with the last line of the verse, *they swing away from men.* —*a shaft:* i. e. a passage leading into a mine. —*Forgotten by the feet:* i. e. unsupported by the feet. They do not descend by their feet, but are let down by ropes or baskets.

5. -*torn up, &c.:* i. e. Effects are produced by man, in excavating the earth, similar to those produced by subterranean fires. So Pliny: Persequimur omnes ejus (terræ) fibras, vivimusque super excavatam. . . . Imus in viscera ejus, et in sede Manium opes quærimus, tanquam parum benignâ fertilique, quaquâ calcatur [perhaps, secatur]. Hist. Nat. xxxiii. 1.

7. *The path thereto:* i. e. to the place of sapphires, gold ore, &c. Verses 7 and 8 are probably designed to illustrate the intrepidity of man in penetrating these dangerous regions of darkness. The most far-sighted birds could not see them, or find their way to them. The most daring beasts of prey would not venture into them. *Vulture:* I think it better to rely on the Sept. and other ancient versions as to this meaning, than on uncertain etymological conjecture.

9. *Man layeth his hand, &c.* This and the following verses describe the immense labor and difficulty of working a mine. Man overcomes every obstacle which nature has placed in his way.

10. *He cleaveth out streams, &c.* This was done either for the purpose of drawing off the water which impeded their operations, or of washing the impure ore.

11. *—bindeth up the streams, &c.:* i. e. the water which trickles down the shaft of the mine.

12. *But where shall wisdom be found?* Having given an imposing view of the powers of man in regard to natural things, he proceeds to give as emphatic a representation of his inability to fathom the counsels of God, or to understand the reasons which direct him in the government of the world, particularly in the distribution of happiness and misery.

13. *Man knoweth not the price thereof:* i. e. He hath no means or ability to obtain it.

21. *And kept close from the fowls of the air:* i. e. The residence of wisdom is beyond the flight of the swiftest and strongest birds. This is saying, in a poetical and perhaps a proverbial manner, that this wisdom is not to be found within the limits of our world. *Scott.*

22. *Destruction and Death:* i. e. the under-world, Hades. — *We have heard a rumor, &c.:* i. e. It is at such an immense distance from us, that we have only heard a rumor respecting it.

23. *God knoweth the way to it:* i. e. God only knoweth the reasons of his dispensations to men.

27. *— and make it known:* i. e. to his angels. Or, He made his wisdom visible in his works.

28. *— that is wisdom:* i. e. The wisdom of man does not consist in the knowledge of the reasons of the divine government, but in piety and holiness.

XX.

Job now returns to his own case, as a striking illustration of the mysterious ways of Providence, of which he had spoken in the last chapter. His aim is to show that all his pleadings and complaints were well founded. He beautifully descants upon his former prosperity, ch. xxix., and exhibits the striking contrast between it and his present affliction and debasement, ch. xxx. Lastly, in answer to the unfounded insinuations and false charges of his friends, he relates the principal transactions of his past life, asserts his integrity, as displayed in the discharge of all his duties relating to God and man, and again appeals to the omniscience and justice of God in attestation of his sincerity. Ch. xxxi. *Lowth.*

Ch. XXIX. 3. *When his lamp shone over my head.* The houses of Egypt, according to Maillet, are never without lights in the night-time. If such were the ancient custom, not only of Egypt, but of the neighboring countries of Judea and Arabia, it will strongly illustrate this passage. Mr. Scott, however, thinks that there is probably an allusion to the lamps which hung from the ceiling in the banqueting rooms of the wealthy Arabs. — *walked through darkness.* Here is reference probably to the fires, or other lights, which were carried before the caravans in their night-travels through the deserts. The extraordinary favor of God and his protecting care are denoted by the metaphors in both parts of this verse.

4. *The autumn of my days,* i. e. the ripeness, the maturity of my age. Comp. the Greek ὀπώρα. Or *autumn* may refer to the time of his greatest outward prosperity ; of the ripest fruits of life.

6. *When I bathed, &c. :* i. e. When streams of milk met me, as it were, wherever I went. Olive groves and abundance of cattle made the principal wealth of the Arabs. The best olives grew upon the rocky mountains. Hence the bold figures by which the Arabs express a condition of uncommon felicity. See Deut. xxxii. 13, 14. *Scott.*

7. — *to the gate :* i. e. the forum, or place where the courts were held. — *And took my seat, &c.* "Job here speaks of himself as a civil magistrate, who had a seat erected for him to sit upon whilst he was hearing and trying causes ; and this was set up in the street, in the open air, before the gate of the city, where great numbers might be convened, and hear and see justice done. The Arabs, to this day, hold their courts of justice in an open place under the heavens, as in a field, or a market-place." *Burder's* Oriental Customs, No. 515.

8. *The young men, &c.* Savary, in his Letters on Egypt, Vol. I. p. 149, says, "The children are educated in the woman's apartment, and do not come into the hall, especially when strangers are there. Young people are silent when in this hall ; if men-grown, they are allowed to join the conversation ; but when the Sheik begins to speak, they cease, and attentively listen. If he enters an assembly, all rise ; they give him way in public, and everywhere show him esteem and respect." — *And the aged arose and stood.* This is a most elegant description, and exhibits most correctly the great reverence and respect which was paid, even by the old and decrepit, to the holy man in passing along the streets, or when he sat in public. They not only rose, which in men so old and infirm was a great mark of distinction, but they stood ; they continued to do it, though the attempt was so difficult. *Lowth.*

14. *I clothed myself, &c.* i. e. I was clothed with righteousness, as with a garment without, and it wholly filled me within. I was altogether

righteous within and without. This meaning is made probable by the paronomasia of the Hebrew, and also by such expressions as Judges vi. 34. "The spirit of Jehovah *put on* Gideon." By altering the vowel points so as to change the conjugation from kal to hiphil, one might sustain the rendering of the common version. — *robe and diadem.* A proverb still in use among the Arabs is, "Knowledge is a diadem to a young person, and a chain of gold about his neck." *Scott*, referring to Schultens.

18. — *I shall die in my nest.* Schultens remarks that the image is taken from the eagle, who builds his nest on the summit of a rock. Security is the point of resemblance intended. See ch. xxxix. 27, 28; Numb. xxiv. 21; Obad. ver. 4.

19. *My root is spread, &c.* A tree planted by the rivers of waters, and bringing forth its fruit in its season, is a beautiful emblem of prosperity. See Ps. i. 3. The dews, which fall very plentifully in the night, contribute greatly to the nourishment of vegetables in those hot climates where they have scarcely any rain during the summer. *Scott.*

20. *My glory is fresh.* A flourishing evergreen was the image in the preceding verse, and is carried on in this. — *And my bow gathers strength in my hand.* By the state of the weapons commonly used, the Orientals express the condition, as to strength or weakness, prosperity or adversity, of the person who uses them. See Gen. xlix. 23, 24. The figure is very common in Arabic poetry, as may be seen in Schultens' note upon this verse.

22. *When my speech dropped down upon them.* So Deut. xxxii. 2, "My doctrine shall drop as the rain." So Homer speaks of Nestor's eloquence, Iliad, I. 249.:

Τοῦ καὶ ἀπὸ γλώσσης μέλιτος γλυκίων ῥέεν αὐδή·

Words, sweet as honey, from his lips distilled. ***Pope.***

So also Milton, Par. Lost, II. 112.:

—— though his tongue
Dropt manna, &c.

23. *They waited, &c.*: i. e. They waited for my opinion with the same eager desire with which the husbandman doth the showers after he hath sown his seed; they gaped for it, as the thirsty earth doth for the latter rain to plump the corn. *Patrick.* Among the Egyptians, the heavens pouring down rain or dew was the hieroglyphic of learning and instruction. *Burder.*

24. *If I smiled upon them, they believed it not.* The reverence in

which I was held was so great, that, if I laid aside my gravity and was familiar with them, they could scarcely believe that they were so highly honored; my very smiles were received with awe. — *Nor did they cause the light of my countenance to fall.* In the Scriptures *to lift up the light of the countenance* means to show favor. The opposite expression, therefore, *to cause the light of the countenance to fall*, must mean to provoke displeasure by unbecoming behavior; to bring a cloud upon the countenance.

25. *When I came among them:* lit. *I chose their way;* the particle אִם being understood. Or rather it is a common idiom of the Hebrew to omit the conditional particle, just as when in English one puts the verb before the pronoun. *Smiled I upon them, then they believed it not. Came I among them, then I sat, &c.*

Ch. XXX. 1. —*younger than I.* The veneration paid to the aged by the Orientals quickened their sensibility with respect to contempt and indignities offered by the young.

2. *Of what use, &c.:* i. e. If I have a mind to employ them, they are so reduced and enfeebled by their wretched condition as to be incapable of rendering me service. *Old age, &c.:* i. e. who are so much emaciated by famine, as to have no hope or prospect of old age.

3. —*famished:* גַּלְמוּד, primarily, *hard;* and is applied to a dry, stony soil; and hence it denotes, *barren, dry, emaciated,* according to the connection. It occurs in ch. xv. 34, and Is. xlix. 21. — *The darkness of desolate wastes:* more literally, *Darkness, wasting, and desolation;* or, *The night of wasting and desolation.* See note on ch. iii. 7. See Merc. or Ges. upon אֶמֶשׁ.

4. —*purslain.* It is most probable that it denotes the plant *atriplex halimus*, or sea-orach, or purslain, which Dioscorides describes as a kind of bramble without thorns, the leaves of which used to be boiled and eaten. It has a saltish taste. מַלּוּחַ is a denominative from מֶלַח, *salt.* So we have in English *salad*, and in French, German, Italian, *salade, salat, insalata.* See Harris's Nat. Hist. of the Bible, p. 285. —*the broom.* This is a plant abounding in the desert and sandy plains of Egypt and Arabia. Its root is very bitter. See Ros.

8. —*beaten:* i. e. driven out with blows.

10. —*spit before my face.* The association between *spitting* and *shame* is such now in the East that we can scarcely conceive of it. Monsieur d'Arvieux tells us, "The Arabs are sometimes disposed to think, that, when a person spits, it is done out of contempt; and they never do it before their superiors." But Sir J. Chardin's MS. goes much farther.

He tells us, in a note on Numb. xii. 14, that "spitting before any one, or spitting upon the ground in speaking of any one's actions, is, through the East, an expression of extreme detestation." It was probably all that the law required in Deut. xxv. 9. בְּפָנָיו often denoting *before one, in one's presence*. See Josh. xxi. 44, xxiii. 9; Esth. ix. 2. See Harmer's Observ. ch. xi., obs. xcviii.

11. *They let loose the reins, and humble me.* They insult and afflict me without restraint, and in an unbridled manner. Thus the meaning is the same as that of the other clause of the verse.

12. — *the brood.* The youth are thus called by way of reproach. *They cast up against me their destructive ways.* The metaphor is drawn from the advance of a besieging army against a city.

13. *They break up my path:* i. e. They oppose all my plans, and hinder me from taking any course for my relief or benefit. — *They that have no helper!* Schultens has shown that the phrase, *one who has no helper*, was proverbial amongst the Arabs, and denoted a worthless person, or one of the lowest class. It is probably so used here.

15. *They pursue my prosperity:* i. e. They come upon me with unrelenting violence, destroying my peace. The image is borrowed from a person buffeted by a violent storm.

16. — *poureth itself out upon me.* So in Ps. xlii. 4. In our language we say that one is *dissolved* in grief. The foundation of the metaphor is, that in excessive grief the mind loses, as it were, all consistence. The Arabians style a fearful person *one who has a watery heart*, or *whose heart melts away like water.*

17. — *my gnawers:* i. e. my gnawing pains. *Et qui me comedunt non dormiunt.* Vulg.

18. — *is my garment changed:* i. e. his skin which was affected by the leprosy, so that he cou'd scarcely be recognised. Some, however, suppose the meaning to be that his outer garment, the mantle, had become close like the tunic. Schultens renders it, *it* (pain) *hath become my garment.* He has shown that it is a common metaphor in Arabic poetry. It agrees well with the parallel clause. — *like the collar of my tunic.* The allusion probably is to that kind of Eastern tunic which was seamless, and all of a piece, and had an opening at the top, with a sort of collar which was fastened close around the neck. Comp. Exod. xxviii. 32.

19. — *I am become like, &c.:* i. e. more like a mass of inanimate matter than a living man. See ch. ix. 31, and note.

20. *I stand up.* Standing being the usual posture of prayer amongst the Hebrews, *to stand*, or *stand up*, is sometimes used for *to pray*, as Grotius remarks in his note on Matt. vi. 5. See Gen. xviii 22; Jer. xv. 1. *Scott*

22. *Thou liftest me up, &c.* He represents his miseries under the image of a person caught up into the air by a tempest, and driven like stubble, or like a cloud, by the wind. — *Thou meltest me away:* i. e. my strength of body and mind. Thou leavest nothing solid or firm in me. Some think this to be a continuation of the metaphor in the first clause, referring to a cloud, which, having been driven about by the wind, melts away and disappears. — *in the storm:* or more literally, *the rattling*, or *clashing*, or noise of the tempest. With considerable hesitation I have concluded to adopt this rendering, proposed by Stuhlmann, in his Translation published in Hamburg, 1804, as being on the whole more probable than any of the various meanings assigned to the Hebrew in ancient or modern versions. It is obtained by altering the vowel points so as to read תְּשֻׁוָּה, and regarding this as equivalent to תְּשֻׁאָה, or תְּשׁוּאָה, which is found in the plural in xxxv. 29, referring to the *noise, rattling*, or *clashing* of Jehovah's tabernacle, and xxxix. 7 referring to the shoutings of the driver, and in Is. xxii. 2 to the *tumult* of a multitude, and in Zech. ix. 7 to *shouts* of joy. As to the omission of the א, which this rendering supposes, it occurs often in Job. See xxii. 29, xxxi. 35, xxxiii. 17, xxxiv. 36, xxxix. 7. A considerable number of modern Hebraists, such as Ewald, Heiligstedt, Hirzel, Schlottman, and others have adopted this rendering. If it be liable to objections, are not other renderings liable to greater? The rendering of the Common Version — *my substance*, or the similar rendering — *my safety — my strength, &c.* involves the unusual construction, Thou meltest *me* away *as to* substance or safety, and besides is not in accordance with the preceding figure.

24. For a defence of this rendering, see Ros., and Ges. Lex. upon בְּעִי. It is also adopted by De Wette.

26. *But when I looked, &c.* He expected to be made happy all his life, through the divine benediction, on account of his charity and other virtues; but, instead of that, he was made most miserable.

27. *My bowels boil, &c.* These expressions, in their literal meaning, describe the violent inward heat caused by his inflammatory disease. They may likewise include the ferment of his mind ever since his afflictions came upon him. *The heart* and *the reins*, in the Oriental figurative style, denote the thoughts and passions. *Scott.*

29. *I am black, but not by the sun.* His disease had made his complexion as swarthy as that of the poor laborers in the field, who are exposed to the scorching sun in that hot climate; and so sharp were his pains, that he was obliged to shriek out, even in a public assembly.

29. *I am become a brother to jackals:* i. e. I am like the jackal with respect to his mournful cries. Dr. Shaw observes that jackals make a

hideous howling in the night. Dr. Pococke observes, in his note upon Micah i. 8, "The ancient Syriac describes it by a word, which, in that language, as their own authors tell us, signifies a kind of wild beast, between a dog and a fox, or a wolf and a fox, which the Arabians call, from the noise they make, *Ebn Awi*, or *wawi*, and our English travellers and other Europeans, by a name borrowed from the people of those countries, where they are more known than in Europe, *jackales*, which, abiding in the fields and waste places, make in the night a lamentable howling noise, insomuch that travellers, unacquainted with them, would think that a company of people, women or children, were howling one to another, as none that have travelled in those parts of Syria, &c., can be ignorant. This translation seems to carry more reason with it than the rendering it *dragons;* because of *the hissing of dragons*, as of other serpents, we hear and read, but nowhere in any creditable author of their *howling*, or making such a noise as may be called *wailing*, or like to it." See also תַּן in Ges. Lex., and Harris's Nat. Hist. p. 113. — *And a companion to ostriches. Companion* is used like *brother* in the preceding line, to denote resemblance. See Ges. upon יַעֲנָה. "During the lonesome part of the night," says Dr. Shaw, "they (the ostriches) make very doleful and hideous noises; which would sometimes be like the roaring of a lion; at other times it would bear a nearer resemblance to the hoarser voice of other quadrupeds, particularly of the bull and the ox. I have often heard them groan as if they were in the greatest agonies." *Shaw's* Travels, Vol. II. p. 348. 8vo.

30. —*is black, and falleth from me:* lit. *is black from upon me.* Construct. Præg.

31. *My harp, &c.* These were probably proverbial expressions, denoting a change from happiness to misery.

Ch. XXXI. The apology of Job in this chapter, says Mr. Scott, which turns chiefly on his behavior in private life, is not the effusion of vanity and self-applause. It is, in regard to his antagonists, necessary self-defence and solid refutation. Yet I think, from its connection with the foregoing account of his sufferings, and from verses 35-37, his favorite design evidently is to show that God *had multiplied his wounds without cause.* In this view he is chargeable with justifying himself more than God; that is, with making his own cause to be more just than that of Providence. If we except this fault, however, the picture which he has drawn is a masterly piece of moral painting. Nothing can be more finished and amiable than the character here represented. It is an exemplification of the most disinterested virtue, inspired and ennobled by the most rational and exalted piety. In short, this apology may be justly styled a fine epitome of morality and religion.

1. *How then, &c.* : or, *That I would not, &c.*

6. *Let him weigh me, &c.* Some suppose this verse to be parenthetical, and that the imprecation in verse 8 relates to verse 5, as well as to verse 7. Others, that this verse includes a tacit imprecation : *Let him weigh me, &c.*, and if I am found guilty, *May he do so to me, and more also !*

7. —*from the way :* i. e. of rectitude. — *Or if any stain :* i. e. any unjust gain. If I have taken the property of others by fraud or violence. The Sept. renders the clause, *If I have touched gifts with my hands :* i. e. taken bribes.

9. — *a woman.* *A woman* here means a married woman. It stands opposed to *a maid* in verse 1, and is rendered *wife* in ver. 10. — *watched, &c.*, to see when the husband was absent, and when there was an opportunity for committing adultery.

10. *Then let my wife grind for another :* i. e. let her be his abject slave. The ancients ground their corn with hand-mills. This was the work of female servants. See Ex. xi. 5 ; Is. xlvii. 2 ; Matt. xxiv. 41.

12. *Yea, it were a fire, &c.* The commission of such a crime would have provoked God to send destruction, like a consuming fire, upon my family and estate. See Ps. lxxxiii. 14.

14. — *riseth up :* i. e. as a judge, to inquire into and punish the sins of men.

16. *Or caused the eyes of the widow to fail :* i. e. If I refused her the relief which she implored of me with earnest eyes.

17. *Have I eaten my morsel alone ?* " No sooner was our food prepared, whether it was potted flesh, boiled with rice, a lentil soup, the red pottage, Gen. xxv. 30, or unleavened cakes, served up with oil or honey, than one of the Arabs, after having placed himself on the highest spot of ground in the neighborhood, calls out thrice with a loud voice to all their brethren, *the sons of the faithful*, to come and partake of it, though none of them were in view, or perhaps within a hundred miles of them." *Shaw's* Travels, Vol. I. p. xx. Burckhardt informs us that in Kerek, a city in Arabia, " when a stranger enters the town, the people almost come to blows with one another, in their eagerness to have him for their guest; and there are Turks who every other day kill a goat for this hospitable purpose."

18. —*helped the widow :* lit. *assisted her*, the antecedent being in verse 16.

21. *Because I saw my help in the gate :* i. e. When, on account of my influence in the courts of justice, I could commit any act of injustice with impunity.

22. *And my fore-arm, &c.* There is a striking grandeur in this im-

precation on the arm that was lifted up to threaten an orphan in a court of justice. *Scott.* —*from its bone:* i. e. from the upper arm, to which it was appended.

26. *If I have beheld, &c.* See Deut. iv. 19. Sabaism, or the worship of the heavenly bodies, was doubtless the most ancient species of idolatry. The Arabs went early into it. They adored the sun and moon, the planets, and the fixed stars. See Encyclop. Amer. Art. *Sabaism.*

27. *And my mouth have kissed my hand.* Kissing the idol was an act of religious homage. The Mahometans, at the present day, in their worship at Mecca, kiss the black stone, which is fastened in the corner of the Beat-Allah, as often as they pass by it, in their rapid walks round that sacred building. If they cannot come near enough to kiss it, they touch it with their hand, and kiss that. This seems to be a remnant of the ancient idolatry, though not practised as such by them. The heavenly bodies, being at too great a distance for a salute of the mouth, their worshippers substituted kissing their own hands in place of that ceremony. *Scott.* Minutius Felix (De Sacrif., cap. 2, ad fin.) remarks, that, when Cæcilius observed the statue of Serapis, "according to the custom of the superstitious vulgar, he moved his hand to his mouth, and kissed it with his lips."

32. *The stranger, &c.* See note on ver. 17.

33. —*after the manner of men.* See Is. viii. 1; Ps. lxxxii. 7. Otherwise, *Have I, like Adam, hidden my transgressions.*

34. I have followed Schultens, Dathe, and Scott, in rendering this verse in the imprecatory form. Some confine the imprecation to the last line of the verse.

35-37. Job here renews the wish, which he had expressed in ch. xvii. 3, and elsewhere, that God would enter into judgment with him. He is convinced that the result of a trial would be honorable to him. "Bolder words than these Job had not uttered in the whole dispute. These provoked Elihu to renew the debate, and these are the expressions for which the Almighty chiefly reprimanded him, in ch. xl. 2, 8, taking little or no notice of the rest." *Michaelis.*

35. —*signature,* תָּו. This is the name of the Hebrew letter ת, which has the form of a cross in the Phœnician Alphabet, and on the coins of the Maccabees. See in Stuart's Grammar the Hebrew coin-letter. This mark, or cross, was used, probably, to denote the name of the person who used it, when he was unable to write his name. Hence it denotes a subscription to a writing of complaint or defence, or, by metonymy, the writing itself, as in this passage. I should understand it here a bill of defence, rather than of complaint, as Ges. explains it. Job hardly goes so far as to offer to bring a bill of complaint against God. It is more probable that he offers a bill of defence, and invites the Deity to answer

him, i. e. to refute what he has said in his defence, if he can, and to bring what charges he can against him. —*And let mine adversary, &c.:* i. e. Let the Almighty, as adversary or opponent in court, charge me with any sins on account of which I suffer my extraordinary afflictions.

36. *Truly I would wear it upon my shoulder, &c.:* i. e. Instead of being ashamed of it, or endeavoring to conceal it, I would wear it as an ornament about my person. I would glory in it, as affording me the long desired opportunity of vindicating my character.

37. —*all my steps:* i. e. the whole course of my life. —*I would approach him like a prince:* i. e. with confidence and cheerfulness, as being conscious of innocence, and not as a self-condemned malefactor, as I am regarded by my friends.

38–40. It is not improbable that these verses have accidentally been transferred from their original place in the chapter, and that the speech of Job ended with verse 37. The natural place for the passage, according to modern ideas of arrangement, would be after verse 23 or 25.

38. —*cry out against me:* i. e. to God for vengeance, because I have obtained it from its rightful owners by fraud or violence. See Gen. iv. 10; Hab. ii. 11. —*bewail together:* i. e. of my injustice in keeping the land dishonestly acquired.

39. —*without payment:* i. e. without paying the price which I promised to give the owner of the land. Or, without paying the laborers their wages. —*And wrung out the life of its owners:* Literally, *caused the life of the owners to breathe forth:* i. e. by depriving them of their land; drained their life-blood, as we should say. The common version gives the literal meaning of the words. But the expression is probably hyperbolical, meaning *to inflict great distress.*

40. —*noxious weeds:* בָּאְשָׁה, from בָּאַשׁ, *to have a bad smell.* So the Chald.

XXI.

With chapter thirty-second commences a new division of the poem, the design of which seems to be to prepare the way for the appearance of the Deity in the latter part of it. A new speaker is introduced, of whose extraction, and of whose motives for renewing the debate, an account is given in the first five verses. In the last chapter Job had triumphantly closed his defence against the accusations of his friends, and they are now represented as renouncing the discussion with him, "because he was righteous in his own eyes;" that is, because he contended that he had been guilty of no wickedness which could call down upon him the heavy vengeance of God. Elihu now steps forward, as a sort of mediator, or arbiter in the controversy. He expresses his dissatisfaction with both parties ; with Job, "because he had pronounced himself righteous, rather than God," that is, because he had defended so vehemently the justice of his own cause, that he seemed in some measure to arraign the justice of God ; and with the three friends "because they had not found an answer, and yet had condemned Job;" that is, they had concluded, in their own minds, that Job was impious and wicked, although they had nothing specific to object against his assertions of his own innocence, or upon which they might safely ground their accusation.

Elihu professes, after a slight prefatory mention of himself, to reason with Job, unbiassed either by favor or resentment. He therefore reproves Job from his own mouth, because he had attributed too much to himself ; because he had insisted too strongly upon his freedom from guilt and depravity; because he had presumed to contend with God, and had not scrupled to insinuate that the Deity was hostile to him. He asserts that it is not necessary for God to explain and develop his counsels to men; that he takes many occasions of admonishing them, not only by visions and revelations, but also by the visitations of his providence, by sending calamities and diseases upon them, in order to repress their arrogance, and turn them from those evil purposes which would end in their ruin. He seems to regard afflictions, not as punishment for past offences, nor as evidence of a guilty character; but rather as preventives of those sins which the best men sometimes commit, and as salutary discipline for the correction of those faults of which a man may be unconscious, until his attention is awakened by adversity. Ch. xxxiii. He next rebukes Job, because he had pronounced himself innocent, and affirmed that God had acted inimically, if not unjustly, towards him. He brings forward various considerations to show that the Governor of the world can do nothing inconsistent with justice and benevolence. From these considerations he infers the duty of a man in Job's situation. Ch. xxxiv. He then objects to Job, that, from the miseries of the good and the prosperity of the wicked, he has falsely and perversely concluded that there is no advantage to be derived from the practice of virtue. On the contrary, he affirms, that, when the afflictions of the just continue, it is because they do not place a proper confidence in God, ask relief at his hands, patiently expect it, nor demean themselves before him with becoming humility and submission. This observation alone, he adds very properly, (xxxv. 4,) is at once a sufficient reproof of the contumacy of Job, and a full refutation of the unjust suspicions of his friends. Ch. xxxv. Lastly, he explains the purposes of the Deity in chastening men, which are, in general, to prove and amend them, to repress their arrogance, to afford him an opportunity of exemplifying his justice upon the obstinate and rebellious, and of showing favor to the humble and obedient. He supposes God to have acted in this manner towards Job; on this account he exhorts him to humble himself before his righteous Judge, to beware of appearing obstinate or contumacious in his sight, and of relapsing into a repetition of his sin. He entreats him, from the contemplation of the divine power and majesty, to endeavor to retain a proper reverence for the Almighty, and to submit to his mysterious allotments. Ch. xxxvi., xxxvii. To these frequently intermitted and often repeated admonitions of Elihu, Job makes no reply. *Lowth.* Bouillier observes that Elihu did not hit upon the precise cause of Job's afflictions, though he gave a more rational conjecture than the three friends of Job. Thus one purpose of the poet is answered, viz. that of showing, that it is better to submit to the wisdom of Providence than curiously to pry into it

Ch. XXXII. 2. *Then was kindled the wrath.* These expressions do not mean that he was in a passion. They are the strong Oriental manner of denoting high disapprobation. At most, they signify no more than a becoming warmth. *Scott.* — *Elihu . . . the Buzite.* We know nothing more of Elihu than is here mentioned. Buz was the second son of Nahor, the brother of Abraham; and the city of this name, probably derived from the same family, is mentioned in Jer. xxv. 23, in conjunction with Dedan, which we know to have been in Idumæa. *Good.*

4. — *till Job had spoken:* Supply, *and his three friends.*

8. — *the spirit in man.* By supposing רוּחַ to mean *the divine spirit,* so as to be synonymous with *the inspiration of the Almighty,* in the other clause of the verse, the parallelism is preserved, and a sense well suited to the connection afforded. Having said, in the preceding verse, that he had expected to find wisdom in age and in experience, he now intimates that he is disappointed; that he finds that wisdom is not the attribute of age or station; that it is the gift of God; and that what is denied to the great and the aged may be found in a youth. The expressions, *the spirit*, and *the inspiration of the Almighty*, may denote the divine gift of natural genius and endowments, or extraordinary illumination from the Father of lights. The connection seems to be in favor of the latter sense here. The ancients used to ascribe all extraordinary endowments to divine assistance. Thus in Homer, a person is wise by the assistance of Minerva, &c. Milton has a similar sentiment in the preface to the *Reason of Church Government, urged against Prelaty:* "And if any man think I undertake a task too difficult for my years, I trust, through the supreme en-

lightening assistance, far otherwise; for my years, be they few or many, what imports it? So they bring reason, let that be looked on." Some render the verse thus:

There is, indeed, a spirit in man;
But it is the inspiration of the Almighty that giveth understanding.

13. *God must conquer him, not man:* i. e. Do not excuse your ceasing to reply, by alleging that the wisest course which can be taken with Job is to leave him to be humbled by God, as being too obstinate to be re claimed by man. So Scott, though not with the best taste,

Say not, "'T is wisdom that we leave to God
To humble this stiff sinner with his rod!"

Otherwise, *God hath thrust him down, not man:* i. e. Say not that ye have gone to the root of the matter, and proposed an unanswerable argument against Job, and proved him to be a bad man, by the assertion that his misery is inflicted by a just God. So Merc.

14. *And with speeches like yours will I not answer him.* Their speeches were levelled against his whole moral character, aiming to prove him a wicked man from the similarity of his sufferings to those of notoriously wicked men. Elihu takes another course. He limits his censure to Job's answers in this dispute. He fixes upon some of the most obnoxious passages, such as seemed to betray too high conceit of his own virtue, want of respect to God, and dishonorable sentiments of Providence, and takes occasion from these passages to vindicate the divine goodness, equity, and justice. *Scott.*

15. *They were confounded! &c.* Elihu here ridicules the friends of Job, because they were unable to answer him. Some suppose that Elihu here addresses an audience who were listening to the discussion, and desires them to observe the confusion of the three friends. There is no objection to this explanation, except that it is unnecessary. For the third person is often used for the first or second in Hebrew poetry, and particularly when censure or contempt is expressed. See ch. xiii. 28, xviii. 4, xli. 9.

18. *The spirit within:* i. e. My soul, which is full of ardor, and powerfully impelled to make known my views.

19. *Like bottles of new wine:* literally, *new bottles.* These bottles, being made of skin, were liable to burst, when they had become old, and were filled with new wine. See Mat. ix. 17.

21. *I will not be partial, &c.:* i. e. I will deliver my sentiments with freedom and impartiality.

22. —*take me away:* i. e. destroy me.

Ch. XXXIII. 3. — *knowledge purely:* This may mean that he utters what he knows sincerely, or that he gives a true view of the subject.

4. *The spirit of God made me, &c.:* i. e. I am thy fellow-creature, dependent like thee upon God, and therefore fit to discourse with thee upon equal terms.

6. *Behold, I, like thee, am a creature of God.* Lit. *I, like thee, am by God,* i. e. created by God. This meaning accords with that of the parallel clause. He intimates that Job might engage him upon equal terms, having nothing to fear but the strength of his arguments.

7. *Behold, my terror, &c.:* i. e. You are in no danger of being confounded by the terror of my appearance, or of being borne down by the weight of my authority. In order to see the force of this declaration, we must call to mind the bold challenge of Job in ch. ix. 34, 35, xiii. 20 – 22.

9. *I am pure, and without transgression.* Job had not used these very expressions, but he had used others equivalent to them, in ch. ix. 30, x. 7, xiii. 23, xvi. 17.

10. *Behold, he seeketh causes of hostility against me, &c.* See Ges. upon תְּנוּאָה, and Ros. He refers to the language of Job in ch. xiii. 24, 25, xiv. 16, 17, xix. 11.

11. *He putteth my feet, &c.* See ch. xiii. 27.

12. *Behold, in this thou art not right:* i. e. Your language to the Deity is wholly inexcusable. It is inconsistent with the reverence which is due to so great a Being. — *God is greater than man.* "This is one of those expressions which imply much more than is expressed. There is a kind of ironical castigation in it. As if he had said, "You talk to God as an equal; but methinks he is somewhat superior to us." *Scott.*

13. *Why dost thou, &c.* To convince Job how culpable his behavior is, Elihu argues that it is irreverent and fruitless. God, says he, will never stoop to defend his measures against murmurers, nor will he communicate the reasons of them to those who cavil at his dispensations. *Scott.*

14. *For God speaketh, &c.* He alleges another argument against striving with God. There is no just cause for it. God has sufficiently manifested his goodness and care of mankind, by the methods which he takes to show them their duty, to recover them from their wanderings, and thereby to save them from destruction. *Scott.*

16. — *sealeth up, &c.:* i. e. secretly admonishes them.

17. *And hide pride from man.* Pride may comprehend insolence towards God and towards man. But I apprehend that Elihu had his eye on the former; and that he glances at Job's too high opinion of his own rectitude and merit, which gave rise to his complaints against God. *Scott.*

18, 22. —*his life*—*his soul.* These words denote the person himself, and are equivalent to the personal pronoun *he.* See Stuart's Gram. § 186.

22. —*the destroyers :* i. e. angels of death, or the instruments or causes of death generally.

23. —*a messenger, an interpreter :* מַלְאָךְ מֵלִיץ. Some render these words *a mediating angel*, so called from being the medium of communication between God and man. As Satan is represented as going round the earth, and accusing the pious before God, it is said to be natural that good angels should be employed on errands of mercy. This may be the true meaning. But as a prophet or religious teacher is often called by this name, (see Eccl. v. 6 ; Hag. i. 13 ; Mal. ii. 7,) and is the usual person employed for the instruction of men, it is most probable that such a person is denoted here. Elihu may refer to himself, and to the office which he was then performing towards Job. Throughout his speech he is represented as thinking very highly of himself, and I am persuaded that he was thinking of himself here. —*an interpreter :* i. e. a teacher, one who makes known the will of God. —*one of a thousand :* i. e. a rare person, one well qualified to be a religious monitor. See Eccl. vii. 28. —*his duty :* i. e. what reason and religion require of a man in his situation ; repentance, submission, and prayer to God for pardon. In Cranmer's Bible, *to show him the right way.* The instruction is supposed to be effectual, as appears from the following verses.

24. —*and say, Save him :* i. e. he shall be saved.—*I have found a ransom :* i. e. I am satisfied with his repentance ; he has been sufficiently humbled by his afflictions. Whatever is a means of averting punishment, or of procuring deliverance from evil, and conciliating the divine favor, is termed in Scripture *a ransom*, or *atonement.* The intercession of Moses and the act of Phineas are so called, and here the sick man's repentance. See Ex. xxxii. 30 ; Numb. xxv. 13. So Ecclesiasticus xxxv. 3, "To depart from wickedness is a thing pleasing to the Lord ; and to forsake unrighteousness is a propitiation" (*ἐξιλασμός*).

26. —*to see his face, &c. :* i. e. to enjoy his favor. The expression is borrowed from Oriental ideas respecting kings and great men ; to be admitted into whose presence, or to see whose faces, was esteemed a mark of favor. a privilege. —*And restore unto man his innocence :* i. e. regard and treat him as innocent.

27. *He shall sing.* See Ges. upon שִׁיר.

29. *Time after time :* lit. *Twice and thrice.* The Sept. renders it, *ὁδοὺς τρεῖς, three ways*, referring to three ways in which men are said to be admonished, viz. by dreams, ver. 15, by sickness, ver. 19, and by a religious teacher, ver. 23.

Ch. XXXIV. 6. — *I am made a liar :* i e. I am regarded as a wicked man on account of my misery, notwithstanding my innocence. See ch. xvi. 8. — *My wound, &c.* See ch. ix. 17.

8. *Who goeth in company, &c. :* i. e. Who speaks like the wicked men, who call Providence in question.

> " Marmoreo tumulo Licinus jacet, at Cato nullo ;
> Pompeius parvo. Quis putet esse Deos ? "

9. *A man hath no advantage, &c.* Job had not used this language ; but in ch. ix. 22, and ch. xxi., he had expressed nearly the same sentiment.

13. *Who hath given him the charge, &c.* Elihu's first argument, to prove that God cannot be unjust, is taken from his *independence.* Were God a subordinate governor, he might be tempted to commit injuries, to gratify the avarice or resentment of his superior. *Scott.*

14. *Should he set his heart against man :* i. e. Should he deal severely with him. His second argument is from the divine *benevolence.* If God were unjust, revengeful, and cruel, the earth would be a dreadful scene of universal desolation. So in Wisdom of Sol. xi. 24 – 26, " For thou lovest all things that are, and abhorrest nothing which thou hast made ; for never wouldst thou have made anything, if thou hadst hated it. And how could anything have endured, if it had not been thy will ; or been preserved, if not called by thee ? But thou sparest all; for they are thine, O Lord, thou lover of souls ! " Others render the line, *If he had regard for himself alone.*

17. *Shall he, that hateth justice, govern ?* The argument is similar to that of Abraham, " Shall not the Judge of all the earth do right ? " Gen. xvii. 25. If God were unjust, there would be nothing but disorder and confusion in the world.

19. *How much less, &c.* So Wisdom of Sol vi. 7, 8, " For he who is Lord over all shall fear no man's person, neither shall he stand in awe of any man's greatness ; for he hath made the small and great, and careth for all alike. But a sore trial shall come upon the mighty."

20. — *yea, at midnight, &c.* The allusion seems to be to some capital city overthrown by an earthquake. — *and pass away :* i. e. into the grave. — *without hand :* i. e. by no human hand ; by the invisible power of God. See Lam. iv 6 ; Dan. ii. 34.

23. *He needeth not attend long to a man :* lit. *He doth not fix* his mind *long upon a man ;* לִבּוֹ being understood after יָשִׂים. So Ges., Dathe, and Ros. The circumstance is mentioned to illustrate the omniscience of God, and the suddenness with which he often inflicts punishment. He, in whose sight all things are naked and open, has no need of

a long and formal examination into a man's character before he proceeds to punish him.

24. — *without inquiry:* i. e. without judicial investigation, such as must be resorted to by men.

26. *In the presence, &c.:* lit. *In the place of spectators.*

28. *And caused, &c.* Others render, *So that he (God) caused the cry of the poor to come upon them.*

29. *And when he hideth his face, who can behold him?* i. e. When he withdraws his favor, who can expect or obtain help from him?

31, 32. It is observed by Scott that the petition and confession, which Elihu recommends to Job, would be highly improper for one who knows himself to be guilty of heinous crimes, but highly fit for a person who, though good in the main, has reason to suspect somewhat amiss in his temper and conduct, for which God is displeased with him. It appears plainly that Elihu did not suppose Job to be a *wicked man*, suffering for his oppressions, bribery, inhumanity, and impiety, with which his three friends had charged him.

33. — *and not he:* lit. *and not I;* by *Mimesis.* See Glass. p. 315; Stuart's Gram. § 212; ch. xviii. 4; xxxv. 3.

36. — i. e. that he may not cease to be tried with afflictions, until he is humble or penitent.

Ch. XXXV. 2. *I am more righteous than God.* Job had not used these words; but this was the amount of his complaints against God, and his justification of himself. See ch. ix. 30–35, x. 15.

3. He had already brought the charge contained in this verse, in ch. xxxiv. 9. But there he censured the complaint of Job, as an arraignment of the justice of God. Here it is considered as implying that God was under obligation to him. The charge is, that Job had in effect said: I have been more just to God than he hath been to me. I have discharged my duty to him, but have not met with a proper return from him. My innocence hath been of no advantage to me. Elihu replies, first, that so great a Being cannot possibly be hurt by the sins, or benefited by the services, of men; and, secondly, that our vice and virtue can harm or profit our fellow-mortals only. *Scott.*

4. — *thy companions:* i. e. those who entertain the same unworthy sentiments of God and his providence.

5. *Look up to the heavens, &c.* This is a sublime sentiment in a plain dress. One view, says he, of the magnificent scenery of the lofty sky will extinguish all low conceptions of its almighty Author. It will strike the mind with a vast idea of his infinite superiority to all other beings, and of the impossibility of his gaining or suffering by the good or bad behavior of his reasonable creatures. *Scott.*

9. *The oppressed cry out, &c.* He now passes to another topic, viz. Job's complaint of God's disregard of the numerous oppressions committed in the world, the authors of which he suffers to escape with impunity. Elihu replies, that when God avenges not the oppressed it is owing to their want of piety. He neglects them, because they neglect him. They murmur, but they do not pray. They are clamorous, but they are not humble. This seems an oblique hint to Job that the continuation of his sufferings was owing to his unsubmitting behavior. *Scott.*

10. *Who giveth songs in the night.* Songs are thanksgivings to God for deliverance. The term *night* metaphorically denotes affliction, as in ch. xxxiv. 25.

14. *Much less :* i. e. shalt thou be heard. He alludes to the complaints of Job in ch. xxiii. 8, &c. — *Justice is with him, &c. :* i. e. Although thou complainest that God does not appear to thee for thy deliverance, yet be assured that thy cause is known to him, and that thou shalt receive justice from him, if thou wilt only commit thyself to him.

15. *transgressions.* See Ges. upon פַּשׁ. παράπτωμα, Sept. and Theodotion ; παραπτώματα, Symmachus ; *scelus*, Vulg. Dr. Durell thinks בַּפַּשׁ to be a corruption for בְּפֶשַׁע. Some suppose that he refers to the transgressions of Job by this expression, particularly to his irreverent speeches, &c. Others, that he refers to the transgressions of the wicked, which Job had asserted to be committed with impunity.

Ch. XXXVI. 3. *I will bring my knowledge from afar :* i. e. from remote times, places, and things. I will not confine my discourse to thy particular case, but will justify God by declaring his great and glorious works of creation and providence, both in heaven and earth, and his manner of dealing with men in other parts and ages of the world. *Poole.*

4. *A man of sound knowledge.* Elihu refers to himself, and means that he is unbiassed by prejudice, and will not seek to baffle Job by sophistical arguments.

5. —*but despiseth not any.* He may refer to Job's expressions in ch. x. 3, &c.

12. — *the sword :* i. e. the sword of divine justice.

13. —*treasure up wrath.* This may mean that they retain anger, or persevere in the exercise of angry feelings, or that they treasure up the wrath of God against them. See Rom. ii. 5. —*when he bindeth them :* i. e. bringeth affliction upon them. See verse 8.

14. *with the unclean.* בַּקְּדֵשִׁים. See Ges. ad verb.

20. —*that night :* i. e. the night of death. He warns him against impatient wishes for death, and murmuring against God.

21. But let thy sufferings teach thee caution, and make thee afraid to

go on to provoke offended justice ; for thou hast done it too much already, in choosing rather to accuse divine Providence than to submit patiently to his chastisements. *Patrick*.

22. *Who is a teacher like him?* τίς γάρ ἐστι κατ' αὐτὸν δυνάστης ; Sept. *Et nullus ei similis in legislatoribus*. Vulg. The object of the remaining portion of Elihu's discourse appears to be to convince Job of his ignorance of the ways of Providence, by his ignorance of the works of creation, and to humble him for finding fault with what he did not and could not understand.

24. — *his work :* i. e. that which he does in the natural world, according to the following description. — *celebrate with songs*. שֹׁרְרוּ. See ch. xxxiii.; 27. *de quo cecinerunt viri*. Vulg. *quod laudaverunt viri justi*. Chald. See Schult. and Ges.

27. — *draweth up the drops of water :* i. e. by means of the sun, which changes water into vapor, and causes it to ascend into the air. — *Which distil rain :* i. e. These minute particles of water, drawn up by the sun in the form of vapor, *form*, or, more literally, *pour out*, rain.

29. *And the rattling of his pavilion :* i. e. the thunder. By his *pavilion*, or *tabernacle*, the clouds are intended. See Ps. xviii. 11.

30. — *his light*. See Ps. civ. 2. — *And he clotheth himself with the depths of the sea :* i. e. which he draws up to heaven, and forms into the dark clouds which are his habitation. עָלָיו is to be supplied from the preceding line. Comp. ver. 32. Otherwise, *And he covereth the bottom of the sea :* i. e. with darkness. The power of God in the highest and the lowest regions is denoted.

31. *By these :* i. e. the clouds, rain, &c.

33. *His thunder, &c.* Lit. *His noise maketh known concerning him, Yea, to the herds concerning him, who ascendeth on high.* i. e. the thunder proclaims God even to the herds as he ascends in the tempest. This rendering adopted by Ges., Hitzig, and De Wette, seems closer to th original than any previous one. Though not entirely satisfactory, i may be accepted as the most probable.

Ch. XXXVII. 1. *At this*, i. e. the thunder, lightning, &c., of which he was speaking.

2. *Hear, &c.* Some suppose, that, while Elihu was speaking, thunder is represented as being heard, and the tempest as begun, from which the Deity was about to address Job.

4. *And restraineth it not :* i. e. The lightning.

7. *He sealeth up, &c. :* i. e. The labors of the field are interrupted in consequence of these heavy and continual rains, and the husbandmen remain at home, with their hands, as it were, in their bosom. — *men whom*

he hath made: lit. *men of his work.* — *may acknowledge him;* or *may have knowledge;* viz. of their dependence upon the mighty power of God; or, that it is he who commands the snow, &c.

9. — *the South:* lit. *the secret chamber.* See ix. 9.

10. — *breath of God.* The air seems to have been regarded as put in motion by the breath of God, and hence this appellation is given to the wind, here a cold wind. When the ice is formed, the water is regarded as contracted; or what remains of it is brought into a narrower compass. But some regard the parallelism of this verse as antithetical, and suppose the meaning to be that the breath of God forms ice by cold winds, and dries up the waters by hot winds, like the Simoon.

12. *They move about:* i. e. The clouds, rain, lightning, &c.

13. *Or for the land:* i. e. what is necessary, in the course of nature, for fertilizing the earth.

16. — *the balancing of the clouds:* i. e. how the clouds are suspended in the air in such a variety of forms, and are not borne to the ground by the weight of water which they contain. From our ignorance of the works of nature, Elihu infers our incapacity of judging of the divine counsels. The same kind of reasoning is pursued in the Essay on Man:

> Presumptuous man! the reason wouldst thou find,
> Why formed so weak, so little, and so blind?
> Ask of thy mother earth, why oaks were made
> Taller or stronger than the weeds they shade;
> Or ask of yonder argent fields above,
> Why Jove's satellites are less than Jove.

18. —*firm like a molten mirror.* It must be recollected that mirrors in ancient times were made of metal highly polished. It may be asked, what conception the author of Job entertained respecting the sky, which led him to describe it as firm like a molten mirror. It has been thought that in the book of Genesis the firmament, or blue vault of heaven, is represented as a solid surface, in which the stars are fixed at equal distances from the earth. The chief support of that opinion is, I think, to be derived not so much from the Hebrew term itself, as from the circumstance that a body of waters, like a sea or ocean, seems to be represented as resting upon the firmament, which God *made.* Comp. Ps. cxlviii. 4. The Hebrew term רָקִיעַ, *firmament,* may denote a solid body, as it were, *hammered out,* or, secondarily, any substance *spread out.* See Ges. Lex. ad verb.

19. *Teach us, &c.* This seems to be addressed to Job ironically, by way of reproof for his presumption; as if he had said, We should like to learn from you, you are so well acquainted with the character and pur-

poses of God, in what manner we should address him or discourse with him. —*darkness:* i. e. the darkness of our minds, or of the subject, or both.

20. *If I should speak, &c.:* i. e. Will any one venture to repeat to him my discourses, if I undertake to complain of the ways of Providence? If any one should carry my complaints to his ear, he would certainly be destroyed for his rashness.

21. If the splendor of the firmament, illuminated by the sun, is too bright for man to behold, how can he endure the glorious majesty of its Author?

22. *From the North cometh gold.* This is the literal rendering; and, as the ancients regarded the regions of the North as the peculiar place for gold, Herod. III. 116, Plin. Nat. Hist. 6, 11, 33, 4, we need not seek a figurative sense, however well such a sense might meet the connection. It is rather harsh to use *gold* to denote *golden brightness:* harsher still to make *the North* denote *the Northern hemisphere,* or *sky.* The idea is that men can find out where gold is even in the most distant regions, and procure it; but cannot comprehend God, or endure his majesty. Comp. ch. xxviii.

23. *The Almighty, &c.* This sentiment seems to be the conclusion of the whole discourse in vindication of God. We know but very little of his nature and designs, and it is wrong to censure what we do not understand in his dispensations; especially, since we have abundant proof of his justice and goodness. —*he doth not oppress:* otherwise, *he giveth no account of his doings, &c.* Instead of יְעַנֶּה, some ancient and valuable manuscripts read יַעֲנֶה. See xxxiii. 13.

24. *Upon none of the wise in heart will he look:* i. e. who confide too much in their wisdom. I prefer the present rendering of this ambiguous line, because it better suits the parallelism. Otherwise, *Whom none of the wise in heart can behold:* i. e. they cannot endure the brightness of his majesty. See Ros. ad loc.

XXII.

WHILST Elihu was yet speaking, Jehovah himself is represented as interposing, and addressing Job from the midst of a tempest. He does not, however, at first, address him in the language of encouragement and approbation, which Job's consciousness of integrity had led him to anticipate. Job had defended a good cause in an improper manner. The design of this discourse of the Almighty is, therefore, to reprove his complaints respecting the ways of Providence; to bring him into a proper temper of mind, and thus to prepare the way for his final vindication. Jehovah does not condescend to explain or vindicate the ways of his providence, but aims to convince Job of his inability to judge of them. He requires him, who had spoken so rashly of the divine counsels, to give an explanation of some of the works of nature which are constantly presented to his view; of the nature and structure of the earth, the sea, the light, and the animal kingdom. If he were unable to explain any one of the most common phenomena of nature, it followed that he was guilty of great presumption in finding fault with the secret counsels and moral government of God. He then pauses for an answer from Job.

Ch. XXXVIII. 2. — *that darkeneth counsel:* viz. my counsels or purposes, i. e. speaketh of them in an obscure, erroneous, and improper manner. Gesenius supposes that *to darken* is a metaphorical expression for *to censure.*

7. *When the morning-stars, &c.* It was the custom to celebrate the laying of the corner-stone of an important building with music, songs, shouting, &c. See Zech. iv. 7; Ezra iii. 10, 11. Hence the morning-stars are represented as celebrating the laying of the corner-stone of the earth. They are called *morning*-stars on account of the greater brightness which they have just before the dawn. Some suppose that *morning-stars* denote *angels*, and that the expression has the same meaning as *sons of God* in the next line.

12. *Hast thou, in thy life, given charge to the morning, &c.* The transition from the sea to the morning is not so abrupt as it appears. For the ancients supposed that the sun sets in the ocean, and at his rising comes out of it again. The *morning* and *day-spring* seem to mean the same thing; and the regularity of the appearance of the morning in the east is here referred to.

13. *That it should lay hold, &c.* The first light of the sun, as it strikes upon the verge of the horizon, is represented as laying hold of the ends of the earth, and shaking the wicked out of it, as dust from a sack; light being hostile to thieves and malefactors of every kind, as darkness is favorable to them. See ch. xxiv. 14-17.

14. *It is changed, &c.:* i. e. The earth, which in the darkness of night is a mere blank, but which, when illuminated by the sun, exhibits a great variety of beautiful objects, and appears like sealing-clay which has received the stamp of the seal. — *And all things stand forth as in rich apparel.* See Cocc. Comment., and Ges. upon לְבוּשׁ. Otherwise, *And they* (the morning and day-spring) *come forth as a garment upon it.*

15. — *their light is withheld.* Darkness is the light of the wicked, i. e. that which enables them to accomplish their evil designs. Thus the

strength and courage of the wicked are prostrated by the light, which discovers their evil practices.

17. —*gates of death:* i. e. of hades, the under-world.

19, 20. For similar conceptions see Hesiod, Theog, 748.

24. —*light:* i. e. the light of the rising sun, which, in a moment, as it were, pervades and illuminates the whole hemisphere.

27. The word מֹצָא probably denotes *growth*, not *bud*, and may be omitted in the connection. Literally, *And cause the growth of the tender herb to spring forth.*

31. —*fasten the bands, &c.* Here מַעֲדַנּוֹת is supposed to be by *metathesis* the same as מַעֲנָדוֹת, from עָנַד, *to tie, to bind.* In support of this rendering, Ges. observes that the Asiatic poets often speak of the *band* of the Pleiades. The Sept. has it, δεσμὸν Πλειάδος· and the Chald., שֵׁירֵי, *chains.* —*the Pleiads* (in Hebrew, *Chimah:* i. e. *a heap*, a term corresponding to what we call *a cluster*) are a constellation in the sign Taurus, and make their appearance early in the spring; hence they were called by the Romans *Vergiliæ.* — *Orion* (*Chesil*, in Heb., i. e. *the fool, or impious one*) made its appearance early in the winter, and was considered the precursor of storms and tempests, and is hence called by Virgil *nimbosus Orion.* Æn. I. 535. According to the rendering *sweet influences*, as in the common version, the meaning is, Canst thou forbid the sweet flowers to come forth, when the Seven Stars arise in the spring? or open the earth for the husbandman's labor, when the winter season, at the rising of Orion, ties up their hands? *Patrick.* But the purport of the questions evidently is to ask Job whether his power could do what is actually done by the Almighty.

32. —*the Signs.* מַזָּרוֹת, equivalent to מַזָּלוֹת, *lodgings*, viz. of the sun, in the twelve successive months of his course; thus denoting the twelve signs of the zodiac. —*the Bear with his sons. Bear* is not the literal meaning of the Hebrew עַיִשׁ, which rather denotes *a bier*, which is the name given by the modern Arabians to the constellation of the Great Bear. They also call the three stars in its tail *daughters of the bier.* Here these three stars are called *sons.* See *Niebuhr's* Description of Arabia, pp. 113, 114.

33. —*ordinances of the heavens:* i. e. the laws regulating the places, motions, and operations of the heavenly bodies. —*their dominion:* i. e. the influence which they have in producing the changes of the seasons.

36. The transition from the phenomena of the heavens to the mind of man appeared so great, that in the first edition I departed, with others, from the usual meaning of the words, rendering this verse, *Who hath im-*

parted understanding to clouds, and given to meteors intelligence? the words being supposed to denote the regularity of the clouds in coming and going, and affording the due proportion of rain to the earth. I now regard the rendering *clouds* and *meteors* far too uncertain to be adopted. For טֻחוֹת plainly denotes *reins*, in Ps. li. 8. Besides, if we suppose the reference to be to the mind of Job in particular, the intelligence with which he was able to see and admire all the phenomena which had been recounted, the transition will not appear so very violent. See Ges. Lex. ad verb. טֻחוֹת and שֶׂכְוִי.

37. *Who numbereth the clouds, &c.* The collecting and arrangement of the clouds are expressed by a metaphor taken from a civil or military enrolment. See Ps. cxlvii. 4; 2 Sam. xxiv. 10. The clouds are metaphorically called *bottles*, as containing rain.

38. —*flows into a molten mass:* i. e. when, on account of the copious rains, the dry dust melts, as it were, into one mass.

41. —*the raven.* Bochart observes that the raven expels his young from the nest as soon as they are able to fly. In this condition, being unable to obtain food by their own exertions, they make a croaking noise; and God is said to hear it, and to supply their wants.

Ch. XXXIX. 1. —*wild goats:* i. e. the ibex or mountain-goat. It is, no doubt, the same kind of goat as that described by Burckhardt, in his Travels in Syria, p. 571: "As we approached the summit of the mountain, (St. Catherine, adjacent to Mount Sinai,) we saw at a distance a small flock of mountain-goats feeding among the rocks. One of our Arabs left us, and by a widely circuitous route endeavored to get to the leeward of them, and near enough to fire at them; he enjoined us to remain in sight of them, and to sit down in order not to alarm them. He had nearly reached a favorable spot behind a rock, when the goats suddenly took to flight. They could not have seen the Arab; but the wind changed, and thus they smelt him. The chase of the beden, as the wild goat is called, resembles that of the chamois of the Alps, and requires as much enterprise and patience."

3.— *their pains:* i. e. their young, which cause their pains.

5. The following account of the wild ass is given in Robinson's Calmet, on the authority of the Russian professors, Pallas and Gmelin: "These animals inhabit the dry and mountainous parts of the deserts of Great Tartary, but not higher than about lat. 48°. They are migratory, and arrive in vast troops to feed, during the summer, in the tracts to the east and north of the sea of Aral. About autumn they collect in herds of hundreds, and even thousands, and direct their course southward towards India, to enjoy a warm retreat during the winter. But they more usually

retire to Persia, where they are found in the mountains of Casbin, and where part of them remain the whole year. . . . They assemble in troops under the conduct of a leader or sentinel, and are extremely shy and vigilant. They will, however, stop in the midst of their course, and even suffer the approach of man for an instant, and then dart off with the utmost rapidity. They have been at all times celebrated for their swiftness. Their voice resembles that of the common ass, but is shriller."

"Xenophon says, Cyrop. Lib. I., that he has long legs, is very rapid in running, swift as a whirlwind, having strong and stout hoofs. . . . Martial gives the epithet handsome to the wild ass, 'Pulcher adest onager,' L. xiii., Epig. 100 ; and Oppian describes it as 'handsome, large, vigorous, of stately gait, and his coat of a silvery color, having a black band along the spine of his back ; and on his flanks patches as white as snow.' Mr. Morier says, 'We gave chase to two wild asses, which had so much the speed of our horses, that, when they had got at some distance, they stood still and looked behind at us, snorting with their noses in the air, as if in contempt of their endeavors to catch them.'" *Robinson's Calmet.*

9. —*the wild-ox :* רֵים, *reem.* Otherwise, *the rhinoceros.* See Harris's Nat. His. p. 421. According to others, *the wild oryx.* But it is probable, from the nature of the description, that an animal of the beeve kind is intended ; i. e. one which appears, from its form and strength, to be qualified to do the business of the tame ox. So the wild ass is, by implication, compared with the tame, in verse 7. In other passages where it occurs, it is parallel with animals of the beeve kind, and is mentioned as having horns, whereas the rhinoceros has but one short one. See Numb. xxiii. 22, xxiv. 8 ; Deut. xxxiii. 17 ; Ps. xxii. 21, xxix. 6, xcii. 10 ; Is. xxxiv. 7. For other arguments, see a long and highly satisfactory article in Robinson's Calmet.

13. *The wing of the ostrich moveth joyfully.* For an excellent description of the ostrich, see Harris's Nat. His. p. 318. Dr. Shaw observes : "When I was abroad, I had several opportunities of amusing myself with the actions and behavior of the ostrich. It was very diverting to observe with what dexterity and equipoise of body it would play and frisk about on all occasions. In the heat of the day, particularly, it would strut along the sunny side of the house with great majesty. It would be perpetually fanning and priding itself with its *quivering, expanded wings*, and seem, at every turn, to admire and be in love with its own shadow. Even at other times, when walking about, or resting itself on the ground, the wings would continue their fanning and vibrating motions, as if they were designed to mitigate and assuage that extraordinary heat wherewith their bodies seem to be naturally affected." —*But is it with loving pinion and feathers?* This is the most literal meaning, and now most generally received by commentators on Job. The allusion

is to the stork, which was called the *affectionate* or *loving* bird on account of her extreme devotedness to her young. She was called *avis pia* by the Romans. But because *pia* is a good representative of the Hebrew חֲסִידָה, it does not follow that *pious* is; as some translators render it. The point of the allusion is, that the ostrich, which resembles the stork so much in the structure of her body and the color of her wings, should yet be destitute of affection for her young.

14. — *she layeth her eggs on the ground.* The verb תַּעֲזֹב here means, I suppose, *to commit to* or *to deposit upon,* not *to abandon in.* The meaning is, that the ostrich, instead of building her nest on some high rock or tree, like other birds, deposits them upon the ground, where they are exposed to the view of every traveller, and the foot of every wild beast. — *She warmeth them in the dust.* I do not understand the meaning to be, that she abandons her eggs, to be hatched by the warmth of the sun heating the sand or dust; but rather that she broods over them in so exposed a place. The fact is, that the ostrich usually sits upon her eggs as other birds do; but then she so often wanders, and so far, in search of food, that frequently the eggs are addle by means of her long absence from them. To this account we may add, when she has left her nest, whether through fear, or to seek food, if she light upon the eggs of some other ostrich, she sits upon them and is unmindful of her own. The Arabian poets often allude to this peculiarity of the ostrich. The following is quoted from Nawabig by Schultens :

> There are, who, deaf to nature's cries,
> On stranger tribes bestow their food;
> So her own eggs the ostrich flies,
> And, senseless, rears another's brood.

"Notwithstanding the stupidity of this animal," says Dr. Shaw, "its Creator hath amply provided for its safety, by endowing it with extraordinary swiftness, and a surprising apparatus for escaping from its enemy. 'They, when they raise themselves up for flight, laugh at the horse and his rider.' They afforded him an opportunity only of admiring at a distance the extraordinary agility, and the stateliness, likewise, of their motions, the richness of their plumage, and the great propriety there was in ascribing to them *an expanded, quivering wing.* Nothing, certainly, can be more entertaining than such a sight; the wings, by their rapid but unwearied vibrations, equally serving them for sails and oars ; while their feet, no less assisting in conveying them out of sight, are no less insensible of fatigue." *Travels*, 8vo. Vol. II. p. 343.

"The surprising swiftness of the ostrich is expressly mentioned by Xenophon in his Anabasis; for, speaking of the desert of Arabia, he states that the ostrich is frequently seen there; that none could take them, the horsemen who pursue them soon giving it over; for they escaped far away, making use both of their feet to run, and of their wings, when expanded, as a sail to waft them along." *Robinson's Calmet.*

In regard to the proverbial stupidity of the ostrich, Dr. Shaw observes, that, in addition to her neglect of her young, "she is likewise inconsiderate and foolish in her private capacity, particularly in the choice of food, which is frequently highly detrimental and pernicious to it; for she swallows everything greedily and indiscriminately, whether it be pieces of rags, leather, wood, stone, or iron. When I was at Oran, I saw one of these birds swallow, without any seeming uneasiness or inconveniency, several leaden bullets, as they were thrown upon the floor, scorching hot from the mould." *Shaw's* Travels, 8vo. Vol. II. p. 345.

16. *She is cruel, &c.* "On the least noise or trivial occasion," says Dr. Shaw, "she forsakes her eggs, or her young ones, to which perhaps she never returns; or if she does, it may be too late either to restore life to the one, or to preserve the lives of the others. Agreeably to this account, the Arabs sometimes meet with whole nests of these eggs undisturbed; some of them are sweet and good, others are addle and corrupted; others, again, have their young ones of different growth, according to the time, it may be presumed, they have been forsaken of the dam. They often meet with a few of the little ones, no bigger than well-grown pullets, half-starved, straggling and moaning about, like so many distressed orphans for their mother." *Travels,* 8vo. Vol. II. pp. 344, 345. This want of affection is also recorded in Lam. iv. 3. — *Her labor, &c.:* i. e. in laying her eggs. The ostrich is naturally a timid bird, but it is here said that *she feareth not:* i. e. she has no affectionate fear for her young; she abandons her nest without fears of what may happen to it.

17. — *hath denied her wisdom.* The Arabs have the proverbial expression, *More foolish than an ostrich.*

18. — *lifteth herself up:* i. e. lifteth up her head and body, and spreadeth her wings, in order to escape the pursuer. The expression does not imply that her feet quit the ground.

19. — *horse.* The whole description refers to the horse as he appears in war. — *Hast thou clothed his neck with his trembling mane?* I am now convinced that the rendering *thunder* is untenable. The neck of the horse must be regarded as *clothed* with what is addressed to the sense of sight. It is not a natural metaphor to represent the neck as clothed with the sound of neighing which comes from the mouth. The noise made by the horse is referred to in another line. רַעְמָה denotes *trembling, quivering,* and is used poetically to denote the mane of a horse, which appears to quiver on the neck of a high-bred one on account of its fatness, or which is erect and trembles in the excitement of running. So the mane of a

horse or lion is in Greek called φόβη. See Ges. Lex. ad רַעְמָה. Some suppose *trembling* to denote that which causes trembling in the spectator, i. e. terror. But this is harsh, and wholly against the *usus loquendi* in Hebrew. Umbreit renders the line, *Hast thou clothed his neck with loftiness?* supposing the word רעמה to be formed from the Chald. רְעַם, equivalent to the Hebrew רוּם. But this is conjecture.

20. *How majestic his snorting! how terrible!* There may, at first view, appear something ludicrous in speaking of the majestic snorting of a horse. But let one conceive of the war-horse, and suppose, moreover, that he has, or will, come against him in war, and the associations will be different. It is to be recollected, too, that the horse was peculiarly an object of terror to the Hebrews, on account of their ignorance of horsemanship. See Is. xxxvi. 8, and the note. Jeremiah says, ch. viii. 16,

> From Dan is heard the snorting of their horses,
> At the sound of the neighing of their steeds the whole land
> trembleth.

See Virg. Georg. III. 85, &c. Æn. XI. 496.

24. —*he devoureth the ground.* This expression is still used in Arabia to denote prodigious swiftness. See also Virg. Georg. III. 143. *He will not believe, &c.*, i. e. he is so full of joy when he hears the sound of the trumpet that he scarcely trusts his ears. Comp. ix. 16; xxix. 24.

26. —*towards the south.* Most of the species of hawks are said to be birds of passage. The instinct which teaches such birds to know the proper time for migrating in search of food, or of a warmer climate, or both, is probably referred to.

29 —*discern it from afar.* See Iliad, xvii. 674:

> —ὥστ' αἰετὸς, ὅν ῥά τε φασὶν
> Ὀξύτατον δέρκεσθαι ὑπουρανίων πετεηνῶν.

> As the bold bird, endued with sharpest eye
> Of all that wing the mid aërial sky. *Pope.*

XXIII., XXIV.

The Almighty is now represented as pausing, and demanding of Job an answer to his questions, and inviting him to defend his cause. But the admonitions of Elihu and of the Almighty have produced their proper effect; Job is impressed with the most profound reverence of the majesty of God; he has lost that boldness and presumption with which he once challenged the Almighty to a controversy; and he acknowledges his weakness, and the rashness of his complaints, and bold appeals to God. But to make his submission and penitence more complete and impressive, the Almighty is represented as addressing him in a still severer tone of reprehension. In reference to his boldness in desiring to enter into a controversy with him, the Deity challenges him to emulate a single exertion of the Divine power. He adds the description of the river-horse and the crocodile, by which his power is strikingly illustrated. From the whole discourse it follows, that it is better for man to submit without murmuring to the will of so great a Being, than to contend with him, and require him to give an account of his doings.

Ch. XL. 15. — *the river-horse.* This animal is usually mentioned by the ancients in connection with the crocodile, which is supposed to be denoted by the leviathan. The description seems to apply to the river-horse rather than to the elephant, in several particulars, which are well stated by Herder.* "In general, the description is undoubtedly that of an animal whose usual resort is the river, since it is introduced, as something singular, that he eateth grass like the ox, that the mountains bring him forth food, and the beasts of the field play around him. He sleeps among the reeds, and lies concealed among the marshes on the shore of the river, which clearly does not suit a description of the elephant. He goes against the stream, as if he would drink up the river with his enormous mouth, a character not well fitting a land-animal. His strength too is in his loins, and his force is in the navel of his belly, where, on the contrary, the elephant is weakest. He that made him has furnished him with a sword; for the sharp-pointed and projecting tusks of the hippopotamus may be considered his weapons; and the language applies better to these than to the weapons of the elephant. Since, moreover, the name behemoth

* Spirit of Hebrew Poetry, Vol. I. p. 107, Marsh's Translation.

itself is probably the Egyptian name of this animal, *p-ehe-mouth*, (river-ox,) here modified, as all foreign words were by the Hebrews and Greeks, to suit their own forms, and since, in company with the crocodile, it is placed apart from the land-animals, which also are arranged in a separate discourse by themselves, and represented, as all creatures of the watery realm are by the Orientals, as something foreign and monstrous, it seems to me that this opinion has at least a balance of probabilities in its favor, and will soon become the prevailing one." See *Robinson's Calmet*, Art. *Behemoth*, where is an interesting description, extracted from the Travels of Rüppell, the German naturalist, of the capture of one of these animals, which measured from the snout to the end of the tail fifteen feet; and his tusks from the root to the point, along the external curve, twenty-eight inches. See also, in Dr. Shaw's Travels, Vol. ii. p. 294, or Montfaucon's Antiquities, Vol. vii. p. 476, an engraving of the mosaic pavement at Præneste, in which the river-horse and crocodile are placed in company, the former being *in the midst of reeds and fens*, and plants, which correspond to the descriptions of the Egyptian lotus.

17. —*like the cedar.* "The tail of the hippopotamus, although short, is thick, and may be compared with the cedar for its tapering, conical shape, and its smoothness, thickness, and strength. But although it is thick, short, and very firm, yet he moves and twists it at pleasure; which is considered, in the sacred text, a proof of his prodigious strength." *Scheuchser.*

19. —*his sword.* This refers to the long, bending teeth of the animal, with which he, as it were, mows the grass. The ἅρπη, i. e. *the sickle*, or *scythe*, was ascribed to this animal by some of the ancient Greek writers. Thus Nicander, Theriac. ver. 566, quoted by Ros.:

Ἢ ἵππου, τὸν Νεῖλος ὑπὲρ Σάϊν αἰθαλόεσσαν
Βόσκει, ἀρούρῃσιν δὲ κακὴν ἐπιβάλλεται ἅρπην.

In the next verse the reason of his being furnished with it is given, viz. that, although he was an aquatic animal, he procured his food, not from the rivers, but from the grassy mountains.

21. It has been doubted whether צֶאֱלִים denotes *the lote-tree*, *Rhamnus lotus*, Linn., or the *lote-plant*, the Egyptian water-lily, which grows in the water, or in places overflowed by water. See note on ver. 15, and. Wilkinson's Customs and Manners, &c. Vol. III. p. 71.

23. — *Jordan:* i. e. a river as large as the Jordan; for the river-horse could not have lived upon the Jordan. Undoubtedly, the author understood, that, like the crocodile, he was found upon the Nile. He mentions the Jordan as an instance of a great river; and it seems to be an argu-

ment that the writer was a native of Palestine, and wrote for those who were familiar with the Jordan, that he mentions it as an instance of a great stream. The overflowing of it would not frighten the river-horse, because he was amphibious.

Ch. XLI. 1. —*the crocodile.* See note on ch. iii. 8. The crocodile is here described in the hyperbolical style of Eastern poetry. See Harris's Nat. Hist., p. 245. The following description of the crocodile is from Shaw's Zoölogy, Vol. III. p. 184 : "The crocodile, so remarkable for its size and powers of destruction, has in all ages been regarded as one of the most formidable animals of the warmer regions. It is a native of Asia and Africa, but seems to be most common in the latter; inhabiting large rivers, as the Nile, the Niger, &c., and preying principally on fish, but occasionally seizing on almost every animal which happens to be exposed to its rapacity. The size to which the crocodile sometimes arrives is prodigious ; specimens being frequently seen of twenty feet in length; and instances are commemorated of some which have exceeded the length of thirty feet. The armor, with which the upper part of the body is covered may be numbered among the most elaborate pieces of Nature's mechanism. In the full-grown animal it is so strong and thick as easily to repel a musket-ball. The whole animal appears as if covered with the most regular and curious carved work. The mouth is of vast width, the gape having a somewhat flexuous outline, and both jaws being furnished with very numerous, sharp-pointed teeth. The number of teeth in each jaw is thirty or more, and they are so disposed as to alternate with each other, when the mouth is closed. The legs are short, but strong and muscular. In the glowing regions of Africa, where it arrives at its full strength and power, it is justly regarded as the most formidable inhabitant of the rivers. It lies in wait near the banks, and snatches dogs and other animals, swallowing them instantly, and then plunging into the flood, and seeking some retired part, where it may be concealed, till hunger again invites it to its prey." — *Or press down, &c.* : i. e. Canst thou put a cord into his mouth, so as to draw him with it as with a bridle ? See Ges. upon שָׁקַע.

2. —*a rope — a ring :* i. e. by which he might be fastened to the land, after he was caught.

5. —*for thy maidens :* i. e. for their amusement.

6. —*lay snares for him ? &c. :* i. e. Do the fishermen in company catch him, and sell him like fish ?

8. *Thou wilt no more think of battle :* i. e. thy first attack on the monster will have such an issue, that thou wilt not dare to try a second.

9. *Behold, his hope :* The third person for the second. The meaning is,

Thy hope (of taking him) *is vain.* See ch. xxxii. 15, and note. See also Glass. Phil. Sac. pp. 318, 647. Ed. Dath.

13. —*his garment:* i. e. his skin. —*his jaws:* lit. *his double bridle,* which his jaws resembled.

15. —*shields:* i. e. scales.

18. —*eyelashes of the morning.* This may happen, says Schultens, when the crocodile lifts his head above water in the night. His staring eyes, which are the first object that strikes the beholder, may then be compared to the dawning light. The eyes of the crocodile are said to be small. But, as Bochart observes, they are so remarkable, that, when the Egyptians would represent the morning by a hieroglyphic, they painted a crocodile's eye.

19–22. Here the crocodile is described as in pursuit of his prey on land. His mouth is then open, his blood inflamed, his breath thrown out with prodigious vehemence, like volumes of smoke, and heated to such a degree as to seem a flaming fire. *Strength* and *Terror* are represented as animated beings, the one seated on his neck, and the other bounding before him.

20. — *heated:* Lit. *blown up.*

23. —*flakes:* i. e. the pendulous parts of his flesh.

26. — *doth not hold:* i. e. will not pierce him and remain fixed in him, but is repelled and beaten back by the excessive hardness of his skin.

30. —*potsherds.* His scales are compared to fragments of broken earthen vessels. —*thrashing-sledge.* חָרוּץ. His outer skin, or coat of mail, is represented as rough and pointed like a thrashing-sledge. This was an instrument for rubbing or beating out grain upon the thrashing-floor. It consists of three or four rollers of wood, iron, or stone, made rough, and joined together in the form of a sledge or dray; and is drawn by oxen over the grain in order to separate the kernels from the ear. See Ges. ad verb.

32. —*shining path:* viz. the white foam which he stirs up in his passage through the water.

34. *He looketh down, &c.:* i. e. Although a reptile, he is not afraid of the fiercest wild beasts.

XXV., XXVI.

Job is now represented as impressed with a deep sense of his presumption and irreverence in his former discourses, and expressing his penitence in the strongest terms of self-condemnation. The way is thus prepared for the vindication of the integrity and piety of Job by the Deity, and consequently for the decision of the question which had been the great subject of controversy. The Almighty decides that the friends of Job *had not spoken that which was right*, in contending that the misery of Job was inflicted by God as the punishment of his sins; and that Job had spoken the truth, in maintaining that no man's character can be ascertained by his external condition. He confirms his decision by restoring him to his former prosperity.

Ch. XLII. 3. *Who is he, &c.* This is repeated from ch. xxxviii. 2, where the question is asked by the Deity. As if Job had said, Alas! who is it, as thou sayest, that hideth, &c. I am the presumptuous man.

4. *I will ask thee, &c.* I will no more dispute and endeavor to contend with thee with the pride of an equal, but inquire of thee with the humility of a scholar. The words which Jehovah had spoken to Job by way of challenge, ch. xxxviii. 3, and xl. 7, Job uses in the spirit of deep submission.

5. *— hearing of the ear — eye seen.* This may mean only, that Job had a much more perfect knowledge of the Deity than before, as knowledge which is gained by seeing is proverbially more accurate and thorough than that which comes to us by the report of others. It is said that Jehovah spake from the whirlwind, but no visible form is mentioned.

6. *— I abhor myself:* i. e. on account of my former rash speeches respecting thee. The general meaning will not be altered if we supply "it" instead of myself as the object of the verb.

7. *— ye have not spoken concerning me that which is right, as hath my servant Job.* This language is to be understood comparatively, for Job has just been censured for rashly complaining of the ways of God; and it is to be understood relatively, i. e. with reference to the main subject of discussion. They had not spoken right, in maintaining that misery is

always a proof of guilt, and in condemning an apparently upright and good man, merely because he was afflicted. They had not spoken so well in supporting such a proposition, and in heaping unmerited reproach upon a good man, as Job had in denying the proposition, and in maintaining his innocence. See Introduction, p. 15.

10. —*turned the captivity, &c.:* i. e. delivered him from his distress, and restored to him his former prosperity.

11. —*a kesita — a ring of gold:* i. e. as tokens of regard. This probably denoted a lump of silver of a certain weight. Gesenius, from a comparison of Gen. xxxiii. 19, xxiii. 16, supposes it to be about 4 shekels.

14. The names of Job's daughters have reference to their loveliness; Jemima denoting *dove*, or, as some suppose, *fair as the day ;* Kezia, *cassia;* and Kerenhappuch, *horn of beautiful paint*, i. e. beautiful as those whose persons are adorned to the utmost extent.

15. —*among their brethren.* This, being contrary to custom, is mentioned for the purpose of showing the extent of Job's wealth, as well as the excellence of his daughters. See Numb. xxvii. 8.

NOTES ON ECCLESIASTES.

1. The term *Ecclesiastes* is the Greek translation of the Hebrew קֹהֶלֶת, *Koheleth,* which is the title of the book. The word *Preacher* conveys the meaning of the original as well as any English term. The Greek rendering, *Ecclesiastes,* is the more literal, as the Hebrew noun is derived from a verb signifying *to call together, to assemble;* and the secondary meaning, *preacher,* comes from the purpose for which the assembly is called, namely, to be addressed. As no son of David was king at Jerusalem except Solomon, there can be no reasonable doubt that he is designated as the Preacher, in reference to the contents of the book which is here ascribed to him. As to the feminine form, *Koheleth,* it is supposed by Hitzig, Fürst, and others, to have been originally applied to *wisdom,* regarded as calling around her the lovers of instruction, as in Prov. i. 20, viii. 1, ix. 1, and transferred to Solomon as the embodiment of wisdom. Gesenius regards the term, thus put in the feminine, as a name denoting office, according to a common Hebrew idiom. The former view is not so satisfactory as it would have been if any instance had been adduced in which wisdom was actually called Koheleth. I leave the matter doubtful.

In ch. i. 2–11, the Preacher announces the principal subject of his book, the vanity of human things, and illustrates it by the unprofitableness of human striving and labor, ver. 3; and by the instances of perpetual change and wearisome vicissitude in the natural world, while nothing new is brought to pass, and no rest is attained. In endeavoring to illustrate the idea, that the mind of man receives no satisfaction from his labors and experiences, the writer seems to impart his own feelings to inanimate nature, and to represent it as wearying itself with incessant change, without effecting any thing new; as it were, without satisfying itself, or gaining any thing by its labors. All is perpetual change, wearisome labor, and no rest. The sea is not made full by the streams, and the mind of man is not satisfied by all which it learns or enjoys in the world.

Knobel regards the reference to the sun, the wind, and the streams as designed to show the fruitlessness of human efforts, in consequence of the unchangeableness of nature's operations, and the impossibility of man's altering what is fixed by an established law of nature. But the author seems to describe, not the constancy of nature, but of her changes. Besides, the mere constancy of outward nature does not seem to present a strong reason against human striving in general, but only against striving in opposition to natural laws.

2. *Vanity of vanities;* i.e., mere vanity, extreme vanity.

3. *What profit;* i.e., what advantage which can compensate him for his labor, and leave a balance in his favor? Or, what advantage which he would not have had without anxious and laborious striving?

4. *One generation,* &c. Some connect this verse with the preceding one, supposing it to illustrate the vanity of human exertions, from the consideration that man at death must leave the results of them. It appears to me more natural to suppose, that the writer adduces the fact of the continually changing generations of men as an illustration of the vanity of human things.

7. — *to the place,* &c.; i.e., by subterraneous passages and channels, or by evaporation and rain, they return to the fountains and streams. It is mentioned as an instance of the vanity of human things, that the waters, when they have arrived at the sea, where they had so much desired, as it were, to arrive, hasten back to their springs, where again they do not rest, but return again to the sea. "Thus all things in the world are movable and mutable, and subject to a continual toil and toss, constant in nothing but inconstancy, still going, never resting."

8. *All words become weary.* This is the most literal rendering, and most probable from the connection. Otherwise, *All things are full of labor;* all other things, as well as the sun, the wind, and the streams, are in perpetual motion and wearisome agitation. There is no rest to material things, and no satisfaction to the mind of man. — *express it;* i.e., the subject of the preceding and following verses, namely, the perpetual changes of things without novelty or improvement.

9. *The thing that hath been,* &c. The writer seems to regard it as an additional illustration of the vanity of human things, that, while there is perpetual change, there is no novelty; that there is a perpetual recurrence of the same things. The passage seems to express the feeling of satiety and disgust with which human life is sometimes regarded.

The following passage from Seneca, Epist. XXIV., is quoted by Rosenmüller to illustrate these verses: "Quosdam subit eadem faciendi videndique satietas, et vitæ non odium, sed fastidium; in quod prolabimur, ipsa impellente philosophia, dum dicimus: Quousque eadem? Nempe expergiscar, dormiam, satiabor, esuriam, algebo, æstuabo; nullius rei finis est; sed in orbem nexa sunt omnia; fugiunt ac sequuntur. Diem nox premit, dies noctem; æstas in autumnum desinit, autumno hyems instat, quæ vere compescitur. Omnia transeunt, ut revertantur; nihil novi video; nihil novi facio. Fit aliquando et hujus rei nausea. Multi sunt qui non acerbum judicent vivere, sed superfluum."

10. *It hath been*, &c.; i.e., if any one supposes any thing which takes place to be new, he is deceived. For it certainly has occurred long before.

11. — *no remembrance.* A reason seems to be assigned here why some esteem things new which are really old; namely, ignorance of ancient times, want of records of the past.

12–18. Having illustrated his declaration, that all was vanity, by general arguments, drawn from the phenomena of the world, the author now represents Solomon as appealing to his own experience as an additional illustration of what he had said. And, first, from ver. 13 to the end of the chapter, he aims to show how vain and unsatisfactory are the pursuit and acquisition of knowledge. The fame of Solomon for wisdom makes his example a striking illustration of the sentiment which it is brought to illustrate.

13. — *an evil business*, &c.; i.e., a source of pain and vexation. Knowledge seems to be thus represented, 1. On account of the labor and weariness which attend its pursuit, ch. xii. 12; but, 2. chiefly, on account of the perplexing, imperfect, painful subjects of contemplation which it presents to the mind, ver. 14, 15. Dr. South, in his Sermon on the Evils of Knowledge, observes: "Knowledge is the parent of sorrow from its very nature, as being the instrument and means by which the afflicting quality of the object is conveyed to the mind; for, as nothing delights, so nothing troubles, till it is known. The merchant is not troubled as soon as his ship is cast away, but as soon as he hears of it. The affairs and objects that we converse with have most of them a fitness to afflict and disturb the mind. And, as the colors lie dormant and strike not the eye till the light actuates them into a visibility, so those afflictive qualities never exert their sting, till knowledge displays them, and slides them into the apprehension." But if good predominates over evil in the universe, (and who can doubt

it?) then knowledge, regarded in this light, must be the source of more pleasure than pain."

14. — *all the things*, &c.; i.e., I saw that all human pursuits, all the business in which men engage, and all the objects from which they expect happiness, were vain, unsubstantial, incapable of yielding satisfaction to the mind. In fact, the desire and endeavor to catch and possess something so intangible and unsubstantial as air represent the vanity of human actions and pursuits. — *striving after wind.* This rendering is preferred by Gesenius, De Wette, Rosenmüller, and Knobel. (Comp. ver. 17, and, in the Hebrew, ch. ii. 22; iv. 16.)

15. The design of the proverbial expressions in this verse seems to be to assign a reason why human striving should be vain, and human pursuits should be so incapable of affording satisfaction; namely, the perverseness of human nature, and the imperfections of human things. As that which is by nature crooked cannot by human endeavors be straightened; as the vine, for instance, cannot be made to grow up straight, like the poplar; and as that which is naturally wanting to any thing cannot be supplied by human exertion; for instance, as man cannot be made to possess wings, like a bird, or more than two hands or two feet; so there are incongruities, discords, imperfections in human life and the course of human things, which are irremediable, and render it impossible for man to find complete satisfaction. Hence, the knowledge of the things that are done under the sun gives pain.

17. — *senselessness and folly;* i.e., to observe senseless and foolish conduct, and its consequences.

18. See the note on ver. 13. Henry closes his notes upon this chapter with the following good remark: "Let us not be driven off from the pursuit of any useful knowledge, but put on patience to break through the sorrow of it; yet let us despair of finding true happiness in this knowledge, and expect it only in the knowledge of God, and the careful discharge of our duty to him. *He that increases* in heavenly wisdom, and in an experimental acquaintance with the principles, powers, and pleasures of the spiritual and divine life, *increases* joy, such as will shortly be consummated in everlasting joy."

Ch. II. 1–26. Not having found happiness, or the chief good, in the pursuit and acquisition of knowledge, Solomon is represented in this chapter as seeking it in the pleasures of sense, united with the pursuits of knowledge or philosophy. The result of this pursuit, 1–11. He then compares wisdom and folly, and, while asserting the infinite superiority of the former, yet perceives its insufficiency in regard to the attainment of happiness. For the wise man and the fool have a common lot, and a fool often enjoys that for which a wise man fatigues himself, 12–23. He then recommends the tranquil, contented, cheerful enjoyment of life's blessings, without anxiety and care about distant objects and perplexing subjects, 24–26.

2. *It is mad;* i.e., it is an indication of madness; more appropriate to a madman than to a rational being. — *What availeth it?* i.e., what good does it do? what happiness does it confer? At first view, there may appear some inconsistency between this and ver. 24. But here the author is speaking of the pleasure which is pursued and striven for; but, in ver. 24, of that which comes unsought.

3. — *strengthen,* &c. So Gesenius. If, with Fürst in his Lexicon, we suppose מָשַׁךְ to mean *to bestow protracted care upon,* or *to nurse,* the sense will be nearly the same. — *while my heart cleaved to wisdom.* (Comp. ver. 9.) Some suppose the meaning to be, that he was wise in the choice of pleasures, and in the degree to which he pursued them. I rather think the meaning to be, that he united the pursuits of wisdom or philosophy with the pleasures of the senses. — *see what was good,* &c.; i.e., till I should find out by trial whether that supreme good which men ought to propose to themselves and prosecute in life consisted in the pleasures of sense; i.e., in pleasures derived from objects addressed to the senses.

6. — *pools of water.* "At about an hour's distance to the south of Bethlehem are the pools of Solomon. They are three in number, of an oblong figure, and are supported by abutments. The antiquity of their appearance entitles them, Dr. Richardson thinks, to be considered as the work of the Jewish monarch." Modern Traveller. (See more in Bush's Illustrations ad loc.) Maundrell observes: "As to the pools, it is probable enough they may be the same with Solomon's; there not being the like store of excellent spring-water to be met with anywhere else throughout all Palestine. But, for the gardens, one may safely affirm, that, if Solomon made them in the rocky ground which is now assigned for them, he demonstrated greater power and wealth in finishing his design, than he did wisdom in choosing the place for it." Travels, p. 151, Amer. edit. — *the grove that produceth trees;* young plantations, or perhaps nurseries, may be intended.

8. — *a chosen woman, and chosen women.* The words thus rendered do not elsewhere occur. From their probable derivation, as well as from the circumstance that the harem is nowhere alluded to as a source of pleasure, if not here, we think we have given the words their

true meaning. The singular probably refers to the queen, and the plural to the king's other wives and his concubines. (See Gesen. ad verb. שִׁדָּה.)

10. — *my portion*, &c.; i.e., the present temporary enjoyment of them was all the benefit I could expect or receive from all my labors. There was no permanent, abiding good.

11. All that he did was performed with labor and preserved with anxiety; and, above all, the pleasure arising from it was transitory. After the freest enjoyment of what is called pleasure, he felt the inward thirst and torment still.

12. Having tried what satisfaction was to be found, first in knowledge and then in the pleasures of sense, he here compares these two sources of happiness one with another, and passes judgment upon them. — *cometh after the king;* i.e., succeeds me in this inquiry or trial respecting happiness. No mere private man can be expected to have a larger experience than so great a king, or be better able to form a judgment respecting the subject of which he is treating. — *already done*, i.e., in the way of experience and discovery as to what is true good.

14. — *in his head;* where they ought to be, in order that he may guard against danger or foresee advantages. The eyes of the fool are, as it were, in his heels, or in the ends of the earth (Prov. xvii. 24), so that he is likely to stumble or fail of advantages. — *one event*, &c.; i.e., both are subject to many of the same calamities, and especially to death and oblivion.

15. — *wiser than others;* i.e., to what purpose have I taken so much pains to acquire wisdom. — *This also is vanity;* i.e., Although wisdom excels folly, yet it is liable to the charge of vanity, since it has no power to secure its possessor from many of the calamities to which the fool is subject.

18. — *leave it;* i.e., what was obtained by my labor, my possessions.

24. — *to eat and drink, and let his soul enjoy good in his labor.* The drift and meaning of this language is very different from that of ch. ii. 1, &c. It is no Epicurean indulgence, no addiction to the mere pleasures of sense, which the author here pronounces to be the best course a man can pursue in order to make the best of a vain world. But, in opposition to the anxious and strenuous pursuit of wisdom or pleasure or wealth, he advises to give up anxious cares for distant objects and about perplexing subjects, and to enjoy, with a tranquil,

contented, cheerful mind, the blessings of life, as he goes along. And this tranquil, contented, cheerful spirit, he says, is the gift of God, i.e., "to those who are good in his sight," ver. 26; i.e., it cannot be had without religion and virtue. This is an important sentiment of the book, and recurs repeatedly as the result of the author's meditations upon life. (See ch. iii. 12, 13, 22; v. 18–20; vii. 14; viii. 15; ix. 7–10; xi. 9.) From a comparison of these passages, together with ch. v. 1–7, and the whole of ch. xii., it is manifest that it is not mere sensual or selfish indulgence which the author commends as the best thing which a man can attain in a world of vanity, but only such a cheerful, joyful participation of present blessings as is consistent with the thought of God and retribution, or with obedience to the commands of the Creator. The cheerfulness and the joy which he commends is in opposition to anxious cares about the future or about unavoidable evils, or to the ambitious, eager pursuit of distant good.

25. *For who can eat,* &c. The meaning seems to be, that Solomon, from his large experience, could tell as well as any one whether "to eat and drink, and let one's soul enjoy good in his labor," did or did not come from the hand of God; whether those who were not "good in his sight" could have such enjoyment. Instead of *more than I,* חוּץ מִמֶּנִּי might be translated *except I;* i.e., I who have labored for it. — *who can hasten* [thereunto], &c. The plain and common meaning of חוּשׁ is *to hasten,* and hence *to be eager.* It is elsewhere used to qualify another word. (See Ps. xxii. 20; cxix. 60.) I cannot find that in the later, more than in the ancient Hebrew, it means *to enjoy one's self,* or *to enjoy pleasure,* as Stuart and others have it. Buxtorf, in his Lex. Chaldaicum et Talmudicum, says that it means simply *to perceive,* and that the noun חוּשׁ denotes the five senses. But to perceive pleasure or enjoyment is another thing. The conjectural reading, מִמֶּנּוּ in place of מִמֶּנִּי, as making the meaning to be, *who can eat,* &c., *without him,* i.e., without God, is unnecessary, and therefore inadmissible.

26. *For — God giveth,* &c. "For this is a blessing which God reserves for him whom he loves; whose sincere piety he rewards with wisdom to judge when, and with knowledge to understand how, he should enjoy and take the comfort of all that he hath; especially with inward joy, satisfaction of heart, and tranquillity of mind, in this favor of God to him, whereby the troublesome affairs of this life are tempered and seasoned: but he delivers up him that regards not God to the most

cruel tormentors, which are his unsatiable desires and anxious cares, with busy labors and incessant pains to increase his estate without end, and to heap up vast treasures, which God disposes afterward to those who approve themselves to him in a pious, just, and charitable life, with contented minds." Patrick. — *good in his sight*, &c. That this refers to the *moral* character is evident, not only from its contrast with חוֹטֵא, which usually means *sinner*, and never simply *odious* or *offensive;* but also from vii. 26, and especially viii. 12, 13, where the same two characters are contrasted, and where חוֹטֵא, *sinner*, is defined by עֹשֶׂה רָע, *evil-doer*, and contrasted with *those who fear God.* (See also ix. 2.) To say with Stuart, following Hitzig, that "good in his sight" here means "one who is regarded with favor," seems to me quite arbitrary. — *This also is vanity;* i.e., to the sinner, to get riches for those for whom he never designed them. Some suppose the meaning to be, that "to eat and drink, and enjoy good from all his labor," (ver. 24), is "vanity, and striving after wind." This seems to me harder than to refer it to a subordinate part of the sentence, as I have done.

Ch. III. 1–15. The design of this passage seems to be to show the vanity of human efforts and anxieties respecting the future, in consequence of the fixed course and established, unavoidable changes of human things. A higher power than man's controls human efforts and destinies. Hence, a quiet enjoyment of life is recommended as true wisdom.

1. — *a fixed period*, &c. — *appointed time.* This does not mean a *fit* season, an *appropriate* time, when men may and ought to do the things therein mentioned, and which, if neglected, will not again recur. For this meaning will not apply to several of the subjects which are enumerated in the following verses. What, for instance, is the appropriate time *to kill* or *to hate?* The author is speaking, I conceive, not of a *fit* time, an *appropriate, opportune* season, but of a *necessary* change, a period that *must* recur. Every thing remains but for a time. Every condition soon passes away. Nothing is stable and enduring. The thought is somewhat similar to that which is contained in the proverbial expression, that "all things have their *day.*"

3. — *to kill.* In ver. 1, natural death was spoken of; here, that which comes by violence, as by robbers, assassins, or by course of law, or by accident. — *to break down*, &c. At one time, buildings are de-

stroyed in war, or by hurricanes, floods, or conflagrations; at another, new edifices are erected in their place.

4. — *to weep*, &c. There are changes in life, such as sickness, loss of relations, &c., moving us to tears, which are succeeded by others effacing the memory of trouble, and leading to joy. — *to mourn*, &c. This may be distinguished from weeping, as being a formal, public expression of grief, as dancing is of joy.

5. — *to cast stones asunder;* as in the case of edifices, fortifications, &c., which fall into ruin; or they are brought together for building new walls, &c. — *to embrace*, &c.; i.e., a time when we embrace our friends after a long absence, and a time when they are again absent from us. Or, possibly, a time when we live in friendship with any one, and a time when, by change of pursuits or character, we become estranged from him.

6. — *to keep*, &c.; i.e., from attachment to the object, or expectation of benefit from it. — *to cast away;* i.e., as worthless.

7. — *to rend;* as in great and sudden grief, as Gen. xxxvii. 29; Joel ii. 13. — *to sew;* i.e., when the grief is over; or, perhaps, making new garments on some occasion of joy. — *silence;* when men will keep silence through grief, sickness, &c.

8. — *to love.* Love is often followed by hatred.

9. *What profit*, &c. What can his utmost efforts to obtain good or avoid evil avail, while there is such a system of vicissitude and change by the appointment of Providence?

10. — *the labor;* i.e., the labor of the human mind in endeavoring to explore the ways of God in the government of the world, and the appointment of the various vicissitudes of human life.

11. — *maketh every thing good in its time.* The meaning seems to be, that every thing which takes place in the course of providence, by Divine appointment or permission, is right; so that, all things considered, it could not have been done better, ver. 14; and would appear so, if viewed in relation to its season, tendencies, and relations: —

> "And spite of pride, in erring reason's spite,
> One truth is clear, Whatever is, is right."

— *but.* For this use of the Hebrew particle, see ch. iv. 16. — *but he hath put the world into the heart of man, so that he understandeth not*, &c. The translation and interpretation of this passage are attended with much difficulty; first, on account of the ambiguity of the Hebrew term עֹלָם, rendered *world*, and, secondly, on account of the Hebrew negative particles; whether both have their separate force, or whether they unite their force to form one negative. The Hebrew term, in all other instances in which it occurs in the Scriptures, denotes duration, indefinite duration, whether past or future, and sometimes eternal duration; but in the Chaldee and Rabbinic usage, *the world, worldly things,* like the Greek *αἰών*, in Eph. ii. 2; Heb. i. 2; xi. 3 (see also Buxtorf's Lex. Chald. et Talm., especially on עוֹלָם); i.e., things which exist in a given period of duration, more or less definite. If we suppose this rendering correct, and that there is but one negation in the sentence, according to the Common Version, which I follow, the meaning will be, that, according to the same idiom by which he is said to harden the heart of Pharaoh, God has put the cares, or the love, of the world into the hearts of men; so that they cannot discern the propriety and the beautiful harmony of his dispensations, and cannot understand the whole that he does in his providence from beginning to end, but only a part of it. Others give to the term עֹלָם a signification more nearly allied to the common meaning, and render the passage, *And God hath put futurity* or *duration into the heart of man;* i.e., the capacity of looking back upon the past, and forward into the future, *except that he cannot understand the work which God doeth from the beginning to the end;* i.e., God has given man the capacity of looking back upon the past and forward into the future, but not in such a measure or degree that he can understand the work of God from beginning to end. This seems to me to be strained, to make *eternity* mean *a capacity to look into eternity.* Others resort to the Arabic, making עֹלָם mean *understanding* or *reason;* translating, "He hath put intelligence in their heart, without which no man can find out the work which God doeth from beginning to end." So Stuart and Fürst, following Hitzig. But to this there are two objections, of which the first is decisive with me. 1. There is a great abundance of words in Hebrew to denote *intelligence, insight, reason* Why, then, should the writer use an Arabic word? 2. Though I am not such a reader of Arabic as to be able to affirm that עֹלָם never means *reason* or *intelligence* in that language, I can say that there is no such meaning assigned to it in Freytag's Lexicon; but only that of *learning, art,* and *science,* in the objective sense, as the science of physics, theology, &c. (See Freytag, iii. p. 213.) As to the double negative contained in מִבְּלִי אֲשֶׁר לֹא, every one knows the general rule in Hebrew to be, that two negatives strengthen the negation. (See Gesen. Grammar, § 152.) It seems to me that Hitzig's remarks are by no means conclusive against the construction which I have adopted, being that of the Common Version and of most scholars. Besides, the translation of Hitzig and Mr. Stuart gives a sentiment in opposition to the current of the whole book and of other writers of the Old Testament. According to these critics, the meaning is, that without intelligence or reason "no man can find out the work which God doeth from beginning to end." Surely it needed no Solomon to tell us that. But is it the doctrine of the Preacher, or of the Book of Job, or of any sacred writer, that *with* reason "a man can find out the work that God doeth *from beginning to end*"? (See viii. 17, already cited; i. 17, 18; iv. 1–3; Job xxxvii.; xxxviii.) The main design of the passage, whichever explanation may be adopted, is illustrated by ch. viii. 17: "Then I saw the whole work of God, that a man cannot comprehend that which taketh place under the sun: how much soever he labor to search it out, yet shall he not comprehend it; yea, though a wise man resolve to know it, yet shall he not be able to comprehend it."

12. — *enjoy good.* (Comp. ch. ii. 24, and the note.)

13. — *gift of God*; i.e., "to him that is good in his sight. (See the note on ch. ii. 24.)

14. — *whatever God doeth.* The context seems to require this to be understood as referring to the course of things under the Divine government, rather than to the works of creation. It sets forth the perfection and uniformity of his conduct in the government of the world. — *for ever;* i.e., is unalterable. Patrick has given a good paraphrase of the verse: "It is not only very foolish and vain, but a great plague, to be discontented that things go otherwise than we desire; for certain it is, God hath settled them by such an eternal and immutable law, in that course and order before described, ver. 1–3, &c., in which nothing is superfluous, nothing wanting, that it is not in the power of man to make the least alteration one way or other; therefore we must alter ourselves, and not murmur that we cannot change the course of things, which God hath thus immovably fixed, not to make us miserable, by fretting at it, but happy, by reverent submission to the Divine government, and humble patience under those troubles which we cannot honestly avoid, and a due care not to offend the Divine majesty, whose will shall be done, one way or other, if not by us, yet upon us."

15. — *recalleth that which is past;* i.e., he repeats it; makes the future resemble the past, and substantially the same with it, so that there shall be "nothing new under the sun." "This alone is sufficient to silence all our unprofitable, as well as undutiful, complaints about that which hath always been and ever will be. For we, in this present

age, are subject to no other laws than those by which God hath governed the world from the beginning; nor will the next produce any other method than that wherein he hath already proceeded: but, though that which succeeds thrusts out what went before, it brings the very same things about again, as constantly as spring and fall, summer and winter, return in their seasons." *Patrick.*

16–22. The vanity of human things is illustrated in this passage from the prevalence of injustice, and the resemblance of men to brutes in respect to hardships and death. Hence the usual inference of the writer, that man should lead a quiet, cheerful life, without anxiety concerning the unknown future.

16. — *in the place of justice;* i.e., where justice ought specially to be, where rulers or judges professed to administer justice. The meaning may, however, be more general, referring to justice between man and man. The fact to which he refers seems to be introduced as a new instance of the vanity of human things.

17. — *a time;* i.e., of judgment. — *hath he appointed.* This rendering is obtained merely by changing the diacritic point, reading שׂ for שׁ. (Comp. ch. xii. 14; xi. 9; Dan. vii. 9, 10; Job xix. 29.) It is a question whether the judgment or retribution here spoken of was expected by the writer to take place in the present or in the future world. From the context, ver. 18–21, and from other passages in the book, I think it most probable that the present life was exclusively in his view. The passage in Daniel, above referred to, is a good illustration of a time of judgment; for undoubtedly it relates to a judgment in the present world. So the Book of Job, ch. xix. 29, contains mention of a judgment, although the plan and the contents of that work exclude the idea of a retribution after death. If the Preacher had held a belief in a state of retribution after death, his faith must have been manifested in other parts of the work, and applied to the solution of the doubts and difficulties relating to the course of human things which perplexed him. It seems to me certain that, if the Preacher had believed in a future state of righteous retribution, he could never have written such a book as this. "Life and immortality were brought to light by the gospel." The phrase, *will judge the righteous and the wicked,* means will acquit and deliver the righteous, and condemn and punish the wicked.

19. — *one spirit in them;* i.e., the spirit of life. (Comp. ch. viii. 8; xii. 7; Judges xv. 19; 1 Sam. xxx. 12; Ezek. xxxvii. 8; Hab. ii. 19.) Sometimes this *vital spirit* is called *the spirit* or *breath of God,* as having been imparted by him, breathed by him into the nostrils of

men, and as returning to him again. (See Job xxvii. 3.) In Job xxxiv. 14, he is said to *take back his spirit,* when men die. (Comp. Ps. civ. 29, 30.) From a comparison of the preceding references, it will appear, that, according to Hebrew usage, the return of the spirit to God denotes simply *death,* and not a return to a state of happy existence with God after death.

21. — *whether it goeth upward,* &c. This is the rendering of the Septuagint and all the ancient versions, as also of the Geneva Version, and of Luther. It appears to agree better with the Hebrew idiom, and with the connection, than that of the common version. The term *spirit* in this verse is the same in the original as in ver. 19, where it is said that *one spirit* is in men and brutes. In both cases, I understand it as denoting the animal or vital spirit. It seems to me improbable, that, in a sentence so closely connected with ver. 19, there should be any change in the meaning of the term *spirit,* especially as it is here applied to brutes as well as to men, and as the spirit of all mankind, the bad as well as the good, seems to be spoken of in comparison with that of brutes. The Preacher seems to me to express a doubt, whether man, whom he represents to be like the brutes in many respects, differs from them in this, that the spirit of men ascends upward, or returns to God, and that of brutes goes downward, or mingles with dust. I do not understand him to refer to the personal, conscious immortality of either; for, in ver. 19, he says, "One lot befalls both. As the one dies, so dies the other. Yea, there is one spirit in them, and a man has no preeminence above a beast." The doubt is, whether the vital spirit of man is more honorably disposed of after death than that of a brute. In ch. xii. 7, it is true, he positively affirms that the spirit of man "shall return to God." But it is not very probable that he doubts here what he affirms there. The doubt is, whether any different disposition is made of the soul of a man and that of a brute; whether the latter may not go upward as well as the former. The foregoing exposition of the passage seems to be confirmed by the inference which is drawn from it in ver. 22. If the writer had believed that man was distinguished from beasts by a destiny to an immortal, conscious, desirable existence, and to a state of righteous retribution, and had, as many suppose, intended to express his surprise that so few regarded, as the writer did, the different destiny of the spirits of men and brutes, would his inference from the passage have been exactly what it is in ver. 22? Is not this inference rather drawn from what the writer considers as the resemblance of man to the brutes in all the points in which he compares them? It ought not to appear strange to any one, that the

writer did not believe in doctrines which had never been revealed tc him or to his countrymen. The other mode of understanding the verse is expressed in the paraphrase of Patrick: "As for the spirit, which makes all the difference between the beasts and us, that is invisible; and where shall we find a man, especially among those great persons spoken of before, who seriously considers it, and believes that the souls of all mankind go to God that gave them, to be judged by him, whereas the souls of beasts perish with them?" If we were to allow that *who knows* may here denote *who considers* or *regards*, the verse as thus expounded seems to be quite inconsistent with the writer's train of thought. (See the note on ch. xii. 7.)

22. And therefore, considering that such is the vanity of human life, and that man in his condition and his end so much resembles the brutes, "I was confirmed in my former opinion," ch. ii. 23, "that it is best for a man herein also to imitate the beasts, by enjoying freely the good things God has blessed him withal, and taking all the comfort he can find in them at present, without solicitous care about the future; for this is all he can be sure of: he shall not enjoy that hereafter which he makes no use of now; much less, when he is dead, can he be brought back again to take any pleasure in the fruit of all his labors, or see what becomes of them." *Patrick.* (See the note on ch. ii. 24.)

Ch. IV. In this chapter, the author goes on to illustrate the vanity of human things, or the obstacles which prevent a tranquil and happy life, by referring to the sufferings of the oppressed; to the envy which is excited towards the prosperous; to the evils of avarice and of solitude; and those which attend royalty, arising from the infirmities of its possessor and the fickleness of the people.

1. *Then I turned;* i.e., from the preceding subject of contemplation and remark to that which follows.

2, 3. (Comp. Job iii. 11–23.)

4. *This also is vanity;* namely, that an industrious and successful man should meet with envy and obloquy instead of good-will and applause.

5. — *eateth his own flesh.* This may mean that the fool is so tormented with envy, that he is, as it were, consumed or devoured by it. So, ὃν θυμὸν κατέδων, Hom. Il. vi. 202: "Quisnam illic homo est, qui ipsus se comest, tristis, oculis malis?" (Plaut. Trucul. ii. 7, 36.) Gesenius observes that such a man is called by the Arabs *a devourer of himself;* but he does not, as he ought, produce the proof of this asser-

tion. Another meaning of the verse may be, that the fool, perceiving that diligence is attended with envy, goes to the opposite extreme of folding his hands and doing nothing, and thus is reduced to such poverty, that he is ready to eat his own flesh through extremity of hunger. This seems better suited to the connection.

6. *Better*, &c.; i.e, in reference to ver. 4, "Better is a moderate estate, gotten honestly with moderate diligence, and enjoyed handsomely with perfect contentment, than the greatest treasures, gotten by oppression or with infinite toil, and enjoyed with anxious thoughts and fretting cares, and exposing a man either to the hatred or the envy of others." *Patrick.*

7–12. In these verses is described the vanity of avarice, especially in one who lives in solitude, and has no near friend to whom he may leave his wealth. The state of solitude is then contrasted with the advantages of social and married life.

8. [*saith he*]. The ellipsis of these words, for the sake of vivid representation, is not very unusual. The miser who is without descendants is represented as speaking.

9. — *good reward;* i.e., profitable results. By mutual counsel and assistance they effect much more than they could separately.

12. — *threefold cord,* &c. No more than a bundle of arrows or sticks; though each single thread, arrow, or stick may easily be broken.

13. *Better,* &c. The author draws a new illustration of the vanity of human life from the contempt of royalty, when mental vigor is wanting in the possessor of it, and from the general uncertainty and inconstancy of popular favor towards kings.

14. — *out of prison;* i.e., from a very low condition, as was not uncommon in the despotisms of the East, and has not been uncommon in modern times. — *such a one;* i.e., one poor but wise. — *for in his own kingdom,* &c.; i.e., that in which he afterwards reigned.

15. — *with the child;* i.e., following him, paying their court to him, worshipping the rising rather than the setting sun. — *in his stead;* i.e., instead of the old and foolish king, ver. 13.

16. — *went forth;* i.e., as a leader. — *not rejoice in him;* i.e., by reason of the love of novelty, the flattery of human hopes, and other circumstances, they will be as weary of the successor, though a wise and worthy prince, as their parents were of his foolish predecessor.

Ch. V.–XII. The remainder of the book is chiefly preceptive, rather than speculative. The author seems to be giving his advice as to the way in which we may best pass through the life of vanity which he has described.

1. *Look well to thy feet*, &c.; i.e., Walk circumspectly. Make sure and straight steps. Engage in the services of religion with attention, seriousness, deliberation, and sincerity. The metaphor seems to be drawn from the condition of one who is walking in a very slippery path, in which more than ordinary care is necessary to keep him from falling. The expression will thus be similar to that of *taking heed to one's ways*. Some, however, suppose the metaphor to be drawn from the impropriety of entering the houses of the great with dirty feet; others, from the practice of putting off the shoes on entering a sacred place. — *to hear*. *To hear* is often used in the sense of *to obey*. (See 1 Sam. xv. 22.) In this place, it denotes *to obey* the law which is read, rather than simply to hear it, though the latter is implied. — *as fools;* who offer splendid oblations as substitutes of piety and obedience. This does not imply that the writer regards the offering of sacrifice as itself folly, but only irreverent sacrifice, with no desire "to hear" or obey.

2. — *words be few*. As you would not, if admitted to the presence of a king, use many words, words which are not weighed and chosen, much less should you multiply words, without care, thought, and reverence, in the presence of him who is higher than the highest.

3. — *with much bustle*; i.e., thoughtless and profitless activity. This rendering of the verse is strictly literal; and the meaning is, that as a dream is attended with, sets forth, or brings forward, many thoughtless and trifling matters, so a fool utters many thoughtless and trifling words. (Comp. ver. 7.) The objection to the common version is, 1. That it requires too much to be supplied; and, 2. That it neglects the studied antithesis of the original. It makes business the cause of the dream; but the multitude of words is not the cause, but the consequence, of folly. In the Hebrew idiom, *to come with* is often used to denote *to bring forward, to set forth*. Ps. lxvi. 13, lxxi. 16, where *I will come with thy mighty deeds*, means, *I will set forth, celebrate, thy mighty deeds*.

4, 5. (Comp. Numb. xxx. 2, &c.; Deut. xxiii. 21, 22.)

6. — *to bring punishment*, &c. So Hitzig, according to a Hebrew idiom, which is common in the noun. (Comp. in the Hebrew, Isa. xxix. 21.) The mouth, by uttering inconsiderate or false vows, might bring punishment on the body, on the whole man. — *before the angel;* possibly before the priest, regarded as the messenger of God, the announcer of his will. (See Mal. ii. 7.) It may be, however, that there

is reference to some angel, supposed to preside over the temple. (Comp. "angel of the Church" in Rev. iii.) See Christian Examiner for November, 1838, pp. 210, 211. — *It was a mistake;* i.e., I made a mistake; I acted foolishly and inconsiderately in making such a vow, and therefore hope God will excuse me from paying it. — *the work of thy hands;* i.e., the product of the work of thy hands, thy estate.

7. — *fear thou God;* i.e., manifest thy fear of God by abstaining from rash and inconsiderate vows.

8. — *alarmed at the matter;* as though injustice would be finally triumphant, and sentence would never be executed against the evil work. — *a higher, who watcheth;* i.e., over subordinate magistrates there is a higher, or the king, who will call them to account; and over them all is God, who will bring every work of the king as well as of the subject, into judgment.

9. — *a king over cultivated groud;* i.e., one who does not make his country desolate and barren by oppression. So the Sept. *βασιλεὺς τοῦ ἀγροῦ εἰργασμένου.* נֶעֱבָד denotes *tilled,* in Ezek. xxxvi. 9, 24; Deut. xxi. 4. (See Fürst's Lex.) The rendering adopted by me in the former edition, "honored by the land," seems to be not sufficiently sanctioned by Hebrew usage.

11. — *that eat them.* "The more meat, the more mouths. The more men have, the better house they must keep; the more servants employ, the more guests entertain; the more give to the poor, and the more will they have hanging on them; for where the carcass is, the eagles will be. What we have more than food and raiment, we have for others; and then what good is there to the owners themselves, but the pleasure of beholding them with their eyes? And a poor pleasure it is; an empty speculation is all the difference between the owners and the sharers." *Henry.*

> "*P.* What riches give us, let us then inquire;
> Meat, fire, and clothes. *B.* What more? *P.* Meat, clothes, and fire.
> Is this too little? would you more than live?"
>
> Pope's Moral Essays, Epist. iii. 79.

> ——— "Congestis undique saccis
> Indormis inhians, et tanquam parcere sacris
> Cogeris, aut pictis tanquam gaudere tabellis."
>
> Hor. Sat i. 1, 70

> "On every side the numerous bags are piled,
> Whose hallowed stores must never be defiled
> To human use; while you transported gaze,
> As if, like pictures, they were formed to please."

12. — *repletion;* i.e., of his stomach with various delicacies, more than can be digested. This is the literal rendering. Some, however, understand abundance of wealth, which brings cares and fears.

"An vigilare metu exanimem, noctesque diesque
Formidare malos fures, incendia, servos,
Ne te compilent fugientes; hoc juvat? horum
Semper ego optârim pauperrimus esse bonorum." Id. 76.

"But, with continual watching almost dead,
House-breaking thieves, and midnight fires to dread,
Or the suspected slave's untimely flight
With the dear pelf; if this be thy delight,
Be it my fate, so Heaven in bounty please,
Still to be poor of blessings such as these."
Francis's Translation.

13. — *to his hurt;* by exposing him to danger from thieves, as represented in the last quotation from Horace; or, by causing mental distress when he loses them, as described in the next verse.

14. — *in his hand.* There seems to be no consideration which decides conclusively whether *his* refers to the father, who, by calamity, is deprived of the power of leaving any thing to the son for whom he endured all his labors, or whether it refers to the son, who has nothing in his possession after his father's death. I incline to the former supposition.

15. These things, indeed, do not always happen; but it is at least certain, that, though he died possessed of all that he has acquired, yet he cannot carry one farthing away with him. (See Job i. 21; 1 Tim. vi. 7.) So Propertius, l. iii, Eleg. 3, vs. 13, 14: —

"Haud ullas portabis opes Acherontis ad undas,
Nudus ab inferna, stulte, vehere rate."

16. — *for wind;* i.e., for riches, which are empty and unsatisfying, uncertain and transitory, which no man can retain more than he can wind. (Comp. Prov. xxiii. 5.)

17. — *he ate in darkness;* i.e., lived in disquietude, vexation, and fear.

18. (See the note on ch. ii. 24.) — *his portion;* i.e., the use and enjoyment of one's possessions is all that can be truly called his own; all the good which he can receive from them.

19. — *gift of God;* i.e., to the good man. (See ch. ii. 26.)

20. — *will not much remember,* &c. He does not torment himself with useless grief about the past misfortunes of his life, which he can-

not remedy, nor with vain anxiety about future ones, which he cannot avoid. — *answereth him with;* i.e., bestows upon him joy, as it were, in answer to his desires. Otherwise, *occupieth him with*, &c.

Ch. VI. 1-6. The folly and misery of avarice; of hoarding, without enjoying or using.

1. — *lieth heavy.* (See viii. 6.) — *God giveth him not to taste*, &c.; on account of his avaricious mind, his temper ever anxious about the future, his disposition to neglect the present use and enjoyment of his wealth.

3. — *his soul be not satisfied with good;* i.e., if he have not a cheerful, contented mind, if he do not enjoy his property, &c. — *and he have no burial;* either because the strangers to whom his property is left have grudged him the expense of a decent burial, or because he has died in foreign lands, or drowned in a foreign sea, whither he had gone in quest of wealth. How much importance the Hebrews attached to a decent burial appears from Isa. xiv. 19, 20; Job xxvii. 19; Ps. lxxix. 2.

4. — *cometh in nothingness;* i.e., the abortion has no real existence as a human being. — *goeth down into darkness;* i.e., is immediately buried, put out of sight. — *its name is covered*, &c.; i.e., no mention is made of it.

6. — *and see no good*, &c.; i.e., enjoy no good, have no enjoyment of the good things of life. — *to one place;* i.e., the grave. And if they who live long have no enjoyment of life, it follows that they who die soonest have the most rest. "Omnes eodem cogimur." (Hor. Carm. ii. 3, 25.)

> "Serius aut citius sedem properamus ad unam;
> Tendimus huc omnes; hæc est domus ultima."
> Ovid. Metam. x. 33, 34.

7. — *for his mouth*, &c. Although all that a man can get by his labors is food necessary for the support of life (see ch. v. 11, and the note), yet such is the vanity of the world and the folly of mankind, that the desires of men are insatiable.

8. *For what advantage*, &c. The most natural meaning of this verse seems to be this: Since the support of life, or meat, clothes, and fire, is the chief advantage of wealth, what advantage has the wise man over the fool, or what advantage has the poor man who knows how to walk before the living, i.e., who is ingenious, enterprising, knowing how to gain the favor of the rich over the poor man who is destitute of these advantages, who does not know how to walk before the living?

For the most foolish, and the most ignorant and rude of the poor, can, by the labor of their hands, find bread to fill their mouths, &c.

9. — *sight of the eyes*, &c.; i.e., the enjoyment, the making the best, of what is present is better than the wandering of the soul after things at a distance, and affecting a variety of imaginary gratifications which usually end in vexation.

10. *That which is;* i.e., relating to man. — *was long ago called by name.* The meaning of this sentence is not very obvious. It seems, however, to intimate that the condition and fortunes of every man are known and appointed by the Almighty; that they depend more upon an established course of things than upon his personal striving. (Comp. ch. iii. 1–9.) Hence the folly of excessive exertion and anxiety. Others suppose the meaning to be, Man is frail, earthy, mortal, according to the name *Adam*, which God gave him when he formed him out of the dust; *Adam* being supposed to denote *earth.* (Gen. ii. 7.)

11. — *increase vanity*, &c. Ver. 11 and 12 seem to be added as a conclusion of all that he has said respecting the toil, care, and anxiety which what are called the good things of this life bring with them. (Comp. ver. 8 and the note.)

12. — *after him under the sun;* i.e., he knows not who shall possess his acquisitions, or whether the future owners of his possessions will use or abuse them. Whence it follows, that it is best for a man to live a tranquil, unambitious life, agreeably to ver. 7–9. (See ii. 18; iii. 22; xii. 14.)

Ch. VII. 1–VIII. 13. The design of this portion is to give certain proverbs or precepts for the guidance, consolation, or support of men in their passage through the world, whose vanity he has described, and continues to set forth by incidental remarks. The general purport of these precepts is to inculcate the necessity of regulating our thoughts, dispositions, desires, even to an extent which may seem paradoxical to the mass of mankind, and conforming them to the course of things, or the appointments of the Creator. For precepts, just, comprehensive, and complete, having a certain resemblance to those of the Preacher, see the Sermon on the Mount.

1. — *precious perfume;* such as was used in the East, as a part of personal comfort, elegance, and dress. "The custom of anointing with oil or perfume was also common among the Greeks and Romans, especially the anointing of guests at feasts and other entertainments." (See Potter's Grec. Ant., vol. ii. p. 385; Adam's Rom. Ant., p. 144; Hor. Od., ii. 7, 11; iii. 29; Joseph. Ant., xix. 4, 1, and 9, 1; Iliad, xiv.

171.) The same custom is still prevalent in the East. Tavernier says, that "among the Arabs olive-oil is regarded as a very agreeable present. When any one offers it to them, they immediately take off their turban, and anoint their head, face, and beard, raising their eyes to heaven at the same time, and exclaiming, 'Thanks be to God.'" (Rosenmül. A. ü. N. Morgenland, vol. iv. p. 117.) — *day of one's death.* Since life is so full of vexation and misery, it is a more desirable thing for a man to go out of it than to come into it, although it is the practice of almost all mankind to celebrate their own or children's birthdays with solemn feasts and rejoicings, and their deaths with all expressions of sorrow.

2. —*for that;* i.e., death. In Schultens's Anthologia, &c., is the following sentiment of an Arabic poet:—

> "When thou hearest lamentations for the dead, be there!
> But, if thou art invited to a feast, beware!"

See Ros. ad loc.

4. *The heart of the wise,* &c.; even when their bodies are absent. There is no inconsistency between this remark and those passages which inculcate the enjoyment of the present; because by the enjoyment of the present the writer means not sensual or riotous pleasure, but the grateful use of the good which Heaven sends, in opposition to excessive striving and anxiety about the future.

5. — *song of fools;* i.e., the music, songs, and jests of merry companions, which are commonly regarded as delightful.

6. — *crackling of thorns;* which make a great noise and blaze, as if they would produce a mighty heat, but leave the water as cold as they found it. — *laughter of a fool;* i.e., quickly passing away, doing no good, but rather terminating in a sad silence.

7. — *the gain of oppression.* From speaking of fools, the Preacher is led to a particular instance of folly, namely, the grasping at unjust gain, bribes, &c., which take away from wise men their judgment and reason. (Comp. Exod. xxiii. 8; Deut. xvi. 19; Prov. xv. 27.)

8. *Better is the end.* If this verse is connected in sense with the preceding, the meaning is, that the end of the practice of bribery will show that he who takes it is not a gainer by it. But as there is often no connection between one proverb and the preceding, the meaning may be general, that we cannot judge well of things till they are brought to a conclusion. Some things, which are pleasant and promising at first, end in ruin; and some things, difficult and painful at first, have a happy termination. — *patient in spirit;* who quietly waits for the end

of things. — *proud in spirit;* pride being the chief cause of impatience. Or this last line may be understood more generally.

9. — *anger resteth;* i.e., dwells, has its abode; is ever at hand on all occasions.

10. In this verse the Preacher condemns a querulous, repining spirit, which indulges itself in unavailing wishes that it had lived in what it regards the good old times, instead of accommodating itself to the present state of things. Perhaps complaints even against the Governor of the world may be referred to. This spirit has been common in all ages. (Comp. Hor. Ars Poet., 173.)

> "Difficilis, querulus, laudator temporis acti
> Se puero, censor castigatorque minorum."

The notion of the superiority of former ages is still prevalent in the East. "The Hindoos have four ages, which nearly correspond with the golden, silver, brazen, and iron ages of the Western heathen. In the first age, called *Kretha,* they say the corn sprang up spontaneously, and required no attention; in the second, named *Treatha,* the justice of kings and the blessings of the righteous caused it to grow; in the third, called *Tuvara,* rain produced it; but in this, the fourth age, called *Kally,* many works have to be done to cause it to grow. 'Our fathers,' say they, 'had three harvests in the year: the trees also gave an abundance of fruit. Where is now the cheapness of provisions? the abundance of fish? the fruitful flocks? the rivers of milk? the plenty of water? Where the pleasures? Where the docility of animals? Where the righteousness, the truth, and affection? Where the riches, the peace, the plenty? Where the mighty men? Where the chaste and beautiful mothers, with their fifteen or sixteen children? Alas, alas! they are all fled.'" (Roberts's Illustrations ad loc.)

11. — *as good,* &c.; it is as desirable to possess wisdom as to inherit a fortune; yea, even more so. — *that see the sun;* i.e., that live.

12. — *giveth life,* &c.; literally, *vivifieth;* i.e., makes them flourishing, contented, happy. So the noun *life* is used in Prov. iv. 22, 23; xii. 28, and many other places. "It marvellously supports, revives, and comforts the souls of those who are owners of it, under all the evils which it could not help them by honest means to avoid." *Patrick.*

13. From the praise of wisdom the Preacher passes to the principal exercise of it, namely, the contemplation of the providence of God. — *the work of God;* i.e., *what God doeth;* i.e., in the circumstances and events which we witness. We are instructed in this verse to regard

our condition as appointed by God, and to suit our minds to it; for we cannot bring things to our minds, and therefore it is best to strive to conform our minds to our condition, whether it be one of prosperity or adversity.

14. — *be joyful.* (See the note on ch. ii. 24.) — *look for a day of adversity.* So I translate, because I doubt whether the verb רָאָה, which literally means *to see*, is ever used to denote what we understand by the term *consider*. It would be against the author's views to recommend anxiety about the future; but it is not anxiety to remember in the day of prosperity that it may not always last. We are the better prepared to endure the storm when it comes, if we remember that sooner or later it will come to all. — *what shall be after him;* i.e., God has ordained that prosperity and adversity shall succeed each other in the course of men's lives, so that they cannot foresee what shall take place in the future, or after they have left the world, and thus may live in constant dependence upon God, and submission to his will. (Comp. vi. 12.)

15. *All this;* i.e. All that I have mentioned, and am about to mention. — *my days of vanity;* i.e., my vain life. — *in their righteousness;* or, *by* their righteousness. The meaning assigned to ver. 15, 16, and 17, by Patrick, in his paraphrase, seems to me as probable as any: "It seems very hard that a just man's integrity should not be able to preserve him, but he is therefore perhaps destroyed because he is better than others, when a wicked man escapes, nay, is countenanced and encouraged, or suffered to prolong his days in (and perhaps by) his wickedness. But besides other things which may be replied to this (as that good men are sometimes removed from, and wicked reserved unto, future evils), it must be noted also, that some pious men are more strict and rigid than they need be, and not so prudent as they ought to be, but necessarily expose themselves to danger. And therefore it is good advice, in order to a safe and quiet passage through this life, to be temperate in thy zeal, and not to overdo, either by extending thy own duty beyond the divine commandment, or by correcting the inveterate vices of others, and opposing the vulgar opinions too severely or unseasonably, whereby they are only exasperated and enraged, but not at all amended; for why should a man bring a mischief upon himself without any benefit unto others? And, on the other side, let not impunity tempt any man to presume to grow so enormously wicked and foolish as to embrace and follow the lewdest opinions; for this may awaken the public justice against him, even for the common

safety; or the divine vengeance, nay, his own excessive wickedness, may cut him off before he come to the natural term of his life." Rosenmüller supposes these precepts to have particular reference to judges and rulers in the administration of laws. But this supposition does not seem to be supported by verse 17.

18. — *take hold of this;* i.e., the counsel about avoiding wickedness and folly, ver. 17. — *from that;* i.e., the advice in ver. 16. — *escape,* &c. For יָצָא with the accusative, see Gen. xliv. 4; Exod. ix. 29, 33; Amos iv. 3 The rendering *shall make his way,* i.e., order his life, which Stuart adopts from Hitzig, seems to me more forced than the somewhat unusual construction which it aims to avoid. *To walk* means to order the life; but *to come out* has not this meaning. — *all those things;* i.e., the extremes which have been mentioned, and their evil consequences.

21. *Give no heed,* &c. Lord Bacon, as quoted by Patrick ad loc., thus remarks on this verse: "It is a matter almost beyond belief, what disturbance is created by unprofitable curiosity about those things that concern our personal interest; that is, when we make a too scrupulous inquiry after such secrets, which, once disclosed and found out, do but cause a disquiet of mind, and nothing conduce to the advancing of our designs. For, first, there follows vexation and disquiet of mind; human affairs being so full of treachery and ingratitude, that, if there could be procured a magical glass in which we might behold the hatreds and whatsoever malicious contrivances are anywhere raised up against us, it would be better for us if such a glass were forthwith thrown away and broken in pieces. For things of this nature are like the murmurs of the leaves of trees, which in a short time vanish! Secondly, This curiosity loads the mind too much with suspicions and ungrounded jealousies; which is the most capital enemy to counsels, and renders them inconstant and involved. Thirdly, The same curiosity doth sometimes fix those evils which otherwise of themselves would pass by us and fly away. For it is a dangerous thing to irritate the consciences of men; who, if they think themselves to lie undiscovered, are easily changed for the better; but, if they perceive themselves to be detected, drive out one mischief by another. And therefore it was deservedly esteemed the highest wisdom in Pompey the Great, that he instantly burnt all Sertorius's papers, unperused by himself, or suffered to be seen by others." — "Be not solicitous or inquisitive to know what people say of thee: if they speak well of thee, it will feed thy pride; if ill, it will stir up thy passion." *Henry.*

23. — *it was far from me;* i.e., I fell far short of the perfection of wisdom to which I aspired.

24. — *far off,* &c.; i.e., perfect wisdom, a knowledge of the reasons of all that occurs in the world. (Comp. ch. i. 13.)

25. — *wickedness and folly,* &c. Otherwise, *to know wickedness as folly, and folly as madness.* This could scarcely be said to be the *purpose,* though it would be the certain *result,* of diligent investigation. The result of the Preacher's investigation seems to be in the next verse.

27. — *to find out knowledge;* perhaps, *the computation, result,* or *conclusion.*

28. — *is this;* namely, a wise and virtuous woman. This is spoken in conformity with the Oriental notions of the female sex. (See Job xiv. 1, and the note.)

29. — *God made man upright.* That *man* is used in the collective sense, denoting all mankind, including especially the men and women who are just before mentioned, is evident from the plural verb, *they have sought out.* — *devices;* i.e., perverse and evil pursuits. Jerome remarks on this passage: "Ne videretur communem hominum damnare naturam, et Deum auctorem facere mali, dum talium conditor est qui malum vitare non possint, argute præcavit, et ait, bonos nos a Deo creatos; sed quia libero sumus arbitrio derelicti, vitio nostro ad pejora labi, dum majora quærimus, et ultra vires nostras varia cogitamus."

Ch. VIII. 1. — *brighteneth his countenance;* i.e., enlivens it, makes it cheerful and mild, beaming kindness. (Comp. Ps. lxxx. 3, 7, 19.)

2. — *oath of God;* i.e., the oath of allegiance to the king, which you called God to witness.

3. — *to depart from his presence;* i.e., in dislike or discontent, quitting his service or obedience. — *persist not,* &c. Less probably, *stand not up;* i.e., show no resentment, *on account of a grievous word.*

4. — *powerful;* i.e., he has instruments enough to execute all he commands, and there is none to call him to account for his conduct.

5. — *time and judgment.* Most modern interpreters translate *time and manner;* i.e., a wise man will attempt to correct what he sees to be wrong in government, only at a fit time and in the best way. He will not be rash and violent in opposition to the powers that be. The passage thus has a good meaning. But it is doubtful whether this signification, *manner,* be justified by the usage of the term מִשְׁפָּט in the Scriptures. In this book it has a different sense in all other passages

in which it occurs. The word *time* seems also to be used in a peculiar way. Thus, in ch. iii. 17, "For there shall be *a time* for every employment and for every work." Here the connection seems to require us to understand a time *of judgment*. So, in ch. ix. 12, "Man knoweth not *his time;*" i.e., the time when calamity or death shall come upon him. So, in Job xxiv. 1, the term denotes the time when one may experience the evil consequences of imprudence, rashness, or misconduct. *Judgment*, it is well known, often denotes retribution or punishment.

6. *For to every thing there is a time and judgment;* i.e., time when the consequences of it shall be experienced, and retribution take place. (See the note on the preceding verse.) Otherwise, *time and manner*, in the sense above referred to. — *the misery*, &c. Otherwise, *the wickedness*, &c.

8. We need not seek for any closer connection of this verse with the preceding than to suppose it an illustration of human misery, mentioned in ver. 6, or of man's ignorance of the future, in his being unable to predict the day of his death. — *the spirit;* i.e., his vital spirit, breath of life. (See ch. iii. 19.) Otherwise, *the wind.* — *discharge*, &c.; in the conflict between life and death, all must engage, and all be subdued.

9. — *to his hurt;* i.e., to the injury and oppression of the governed. Man oppresses his fellow-man.

10. — *the wicked buried;* i.e., I saw those who deserved infamy obtaining an honorable burial. The Hebrews held the burial of the dead to be a subject of the utmost importance. To be cast out unburied was considered as in the highest degree ignominious and terrible. (Isa. xiv. 19, 20; Jer. vii. 33, xxii. 19.) — *came and went from the holy place;* i.e., came into life and went out of it, from the sacred city of Jerusalem, or perhaps from the royal palace. The verb signifying *to go*, in Hebrew, as in the Greek, English, and other languages, is often used as a euphemism to denote death. — *were forgotten;* i.e., did not receive that place in the memory of their fellow-citizens which their virtues deserved. (Comp. Isa. lvii. 1.) The sentiment of the verse I understand to be similar to that in ver. 14. In regard to the rendering, *the righteous*, literally, *they who did right*, the Hebrew word כֵּן means *right*, or *so*, according to the connection. (Comp. Numb. xxxvii. 7; 2 Kings vii. 9.) Those who prefer the latter rendering will regard the whole verse as relating to the wicked. It will then refer to ill-gotten or ill-used honor and power. They who possess

the highest degrees of either will soon come to the grave and be forgotten.

11. *Because sentence,* &c.; i.e., of retribution, punishment. (Comp. ch. xii. 14.) The sentiment of this verse is of universal application in regard to evil-doers, but probably refers in this place more particularly to tyrants.

12. — *and have his days prolonged;* i.e., in or by his wickedness. (Comp. ch. vii. 15.) Or, though no evil happen to him for a long time. The verse evidently refers to retribution in this life, as appears from the next verse.

13. — *shall not prolong his days;* i.e., he shall come to a sudden and violent end. (Comp. Prov. x. 27; Ps. lv. 23.) Some understand this verse as an imprecation, in order to avoid a seeming inconsistency between it and the last. But the wicked may have his days prolonged *for a time,* and yet come to an untimely end. (Comp. pp. 105–109.)

Ch. VIII. 14–IX. 10. In this section the Preacher goes on to illustrate the vanity of earthly things, as exhibited in the apparently equal prosperity of the righteous and the wicked, and the difficulty of understanding the Divine proceedings in the affairs of the world. He repeats and farther illustrates these ideas, and proceeds to recommend the present enjoyment of life's blessings as wiser than to live in anxiety about distant good, or perplexity about the mysteries of human affairs. (See p. 117.)

14. On the consistency of this sentiment with the preceding verses, see pp. 105–109.

15. *Then I commended joy,* &c. Some understand this as the cavil of an objector, but without reason. The meaning is, Since a man has so little power over his condition, since he can understand so little of the reasons upon which the outward condition of the righteous and the wicked is allotted, it is best for him not to perplex and torment himself about these seeming disorders of the world, but to live in cheerfulness and tranquillity, freely enjoying the present good things which are allotted him, without anxious cares respecting the distant future, or painful efforts to discover the reasons of the Divine proceedings. (Comp. ch. ii. 24, and the note.) — *it is this that abideth with him,* &c.; i.e., the use and enjoyment of what a man obtains by his labor is all that can properly be called his own. Whatever estate, possession, &c., he may acquire will be left to others. The use and enjoyment only are his own.

16. — *to know wisdom, and to see the business,* &c.; i.e., to advance

myself in wisdom, and to observe the vain and wearisome labors of men. I suppose that *wisdom*, in this verse, refers particularly to a knowledge of the causes and reasons of the Divine proceedings; and that *to see the business which is done* is pursued for the purpose of finding out the work of God, as mentioned in the next verse, and the mysteries of his government of the world. — *doth one see sleep with his eyes.* The restless, anxious activity of men in general is denoted. Some translate, *doth it*, i.e., the mind, *see sleep with its eyes;* but this seems to be too harsh a metaphor.

17. — *the whole work of God;* i.e., the method and reasons of his proceedings in administering the affairs of the world; why, for instance, he suffers the wicked to prosper and the virtuous to be oppressed, as in ver. 9, 14. This the Preacher maintains to be beyond the comprehension of man. — *is done,* namely, by God in his providence.

Ch. IX. 1. — *in the hand of God.* This phrase denotes sometimes, *to be in the power of God;* sometimes, *to be under his protecting care.* Both senses are applicable here. — *yet neither his love nor hatred doth any man know;* i.e., from the good or bad outward condition of a man it cannot be determined whether God loves or hates him. — *all is before them;* reserved in the dark, uncertain future.

2. *All* [cometh to them] *as to all;* i.e., to the righteous as to all other men. "For there is no certain and constant distinction made between one man and another in the distribution of things in this world; but they all fare alike, especially in public calamities. A righteous man, for instance, perishes in a battle as well as the wicked; he that keeps himself pure and undefiled dies in a pestilence as well as the filthy and unclean; he that worships God in sincerity and truth suffers by storms, shipwrecks, and inundations, &c., as well as a profane person or a hypocrite: and, on the contrary, a blasphemer of God, nay, a perjured wretch, prospers and thrives as much as he that dreads the holy name of God, and dare not rashly, much less falsely, take it into his mouth." *Patrick.* The rendering of Stuart, "all are like to all," does not well accord with the meaning of כַּאֲשֶׁר, literally, *according to what, that which,* is to all. In regard to the seeming inconsistency of the Preacher, see the Introduction (pp. 105, 106, &c.). — *to the clean, and to the unclean.* There is probably reference here to legal purity or impurity, according to the statutes of the Mosaic code. Of the difficulty in regard to the Divine government arising from the facts which he here states, the author proposes no solution. He says expressly, that

he cannot find out or comprehend the work of God in regard to it. The solution which occurs to the mind of the Christian does not appear to have occurred to him. He seems rather to deny a future life in the following verses, namely, 5 and 6. A Christian, stating such facts, would naturally be led to speak of a retribution after death, and to excite his readers to look to it, as a motive to perseverance in well-doing, and a relief to his doubts or difficulties relating to the government of God. The only inference which the author seems to draw from the perplexing facts which he states is, that it is best to give up all anxiety about such dark and difficult subjects, and to enjoy the good things of life while they last. From what the writer asserts, and from what he omits in the first ten verses of this chapter, it seems very doubtful whether he had any belief in a desirable future life, or a state of retribution after death. Some writers among the Jews and Christians have supposed these verses to be spoken in the character of an impious Epicurean. But there seems to be no ground for this supposition. The writer is speaking of what he himself searched out (ver. 1), and not of what an objector might say. On the difficulty presented by this passage and similar ones, in relation to the mode in which the author reconciles the sentiments contained in it with his own doctrine of retribution as elsewhere expressed, "that it shall be well with them that fear God," and that "it shall not be well with the wicked," and that "God will bring every work into the judgment, which there is upon every secret thing, whether it be good, or whether it be evil," ch. viii. 12, 13; xii. 14, — see the Introduction (pp. 105–109).

3. — *madness*, &c.; i.e., great wickedness. The sentiment of the verse is the same as that in ch. viii. 11. — *and afterward;* i.e., after the vicissitudes of life. — *they go down to the dead.* This may be added to illustrate the vanity of human things, or to illustrate the sentiment, that a common lot happens to the righteous and the wicked; both being under the necessity of going down to the dead.

4. *For who is there that is excepted;* i.e., exempted from death. — *there is hope.* However miserable may be a man's condition while living, he has this advantage over the dead, that he can hope for a change for the better. (Comp. Job vii. 6–10.)

5. — *know that they shall die.* They know that they must die, and of course they know and feel that they are alive, and may have much enjoyment before death arrives. — *advantage;* i.e., from their possessions, &c., all of which are left to their heirs. — *for their memory is forgotten;* i.e., so far are they from having any enjoyment of their possessions, that it is altogether forgotten by their successors that such persons ever lived.

6. — *which taketh place under the sun.* Some have erroneously supposed that this expression is used in contradistinction to another world, in which the dead might have a portion. But the phrase is not used in this emphatic sense. Thus, in ch. i. 9, the author says, "There is no new thing under the sun." (See also ch. ii. 18.) When I consider that this description of death, as the end of man's activity, faculties, feelings, and enjoyments, is made without any qualification; that it follows the statement of the mysterious conduct of Providence in allotting the condition of the righteous and the wicked; and that, instead of being followed by any reference to a future life, by way of encouragement to the virtuous, or of terror to the wicked, or of explanation of the Divine proceedings, it makes the certainty of death only a motive for enjoying the present life, while it lasts,—it is very difficult for me to believe, that the doctrine of a desirable future life, or of a retribution after death, was a part of the faith of the Preacher. (See the caption to Job xii.)

7. *Go thy way,* &c. "And therefore, shaking off both all anxious cares, and also all perplexing thoughts about God's providence (ver. 1), excite thyself by the remembrance of death to a cheerful enjoyment of those good things present which thou justly possessest; use them, while thou hast them, with a well-pleased, contented, nay, joyful mind." *Patrick.* (Comp. ch. ii. 24, and the note.) —*for long since hath God been pleased with thy works;* i.e., with thy labors, and given them success; and, by giving you the means of cheerful enjoyment, shown his intention that you should use them.

8. — *garments be always white.* This is an exhortation to cheerfulness and joy; as it was the custom for the rich and powerful to robe themselves in white cotton, especially on festival days. (See Jahn's Archæology, § 119; also Esther viii. 15; Rev. iii. 4, 5; vi. 11. See also Hor., Sat. ii. 2, 60.)

"Ille repotia, natales, aliosve dierum
Festos albatus celebret."

—*fragrant oil;* which it was the custom of the Hebrews to pour upon their heads on days of rejoicing and festivity. (See Isa. lxi. 3; Amos vi. 6; Ps. xxiii. 5.)

9. *Enjoy life with the wife whom thou lovest.* "Seek for such a wife as thou canst love; and, when thou hast her, delight thyself in her company, with such unalterable kindness as may help to sweeten the afflictions to which we are subject." *Patrick.* — *thy portion;* the enjoyment of what you obtain by your labor is all that you can call your

own. You can take nothing with you when you go down to the grave. (See ch. viii. 15.) "Here is a new proof that this is not the speech of voluptuaries; for they love not to be confined to a wife, as the Preacher here advises this happy man to be; making her his partner in all the joys and comforts he hath, as she will be in his grief and sorrows." *Patrick.*

10. — *thy hand findeth to do;* i.e., what thou hast opportunity and ability to do at present, without scheming and anxiety respecting the future. Here the Preacher makes it evident, that he does not persuade men to an idle and sensual life, but only to a sober enjoyment of their blessings in an industrious prosecution of their vocations.

Ch. IX. 11–XI. 6. The Preacher now adduces a new illustration of the vanity of human life in the circumstances, that success does not always answer to a man's strength, wisdom, and other advantages; and that wisdom, with all its benefits to the public, often brings but little consideration to its possessor. He adds various proverbs showing the advantages of wisdom and prudence. He speaks of the evil of rulers unfit for their stations, and gives various maxims for the regulation of conduct in private and public. This section closes with a recommendation of liberality to the poor, and diligent exertion, without an over-anxious solicitude respecting the issue of our labors.

11. — *nor favor to men of knowledge;* i.e., the esteem and respect of mankind are not always gained by the wise. Sometimes neglect, envy, and hatred are their portion. — *time and chance.* In this connection the author has in mind *a time* of misfortune, an unfortunate *chance* or occurrence. Lord Bacon, as quoted by Patrick, remarks upon the maxim, "Faber quisque fortunæ suæ, "Every man makes his own fortune," that we ought to look upon it as "an insolent and unlucky saying, except it be uttered as an hortative or spur to correct sloth. For otherwise, if it be believed as it sounds, and a man enters into a high imagination that he can compass and fathom all accidents, and ascribes all successes to his own drift and reaches, and the contrary to his errors and slippings, it is a profane speech; and it is commonly seen, that the evening fortune of that man is not so prosperous as of him that, without slacking his industry, attributeth much to felicity and providence above him."

12. — *knoweth not his time.* We need not confine this remark exclusively to the time of one's death. It more probably refers to the time of any misfortune or calamity. Some understand it in the sense of *suitable time* or *opportunity; εὐκαιρίαν.*

13. — *even wisdom;* i.e., I have observed the nature and effects of wisdom, and estimated its exceeding value.

15. — *yet no man remembered,* &c.; i.e., no man thought of him after the danger was past. Thus the remark in ver. 11 is illustrated, that favor is not always to the wise.

17. — *are sooner heard;* i.e., in times of danger and distress, though they may be disregarded in times of prosperity. — *foolish;* literally, *who is among fools.* So in Ps. cxviii. 7, the literal rendering is, *Jehovah is among my helpers;* i.e., *Jehovah is my helper.* (See Gesen. Lex. on the preposition ב.)

18. *But one offender;* i.e., against the rules of wisdom and prudence, as the connection seems to require. One man, by his rashness and imprudence, may bring ruin, not only upon himself, but upon many, even upon whole nations.

Ch. X. 1. — *nauseous;* more strictly, *fetid.* — *a little folly.* The Preacher seems in this verse to intend to illustrate the evil which a foolish man may occasion to the cause in which he is engaged. He is a marplot, and often does more mischief than many wise counsellors can remedy. Otherwise, a little folly in the wise man destroys the fruits of his own wisdom, and ruins his reputation. The rendering of the Common Version, which has no better support from the Hebrew than mine, is less agreeable to the connection.

2. — *wise man's mind;* literally, *heart,* which was regarded as the seat of the mind by the Hebrews, as the brain is by the moderns. — *at his right hand;* i.e., he can use his mind to some purpose, can exercise a ready judgment on every occasion; as men in general can readily and efficiently use their right hand, but not their left.

3. — *walketh in the way.* I should understand this literally of the gait, behavior, and talk of a person, as he passes through the streets. — *saith,* &c.; i.e., by his behavior, that he is himself a fool. Otherwise, *saith of every one,* &c., he thinks and declares that all are fools except himself.

4. — *leave not thy place;* i.e., in anger and discontent. Do not abandon his service hastily and rashly, but continue in the faithful and quiet discharge of the duties of thy station. (Comp. ch. viii. 3.) — *great offences;* i.e., such as he supposes thou hast committed against him. Let not, therefore, a false opinion of implacability make thee desperate, and draw thee into rebellion.

5. — *from a ruler;* in appointing unworthy and incapable persons

to places of honor and power; or in suffering them to rise to such places.

6. — *set in many high stations;* i.e., raised to honorable stations. — *the noble;* in character, birth, and advantages of possessing wisdom, which it is here presumed that they have used. "Many kings," says Grotius, "suspect those who are distinguished for nobility or wisdom or wealth." "Aliena illis virtus formidolosa est," "The virtue of others is feared by them." *Sallust.*

7. — *servants upon horses;* i.e., slaves who had been raised from their servile condition to such eminent stations, that they rode upon horses. Riding upon horses was regarded as the privilege of the higher ranks in the East. (See Jer. xvii. 25; Ezek. xxiii. 23.) — *princes;* i.e., persons of high rank and former opulence, who have been depressed by the injustice of the ruler. It has been observed by several writers, that persons of high rank and opulence in the East, at the present day, are distinguished from their inferiors by riding on horseback when they go abroad; while those of meaner stations, if not on foot, are obliged to content themselves with the ass or the mule.

8. *He that diggeth a pit,* &c. The proverbs which follow (to ver. 20) have been supposed to be cautions against sedition and rebellion against kings, having reference to ver. 4. But such an application of them is rather forced and arbitrary. It seems more probable that they are general maxims for the wise conduct of life, in the midst of the vanities and dangers of the world, which the Preacher has described. (See Prov. xxvi. 27.) — *breaketh down a wall;* i.e., with the design of stealing fruits. — *a serpent;* such as is usually found in hedges. The proverb shows the evil consequences of dishonesty to him that practises it.

9. *Whoso removeth stones,* &c.; i.e., from their earth-bed great stones, for the handling of which their strength is insufficient. The design of both the proverbs in this verse is to show that rash and imprudent men, who engage in difficult and dangerous undertakings, often injure themselves thereby. — *cleaveth wood,* &c. This proverb amounts to the same thing with the common one, that it is dangerous to meddle with edge-tools.

10. *If the iron be blunt,* &c. "This is sufficient to show how unprofitable all our endeavors are without true judgment. For as a rusty tool, though managed by the strongest man, is so far from effecting his desires that it only tires his arm, unless he file and whet it to recover its edge; so all the power in the world rather hurts than advantages him that has it, unless it be guided and directed by prudence." *Patrick.* (See ch. ix. 16, 18.)

11. *If a serpent bite*, &c. This proverb is in commendation of wisdom. As the poison of the serpent is avoided only by the utmost care and circumspection, so is it with the dangers arising from intercourse with men. It is equivalent to the common one, that an ounce of prevention is worth a pound of cure. It is too late to begin to enchant when the poisonous bite is given. Perhaps there may be reference to the avoiding of danger from the powerful by turning away their wrath with conciliating language. (See the next verse.) — *the charmer*, literally, *the lord of the tongue*, has in this case no advantage from his art, but rather severe injury. (Comp. Sirach xii. 13; Ps. lviii. 4, 5; Jer. viii. 17.) For some very remarkable accounts given by travellers in Egypt and the East, respecting the power which certain persons possess of charming serpents, and depriving them of the power of poisoning by music and other means, see Robinson's Calmet, art. "Inchantments."

12. — *gracious;* i.e., mild, kind, agreeable, and thus conciliate favor; while those of the fool are harsh and offensive, and bring evil upon him.

13. *The beginning*, &c.; i.e., All his talk, from beginning to end, is folly, and he proceeds from bad to worse, from folly to rage, which ends in mischief to himself or to others.

14. — *multiplieth words*, &c. The Preacher seems to allude to the folly of those great talkers who speak with confidence of their intentions and plans for the future, or who are fond of predicting what will happen in time to come. — *what shall be after him.* This phrase seems to mean, *what shall happen to him in future.* (Comp. vi. 12, viii. 7.)

15. — *knoweth not how to go to the city.* This language probably had the emphasis and point of a proverb. *To go to the city* is an instance of what ought to be familiar and well known. The meaning is, that the foolish man, in his labors and pursuits, is like a traveller ignorant of the road, who, in going to a city, takes difficult, troublesome, or dangerous circuits, which bring him no nearer to the end of his journey.

16. — *king is a child.* This may be understood literally, as setting forth the evils of having a child for a king. But I should rather understand it of a king resembling a child in disposition, character, and conduct; one who gives himself up to amusements, and neglects the weighty concerns of government. Rosenmüller quotes from the Arabic Anthology a similar proverb: "The blow of an axe upon the head is lighter than the government of one of the young colts." — *feast in the morning.* Jahn, in his Archæology, § 145, says, "Not only the inhabi-

tants of the East generally, but the Greeks and Romans also, were in the habit of taking a slight dinner about ten or eleven o'clock of our time, which consisted of fruits, milk, cheese, &c. Their principal meal was about six or seven in the afternoon." Hence, *to eat*, i.e., to feast, *in the morning* was regarded as intemperance, and as consuming the time which ought to be devoted to affairs of government. (Comp. Isa. v. 11; Acts ii. 13–15.)

17. — *a noble;* i.e., resembles those who are truly noble in disposition and character, according to a well-known Hebraism.

19. — *money answereth all things;* i.e., procures, supplies, all things. From the condemnation of idleness the Preacher passes to the commendation of that which is procured by diligence, i.e., money; affirming that, while of other good things one procures one advantage and another another, money procures all. So Hor., Epist. i. 6, 36:—

> "Scilicet uxorem cum dote, fidemque, et amicos,
> Et genus, et formam, regina pecunia donat."

20. There is probably no allusion here to the custom of sending letters by pigeons, as some suppose. The idea is, that the king will get intelligence of what is said against him in some unknown and unsuspected way, as if a bird of the air was passing by the window and carried it. There are in English the proverbs, "Hedges have ears;" and "The walls will speak."

Ch. XI. 1. *Cast thy bread upon the waters.* There can be little doubt that this verse is a recommendation of liberality in giving to the needy; but, respecting the explanation of the proverb, there are different opinions. Some suppose the allusion is to the planting of corn or rice upon wet places, or such as are even covered with water, which yield an abundant harvest. The objection to this is, that, if there be an allusion to any custom of this kind, it would not be practised without the confident expectation of a harvest; in which case the precept would relate to industry rather than to generosity. Besides, the language is, "Cast *thy bread*," &c., not thy grain. It may not be amiss to observe, that the cakes of the Hebrews were thin and light, such as would float for a time on the water. "The cakes when made were round, and nine or ten inches in diameter. The unleavened cakes were not thicker than a knife, but the leavened were as thick as a man's little finger. Hence they were not cut with a knife, but broken." (Jahn's Archæology, § 140.) Thus the meaning of the proverb may be, Bestow thy gifts with the utmost liberality, even upon those who, by reason of their ingratitude or their extreme poverty, may seem to be as unlikely to make any returns to thee as the water upon which it might be cast. Win the good-will of all, even of the lowest, by acts of kindness. You may receive a return from them; if not, you will be rewarded by God. Rosenmüller observes that the Arabs have a similar proverb: "Do good; throw bread into the water; it will one day be repaid thee." The Turks have borrowed it from the Arabs, with a slight alteration: "Do good; throw bread into the water; even if the fish does not know, yet the Creator knows it."

2. — *a portion;* i.e., a part of thy good things or provisions. — *to seven,* &c.; i.e., to many, not limiting your beneficence, except by your ability. (Comp. Mic. v. 5.) — *thou knowest not what evil,* &c.; i.e., some calamity may strip thee of thy property, and make thee an object of charity, when thou mayst receive aid from some one of those whose good-will thou hast secured by thy beneficence.

3. *When the clouds,* &c. As both clauses of this verse seem designed to express the same thought, the meaning seems to be, that calamities, referred to in the preceding verse, will certainly come; that they cannot be prevented by any foresight, or remedied by human care; and that what cannot be cured must be endured. When the cloud is full, the rain will fall, without regard to our wishes; and where the tree has fallen, there it will stay, whether we like it or not. (Comp. ver. 6.)

4. — *watcheth the wind,* &c. This proverb may imply a recommendation not to be overscrupulous in the exercise of charity. But it is, perhaps, more probable that it relates to human conduct in general, in relation both to business and duty. He that is deterred from any undertaking by every appearance of hazard or inconvenience will never accomplish any thing; as he that will not sow till the wind comes from exactly the right quarter may let the seed-time pass by; and he that will not reap because he is afraid of every cloud that threatens rain may lose his harvest.

5. — *the way of the wind;* i.e., whence it comes and whither it goes. (Comp. John iii. 8.) Both of the images in this verse are designed to set forth the incomprehensibility of Providence, or the uncertainty how God will order the course of things, what evil he will send, or what good, whether storms or sunshine, rain or drought, or whether life itself will be continued. The inference seems to be, that we are to be active in duty and business, and leave events to the care of Providence.

6. — *whether this shall prosper, or that;* i.e., that which is sown early, or that which is sown late. (See the note on ver. 4 and 5.)

Ch. XI. 7-XII. 8. In this portion of the book the Preacher passes to a new topic, and exhorts to a cheerful enjoyment of life while it lasts, in the participation of pleasures which in their nature and degree are consistent with the thought of retribution and the remembrance of the Creator. The consideration of the long night of death and the grievous infirmities of age are urged as a reason for dispelling anxiety and sorrow while the opportunity for enjoyment lasts. (Comp. ch. ii. 24, and the note.)

7. — *the light*, &c.; i.e., life is dear to all. To see the light, to behold the sun, is figurative language for *to live.*

8. — *let him rejoice in them all;* i.e., let him not indulge in anxiety and gloom, but take all the enjoyment which life can give, since it is the only opportunity for enjoyment. (Comp. iii. 12.) — *the days of darkness;* i.e., the long night of death which succeeds life. (Comp. Job x. 21; Ps. lxxxviii. 12.) *All that cometh is vanity.* The connection seems to show the meaning to be, All the future, after the present life is closed, is vanity or nothingness. (Comp. ch. ix. 4-6.)

9. *Rejoice, O young man! in thy youth;* i.e., in the time of thy youth. This verse is commonly understood in an ironical sense, like the language of Elijah to the priests of Baal, "Cry aloud, for he is a god." But from the connection in which the verse stands, and from a comparison of it with other passages in the book, in which the writer recommends *present enjoyment*, in opposition to anxious care, as a man's only portion in the midst of the vanities and uncertainties of life, it is far more probable that the exhortation is serious. (See ch. ii. 10, 24; iii. 12, 13, 22; v. 18; vi. 9; vii. 14; viii. 15; ix. 7-9.) So the verse is understood by Jerome, Martin Luther, Bishop Patrick, and other interpreters. The Preacher regards the season of youth as the peculiar season of enjoyment; but he would have all the pleasures of youth consecrated by the remembrance of the Creator, being innocent in their nature, and pursued only to such an extent as is consistent with the Creator's laws, and with the retribution which attends the violation of them. The expression, "Walk in the ways of thy heart and in the sight of thine eyes," to one accustomed to the Christian sentiment of faith in a future life, would seem at first to be used in an ironical sense. But it is susceptible of a good one, namely, Pursue such things as will gratify your desires and delight your senses; and the necessary qualification is immediately added, namely, that the pursuit of enjoyment is to be in consistency with the thought of judgment or retribution from God; that he will bring us into judgment in relation to the virtuous use or sinful abuse of our blessings. The laws of the Creator, and the

penalties or consequences annexed to their violation, are to be kept in mind. In Numb. xv. 39, "to seek after one's own heart, and one's own eyes," is used in express opposition to "remembering the commandments of the Lord," and of course should have no influence on the explanation of these phrases when used in a different connection.

10. — *sorrow from thy heart,* — *evil from thy body.* The connection, as well as such passages as ch. ix. 7–9, and others referred to in the preceding note, seems to require us to understand the verse as an exhortation to banish anxiety and sorrow from the mind, and from the body whatever is painful or noxious; in other words, to recommend a cheerful enjoyment of life, from the consideration, that the season of youth is transitory, passing away like a vapor.

Ch. XII. 1. *Remember,* &c. This sentiment is to be connected with what goes before. Youth is not only the season of enjoyment, but of religion. In that interesting period of life, cheerfulness and joy are to be cherished, the pleasures of life are to be enjoyed, sorrow and pain are to be banished; but the whole conduct in relation to these things is to be regulated by the remembrance of the Creator, of the intimate relation in which the creature stands to him, of the blessings which he has received from him, of the duties which he owes to him, and of the judgment appointed by him, into which he is to be brought.

2. In ver. 1, the Preacher has exhorted the young to remember the Creator in the peculiar season of their enjoyments and capacities, which is also the season of their temptations, before the troubles and infirmities of age should arrive. He now proceeds to give, in figurative or what may be called enigmatical language, a more particular description of the troubles, decays, and infirmities of old age. — *sun, and the light,* &c. I do not understand this of the dim-sightedness of men, which is alluded to in the next verse. The images in this verse rather set forth the gloom and sadness which belong to old age, when every thing looks dark and cheerless. — *and the clouds return after the rain;* i.e., when one trouble seems to tread upon the heels of another, causing continual sadness; when after the rain no sunshine succeeds, but only perpetual clouds.

3. Here the decay and infirmities of the human body in age are compared to a house decayed and falling into ruin. (Comp. Job iv. 19; 2 Cor. v. 1.) — *keepers of the house;* i.e., the arms, which guard the body from injury, defend it from assault, supply it with food, &c., and which are subject to weakness and trembling in age. — *strong men;* i.e., the

thighs and legs, on which the body rests for support, but which in old men become feeble, bent in walking, and unfit for their office. — *and the grinders cease.* The image is drawn from grinding by the hand-mill, which was performed by Hebrew servants in the house. (Exod. xi. 5.) — *cease;* i.e., cease to grind. It represents the teeth of the aged man, which are too few to discharge their office of preparing the food for the stomach. — *those that look out of the windows;* i.e., the eyes, which look through the cavities of the head in which they are placed, as it were through the windows of a house. They are said to be darkened, in reference to the dimness of sight common to the aged. (Comp. Gen. xxvii. 1; xlviii. 10.)

4. — *when the doors are shut in the streets,* &c. Some understand this literally of the doors of the old man's habitation, in reference to his remaining at home. But it seems best to understand it allegorically of his lips, which are elsewhere in the Scriptures called doors. (See Job xli. 14; Mic. vii. 5.) — *sound of the mill,* &c. The *mill* seems to denote the inner part of the mouth, which gives forth a low sound when the old man speaks. The meaning is, that the old man seldom opens his mouth to speak, as his voice is weak and faint. — *rise up at the voice of the bird.* The aged man's restlessness or difficulty of enjoying sound and long sleep is here described; he is awaked by the earliest chirping of birds in the morning, and so compelled to rise. The pronoun *they,* which I have used for *he* or *one,* to make it conform to the following verses, is implied in the previous description of old age. The rendering, "*it* riseth to the voice of the bird," seems to me much less probable. — *all the daughters of music;* all songstresses, all the women who sing, or perhaps all musical voices, sounds, or songs. — *are brought low;* i.e., sound low, are not heard by him, in consequence of his deafness. So old Barzillai, in 2 Sam. xix. 35, says, "Can I hear any more the voice of singing men and singing women?"

5. — *they are afraid of that which is high;* i.e., on account of their weakness, or short breath, or dizziness, they are afraid to ascend stairs, hills, &c. — *and terrors are in the way;* i.e., terrors for them. They are afraid of walking in a common way, lest they should stumble, or meet with some accident. — *and the almond is despised;* i.e., so rich and delicate a fruit as the almond is rejected by the toothless old man. Others, with the Common Version, *the almond-tree shall flourish;* referring to the white hairs of the old man. This does not agree so well with what follows; and, besides, it is said that the blossoms of the almond-tree are not white, but rose or flesh-colored. (See Pliny, Hist.

Nat. 16, 25.) — *and the locust is a burden;* i.e., the locust, which was a common food with the Orientals, and which may have been regarded as of easy digestion, cannot be eaten or digested by the old man. The locust would hardly be mentioned as an instance of a very light thing resting upon the old man. It would be a disagreeable thing, at least, lighting upon any one. — *and the caper-berry fails;* i.e., to excite appetite, or other natural desire. See Gesen. Lex. ad verb., who refers to Plutarch, Quæst. Symp. 6, 2, and to Pliny, Hist. Nat. 13, 23, ib. 20, 15, as showing that the caper-berry was regarded by the ancients as a provocative of appetite and lust. The translation *caper-berry* is supported by the Sept., Vulg., and Syr. Versions. The Common Version expresses the sense, but not the literal meaning. — *since man goeth, &c.;* i.e., the aged man is on the point of being carried to the grave, his everlasting home (comp. Tob. iii. 6), with the usual mourning solemnities. By *mourners* may be understood not only the relatives, but such hired mourners as are mentioned in Jer. ix. 17, Amos v. 16, upon which see the note.

6. — *before the silver cord be snapped asunder, and the golden bowl be crushed.* From plain language the Preacher now returns to that which is allegorical, setting forth the decline and loss of the vital powers in man by new images. The exhortation, "Remember thy Creator," is to be regarded as repeated at the beginning of this verse. The metaphor, by which loss of life is denoted, is borrowed from a lamp suspended from a ceiling by a silver cord. The golden bowl is the bowl or reservoir of oil, from which it is distributed into the branches, in which the wicks are placed from which the light proceeds. (See Zech. iv. 2, and the note; Job xxix. 3, and the note.) The cord by which this golden bowl or reservoir of oil is suspended being decayed with age, giving way, and so suffering the bowl of oil to fall upon the floor and be broken, and thus extinguish the lamps, affords a striking image of the breaking-up of the human machine, and the extinction of its life, which, by a very common metaphor, is said to be suspended upon a brittle thread. We need not inquire what internal part of the body is denoted by the silver cord or the golden bowl; whether by the former is denoted the spinal marrow, the nerves, the veins, or arteries; or whether by the golden bowl is denoted the heart, the brain, &c., or by the bucket the lungs; since it is extremely doubtful whether the Preacher refers to either. The general image presented by the breaking of the lamp, and of the silver cord which held it up, sufficiently illustrates the extinction of life. — *or the bucket broken at the fountain, or the wheel broken at the well.* By *the fountain* here is denoted a place

from which the water could be obtained only by being drawn up by *a bucket;* an earthen one indeed, and used for carrying water as well as drawing it, but originally for drawing it, as appears from the derivation of the Hebrew term. The water could not be procured when the bucket and the wheel, by which the water was drawn from the well by a line and bucket appended to it, were broken. Water-wheels are still used in the East: Niebuhr has given a picture of one in his Description of Arabia. Indeed, water-wheels are not uncommon in this country. By the images of the broken bucket and wheel, in consequence of which no water could be procured, are set forth the decay and dissolution of the human body through age, by reason of which the life cannot be retained in it. Some have undertaken to point out what internal part of the body was denoted by the bucket, the fountain, the wheel, and the cistern. I do not think the Preacher intended such a particular application of the terms; but any one can conjecture as he pleases.

7. — *and the dust,* &c. This is the most literal rendering; *and* being the translation of the Hebrew conjunction ו. — *and the spirit return to God who gave it.* (See the notes on ch. iii. 19, 21.) In those notes I have given reasons for the supposition, that by *spirit* the author understands the vital spirit, which was breathed into man by the Almighty when he had formed him out of dust, and not the soul, considered as having a conscious and desirable personal existence. In view of the considerations presented in those notes, it seems improbable that this verse expresses the doctrine of the immortality of the conscious soul in a state of retribution. It is more probable that the expression has the same meaning as in Job xxxiv. 14, 15: —

"Should he set his heart against man,
He would take back his spirit and his breath,
Then would all flesh expire together;
Yea, man would return to the dust."

This conclusion is strengthened by the verse which follows. When the Apostle Paul proclaims the Christian doctrine, that this corruptible shall put on incorruption, and this mortal shall put on immortality, he adds, "O death! where is thy sting? O grave! where is thy victory?" If the Preacher had expressed a similar sentiment, would he have added in the very next verse, *Vanity of vanities, all is vanity?* If by the return of the spirit to God he had understood what a Christian would now express by the language, would no joy have been awakened by the thought? Would he not have made use of the doctrine for consolation, in a discourse upon the vanity of earthly things? Would the only way in which he spoke of the return of the spirit to God be that of regarding it as the consequence of the breaking-up of the human system, the last act of the sad drama of life, rather than as the commencement of a happier existence? A review of the passages in which the Preacher alludes to the condition of man after death is, on the whole, inconsistent with his faith in a retributive immortality of the conscious soul. In ch. iii. 18–21, he complains of the sad condition of man, in that the same lot befalls him which befalls the brutes, the body of each returning to the dust out of which it was formed; and in ver. 21 he asks, "Who knoweth the spirit of man, whether it goeth upward, and the spirit of a beast, whether it goeth downward to the earth?" This is the rendering which the Hebrew idiom demands. It seems to imply that some had maintained there was a different residence for the spirit of a man after death from that which was allotted to brutes, but that the writer doubted the correctness of the opinion. In the next verse the same doubt is repeated: "For who shall bring him to see what shall be after him?" In ch. vi. 12, the writer expresses the same doubt in nearly the same words. In ch. viii. 6–9, the Preacher reminds the wicked of a day of judgment which he cannot escape; but he evidently has in view retribution on earth. In ch. ix. 4–6, we have another strong expression of the writer's views, which can hardly be reconciled with faith in the soul's immortality in a state of conscious retribution. The frequent recurrence of his doubts on this subject, and the practical exhortations which are founded on them, indicate that he had no faith in such an immortality of the soul. In ch. xi. 9 and xii. 14, it is most consistent with the tenor of the whole book to regard the judgment spoken of as occurring in the present world. It is also to be observed, that language similar to that of the verse on which we are commenting is used by the ancient philosophers, who had no belief in the soul's conscious immortality. Thus Lucretius, — who, in lib. iii. 418, &c., argues at great length that the soul is mortal like the body, — says, lib. ii. 999, &c.: —

> "Cedit enim retro, de terra quod fuit ante,
> In terras; et, quod missum est ex ætheris oris,
> Id rursum cœli relatum templa receptant."

"For that which was from the earth goes back to the earth; and that which was sent from the regions of the air, being conveyed back, is again received into the temples of heaven." (See also the interesting passages from Greek writers quoted by Le Clerc ad loc.) Similar expressions might be used by Orientals, who now hold the doctrine of the absorption of the soul into the Deity. I do not mean to intimate, however, that Ecclesiastes held this mystical doctrine of absorption. (See the note on ch. iii. 19.) I adduce the passage merely to show that the return of the spirit to God, its author, does not necessarily imply a conscious, much less a retributive, immortality. It would give any one pleasure, without doubt, and perhaps strengthen his faith, to find the doctrines of the Christian revelation anticipated by the Hebrew writers and by all other writers; but no good is permanently gained by disguising or sacrificing the truth. More worthy of a man and a Christian is it to mark the providence of God in the progress of religious knowledge.

Ch. XII. 9–14. This epilogue, on account of the character of its sentiments, is supposed by some critics to have been added to the book by a later writer than the author. But there does not appear sufficient ground for such a supposition. Knobel regards ver. 14 as referring to a retribution in a future life, and therefore inconsistent with the general sentiment of the book. On this account he rejects it as spurious. But, if we consider the broad and indefinite mode of expression which is characteristic of the Preacher, and have regard to the other passages in which he refers to a judgment for evil-doers, there will be no difficulty in supposing that he refers, in ver. 14, to temporal retribution.

11. — *are as goads;* i.e., they have the same power to stimulate men to the acquisition of wisdom and the practice of virtue as the goad has to excite the dull ox to put forth more strength, or to go in the right track. — *as nails driven in;* i.e., they make a deep and abiding impression, stick as fast in the mind as nails or pegs when driven into boards and beams. Roberts informs us that such expressions are common in Hindostan. It is said, "The words of that judge are quite certain; they are like the driven nails." — "I have heard all he has to say, and the effect on my mind is like a nail driven home." — "What a speaker! all his words are nails; who will draw them out again?" (See Roberts's Illustrations ad loc.) — *members of assemblies;* literally, *lords* or *masters of assemblies.* So, in Judges ix. 51, the Common Version correctly translates, "they of the city," where the literal rendering would be "masters of the city." So Joshua xxiv. 11, "the men of Jericho," instead of "the masters of Jericho." These assemblies were probably composed of the most wise and learned men of a place, who met together to discuss questions of religion, morals, philosophy, &c. Perhaps they had some connection with synagogues. The Jewish doctors of the temple, among whom Jesus was found by

his parents, may give us an idea of them. (See Lightfoot, Hor. Heb. et Talmud., on Matt. iv. 23, and De Synagogis.) Otherwise, *masters*, i.e., makers, *of collections.* — *given by one shepherd;* i.e., teacher. The words of the wise, or members of assemblies, such as are uttered by such members among themselves, are said to be *given*; i.e., spoken, or written and published, by one teacher, like the Preacher or the author of the book of Ecclesiastes, i.e., one who feeds the people with knowledge, as a shepherd feeds his flock. (Comp. Prov. x. 21.) Some suppose that, by *one shepherd*, God, the inspirer of wisdom, is intended.

12. *To the multiplying of books*, &c. The design of this sentiment probably is to urge men to be satisfied with a few good books of the wise, whose words are as goads and driven nails, rather than to perplex themselves with reading many books or making new ones. Dr. Channing has a similar sentiment in his Lectures on the Elevation of the Laboring Portion of the Community: "We need not many books to answer the great ends of reading. A few are better than many; and a little time given to a faithful study of the few will be enough to quicken thought and enrich the mind." — "Few of the books read among us deserve to be read. Most of them have no principle of life, as is proved by the fact that they die the year of their birth. They do not come from thinkers, and how can they awaken thought?"

13. — *the end.* This word is used literally, where it elsewhere occurs in this book. (Ch. iii. 11; vii. 2.) The meaning may be thus expressed: My discourse has come to an end. I have nothing more to say except this, the most important thing which can be said, *Fear God*, &c. — *of every man.* Others translate, *the whole of man;* i.e., his whole business or duty. But such a form of expression is hardly met with in Hebrew, or in other languages.

14. — *into the judgment*, &c. (See the notes on ch. iii. 19, 21; ix. 2; xii. 7.) To those who are familiar with the Christian doctrine of retribution after death, the Preacher may seem to allude to it here. A Christian could mean nothing else by such an utterance. But, for the reasons which have been given in the notes referred to, it is far more probable that he refers to retribution in this world. (Comp. iii. 17; viii. 5, 6; xi. 9; Isa. ii. 12; iii. 14; xxvi. 8; lxvi. 16; Jer. xxv. 31; Ezek. xvii. 20; xx. 35; xxxviii. 22; Ps. i. 5; vii. 8; ix. 4, 8, 19; xxxv. 23; l. 4; cxliii. 2; Job xiv. 3.) So Luther understood it. "He does not speak of the last judgment, but according to Scripture usage, and generally, of any judgments whatever, whether those by which heretics are judged and destroyed, or any other ungodly men." (See Luther's Comment. in loc. Opera, vol. iv. p. 46, edit. Wittenb.) — *which there*

is upon. Upon is the strict rendering of the Hebrew עַל. I doubt whether it will bear the rendering *together with* in this or a similar connection. It is true, on the other hand, that the omission of the relative, אֲשֶׁר, is rather hard.

NOTES ON THE CANTICLES.

Ch. I. 2–8. This song seems to set forth the desire of an innocent country maiden to see her shepherd lover, whom she prefers to follow with his flocks rather than to dwell in the abodes of royalty. I do not see how ver. 7, "Tell me where thou feedest," can be reconciled with the supposition, that Solomon, or any king, was the object of the maiden's attachment. It seems rather to be her desire to escape from the palace, and to be with the humble shepherd, tending his flocks.

2. — *one of the kisses;* literally, *from the kisses;* i.e., with one or some of those peculiar kisses which come from his mouth. Sept. *φιλησάτω με ἀπὸ φιλημάτων*, &c. — *thy love;* i.e., as it is expressed in kisses, caresses, love-tokens, &c. The word is in the plural in the Hebrew. The change of person, by which the absent object of affection is addressed as present, belongs to the vividness of poetic representation, and is probably more common in Hebrew than in other poetry. — *better than wine.* The Eastern poets, and even those of Greece, make a frequent use of this comparison. (See Bion, Idyl. A. 49.) The stanza in the song of Ben Jonson is well known: —

"Drink to me only with thine eyes,
And I will pledge with mine;
And leave a kiss within the cup,
And I'll not ask for wine."

3. — *savor,* &c. The fondness of the Orientals for fragrant odors in connection with their dress is well known. (Comp. Ps. xlv. 8; cxxxiii. 2; Prov. vii. 17; Amos vi. 6; Lane's Arabian Nights, vol. i. 405, 536.) But, as the lover is represented as a shepherd in ver. 7, the savor of his perfumes may be a figurative expression, denoting the acceptableness of his person. — *thy name.* In the Hebrew there is a resemblance in sound between the words signifying *name* and *fragrant*

oil, שֶׁם and שֶׁמֶן, which forms what is called in Hebrew grammar a *paronomasia*, and accounts for the remark on the name of the lover. The meaning is, that such is the reputation of the lover, or the regard in which he is held, that the very mention of his name is as grateful as the fragrance of perfumes just poured forth. (Comp. Eccles. vii. 1.)

4. *Draw me*, &c. The maiden seeks some encouragement from the lover, or aid in her flight from the king, who had taken her to his harem. — *we will praise*, &c. The maiden speaks of herself and her female companions.

5. — *of Kedar;* the name of an Arabian tribe, probably so called from being descended from Kedar, the son of Ishmael (Gen. xxv. 13). The tents of the Bedouin Arabs are said by many travellers, quoted by Harmer, Observ. xxiii., to be still covered with black goat's-hair cloth. D'Arvieux says, "The Arabs have no other lodgings but their tents, which they call houses. They are all black, of goat's-hair canvas, which the women weave and spin too." (Travels in Arabia, ch. xii. p. 181.) — *curtains of Solomon;* i.e., of Solomon's tent. That persons of distinction often made use of tents for pleasure may be seen in Harmer's Observations, xxviii. Such tents were often very splendid and costly. (See Robinson's Calmet, art. "Tent.") In regard to the comparison, the meaning evidently is, that the maiden is black as the tents of Kedar, but comely as the curtains of Solomon. Harmer quotes from D'Arvieux, Voy. dans la Palest., p. 214, a passage which illustrates the injury to her beauty which the maiden had suffered by exposure to the sun: "The princesses and the other Arab ladies, whom they showed me from a private place of the tent, appeared to me beautiful and well-shaped: one may judge by these, and by what they told me of them, that the rest are no less so. They are very fair, because they are always kept from the sun. The women in common are extremely sunburnt, besides the brown and swarthy color which they naturally have." (See Harmer's Outlines, &c., ad loc.)

6. *Gaze not*, &c. Addressed to the daughters of Jerusalem, i.e., the ladies who were in company with her, who are supposed to look with wonder upon her presumption, or to assume looks of surprise and doubt. — *my mother's sons;* i.e., my step-brothers. — *my vineyard, my own*, &c.; i.e., my most valued possession, my personal beauty, has been impaired by watching the vineyard of others.

7. — *like a veiled one.* This is the literal rendering and best supported by usage. It is in the margin of the Common Version. Sept. περιβαλλομένη. A veiled one denotes a harlot. (See Gen. xxxviii. 15.)

The maiden expresses her fears, lest, if she should be obliged to go about seeking her lover, unacquainted with the place where he was pursuing his business, she might be taken for a harlot. The custom of reposing in the shade during the heat of noonday is thus referred to by Roberts, a missionary in Hindostan: "Before noon, the shepherds and their flocks may be seen slowly moving towards some shady tree, where they recline during the heat of the day." The custom was not confined to the East. Thus, Virgil, Georg. iii. 331:—

> "Æstibus at mediis umbrosam exquirere vallem,
> Sicubi magna Jovis antiquo robore quercus
> Ingentes tendat ramos, aut sicubi nigrum
> Ilicibus crebris sacra nemus accubet umbra."

8. *If thou know not*; i.e., where he is to be found, take care to feed thy kids by the tents of the shepherds, and he will readily be found there with his flock. In the simple style of pastoral poetry, the preparation for a meeting of the lovers at noon with their flocks is of sufficient importance to form the conclusion of the idyl.

9. *To the horses*, &c. It seems to me that סֻסָתִי may be regarded as a collective noun with י paragogic, as in Lam. i. 1; Isa. i. 21. Otherwise, *To my horse*, or *horses*. In this comparison the resemblance is founded on the splendor of the bride's dress and ornaments, as much as on her personal beauty. (See the next verse.) On this comparison Harmer remarks: "If we may believe Maillet, the horses of Egypt are remarkable for their beauty and stateliness, and are sent, as presents of great value, to the great men of Constantinople; but that strangers cannot procure them, and that he himself, though consul-general, could obtain permission to transport only two of them; and that it appears from the Old Testament they were not less valuable anciently, being eagerly sought for by the kings of Syria. (2 Chron. i. 17.) On the other hand, I would remark, that the Eastern people are excessively attached to their horses, particularly the Arabs, who are fond of them as if they were children. D'Arvieux, in particular, gives a diverting account of the affectionate caresses an Arab used to give to a mare of his he had sold to a merchant at Rama. When he came to see it (which was very frequently), he would weep over it for tenderness, kiss its eyes, and, when he departed, go backwards, bidding it adieu in the most tender manner." It is also observed by Williams, that "the Easterns, so highly valuing their horses, spare no expense to ornament them with the most costly trappings of gold, enriched with pearls and precious stones; and it is very observable that the Arabian and

Turkish ladies decorate themselves in a very similar manner, wearing rows of pearls or precious stones round the head-dress and descending over their cheeks; gold chains, also, upon their necks and bosoms." (Williams ad loc.) In Wilkinson's Manners and Customs of the Ancient Egyptians (vol. i. p. 106), is a plate representing a royal chariot and horses. From the graceful appearance of the horses, and their gay and rich ornaments, one may conclude that the comparison of an Oriental lady in full dress to the horses in a royal chariot was not unnatural. Wilkinson says (vol. i. p. 355), "On grand occasions, the Egyptian horses were decked with fancy ornaments: a rich-striped or checkered housing, trimmed with a broad border and large pendent tassels, covered the whole body; and two or more feathers, inserted in lions' heads or some other device of gold, formed a crest upon the summit of the headstall." Theocritus, speaking of Helen, makes a comparison somewhat similar, but less direct (Idyl. 18, 30), — *ἅρματι Θεσσαλὸς ἵππος.*

10. — *thy cheeks.* In Robinson's Calmet (p. 270) may be seen a representation of the dress of an Eastern lady, which illustrates this verse. "The Persian ladies," says Olearius (Reisebescreib., p. 588), "make use of two or three rows of pearls, which are not worn there about the neck, as in other places, but round the head, beginning on the forehead and descending down the cheeks and under the chin, so that their faces seem to be set in pearls." D'Arvieux also describes the Arab women as wearing pieces of gold coin hanging down the sides of the face; and adds that they have chains of gold about their necks, which hang down their breasts. (La Roque, Voy. dans la Palest., p. 219. See Harmer's Outlines, &c., p. 206.)

12. *While the king reclineth,* &c.; literally, *is in his circle;* i.e., of friends. It is customary for the immediate attendants of an Oriental ruler to stand in a segment of a circle at a small distance before their lord, as he is seated in the corner of the divan. 1 Sam. xvi. 11, "We will not sit down" is literally, "We will not surround." It would seem to be too harsh a figure to suppose *my spikenard* to mean "my personal charms and graces," though such a supposition is favored by the next verse. (See ch. iv. 12, 16.)

13. *A bunch of myrrh;* which was probably suspended from the neck by an elegant chain, as being the most fragrant of perfumes. "There was some inconsistency," says Gesenius, "in the accounts of the myrrh-bearing tree, until Ehrenberg discovered and described it. It is now called *balsamodendron myrrha.*" The myrrh is a substance distilling in tears from a tree growing in Arabia, which tears harden into

a bitter, aromatic gum, which was highly prized, and used in incense. — *abide;* he shall be cherished as the most fragrant perfume, which is constantly in the bosom. It is not so agreeable to the use of language to understand a bunch of the leaves or blossoms of the myrrh-tree to be denoted; for, in ch. v. 5, mention is made of the self-flowing myrrh, i.e., that which distils from the tree in its season, when it is not cut or punctured.

14. — *henna-flowers.* This flower is the *Lawsonia iners* of Linnæus. The Arabic name of this plant is *alhenna*, or, without the article, *henna.* The best description of it is given by Sonnini, who has also furnished an engraved representation of it. (See Voy. dans la Haute et Basse Egypte, tom. i. pp. 291–302.) "The henna is a tall shrub, endlessly multiplied in Egypt; the leaves are of a lengthened, oval form, opposed to each other, and of a faint green color. The flowers grow at the extremity of the branches, in long and tufted bouquets. In truth, this is one of the plants the most grateful to both the sight and the smell. The gently deepish color of its bark; the light green of its foliage; the softened mixture of white and yellow with which the flowers, collected into long clusters like the lilac, are colored; the red tint of the ramifications which support them, — form a combination of the most agreeable effect. These flowers, whose shades are so delicate, diffuse around the sweetest odors, and embalm the gardens and the apartments which they embellish. They accordingly form the usual nosegay of beauty; the women take pleasure in decking themselves with these beautiful clusters of fragrance, in adorning their apartments with them, in carrying them to the bath, in holding them in their hand, — in a word, in perfuming their bosom with them." (See also Shaw's Works, vol. i. p. 113, &c.) It is by the powder obtained from the dried leaves of the henna, and diluted in water, that the Orientals tinge their nails and other parts of the body with a reddish or deep orange hue. (See Lane's Modern Egyptians, vol. i. p. 54; Robinson's Calmet, art. "Camphire.") — *Engedi;* a city near the Dead Sea, fertile in vines and palm-trees. (Pliny, Nat. Hist., v. 17.)

15. — *are doves.* This rendering is rather more in conformity with grammatical usage, and is that of the Septuagint Version. It is adopted by Hodgson, Ewald, and others. That of the Common Version is, however, allowable. The comparison has reference to the brightness, beauty, and quick motion of the dove. So in ch. vii. 4, "Thine eyes are like the pools at Heshbon." So in the Gitagovinda, part vii., as in Clarke's Commentary, "His passion was inflamed by the glances of her eyes, which played like a pair of water-birds with blue plumage,

that sport near a full-blown lotos on a pool in the season of dew." In the same poem the eyes are frequently compared to blue water-lilies. And near the end occurs the sentence, "Whence the antelopes of thine eyes may run down and sport at pleasure."

17. — *cedars*, &c. They were not in a house, but a grove, where the trunks and spreading heads of the cedars and the cypresses are poetically called the beams and the roof of their chamber. Thus Milton, describing Adam's bower: —

> "The roof
> Of thickest covert was inwoven shade,
> Laurel and myrtle, and what higher grew
> Of firm and fragrant leaf." Par. Lost, iv. 692.

Ch. II. 1. — *the rose.* As the name *meadow saffron* would be fatal to the poetic beauty of the verse, I have retained the Common Version, *rose*, although it is probable that a flower of the crocus species is denoted, namely, *Colchicum autumnale*, or meadow saffron, a bulbous plant, with large and delicate flowers of white and violet. (See Gesen. Thes. on חֲבַצֶּלֶת. The maiden does not mean to extol her personal charms, but rather to represent her beauty as nothing extraordinary. The flower arises immediately from the bulb, upon a long, naked tube. A description of the plant, with a colored representation of both the bulb and flower, may be seen in Woodville's Medical Botany, vol. iv. p. 759.

3. — *apple-tree.* The corresponding word in Arabic denotes not only the apple, but orange, quince, citron, peach, and apricot trees. The Hebrew word may have been used in the same general sense. But perhaps the apple, though not so beautiful and fragrant as the citron-tree, may have had a poetic value from the comparative rarity which Forskäll ascribes to it. An apple-tree, loaded with fruit among the barren trees of the wood, would be a sufficient foundation for the comparison. H. B. Tristram, in his Travels in the East, London, 1866, p. 600, gives some weighty, but not decisive, reasons for supposing that the apricot, rather than the apple, tree is denoted here. — *shadow.* It is to be recollected that shade is an essential article of Oriental luxury. Dr. Pococke tells us, "when he was at Sidon he was entertained in a garden, in the shade of some apricot-trees, and the fruit of them was shaken upon him." (Description of the East, vol. ii. p. 95.)

4. — *banqueting-house;* literally, *house of wine.* (Comp. Esth. vii. 8.) There seems, however, to be good reason for the opinion of Döderlein, who understands the expression, *to lead to his banqueting-house*, in a fig-

urative sense, as denoting that the beloved is, as it were, intoxicating the maiden with love. Compare a similar metaphor in Isa. xxix. 9; li. 21. So Umbreit, Gesenius, and Rosenmüller, "Experiri me fecit dilectus meus, quam suavis sit." The verse following seems to favor this explanation. *House of wine* may, however, denote *vineyard.* — *banner over me,* &c.; i.e., I follow the banner or standard of love which my beloved holds up before me, as soldiers follow the standard of their commander and never desert it. — *Strengthen me with raisins;* or, more strictly, *raisin-cakes.* They are mentioned, in 2 Sam. vi. 19, and 1 Chron. xvi. 3, as delicacies with which the weary and languid are refreshed; also, in Hos. iii. 1, as offered in sacrifice. The meaning *cakes* is expressed in most of the ancient versions.

6. *His left hand.* In this situation the spouse is represented as reclining upon a divan, where she falls into a quiet slumber, supported by her beloved.

7. — *by the gazelles.* It is common for different classes to swear by that which is most dear to them, — the warrior by his sword, the prophet by his soul, &c.; so the daughters of Jerusalem are adjured by what is dear to them, namely, beauty, as it is manifested in the gazelles and the hinds. The Hebrew term denoting *the gazelle* originally denoted *splendor* or *beauty;* and the animal is used by the Arabs, as well as the Hebrews, as the emblem of what is extremely elegant and beautiful. To be said to have the eyes of a gazelle is the highest compliment that can be paid to an Eastern lady. (See Gesen. on צְבִי.) — *nor awake,* &c. "In the East," says Roberts, "it would be considered barbarous in the extreme to awake a person out of his sleep. How often, in going to the house of a native, you are saluted with, 'Nittera-kulla-karăr,' i.e., 'He sleeps.' Ask them to arouse him; the reply is, 'Koodătha,' i.e., 'I cannot.' Indeed, to request such a thing shows at once that you are a griffin, i.e., a new-comer. 'Only think of that ignorant Englishman: he went into the house of our chief, and, being told he was asleep, made such a noise as to awake him, and then laughed at what he had done.'"

8. *The voice of my beloved,* &c. Some suppose that these and the following words were the substance of a dream, which the fair one had in the sleep mentioned in the last verse; but it is a mere supposition, and not very probable. As there is no connection between the train of thought in this passage and the close of the last chapter, we conclude that it forms a distinct idyl or song. It adds to the liveliness of the description, that the fair one is represented in a listening attitude, hearing the voice of her beloved before he appears in sight.

9. — *gazelle*, &c. "These animals are elegantly formed, active, restless, timid, shy, and astonishingly swift, running with vast bounds, and springing or leaping with surprising elasticity. They frequently stop for a moment in the midst of their course to gaze at their pursuers, and then resume their flight." (See Robinson's Calmet, art. "Antelope.")

12. — *time of the singing*, &c. As the word זָמִיר denotes *cutting* or *pruning*, as well as *singing*, most of the ancient versions understand the line, "The time for pruning the vines has come." Gesenius also adopts this rendering. But the common rendering is favored by the parallelism, *the voice of the turtle*, i.e., the turtle-dove, &c., also by the circumstance that there is an allusion to the vine in the next verse. As to the objection, that זָמִיר, where it denotes *singing* elsewhere in the Old Testament, refers to the artificial singing of men, the answer is, first, that the singing of birds is not often referred to in the Old Testament by any expression; secondly, if it does usually denote the artificial singing of men, the term may yet be used in a figurative sense by a poet to denote the singing of birds. Nothing is more common in English poetry; for instance, "wood-*notes* wild," "the cock's shrill *clarion*." — *turtle*, &c. The turtle-dove is mentioned as a bird of passage (Jer. viii. 7). Forskäll, the companion of Niebuhr, mentions it as one of the birds of passage which appear at Alexandria about the end of April or beginning of May. (See his Descriptio Animal., p. 9.)

13. — *is spicing*, &c. The Hebrew term חָנְטָה is used in Gen. l. 2, 3, 26, to denote the *embalming* of a dead body; hence it seems to me more probable that it denotes here *to fill with rich, fragrant juice*, rather than, generally, *to ripen*. So Rosenmüller, Umbreit, and De Wette.

14. *O my dove*, &c. Here the wild dove, which hides itself from birds of prey, or from the approach of man in cliffs of rocks, is used as an emblem of the fair one, unwilling to leave her house to meet her lover. (See Jer. xlviii. 28; Hom. Il., xxi. 494; Virg. Æn., v. 213.)

Ὥστε πέλεια,
Ἥ ῥά θ' ὑπ' ἴρηκος κοίλην εἰσέπτατο πέτρην,
Χηραμόν· οὐδ' ἄρα τῇ γε ἁλώμεναι αἴσιμον ἦεν.

"Qualis spelunca subito commota columba,
Cui domus et dulces latebroso in pumice nidi," &c.

15. *Take ye for us the foxes*, &c. The maiden having come forth to enjoy the spring, the vineyards, &c., it is natural for her now to give directions to have the vineyard made as pleasant as possible by the

removal of noxious animals. A similar allusion to foxes is found in Theocritus, Idyl. v. 112:—

> Μισέω τὰς δασυκέρκους ἀλώπεκας, αἳ τὰ Μίκωνος
> Αἰεὶ φοιτῶσαι τὰ ποθέσπερα ῥαγίζονται.
>
> "I hate those brush-tailed foxes, that each night
> Spoil Mycon's vineyards with their deadly spite."

—*now in blossom.* Sept. κυπρίζουσι. So Gesenius, Umbreit, and Ewald. (Comp. ver. 13 and vii. 12.)

16. —*he feedeth,* &c. The Hebrew verb רָעָה has the same ambiguity as the English *feed.* It may mean to feed a flock, as in ch. i. 7, or it may mean to feed one's self. I am inclined to understand it of feeding a flock. Perhaps the flock may have been in an enclosure in the garden or park. It is a recommendation of the beloved to the maiden, that he is a gentle shepherd feeding his flock among the lilies.

17. *When the day breathes.* This is understood by many of the morning; but the more recent commentators, as Gesenius and Rosenmüller, refer it to sunset or the evening. This is most probable; for a grateful, cool breeze is said to spring up at that time. At that time, too, the shadows *flee away,* i.e., continually lengthen themselves, till they are lost in the darkness of the night. So, Gen. iii. 8, *the cool,* literally, *the breeze,* of the day seems to be in contrast with *the heat* of the day, ch. xviii. 1. So here, after the still sultry heat, the day is said *to breathe.* The particle עַד, here translated *when,* seems to be equivalent to עַד אֲשֶׁר, ch. i. 12. —*craggy mountains;* literally, *mountains of division;* i.e., by a well-known Hebraism, mountains divided or cut up, cleft, &c. So the Sept. ὄρη κοιλωμάτων, mountains of cavities.

Ch. III. 1. This is evidently the beginning of a new song. There seems to be no appearance of a dream; and in ancient times a dream was regarded of so much importance, that the author would have mentioned it if he had intended to describe one here. As to any thing inconsistent with probability or propriety, which some have alleged in favor of its being understood as a dream or as an allegory, it appears to me that the author would not be more likely to violate probability or propriety in a poetic dream or in an allegory than in the ordinary products of his imagination.

3. *Have you seen him,* &c. It is a natural circumstance, that the maiden takes it for granted that all the world knows the object of her attachment, though she does not mention his name.

4. — *into my mother's house,* &c. Rosenmüller says, "It is improbable that a modest female among the Hebrews would do such a thing, and therefore it is to be understood allegorically." But it is as improbable that a Hebrew poet would represent a modest female as doing what is improper for an allegorical purpose, as for any other. The passage is, indeed, obscure; but the supposition of allegory does not make it clearer. Hodgson remarks on this verse: "It hath been supposed that this poem was written by Solomon on his marriage with the daughter of Pharaoh. But this passage seems to prove that the person here married was not Pharaoh's daughter; for, if she had been Pharaoh's daughter, her mother's house would have been in Egypt: whereas this scene lies at Jerusalem; for in the next line she addresses the daughters of Jerusalem, and desires them not to disturb her sleeping husband."

Ch. III. 6–11. The design of this song is commonly supposed to be that of describing a nuptial procession, in which the bride of Solomon is led to the palace, in company with himself, in his sedan or carriage. According to the theory of one dramatic poem, Solomon is riding with the Shulamite.

6. *Who is this,* &c. The poet speaks, or perhaps a choir of the daughters of Jerusalem. — *from the wilderness.* מִדְבָּר denotes, not merely a desert, but what we call the country in distinction from the city. (See Gesen. Lex.) Otherwise, *from the wilderness* may denote that the person was coming from the direction of the wilderness. — *pillars of smoke.* It is commonly supposed, that the slender and graceful form of the bride, gradually increasing in tallness as she came nearer, is compared to the light and beautiful column of smoke which ascends from a burning censer of incense. Mercier observes that "it is a tradition of the Jews, that the smoke of incense should go up perpendicularly, and that artists were called from Alexandria to make the smoke of incense ascend as straight as possible." He does not give his authority. But, as the sedan of Solomon is mentioned in the next verse, is it probable that the bride was on foot? Is it not more probable that the dust caused by the approach of the sedan and its attendants is compared to columns of smoke? Or might not the pillars of smoke actually ascend from censers borne in front of the procession? "The use of perfumes at Eastern marriages is common, and upon grand occasions very profuse. Not only are the garments scented, till, in the Psalmist's language, they smell of myrrh, aloes, and cassia, but it is customary for virgins to meet and lead the proces-

sion with silver-gilt pots of perfumes; and sometimes even the air around is rendered fragrant by the burning of aromatics in the windows of all the houses in the streets through which the procession is to pass. In the present instance, so liberally were these rich perfumes burnt, that at a distance a pillar or pillars of smoke arose from them; and the perfume was so rich as to exceed in value and fragrancy all the powders of the merchant." *Williams*. Nothing is said of the bride. It is possible, then, that Solomon alone may have been in the carriage. —*powders;* i.e., aromatic powders.

7. —*carriage;* i.e., a kind of open vehicle, now usually called a palanquin, in which the great men of the East are carried, sometimes upon elephants or camels, and at other times on men's shoulders. Niebuhr says a palanquin, completely ornamented with silver, covered with rich stuffs, and suspended on a handsome bamboo, will cost about two hundred pounds sterling. (Travels, vol. ii. p. 410.)

10. *The railing*. The back and side railing, on which to lean or recline. —*by a lovely one.* (See ch. ii. 7, iii. 5.) So Ewald.

11. —*in the crown,* &c. It was usual with many nations to put crowns or garlands on the heads of new-married persons. The Mishna informs us that this custom prevailed among the Jews; and it seems, from the passage before us, that the ceremony of putting it on was performed by one of the parents. Among the Greeks, the bride was crowned by her mother, as appears from the instance of Iphigenia, in Euripides, ver. 894. "In the Greek Church in Egypt," says Maillet, "the parties are placed before a reading-desk, on which is the book of the Gospels, having two crowns upon it of flowers, cloth, or tinsel. The priest, after benedictions and prayers, places one on the bridegroom's, the other on the bride's, head, covering both with a veil." (See Rosenmüller, Alten und Neues Morgenland, vol. iv. p. 196. Selden's Uxor Hebraica, lib. ii. cap. 15.)

Ch. IV.-V. 1. This canticle seems to include ch. iv. and the first verse of ch. v. It appears to contain a lover's praise of his mistress, and her replies.

1. —*behind thy veil.* So Hafiz: "Thy cheeks sparkle even under thy veil." Sir W. Jones's Works, vol. i. p. 453. Another Persian poet says, "It is difficult to gaze upon the sun without the medium of a cloud. View, therefore, O Saieb! the lovely face of thy mistress through her veil." Orient. Coll., vol. ii. p. 23. —*flock of goats,* &c. Her hair was black and thick, like a flock of goats showing itself on the top of a mountain to one in the distance below.

2. — *teeth;* for whiteness, brightness, fulness, and soundness, they are compared to a shorn flock just coming clean from the washing-place.

3. — *divided pomegranate;* which, in its prime, says Rosenmüller, has a beautiful red color, i.e., when cut in two, equalling or surpassing that of the rose. So Camoens, Lusiad, Cant. ix. 59, translated by Mickle: —

> "The pomegranate of orange hue,
> Whose open heart a brighter red displays
> Than that which sparkles in the ruby's blaze."

4. — *the tower of David;* which was probably built of white marble, high and elegant. Upon the outside of towers it was the custom to hang shields, probably as a terror to enemies. (See Ezek. xxvii. 10, 11.) To the splendid shields and arms with which the tower of David was adorned, are compared the necklaces and jewels which adorned the neck of the maiden.

5. — *gazelles.* (See the note on ch. ii. 7.) Probably the reference is to their general beauty and loveliness.

6. — *day breathes,* &c. See the note on ch. ii. 17. — *mountain of myrrh,* &c. It is said of Pompey the Great, that, when he passed over Lebanon and by Damascus, he passed through sweet-smelling groves and woods of frankincense and balsam. Florus, Epitome Rerum Rom., lib. iii. c. 6: "Per nemora illa odorata, per thuris et balsami sylvas." This quotation is brought to show, not that the bride was actually on a hill of myrrh, &c., but that such hills of myrrh and incense were supposed to exist, and might afford a subject for comparison. The bride seems to be here compared, as respects her general charms, to a mountain of myrrh, &c., to whom the lover says he will return as the antelope flies to the mountain. So Ewald. So some of the Eastern poets represent angels as having bodies of amber and musk Thus the poet Assadi says, "Feridoun and Farrakh were not angels; their bodies were made neither of amber nor musk; it was their justice and liberality that made them celebrated." (See Harmer's Outlines, p. 290.) Grotius, who is followed by Dr. Good, supposes the comparison to be somewhat more definite, referring to her bosom alone: "Sic vocat mammas ob suavissimum odorem." *Grot.* The meaning may be, however, that the lover would return to *the place* where she was, where the odor of her charms was diffused. So Döderlein.

8. *Come with me from Lebanon,* &c. Verses 8 and 9 seem to be introduced very abruptly, and their import in this connection is not very

obvious. Döderlein and others suppose them to be an invitation to the bride to take an excursion with him, in order that they might admire together all that was grand and beautiful in scenery. Others suppose them to be an invitation to the maiden to come from a place of danger to a place of complete security in the arms of her lover.

9. — *taken captive my heart;* literally, *hearted me;* according to the English idiom *to skin*, for *to take off the skin.* Others suppose the word to mean, *Thou hast given me heart*, or *encouraged me.* — *sister;* a term of endearment. So the Romans. (Comp. Tibull. iii. 1, 26.) — *one of thine eyes.* How powerful must be both united when only one does such execution! (Comp. ch. vi. 5.) It has been remarked, that, "supposing the royal bridegroom to have had a profile, or side-view, of his bride in the present instance, only one eye, or one side of her necklace, would be observable; yet this charms and overpowers him." Probably, however, the Hebrew poet intended what others mean to express by *one glance* of the eye, &c. Parallel passages might be quoted from many Eastern poets. The song of Ibrahim says, "One dart from your eyes has pierced through my heart." And, in the songs of Gitagovinda, we find one acknowledging himself "bought as a slave by a single glance from thine eye and a toss of thy disdainful eyebrow." (Asiat. Research., vol. iii. p. 203.) Tertullian, however, mentions a custom in the East of women unveiling only one eye in conversation, while they keep the other covered; and Niebuhr mentions a similar custom as prevailing in some parts of Arabia. (Travels in Arabia, vol. i. p. 262.)

11. *Thy lips*, &c. Here the sweetness of her voice rather than her kisses is denoted. (Comp. Prov. v. 3.) So Hom., Il. i. 249:—

Τοῦ καὶ ἀπὸ γλώσσης μέλιτος γλυκίων ῥέεν αὐδή.

And Theocritus, viii. 82:—

'Αδύ τι τὸ στόμα τοι, καὶ ἐφίμερος, ὦ Δάφνι, φωνά·
Κρέσσον μελπομένω τεῦ ἀκουέμεν ἢ μέλι λείχειν."

12. *A garden enclosed*, &c. The bride is compared to a fragrant garden, a refreshing spring, in respect to her charms; and to a garden *enclosed, a fountain sealed*, in respect to her chastity and fidelity. That fountains or wells, as well as gardens, were sometimes locked up in the East, see Harmer, Obs., vol. i. p. 113. That this kind of distant imagery is common in the East appears from the following passages:— "Feirouz, a vizier, having divorced his wife upon suspicion of infidelity, her brothers apply for redress in the following figurative terms: 'My lord, we have rented to Feirouz a most delightful garden, a ter-

restial paradise; he took possession of it, encompassed it with high walls, and planted it with the most beautiful trees that bloomed with flowers and fruit. He has broken down the walls, plucked the tender flowers, devoured the finest fruit, and would now restore us this garden robbed of every thing that contributed to render it delicious when we gave him admission to it.'" (Miscell. of Eastern Learning, vol. i. p. 12.) In a famous Persian romance, a princess assures her husband of her fidelity in his absence, in these terms: "The jewels of the treasury of secrecy are still the same as they were, and the casket is sealed with the same seal." (Bahur Danush, vol. iii. p. 65. See Williams's Sol. Song, p. 278. See also Prov. v. 18.)

13. *Thy plants;* or *shoots.* I do not understand this of children, as do most of the commentators, but of the graces and charms of the bride. In the last verse she was compared to a garden. In pursuance of the same metaphor, her charms are compared to odoriferous plants. — *Henna,* &c. See the note on ch. i. 14.

15. *A fountain of the gardens;* i.e., a spring that waters many gardens.

16. *Awake, O north wind,* &c. By calling on the north wind at the same time with the south, the maiden expresses the wish that the united influence of the principal winds that blew might shake the plants, and cause the fragrance of the garden to be exhaled and diffused. Having been compared to a garden, she says, in substance, "O that the garden were more fragrant," &c.

Ch. V. 1. — *my spouse;* i.e., betrothed. — *honeycomb,* otherwise, *honey-dripping,* &c.; i.e., that which spontaneously overflows or drips from the combs or hives. (See Ges. and Fürst on יַעַר.) — *drink abundantly, my beloved.* The Hebrew admits quite as well of the rendering, *drink abundantly of love,* or *make yourselves drunk with love.* So King James's translators in the margin. But the parallelism and the connection seem most favorable to the Common Version.

Ch. V. 2-VI. 3. The circumstances introduced into this piece are undoubtedly imaginary; but I perceive no decisive indication that the poet designs to narrate a dream. There is considerable resemblance between this piece and the third ode of Anacreon, beginning, *Μεσονυκτίοις ποθ' ὥραις.*

2. *I slept,* &c. The meaning is, that though the body was asleep, yet the mind was awake and filled with the object of her affection, so that she heard and recognized the knock of her beloved as soon as it was given.

3. *I have taken off my vest.* The frivolous and coquettish excuses

which she gives for not welcoming her lover are here represented. She had prepared herself, and yet pretended she did not like to rise. — *vest;* i.e., the inner garment, reaching to the knees, worn next the skin, commonly with sleeves.

4. — *by the hole of the door*, &c. Le Clerc has a long and learned note on the ancient mode of fastening a door. In this case, the door was probably secured by a crossbar or bolt, which at night was fastened by a little button or pin. In the upper part of the door was left a round hole, through which any person from without might thrust his arm and remove the bar, unless the security of the pin were superadded.

5. — *self-flowing myrrh;* i.e., that which spontaneously flows from the tree, without cutting or puncturing the bark. This was considered the most valuable kind. The myrrh which dropped from her hands was that which her beloved had left upon the wooden bar of the door. This may be understood figuratively, that the moisture of the beloved's hands wet with dew was like fragrant myrrh, perfuming every thing which came in contact with it; or a custom may have prevailed in the East similar to that which is mentioned by Lucretius, iv. 1171:—

> "At lacrymans exclusus amator limina sæpe
> Floribus et sertis operit, postesque superbos
> Unguit Amaracino, et foribus miser oscula figit."

6. *I was not in my senses;* literally, *My soul was gone from me.* The meaning most suited to the connection is, that she acted insanely in not admitting her beloved at his request. It seems to denote that bewilderment of the faculties caused by fear, as in Gen. xlii. 28, or by any other passion; here, by the passion of love.

7. *The watchmen — wounded me,* &c.; i.e., treated me as a lewd, abandoned woman. The same thing is intimated by taking away the veil, in the next line. (Comp. Isa. xxii. 8; Nahum iii. 5.) So Hafiz, in a passage quoted by Dr. Good, speaking of the wife of Potiphar under the name of Zuleikhah:—

> "Led captive by the victor charms
> O'er Joseph's face that play,
> Her veil of chastity at length
> Zuleikhah flings away."

11. — *fine gold;* referring to general splendor and beauty. So Theocritus, Idyl. iii. 28, speaks of the golden Helen. — *palm-branches.* So in Amrolkais, Moallakah, ver. 33, quoted by Rosenmüller, a lover describes the hair of his mistress: "Et capilli, qui tergum

ornant, nigri, carbonis instar, densi sicut racemi palmæ impliciti." Any one who will look at a good representation of the palm-tree — for instance, that in the work of Laborde on Arabia Petræa — will perceive a foundation for this comparison.

12. *Washed with milk.* This is commonly supposed to denote their milk-white color. In Job xxix. 6, to wash the steps in milk denotes to have great abundance of it; and we are told by Roberts, the missionary, that to be washed with milk is now a proverb in Hindostan, denoting to be in a good and happy condition. (See Roberts.) But the former explanation seems most suitable to this passage. — *dwelling in fulness.* יֹשְׁבוֹת עַל־מִלֵּאת. I have rendered this phrase literally, because I consider the meaning as quite doubtful. It seems most probable that it refers to the pigeons, and not to their eyes, and illustrates their plump appearance, arising from their dwelling near full streams or full fields. So the Sept. and Vulg. The translation of the Common Version seems forced. It supposes an allusion to a diamond set in the foil of a ring, denoting that the eyes are neither too much depressed nor too prominent, but well filling the sockets. (See the note on ch. i. 15.)

13. — *a bed of balsam.* Thus paraphrased by Bishop Patrick: "The lovely down upon his cheeks is no less grateful; rising there like spices when they first appear out of their beds; or like the young buds of aromatic flowers in the paradise before described; where the purple lilies are not more beautiful than his lips, from whence flow words more precious and more pleasant than the richest and most fragrant myrrh." The dropping of the lips may, however, refer to the sweet breath. Sadi, the Persian poet, describing a young man, says, "He had just arrived at the opening blossom of youth, and the down had but newly spread itself over the flower of his cheek." Sullivan's Fables from Gulistan, p. 3, quoted by Williams *ad loc.* It is possible, however, that there may be some reference to the beard, which was regarded with almost religious reverence in the East. D'Arvieux says, in ch. vii. of his Travels in Arabia, "One of the principal ceremonies in important visits is to throw some sweet water upon the beard, and then to perfume it with the smoke of lignum aloes, that sticks to this moisture and gives it an agreeable smell." And, in the same chapter, "The women kiss their husband's beards, and the children their father's, when they go to salute them: the men kiss one another's reciprocally, when they salute one another in the streets, or are come from some journey."

14. *His hands are gold rings.* This comparison has reference to the

general beauty of his hands and fingers, and the brilliancy of their ornaments. Some suppose there is a reference to the nails, stained with henna, according to the custom of the Arabians. (See the note on ch. i. 14.) — *sapphires.* The Oriental sapphire is transparent, of a fine sky color, sometimes variegated with veins of a white sparry substance, and distinct, separate spots of a gold color. Hence the prophet describes the throne of God as like sapphire; Ezek. i. 26; x. 1. Pliny, Nat. Hist. xxxvii. 9, says, "Cœruleis, interdum cum purpura, quæ et aureis punctis collucent, ac cœli speciem referunt."

15. — *like Lebanon.* In the manly dignity of his appearance he is compared to the beautiful but majestic Lebanon, with its proud cedars. Volney says, in his description of Lebanon (Travels, vol. i. p. 293), "At every step we meet with scenes in which nature displays either beauty or grandeur." — *like the cedars;* i.e., pre-eminent among men as the cedars among the trees of the forest. Gabriel Sionita, quoted by Dr. Harris, in his Nat. Hist. of the Bible, says, "The cedar grows on the most elevated part of the mountain, is taller than the pine, and so thick that five men together could scarcely fathom one."

16. *His mouth;* literally, *his palate,* which many suppose to be used as the instrument of speech, as in Prov. viii. 7, Job xxxi. 30. But, comparing the word with ch. vii. 9 (10), it seems quite as probable that it is a euphemism, denoting the moisture or saliva of a kiss. (See Gesen. Thes. on חֵךְ, and the note on ch. vii. 9. It is the same word as is here in the Common Version rendered *mouth,* and, in ch. vii. 9, *roof of his mouth.*)

Ch. VI. 4. *Tirzah.* The word itself denotes *pleasantness,* a name given to a city which was the capital of the kingdom of Israel from the time of Jeroboam to that of Omri. It was probably beautiful in regard to its situation as well as its buildings. — *as Jerusalem.* So, Lam. ii. 15, "Is this the city that men called the perfection of beauty, the joy of the whole earth?" — *terrible as an army,* &c. (Comp. ch. ii. 4.) The loved one is represented as conquering, wounding, taking captive the hearts of lovers with her eyes, &c. The idea is carried out in the next verse. So Anacreon, Ode ii.: —

Γυναιξὶν οὐκ ἔτ' εἶχεν.
Τί οὖν; δίδωσι κάλλος
'Αντ' ἀσπίδων ἁπασῶν,
'Αντ' ἐγχέων ἁπάντων·
Νικᾷ δὲ καὶ σίδηρον,
Καὶ πῦρ καλή τις οὖσα.

And again, Ode xvi.: —

Οὐχ' ἵππος ὤλεσέν με,
Οὐ πεζός, οὐχὶ νῆες·
Στρατὸς δὲ καινὸς ἄλλος,
'Απ' ὀμμάτων με βάλλων.

In the same way, the Arabian poets compare the eyes of virgins to swords and darts, their eyebrows to bows, &c., with which they wound and kill. In fact, the same representation is common to all languages. Cupid is armed with his bow and arrow. And yet Dr. Good makes the tasteless remark, that the epithet *terrible* is obviously inappropriate, and gives the term אֲיֻמָּה the forced meaning, *dazzling*.

5–7. (See ch. iv. 1–3.)

8. — *queens*, — *concubines*, — *maidens*. Solomon is said, in 1 Kings xi. 3, to have had seven hundred wives and three hundred concubines. Hence some who regard this piece as written by Solomon, suppose it to have been written at an earlier period of his reign than that referred to in Kings. Rosenmüller, however, supposes an indefinite use of numbers; and this seems most probable.

9. — *the one;* i.e., *the matchless one*. For this use of the term אַחַת, see Ezek. vii. 5, and Gesen. Lex. ad verb.

10. — *like the morning*. So Theocritus, Idyl. xviii. 26: —

'Αὼς ἀντέλλοισα καλὸν διέφαινε πρόσωπον,
Πότνια νὺξ ἅτε, λευκὸν ἔαρ χειμῶνος ἀνέντος,
'Ὧδε καὶ ἁ χρυσέα 'Ελένα διεφαίνετ' ἐν ἁμῖν.

— *as the moon*. So, in Lane's Arabian Nights, vol. i. p. 29, "When I beheld her, I thought that the moon had descended to the earth."

12. — *made me like the chariots*, &c. The meaning seems to be, that her strong desire conveyed her thither as swift as the chariots, &c. — *of the prince's train*. (See Gesen. Thes. on עָם.) Otherwise, *placed me among the chariots of my noble people*.

13. *Return, return*. This seems to be spoken by a chorus of women who regretted her speedy departure. — *as upon a dance of the hosts;* i.e., with eyes as fixed and earnest as upon some very uncommon exhibition or spectacle. This may be the language of one of the company. As to what is meant by *a dance of the hosts*, it is difficult to form a decided opinion: Gesenius, who is followed by De Wette, supposes the angelic host to be denoted, to whom dancing is ascribed, as elsewhere singing. (Comp. Gen. xxxi. 2; Job xxxviii. 7.) Otherwise, *as upon a dance of two companies;* or, *as in a dance of two companies?*

i.e., with such earnest eyes as dancers in two rows look upon each other.

Ch. VII. 1. — *sandals.* How important an article of dress were sandals to an Eastern lady is shown in Judith xvi. 9, where we read that the sandals of Judith ravished the eyes of Holophernes. — *neck ornaments;* i.e., bosses or knobs, of which a necklace was composed. She is also represented as *καλλίπυγος*.

2. — *the spiced wine;* mentioned merely to set off the beauty and richness of the cup. — *heap of wheat,* &c. Perhaps a heap of wheat enclosed with lilies was chosen as an illustration, not merely for its appearance, but as an emblem of fertility. "Wheat and barley," says Selden, "were, among the ancient Hebrews, emblems of fertility; and it was usual for standers-by to scatter these grains upon the married couple, with a wish that they might increase and multiply." (Uxor Hebraica, lib. ii. cap. 15.) It has been conjectured, that the heaps of wheat were, during the joyous time of harvest, covered with flowers, especially with lilies.

4. — *ivory.* So a neck of ivory, *ἐλεφάντινος τράχηλος*, is ascribed by Anacreon to Bathyllus, Ode xxix. — *pools at Heshbon;* i.e., moist, dark, and bright. Burckhardt thus speaks of the remains of this city: "At six hours and a quarter [from El Aal, probably the Elealeh of the Scriptures] is Heshbon, upon a hill bearing southwest from El Aal. Here are the ruins of a large ancient town, together with the remains of some edifices built with small stones; a few broken shafts of columns are still standing, a number of wells cut in the rock, *and a large reservoir of water* for the summer supply of the inhabitants." (Travels, p. 365.) — *tower of Lebanon.* The nose may have been compared to that tower for its height, straightness, and good proportions. The allegorists suppose that the tower-like nose denotes the judgment and discernment of the doctors of the Church.

5. — *Carmel;* with its beautiful and verdant summit of oaks and pines. (See the article in Robinson's Calmet under this word, with its copious extracts from Oriental travellers. Comp. Isa. xxxv. 2.) — *like purple.* As there can be little doubt of the correctness of this translation, I suppose the point of comparison is the glossy brightness of the locks rather than the color of them. Black was the beautiful color for the hair.

7. — *palm-tree.* This tree received its name תָּמָר from its straight, upright growth. It is one of the loftiest of trees, sometimes rising to the height of a hundred feet. It is one of the most celebrated trees

in the world for its beauty and its uses. — *dates;* the fruit of the palm-tree which grows in clusters below the leaves. (See Harris's Nat. Hist., &c., or Robinson's Calmet.)

9. — *that goeth down smoothly*, &c. (See Prov. xxiii. 31.) That the maiden or spouse speaks here, taking up the thread of the discourse, is evident from the fact that דּוֹדִי, *my beloved*, which occurs often in the Canticles, is always applied to the man, never to the maiden. Otherwise, דּוֹדִי must have been brought into the text from the next verse by mistake. —*flowing over the lips*, &c. So, in Lane's Arabian Nights, vol. ii. p. 561, "The moisture of his mouth is like pleasant wine, that would cool me when a fire flameth within me." Gesenius, in his Thesaurus on the word דָּבַב, thus translates and comments: "*Palatum tuum est instar vini dulcis* (significatur saliva palati) *recta fluens ad suavium meum, perreptans labia* una *dormientium* (in eodem toro cubantium). Vereor enim ne recte ita interpretati sint Driessenius in Dissert. Lugd. p. 1101, &c., et Michaelis in Suppl. p. 385, de basio nimirum impudico, neque magis hujus in vetere carmine amatorio mentionem mireris, quam paulo ante (vii. 8) explendæ libidinis. Salivam ab osculantibus imbibendam crebris sermonibus et figuris usurpant Arabes, v. Hug ad Cant. p. 49, v. d. Sloot ad Carm. Togr. p. 134, Ibn Doreid, pp. 113, 114, Scheid. cf. Saad. apud Aben Esram ad Cant. i. 2." (See also Rosenmüller ad loc.)

11. *Come, my beloved*, &c. It is doubtful whether a new piece commences here, or whether what follows to ch. viii. 5, is a part of the preceding canticle. The passage reminds us of one in Milton, Par. Lost, iv. 610: —

> "To-morrow, ere fresh morning streak the east
> With first approach of light, we must be risen,
> And at our pleasant labor, to reform
> Yon flowery arbors, yonder alleys green.
> Those blossoms also, and those dropping gums
> That lie bestrown, unsightly and unsmooth,
> Ask riddance."

13. — *love-apples*. Such is the etymological signification of the word which was given to this fruit from its supposed properties. (See Gen. xxx. 14, &c.) The fruit is that of the *mandragora* (*Atropa mandragora* of Linnæus). Gesenius thus describes the plant: "It has large leaves, like those of a beet; a root like that of a turnip, divided at the lower part, and somewhat resembling the human form; used in the preparation of love-potions, having white and reddish blossoms, vellow and fragrant apples, which may be eaten, about the size of a

small egg, ripening from May to July, and to which the Orientals in ancient and modern times ascribe an efficacy in increasing philoprogenitiveness and fruitfulness." (See Gesen. Thesaurus on the word דּוּדַי, and the numerous authorities, ancient and modern, to which he refers. See also Harris's Nat. Hist. and Robinson's Calmet.) — *kept them for thee*, &c. So Virgil, Ecl. i. 37: —

> "Mirabar, quid, mœsta, deos, Amarylli, vocares,
> Cui pendere sua patereris in arbore poma.
> Tityrus hinc aberat."

Ch. VIII. 1. — *as my brother;* i.e., as a little infant child, whom she might caress in public as well as in private without impropriety.

2. — *teach me;* i.e., how to please thee, &c.

5. *Who is this*, &c. This is probably the language of the poet; or it may be supposed to be the language of a choir. — *from the wilderness;* i.e., the country, in distinction from the city. — *I excited thy love;* i.e., inspired thee with affection to me. This took place under the apple-tree, which has been regarded as peculiarly the tree of love. The following is the note of Rosenmüller: "Cydoniam malum apud alios quoque populos amoribus dicatam fuisse, observat Celsius, *Hierobot.*, p. i. p. 263. 'Apud Ægyptios connubii symbolum fuit. *Ζυγίης σύμβολον παφίης*, *Veneris jugæ tesseram*, appellat Arabicus in Epigrammate. Nempe Veneri, ut Dearum formosissimæ, a Paride addictum fuit. Venus igitur in statuis cydonium dextrâ gerit. Cupidines ex hortis malorum primitias legunt, illisque ludunt. *Οἱ μὲν γὰρ διὰ τοῦ μήλου παίζοντες πόθου ἄρχονται*, *nam qui pomo ludunt, amoris initium faciunt*, dicit Philostratus, Icon. l. i. p. 738. Hinc *τὸ μηλοβολεῖν*, *malis petere, malum mittere, malum dare*, loquutiones frequentes apud Græcos et Romanos. Vid. Theoc., Idyll. iii. 10, v. 88, vi. 6; Virg., Ecl. iii. 64, Aristophanis Scholiastes Nub. p. 180. *Μηλοβολεῖν ἔλεγον τὸ εἰς ἀφροδίσια δελεάζειν, ἐπεὶ καὶ τὸ μῆλον Ἀφροδίτης ἐστὶν ἱερόν· malis petere dicebant ad venerea incitare, quippe malus Veneri est dicata.*'" — *brought thee forth*, &c. So the Sept. *ὠδίνησέ σε*. The meaning seems to be explained by the opinion referred to in the preceding note, namely, that the apple-tree is the tree of love. Thus the birth of the lover under the apple-tree would indicate his power of gaining the love of women. So Apollo is represented as born under a palm-tree. Some suppose that חִבְּלַתְךָ may be rendered *pledged thee*. This would remove a difficulty, but it does not seem to be supported by Hebrew usage. (See Gesenius on חָבַל.)

6. — *set me as a seal*, &c. This denotes intimate, inviolable union. Thus, in Jer. xxii. 24: —

"As I live, saith Jehovah,
Thou Coniah, son of Jehoiakim, king of Judah,
Though thou wert the signet upon my right hand,
Even thence would I pluck thee."

Signet rings were worn by the Orientals not only upon the fingers, but on the bosom, suspended by an ornamental chain from the neck, &c. (See Rosenmül. Alt. und Neues Morgenl., i. p. 183, and iv. p. 190. — *true love;* קִנְאָה, rendered *jealousy* in the Common Version, denotes any ardent feeling. (See Gesen. ad verb.) It is evident from the parallelism and from the connection, that it is here used simply as an intensive term for *love* in the preceding line. Love is strong, like death, inasmuch as it conquers all; and it is firm, like the grave, which never relaxes its hold on its tenants.

7. *Many waters*, &c. Love is compared to fire in the preceding verse. In accordance with this, it is added that water cannot quench it. — *for love;* i.e., to induce one to give up the love she has for a particular person, and transfer it to another.

8–12. The subject of this little piece seems to be a conversation between two worldly-wise brothers, relating to the marriage of their sister, together with her remarks. That the guardianship of females in regard to marriage belonged to their brothers, in the East, in ancient times, may be inferred from Gen. xxiv. 50, xxxiv. 13; Judges xxi. 22.

8. — *spoken for;* i.e., asked in marriage.

9. *If she be a wall;* i.e., if she be inaccessible, unwilling to receive suitors, or to be married. — *a silver tower.* Rosenmüller supposes the meaning to be, "we will ask a high dowry for her." That portions were paid, in the East, to the father for the daughter, is well known. Thus, Jacob served seven years for each of his wives. So it is in modern times. "They bargain," says D'Arvieux, "about the price of the daughter, which the son-in-law is to pay his new father in camels, sheep, or horses. A young fellow that has a mind to marry must in good earnest buy him a wife; and fathers among the Arabs are never happier than when they have abundance of daughters. They are the principal riches in a family: accordingly, when a bachelor is treating with the person whose daughter he is desirous of marrying, he says to him, 'Will you give me your daughter for fifty sheep, for half a dozen camels, or for a dozen cows?' &c. If he is not in circumstances for making such offers as these, he proposes to

him to give him her for a mare or colt, all, in short, according to the girl's merit, the condition of her family, and the income of the intended bridegroom. (Travels, p. 230, English translation.) But perhaps the meaning of *building a silver tower upon the wall* may be simply, that the brothers would adorn the sister with silver, in reward for her modesty. — *an open gate;* i.e., very desirous of being married, and give a very ready reception to a suitor. — *with planks of cedar;* i.e., we will take care to keep her in strict confinement, so that access to her shall be difficult.

10. — *am I become in his eyes,* &c. The idea of the sister seems to be, that, by modesty and difficulty of access to others, she shall the more surely win the favor of her accepted suitor. Perhaps the expression, *as one that findeth peace,* may be a continuation of the preceding metaphor, the suitor being the besieger of the wall and towers.

11. *Solomon had a vineyard,* &c. The vineyard of Solomon, from which he received a great income, seems to be brought in simply by way of contrast to that which the sister regarded as her own vineyard, namely, her beauty or her person (comp. ch. i. 6); and to express the idea, that Solomon was welcome to his income, but that from her vineyard she did not wish for a pecuniary income. She would give her love for love, not for money.

12. *My vineyard is before my eyes;* i.e., I will not let it out to others, but keep in under my own inspection and care.

13, 14. These two verses seem to form a fragment. So far as any general meaning is conveyed by them, it seems to be, that a lover desires a song of his mistress, but is refused and sent away.

13. *Friends,* &c.; i.e., my friends who are with me wait to hear thy voice. Otherwise, thy friends constantly hear it; let me hear it too.

THE END.

www.ingramcontent.com/pod-product-compliance
Lightning Source LLC
LaVergne TN
LVHW010156110826
845151LV00002B/538
* 9 7 8 1 4 2 5 5 3 6 4 4 2 *